T0326974

MYTH AND POETICS

A series edited by
GREGORY NAGY

HEROIC SAGAS AND BALLADS

Stephen A. Mitchell

CORNELL UNIVERSITY PRESS
ITHACA AND LONDON

Cornell University Press gratefully acknowledges a grant
from Harvard University which aided in the
publication of this book.

First published 1991 by Cornell University Press.

International Standard Book Number 978-1-5017-0744-5
Library of Congress Catalog Card Number 91-9899
Printed in the United States of America
Librarians: Library of Congress cataloging information
appears on the last page of the book.

⊗ The paper in this book meets the minimum requirements
of the American National Standard for Information Sciences—
Permanence of Paper for Printed Library Materials, ANSI Z39.48-1984.

To Kristine

Contents

viii   Contents

Foreword

Gregory Nagy

My goal as editor of the Myth and Poetics series is to encourage work that helps to integrate literary criticism with the approaches of anthropology and pays special attention to problems concerning the nexus of ritual and myth. Early volumes in the series set the groundwork for a broadened understanding of the very concepts of myth and ritual as reflected in the specific cultural context of ancient Greek poetics. Stephen Mitchell's *Heroic Sagas and Ballads* now extends the field of vision from the Greek perspective to the linguistically related realm of medieval Germanic poetics, as represented by the Scandinavian heroic sagas and ballads.

Mitchell's book is in the forefront of significant scholarly advances now being made in response to discoveries concerning the nature of oral poetics. Albert B. Lord's *Epic Singers and Oral Tradition* (1991), a volume that shares these scholarly concerns and a distinguished entry in this same Myth and Poetics series, has established, once and for all, the legitimacy and importance of exploring the heritage of Western literature against the backdrop of native oral heritage. Mitchell's understanding of both the historical and the literary background of Old Norse poetics, following in the tradition of Lars Lönnroth's *Njáls Saga: A Critical Introduction* (published in 1976), provides an ideal vantage point for an illuminating case study of interaction between oral and literary traditions.

Preface

In the modern world artistic creativity necessarily implies originality; as a rule, we have great difficulty assessing the works of an age in which such notions were for the most part still quite distant. The heroic sagas taken up in the present volume, the so-called *fornaldarsǫgur* (literally, 'sagas of antiquity'; singular *fornaldarsaga*), reflect a different kind of literary artifice, a kind of creativity practiced in medieval Iceland which drew heavily on commonly known and widely used narrative traditions. It should not be assumed, however, that genius and artistic excellence do not enter into a discussion of the legendary fiction of thirteenth-, fourteenth-, and fifteenth-century Iceland—they do, but the value modern readers place on the originality and uniqueness of a character or an episode makes a very poor standard for evaluating the literary merits of such texts as those taken up in the chapters that follow. One consequence has been that these tales are often relegated to the status of "poor cousins" within the family of Icelandic literature; another is that they are more likely to yield results to extraliterary consideration than to conventional literary criticism.

Moreover, these legendary texts are distinguished from the better-known sagas in that the "cultural moment" on which a discussion of them focuses is not the same as that generally encountered in works of Old Icelandic literature: the most prominent and thoroughly discussed saga genres blossom in the thirteenth century, the Age of the Sturlungs, as it is called, when a renowned figure such as Snorri Sturluson could both write mythological and heroic texts, such as *Snorra Edda* and *Heimskringla* (possibly also *Egils saga Skallagrímssonar*), and play out his own part in them (*Sturlunga saga*). The period under

examination here, its hypothetical present, is in general somewhat
later, by a century or so, a period typically thought of as "postclassical." Of course, works something like the *fornaldarsǫgur* we possess today were known in oral, and in some instances written, forms in
the thirteenth century, as were some texts that have not survived
(marked by an asterisk, e.g. **Hróks saga svarta, *Huldar saga*), of which
we can know little. The extant texts hail from the later Middle Ages.
Even that modest claim is sometimes an optimistic evaluation, for
some of the medieval *fornaldarsǫgur,* such as *Hrólfs saga kraka,* are preserved only in post-Reformation manuscripts, and many have important codicological testimony from the post-Reformation period.

Although popular both before and after the thirteenth, fourteenth,
and fifteenth centuries, these legendary narratives appear to have had a
special appeal to exactly those troubled times in Iceland. The belief that
these heroic texts are best understood through their special connection
to the later period, rather than to the historical settings of the stories
themselves, distinguishes the present volume from many previous
studies, which have tended to regard the Icelandic *fornaldarsǫgur* as
works merely preserved, rather than created, in the high Middle Ages.
That is, I believe we are most likely to understand and appreciate the
fornaldarsǫgur if we examine them within the historical framework of
the fourteenth and fifteenth centuries, not the eighth and ninth. I subscribe wholeheartedly to the view that the *fornaldarsǫgur* are based on
ancient traditions, but the late medieval writers of the extant texts
placed their own authorial stamp on the narratives. At the same time, it
is also true that these sagas and their role in Icelandic literature and
society are unintelligible if we read them without due concern for their
deep roots in Nordic literary consciousness. This orientation also explains why I have drawn only now and then on the testimony of Saxo's
Gesta Danorum and other more fragmentary attestations to preexisting
legendary traditions: rather than attempt to push back the frontiers of
our earliest knowledge about a particular text, my intent here is to
show how the medieval Icelanders of the post-classical period treated
the existing traditions in their literature, and to show how these traditions were transmuted into new genres, the ballads and the *rímur.*

With regard to terminology, 'legendary sagas,' 'mythical-heroic
sagas,' '*fornaldarsǫgur,*' 'Viking romances,' and 'legendary fiction' enjoy various degrees of currency in English in designating some or all of
the texts under discussion here. In general, I have employed the term
fornaldarsǫgur, except in those instances where use of other terms has
been necessary for technical reasons. Likewise, I have used the native

terms for the other saga genres `(thus, *konungasǫgur* for kings' sagas, *biskupasǫgur* for bishops' sagas, *íslendingasǫgur* for family sagas, *riddarasǫgur* for chivalric [or knights'] sagas, and so on). With respect to orthography, I have uniformly employed *ǫ, rather than ö*, a choice I believe to be justified in a discussion of medieval literature; however, I realize that usage of this sort can be jarring when it is carried over to terms such as *fornaldarsǫgur*, which are the product of modern scholarship and lack a medieval heritage. It should be noted too that proper names appear in the text in their normalized form even when surrounding quotations reflect manuscript usage. On that point, I have, where possible, used critical editions of the *fornaldarsǫgur* (rather than Guðni Jónsson's or other normalized texts) for two reasons. First, the arguments presented here occasionally hinge on manuscript variants; the choice of diplomatic editions, reflecting as they do manuscript usage, was therefore already inevitable in these cases. Moreover, it seems to me that the custom developed for the study of West Norse texts in the nineteenth century has ill served Icelandic literary history. The normalizing of all texts to a fictional thirteenth-century "standard" has unfairly promulgated the notion of the 1200s as the classical age of the sagas. Such a choice may be sensible in the cases of the *íslendingasǫgur* and *konungasǫgur*, but it certainly skews our understanding of the *fornaldarsǫgur* and their cultural milieu. Unless noted otherwise, all translations are my own.

Parenthetic annotations in the text of the sort (AT 1137), (ML 5095), and so on refer to the type-indices listed in the Abbreviations. Similar references with a single letter, such as (W11.2 'Munificent monarch'), refer to Stith Thompson's *Motif-Index of Folk Literature* (1932–36) and to Inger Boberg's *Motif-Index of Early Icelandic Literature* (1966). More than fifty years have passed since the last bibliography of the *fornaldarsǫgur* appeared (Halldór Hermansson 1937), nor are they taken up in the most recent bibliographic assessment of Old Norse studies, as the authors ruefully comment in its preface: "Our choice has, however, led to the neglect of several important categories. One is the *fornaldarsǫgur*" (Clover et al. 1985, 8). As a result, although the bibliography of the present volume makes no claim to be comprehensive, it does reflect an inclination to err on the side of inclusion rather than exclusion.

This project began some time ago. Its felicitous conclusion has been aided in a variety of ways by many friends and colleagues; prominent among them are Carol C. Clover, Jürg Glauser, Kaaren Grimstad, Joseph Harris, Nils Hasselmo, Einar Haugen, Bengt R. Jonsson, Peter

Jorgensen, Lars Lönnroth, Albert B. Lord, Gregory Nagy, and Fred C. Robinson. For their hospitality and assistance at Stofnun Árna Magnússonar, I would like to thank Jónas Kristjánsson and Stefán Karlsson. Research for this book was made possible largely through the support of the National Endowment for the Humanities and the Graduate Fund of Harvard University.

STEPHEN A. MITCHELL

Cambridge, Massachusetts

HEROIC SAGAS
AND BALLADS

Introduction

An article of faith in modern folklore studies holds that there is no text without context. In a similar vein, understanding the historical and intellectual context of this book necessitates a few words on the contours of Old Norse studies, particularly for the nonspecialist.[1] Almost all scholarly treatments of the sagas can be characterized as gravitating toward one of two poles, namely, belief in either oral or written sagas. Of course, such terms as the 'oral saga' or the 'written saga' connote much more than the simple equation of the medieval texts with the acts of speaking or writing. The question might be phrased as follows: is the background to the sagas' art to be conceived of as native and essentially spoken (or verbal, or performed, or recited), or is the background based on foreign models in which the key aspects of composition have been shaped by literacy? Neither of these positions is absolute: proponents of the oral saga readily concede that the available works have come down to us in a written medium that cannot have failed to impart something to the text, and even the most strident advocates of the written saga will agree that the texts are frequently informed by oral traditions. In general, these orientations reflect preoccupations with "the folk" and "the court." In the history of the field, these two views have been called many things, but while the labels change, the positions shift, and the interpretations their adherents place on the evidence vary, the divisions (if not their centers of gravity) are

1. Accessible reviews in English are provided in: Andersson 1964 for the early periods; Byock 1984–85 and Clover 1985 for more recent developments. In the case of the newer materials, a balanced view of the situation requires examination of both works.

I

not much different now from what they were at the turn of the century: on the one hand, there are the free-prosists (< *Freiprosa*), or corpus-analysts, or formalists, or traditionalists and, on the other, the book-prosists (< *Buchprosa*), or Continentalists, or members of the Icelandic School (roughly analogous to the 'analysts' and 'unitarians' of nineteenth-century Homeric debate).

Although the technical terminology of the debate does not antedate the twentieth century, the issues are hardly new. In fact, the questions the two groups pose and the political, national, and theoretical concerns on which they rest may already be sensed in the seventeenth and eighteenth centuries. It is possible to place the basic free-prose and book-prose positions in a matrix of political and nationalistic considerations. It was, after all, in just such a political framework that the "study" of the sagas got started in the seventeenth century, with Sweden (and to a lesser degree, Denmark-Norway) trying to use the sagas to bolster claims to Nordic hegemony. Put in the simplest terms, for the Icelanders, the greater the degree to which the sagas can be shown to be innovative, specifically Icelandic works, the greater the degree to which the Icelanders can lay exclusive claim to them as *their* national heritage, rather than as works merely recorded in Iceland. An important element in the rise of this view was the political ferment in Iceland in the twentieth century, which culminated in complete independence and "nationhood" during World War II. It was not without reason that Hjalmar Lindroth wrote of the founding of Hið íslenzka fornritafélag (The Old Icelandic Text Society) in the years before Icelandic independence, that "first of all the Icelandic people themselves must in a more profound manner appropriate their classical literature, so that it can become one of the many factors which develop and strengthen the feeling for national characteristics."[2] This sort of linkage between independence and literary and folk traditions can boast numerous parallels, as, for example, in the case of the *Kalevala* in nineteenth-century Finland, or the successive establishment in the Republic of Ireland of the Folklore of Ireland Society (1926), the Irish Folklore Institute (1930), and the Irish Folklore Commission (1935).

Other Scandinavians, in particular the Norwegians (who achieved relative local autonomy in the early nineteenth century after over four hundred years of Danish domination and gained complete independence and nationhood from Sweden only in 1905) sought to recover their "lost" medieval literature by turning to the sagas. The search was

2. Lindroth 1937, 175.

not an irrational proposition, since most *konungasǫgur* and some *íslendingasǫgur* treat Norwegian topics and characters and are played out in Norway. The greater the degree to which the sagas could be shown to be "traditional," that is, having been given basic form and shape in Norway before being taken up in Iceland as part of an oral tradition that was eventually written down, the greater the degree to which Norway could participate in, and legitimize its claim to, these unique medieval documents. Norwegian literary histories often fill out the section on the Middle Ages through recourse to sagas concerned with Norwegian topics. The same interest in the sagas—although at still greater remove—was displayed by the Swedes, Danes, and others. Typical of such speculation and reconstructed cultural history based on the literary production of medieval Iceland is Jacob Grimm's comment that "Norse mythology [. . .] lies near to us, like the Norse tongue, which, having stood longer undisturbed in its integrity, gives us a deeper insight into the nature of our own."[3] Although such attitudes toward the Old Norse materials were often given their best expressions by scholars, they did not develop in the rarefied atmosphere of the academy, but were shaped by larger societal and political forces such as romanticism, neoromanticism, pan-Scandinavianism, and so on.

The 'Icelandic School,' with its emphasis on the novelistic dimensions of the individual sagas, has been championed by Sigurður Nordal and Einar Ólafur Sveinsson in particular (although they had predecessors, such as Björn M. Ólsen). By the 1950s, the Icelandic School was making real headway, due in part to the Icelanders' production of *Íslenzk fornrit,* the standard edition of the sagas. Certainly their point of view gained important adherents (for example, Peter Hallberg). Parallel to but quite separate from the Icelandic School has been the emergence of the 'Continentalists,' marked by publication of *Norrøn Fortællekunst,* an anthology that points out, for genre after genre, the legacy from the Latin Middle Ages (courtly literature, hagiographic writing, and so on) to Icelandic literature. In a very similar vein, Lars Lönnroth set forth in a series of articles (collected and synthesized into *European Sources of Icelandic Saga-Writing*) the notion that Icelandic literature was indebted in important, and previously unrecognized, ways to European literature.[4]

3. J. Grimm 1883, viii. The question of which nationalities could lay claim to the sagas led to sharp debates in the nineteenth century, especially between J. R. Keyser, P. A. Munch, K. von Maurer, and S. Grundtvig. See, for example, Grundtvig's remarks (1863).

4. Lönnroth 1963–64, 1964, 1965, 1965–69.

The free-prose, or 'traditionalist,' position had been accepted as a matter of faith by several generations of scholars. But the early confidence of such men as Knut Liestøl and Axel Olrik has been replaced in recent decades by hard-won analyses and attempts at new strategies to unlock the oral background to the sagas.[5] The resurgent free-prose position was well expressed when Theodore Andersson concluded, "In fact much of what the Icelanders have claimed as the saga writer's due is compatible with the supposition of oral stories. The writer undoubtedly could and did use written sources, supplementary oral sources, his own imagination, and above all his own words, but his art and presumably the framework of his story were given him by tradition. The inspiration of the sagas is ultimately oral."[6] Nor have the Icelanders remained uniformly committed to the older book-prose stance; they, in turn, have begun to ask the obvious: if oral tradition and written tradition can coexist in modern Iceland, why is it so difficult to imagine a similar situation in the Middle Ages?[7] The greatest weaknesses of the turn-of-the-century free-prose position were its rigid demands for a *fixed, memorized* text, for historical accuracy, and so on. Because the traditionalists had made historical fidelity an important part of their argument, the Icelandic School was able to chip away at this cornerstone of faith by showing flaws in the verisimilitude of the sagas.

On the other hand, today's Continentalists have become equally rigid: lip service is generally paid to some vague concept of oral tradition, but the form and narrative style of the texts are taken to derive more or less exclusively from written foreign models. Although there was much that was right about the book-prose position, a glaring failure was its apparent deemphasis of cultural context. As Lönnroth writes, one could, on reading Sigurður Nordal, believe "that sagawriting took place in a social vacuum, that written sagas were influenced only by other written sagas."[8] Modern Continentalists seem perfectly prepared to leave society out of the equation as well. And in their desire to make the Continentalist case, its adherents threaten to become locked into an arid search for "sources," whether at the level of the

---

5. E.g., Andersson 1966, Hofmann 1976, Bandle 1988. In the context of Old Swedish narrative prose, I have attempted to distinguish oral from written strata (Mitchell 1984).

6. Andersson 1964, 119. Andersson appears to have moved away from his earlier position, although perhaps not with respect to the sagas. See, for example, Andersson 1987.

7. Kristín Geirsdóttir 1979.

8. Lönnroth 1976, 207.

individual motif or of the macrostructure.[9] Source studies are by no means without value nor are such investigations limited to the Continentalists, but whereas traditionalists have tended to employ such studies to illuminate and underscore the generative dimension of saga composition,[10] source studies by the Continentalists would seem to be an intellectual cul-de-sac. Placed in contexts of this sort, literature begins to lack meaning, other than as a sterile warehouse of motifs and structures with which partisans may ratify such displaced concerns as the glory and influence of medieval France.

I do not mean to defend the traditionalist views uncritically. Some objections leveled by the Continentalists have been of great importance, but recent antitraditionalist comments are often based on a kind of negative analogic argument.[11] The idea that the complex interweaving of saga style could not have developed from traditional oral forms, for example, is based on selectively culled evidence from non-European folk traditions: there are counterexamples from Irish and Serbo-Croatian oral traditions which make the point moot. I think it is fair to say that, if they believe in nothing else, the modern-day traditionalists believe in an oral literature that served a nonelite, as well as elite, constituency; in a significant oral impact on the written work; and in a healthy synergism between oral and written saga forms. Obviously, the modern traditionalist position little resembles what Andreas Heusler had in mind at the turn of the century, when he could characterize the saga writers as something like stenographers accurately recording a fixed text word for word from oral narration; if anything, today's traditionalists probably resemble what his generation would have thought of as book-prosists, namely, believers in an individual saga writer employing inherited oral verse and indigenous traditions in the service of a written text.

Among the best expressions of what scholars have learned as a result of all this wrangling is Lars Lönnroth's study of *Njáls saga*.[12] Although a Continentalist early in his career, Lönnroth soon found that if he were to explore this most famous of Icelandic sagas fully, he needed to accommodate the traditional component of the saga as well. His syn-

---

9. An example of such source studies is Clover 1986, and examples of the search for influences on the macrostructure would include Clover 1982 and Kalinke 1990. The latter work appeared only at the editing stage of this book.

10. E.g., Andersson 1967; Lönnroth 1976, 42–103; Byock 1982. Along the same lines, J. Harris (1972) has investigated the *þættir*, short prose narratives.

11. Clover 1985, 272–94.

12. Lönnroth 1976.

thetic view, with its explicit recognition and exploration of the oral and social background to the saga, as well as an appreciation for the work as a literary text, demonstrates the useful synergism to be found in accepting the reality of the sagas as products of both oral *and* written composition.[13] For the most part, the question of orality as a matter of scholarly debate has attached itself more to the *íslendingasǫgur* than to other saga genres, but the influence of that discussion colors virtually every discussion in the area of Old Norse literature, and the issues seem to me to be of the utmost importance in the case of the *fornaldarsǫgur*.

In the history of research on the *fornaldarsǫgur* the tendency has been to focus on specialized questions of motifs and sources;[14] it is an understandable trend, for not only do these texts lend themselves well to such investigation, but, conversely, their diverse and complex character resists consideration and discussion as a group.[15] The preoccupation they display with a long-gone "heroic age" suggests an enigmatic key to their appeal; yet while writing in another context, one expert comments that attempts to answer such questions as those concerning the nature of literary transmission in medieval Iceland and the attitudes of the medieval audience toward the past are likely to invite speculation, but resist documentation and proof.[16] Such suspicion is no doubt well founded, yet the difficulties involved do not seem to me to detract from the importance of the questions themselves or to lessen our obligation to propose answers to them. Still, it is a treacherous path I have taken in this book, which cannot avoid questions of this sort—all the more so, in that I have attempted to synthesize aspects of some thirty separate narrative traditions preserved in a vast array of manuscripts, each with its important peculiarities. I recognize that specialists will protest that alternative interpretations exist for particular texts. The inevitability of such discord was, however, a calculated risk in my undertaking the project in the first place.

Suggesting as it does that it would be better to remain an incurious, if cautious, member of the crowd, the admonition inherent in an Icelandic proverb from a fifteenth-century collection, *vargur sæter þeim saud. sem ur kvium villiz* 'a wolf waylays the sheep who strays from the

13. Cf. Lönnroth 1980.
14. Motif- and source-oriented studies continue to be an integral part of contemporary scholarship (e.g., Davið Erlingsson 1980; Power 1985b), just as they were earlier in this century (e.g., Hollander 1912; Krappe 1928, 1937; Neckel 1920; Schröder 1928).
15. In each its own way, Reuschel 1933; Hermann Pálsson and Paul Edwards 1971; Righter-Gould 1975, 1980; and Buchholz 1980 are exceptions to this tendency.
16. Schach 1982.

fold' (Proverbs, 173) has failed to deter me with regard to either my general view of the historical setting of the texts or the proper methodological approach to them.[17] Thus, with a stubbornness born from the determination to understand how such wonderful texts as the *fornaldarsǫgur,* with their glorification of ancient heroic deeds, legendary monsters, and fabulous adventures, came to be created in the insignificant cultural outpost that Iceland was in the later Middle Ages (and not at the Norwegian, Danish, Swedish, or German courts), I have not allowed myself to be thwarted by the admonition to the field that we abandon such unprovable issues as attitudes toward the past. For it is precisely in such extraliterary questions, in whose accessibility I have a strong measure of confidence, that the justification for studying the *fornaldarsǫgur* resides.

17. Others who have similarly "strayed" include Weber (1978, 490–92; 1981, 480–84) and Glauser (1983). Glauser's analysis, with its underlying tenet that the much-ignored late Icelandic *Märchensagas* could reasonably be treated as an entity and judged within their actual historical and social frameworks, has been of particular importance in the formulation of this book.

CHAPTER I

Definitions and Assessments

What are the *fornaldarsǫgur?* "They are among the dreariest things ever made by human fancy," according to W. P. Ker.[1] Another nineteenth-century student of Old Norse literature, Guðbrandur Vigfússon, calls them "the lowest and most miserable productions of Icelandic pens."[2] Negative remarks about the repetitious character and "conversational tone" of these sagas routinely accompany discussions of them in literary histories.[3] Yet the medieval Icelanders clearly loved these texts, as the great numbers of *fornaldarsǫgur* manuscripts demonstrate. How could such astute modern readers apparently miss something the Icelanders of the later Middle Ages saw and felt? Certainly part of the answer is that Ker and Guðbrandur came to the *fornaldarsǫgur* armed with the critical tools they were used to employing on *Njáls saga* and the other great *íslendingasǫgur,* but these proved to be faulty equipment indeed in the case of the *fornaldarsǫgur.* A reevaluation of these texts is in order, especially as to what kinds of texts the *fornaldarsǫgur* are and how they relate to the other forms of Old Icelandic literature.

1. Ker 1908, 282. He is referring specifically to the "romantic sagas," in which group he includes many of the *fornaldarsǫgur.*
2. Guðbrandur Vigfússon 1878, cxcvi. Guðbrandur is referring to what he terms "the *worthless mythical sagas,*" by which phrase he means most of the *fornaldarsǫgur* except *Vǫlsunga saga, Gautreks saga, Hrólfs saga kraka, Hálfs saga ok Hálfsrekka,* and a few others.
3. So, for example, Finnur Jónsson 1920–24, II, 787; Mogk 1901–9, 740; Paasche 1924, 465; de Vries 1941–42, II, 465.

Genre Analysis and Old Norse Literature

A reevaluation of the *fornaldarsǫgur* must recognize that the manner in which we categorize our world ultimately bespeaks not only how we perceive that world, but also the underlying principles on which our judgments are based. The resulting conceptualization will in turn necessarily influence the way we evaluate the objects so designated. This basic observation is as true of medieval Icelandic literature as it is of the botanical taxonomies of preliterate peoples, to mention but one area that has come under close scrutiny in this regard during the past decades.[4] The significance and implications of classificatory systems with regard to Old Norse creative prose have, however, only slowly been recognized; yet the failure of the discipline to articulate the principles of its literary genera and species has not been without consequence for the nature of its inquiry and findings, as in the cases of Ker and Guðbrandur. Unlike the biological sciences, which had a Linneaus to order what God created,[5] there was no eighteenth- or nineteenth-century equivalent to him in the humanities to establish order on the literary creations of the Nordic Middle Ages. As a result, the taxonomy of saga literature which evolved derived from a combination of native Icelandic tradition, scholarly deliberation, and marketing considerations. Thus, the methodological tool that is to humanistic endeavor what systematics is to the biologist, namely, the very foundation of inquiry and in-depth study, is, in the case of medieval Scandinavian scholarship, a set of somewhat loosely conceived ideals based on convention and convenience.

It was not until the early 1950s that Sigurður Nordal became the first to challenge seriously the prevailing system of Old Norse literary nomenclature. He suggested that instead of *konungasǫgur, íslendingasǫgur,*

4. Ethnobiology, a term coined by Castetter (1944), encompasses many different areas of research; I have in mind the sort described by Berlin, Breedlove, and Raven (1973, 214), as "the detailed study of folk biosystematics, pre-scientific man's classification of his biological universe." For a convenient, and rewarding, review of some of the major theories and works in this area, see Berlin 1978. It should be noted that although the biological sciences provide a convenient parallel for such a discussion, the analogy has limits. As J. Harris (1972, 22) comments, "Genre study in literature can never be as precise as taxonomy in the natural sciences because literature is not entirely self-generated but a product of the synthesizing imagination."

5. Von Linné's contemporaries paid him the greatest of compliments with the admiring epigram "Deus creavit, Linnaeus disposuit." For an overview of the history and theory of systematics in the development of biology, see Mayr 1982, 147–297.

and so forth—categories based only on the status of the protagonist—
an approach be adopted which would base itself solely on the relationship between the time at which a given saga was composed and the
period in which its events purported to take place.[6] Although Sigurður's criticism of the current literary taxonomy was long overdue, his
approach was inherently flawed, despite its clear and uniform set of
principles. The failure of his *system* of genre analysis to be adopted
resulted from its heavy reliance on supposed dates of composition and
its inability in certain instances to distinguish between demonstrably
different kinds of sagas.[7] Equally troublesome, Sigurður's classification
scheme suggests a degree of harmony among other sagas which cannot
be demonstrated. It would be unreasonable to assume, for example,
that one of the *konungasǫgur* such as *Óláfs saga Tryggvasonar* has more in
common with a *fornaldarsaga* such as *Hálfs saga ok Hálfsrekka* than it
does with another of the *konungasǫgur* like *Magnúss saga Erlingssonar,*
merely because the presumed dates of action in the case of the first two
are more widely separated from their probable dates of recording than
is the case with *Magnúss saga Erlingssonar;* yet a rigid application of
Sigurður Nordal's approach would suggest that they do. On the other
hand, if we were to adhere to a strict model of the current system, with
its emphasis on the status of the protagonist, all three might be placed
together in one category, since they all deal with Norwegian kings.

A radically different point of view was taken by Lars Lönnroth, who
was among the first to recognize the significant philosophical state-

---

6. Sigurður Nordal 1953, 180–81. He thus compresses Old Norse prose works into
three basic categories: ancient, early, and contemporary sagas (*oldtidssagaer, fortidssagaer,
samtidssagaer*). Earlier, Felix Genzmer (1948) had suggested the following organization
of Old Norse sagas, which essentially embraces the standard literary taxonomy, but
does classify the unhistorical texts in an interesting manner. He divides the realm of Old
Norse prose works in two, the historical and the unhistorical. Among the former are
the *íslendingasǫgur* and *konungasǫgur*. The unhistorical category is further subdivided
into the "tradition-bound"—the heroic and mythical sagas (*Heldensagas, Göttersagas*)—
and the "untraditional" (*frei erfundene*) texts—Viking, champion, and fictional sagas
(*Wikingersagas, Kämpensagas, novellenartige sagas*).

7. It should be noted that although certain of Sigurður Nordal's *terms* were readily
adopted by other scholars, this usage generally represented no more than an intellectual
"loan-shift," not a reorganization, since the new tags were applied to the old categories
without addressing the rationale for the organization. So, for example, Widding 1965,
esp. p. 80. Although Lönnroth (1964, 9) could write that Sigurður Nordal's system of
genre division had been accepted by modern researchers, most scholarship in the intervening years has continued to rely on the traditional taxonomy of Old Norse texts. Cf.
Hermann Pálsson 1969, 44–48, on Sigurður Nordal's proposal, as well as Hermann's
own suggestions concerning the appropriateness (with some modification) of Northrop
Frye's "Historical Criticism: Theory of Modes" to saga literature.

ment implicit in the system of genre analysis itself: the creation of a taxonomy for Old Norse literature, complete with its own unique terminology, and differing from that applied more generally to medieval European prose, had generated the impression that the composers of the Icelandic sagas subscribed to literary principles substantially different from those of other medieval writers.[8] It was Lönnroth's view in the 1960s that scholars needed to abandon the modern systems of Icelandic genres—both Sigurður Nordal's and the "standard" system—and examine more closely the ethnic system, that is, the usage of the medieval period and the possibility of influence from Continental and clerical modes of thinking.[9] Lönnroth summarized his belief that establishing genre distinctions is in the final analysis a futile industry by arguing that "far-reaching generalisations about the unhistoric concepts of the 'family saga,' 'mythical-heroic saga,' etc." were of little value since each saga would need to be dealt with individually.[10] Whether or not one agrees with this conclusion, it is to be noted that Lönnroth points out two important, and interrelated, features of Old Norse scholarship: that the categories used in discussing the texts had been established externally and did not reflect native usage, and that the subsequent taxonomy silently pressed important philosophical conclusions onto the sagas.

Some years later, the issue of Old Norse literary taxonomy was given a further examination.[11] Lönnroth again reminds us that the terms in current usage, as well as the very categories such terms represent, are, in the strict sense, modern constructs. Although he accepts the likelihood of the current system of technical terms remaining in place, Lönnroth warns that we should not allow these terms to influence our interpretations.[12] This admonition is an important reaffirmation and renewal of his earlier comments: if genre-based distinctions, and analyses, are to be made, they should at least reflect well-

8. See especially Lönnroth 1965, 6.

9. Lönnroth 1964, 1–94 (pp. 9–32 in particular); 1965, 6–11. Lönnroth points out that medieval Icelanders seem to have been emphatically interested in poetic genre distinctions, as evidenced in Snorri's *Edda*, but no corresponding system for the prose texts is anywhere evident in the Old Norse corpus.

10. Lönnroth 1965, 10–11. Cf. Danielsson (1986, 13–15), who rejects the term 'genre,' preferring instead the more general concept of 'group,' but otherwise tends to accept the traditional saga divisions (but see his special treatment of "the *Landnámabók*-group").

11. Lönnroth 1975b, J. Harris 1975, and Andersson 1975. Several other works have also touched on this issue in recent years: Steblin-Kaminskij 1966, J. Harris 1972, 1976b, Weber 1972, Bell 1983.

12. See especially Lönnroth 1975b, 426.

established criteria, and the user must constantly remember what the saga writers themselves would have understood as the "genres" of their works (for example, *ævisaga* 'biography'). In defense of the current system, Joseph Harris focuses on both the theoretical and practical implications of genre definitions based on something other than the nature of the hero.[13] He points out the substantial difference between ethnic and analytic categories, as well as the insurmountable difficulties involved in "resurrecting" the medieval taxonomy, even if it were conceded that such a course were the best one.[14] In his view, and that of many others, genre distinctions are of greater *practical* (as opposed to cognitive and historical) benefit if scholars agree that such classifications are ultimately a modern archival convenience and uniformly regard them as such. In his conclusion, however, Harris admits to having "an unprovable belief that the analytic system intuition has bequeathed to us does to some extent coincide with relevant aspects of the inaccessible ethnic system."[15]

Surprisingly, Theodore Andersson argues that such wranglings over nomenclature are necessarily counterproductive, insofar as they direct our attention and energies away from the sagas themselves and onto a mere academic debate. Thus, for his part, Andersson regards the entire discussion with suspicion, as a "surrogate concern with terms at the expense of literary realities."[16] Andersson notes that critics like Ker managed to produce excellent saga criticism without worrying their audiences over nomenclature. Although Ker's views on the *íslendingasǫgur* may still be insightful, I differ with Andersson's conclusion, at least as to Ker's evaluation of the *fornaldarsǫgur;* moreover, Ker's negative assessment of the *fornaldarsǫgur* is directly predicated on the issue of taxonomy and definition. In fact, Andersson's observation notwithstanding, the prevailing system of genres for Old Norse texts has not always been unbiased or without negative consequences in its treatment of certain sagas. For few genres of Old Norse literature could this fact be truer than for the *fornaldarsǫgur,* surely one of the most problematic and clouded divisions of material from the point of view of

13. J. Harris 1975.
14. Although no terms corresponding to *íslendingasǫgur* and *fornaldarsǫgur* are to be found in the Old Norse texts, *konungasǫgur, riddarasǫgur,* and related terms are regularly used. See Lönnroth 1964, 21–22, for examples, but see also Lönnroth's doubts concerning the extent to which these terms correspond to the modern genre concepts at a significant level (i.e., other than the surface relationship of the terms). For a treatment of ethnic and analytic categories, see Ben-Amos 1969.
15. J. Harris 1975, 435.
16. Andersson 1975, 437.

formal features and genre distinctions.[17] The critical fate of the *forn-aldarsǫgur*, which have suffered much misinterpretation and misunderstanding from the current hero-based organization of Old Norse literature into *konungasǫgur, íslendingasǫgur, biskupasǫgur*, and so forth, and in particular from the lack of precision inherent in the description of these categories, is a prime example of the difficulties that arise from a system that reflects *neither* well-documented native categories *nor* well-discussed analytic categories, but to some extent incorporates unarticulated aspects of both.

The harshness of the assessments by Ker, Guðbrandur, and others derives in large part from the intolerance of literary historians for the folkloric nature of these works, as evidenced again by Ker, who laments the mechanical way in which the romantic sagas repeat "old adventures, situations, phrases, characters, or pretences of character."[18] This negative attitude toward the *fornaldarsǫgur* is strengthened by confusion over several issues, among them, the question of which Old Norse texts should be designated *fornaldarsǫgur* and what such a concept does, or should, designate. As a unique subdivision of Icelandic literature, the term *fornaldarsǫgur* dates only to the early nineteenth century, although few scholars, if indeed any, have ever doubted that these sagas with their traditional heroes, eddic-style poetry, wide-ranging geography, and occasional trips to the Otherworld do indeed constitute a distinct division of medieval Scandinavian literature. Although attempts to ferret out the reasons for this sensation on the part of modern readers are often extremely suggestive, no one has yet been able to say exactly what formal features identify the *fornaldarsǫgur* as a group.[19]

Old Norse is far from unique as regards the problem of genre designation and analysis; indeed, genre has been an enduring area of discus-

---

17. An exception might be the *riddarasǫgur*, the case for which is made by Kalinke 1985, 316–18.

18. Ker 1908, 282.

19. One of the most interesting, and tantalizing, of these discussions is Hallberg (1982). For an early attempt to distill the essential quality of the *fornaldarsǫgur*, see Reuschel 1933. An interesting approach to this same problem is to be found in Righter-Gould 1975, 1980, in which she argues that two basic syntagmatic structures characterize the *fornaldarsǫgur*. A work that to some extent rectifies the situation with regard to the *fornaldarsǫgur*, insofar as it more precisely defines the nature of the hero in them, is Hermann Pálsson and Paul Edwards 1971. Although less concerned with this problem of definition, Schlauch 1934 remains one of the single best attempts to analyze and discuss from an historical perspective the nonrealistic fiction of medieval Iceland. The most extensive recent investigation of the genre is Buchholz 1980.

sion—and controversy—in many fields throughout this century.[20] Although one can still legitimately lament that despite the efforts of scholars, no folklore genre has yet been adequately defined, the theoretical advances have been great.[21] Among the intriguing proposals that have been generated in this regard is the attempt to apply a geometrical and mathematical schema using two axes (sacred/secular, factual/fabulous) to the problem of folklore genres.[22] The resulting graph divides the realm of folk literature into various "ideal types" (myth, legend, folktale, secular history, and sacred history), and although the precise application of such a system is far from clear, one can only agree with the assessment that the idea presents interesting theoretical promise.[23] Indeed, Lauri Honko has recently proposed a refined version of the scheme.[24] It has been objected that the system focuses on European folklore forms and is of doubtful application to materials from outside that area. The culturally specific bias inherent in the approach is, in fact, an asset in the current discussion of the genres of medieval Iceland: because of the vastly more restricted field of factors that impinge on the definition of literary forms in a single culture, the schema suggests an appropriate means of distinguishing the various groups of Icelandic texts.

The great advantage of the two-dimensional approach is that it provides a total system of genre classification for the texts it addresses: each group is defined in and of itself, thereby expressing each genre's distinctive characteristics, yet at the same time the model demonstrates the relationship each group bears to other genres according to these same features. Moreover, each individual text, as a unique constellation

20. Genre definitions in folklore and literature have been much discussed over the years. One of the most important articles on this topic from the point of view of folkloristics is surely Honko 1968. Overviews of the scholarship are provided in Ben-Amos 1976 and Bausinger 1968, 9–64. Convenient reviews of the debates surrounding genre analysis in literature, together with extensive bibliographies, are given in Fowler 1982, Hempfer 1973, and Hernadi 1972. Cf. the debate concerning medieval categories of literature in Jauss 1972.

21. "Thus far in the illustrious history of the discipline, not so much as one genre has been completely defined." Dundes 1964, 252.

22. Littleton 1965. The approach proposed by Littleton is not, however, without forebears. See Ben-Amos 1976, xx–xxiii. For a review of such "maps of modes" from the late antique to the present, see Fowler 1982, 239–46. Independent of Littleton, but reflecting a similar approach to the problem of the saga genres, is J. Harris 1972.

23. "Without agreeing with [Littleton's] conclusions, I find the method technically interesting." Honko 1968, 64.

24. Honko (1979–80) reworks Littleton's system, but accepts the basic premise, calling it "one possible paradigm of ideal narrative genres and their relations" (p. 27).

of features, can be located in relation to other texts in the system. That we need not superimpose elaborate categories from the outside in order to make these distinctions and that the system accounts for the relationships between the Icelandic genres also brings this model of genre analysis in line with Jurij Tynjanov's argument that genres are an *interrelated, dynamic* system that cannot be divorced from the social environment.[25] In addition to its ability to identify the relationship in which the various narrative types stand synchronically, this system also allows us to follow a single heroic figure (or text) diachronically, as it wanders over time through the various categories of folk literature, a concept not without relevance for Old Norse literature.[26] One difference between the folk narrative categories C. Scott Littleton uses in his original proposal and the works of Old Norse literature treated here is that the folk categories are enduring forms, whereas those of Old Norse literature are permeable forms. The *riddarasǫgur*, for example, are not to be found in Scandinavia before the thirteenth century.

The Old Norse prose material to be classified is all decidedly secular (occasional pagan theophanies, religious motifs, and clerical callings of some of their protagonists notwithstanding); therefore, I have replaced the sacred/secular axis in the graph with an axis concerned with tradition.

By 'traditional' narrative materials I mean ones that are *continuous,* or believed to be archaic within a given culture, display *variation* in extant multiforms, and are *communal* to members of the culture. Traditional protagonists would be those heroic figures whose fictionalized lives can be traced over time in Scandinavia (the example par excellence being Sigurðr Fáfnisbani), or whose lives have begun to be molded so as to fit traditional heroic biographies, such as Grettir Ásmundarson. In certain respects, this axis parallels Sigurður Nordal's temporally based concept of *oldtidssagaer/fortidssagaer/samtidssagaer,* insofar as that scale implies a recognition of tradition in its divisions. This approach would thus allow for different native assessments of, for example, *Sturlunga saga* over time, as it and its materials increasingly became part of Icelandic tradition. Moreover, different texts, although ostensibly part of the same genre, could be plotted differently, according to the degree to which their contents related to popular tradition. The less traditional category encompasses those works not of native origin, such as the translated *riddarasǫgur,* even though these same narratives would in other cultural

25. Tynjanov 1971.
26. Cf. Littleton's use of the figure of Alexander the Great in his model.

settings represent traditional material. Such would be the case with the Arthurian romances, for example. It also includes works concerned with less archaic materials, such as *Sturlunga saga*.

The factual/fabulous axis reflects the atmosphere produced by the work: in general, where the action, characters, setting, and time frame are specific and individualized, the work is factual; where these same elements are unspecific and stereotyped, it is fabulous. The fabulous mood is further enhanced by the regular intrusion of the supernatural. Thus, both axes in this model reflect the relationship of the saga genres to forms of reality. The foundation for such an approach is Propp's dictum that "the character of a genre is determined by the kind of reality it reflects, the means by which reality is expressed, the relationship to reality, and its assessment."[27] The results of applying these two axes to Icelandic creative prose of the early fourteenth century are shown in the diagram.[28]

Of course, this approach can at best provide only a rough guide to the "ideal types" of each saga genre, yet such a conceptual map does reveal the essential qualities of the groups in relationship to one another, while at the same time acknowledging that every narrative represents a unique constellation of features.[29] Thus, the position a given saga occupies on the chart will differ somewhat in relation to other sagas, precisely the situation that obtains in reality.[30] The schema thereby not only allows us to perceive readily the relationship of the different *categories* of Old Norse literature to one another, but can also illuminate the relationship in which different saga *texts* stand to one another.

Aware that specific sagas, and especially certain sections of sagas, may not fit as neatly into this framework as its inherent tidiness suggests, we can nevertheless outline the nature of their ideal types:

(1) *Highly traditional, highly fabulous* sagas would encompass those nar-

27. Propp 1984, 41.

28. The underlying divisions that obviously precede the point at which this chart begins are poetry/prose and sacred/secular. Although translated literature (other than the *riddarasǫgur*) is not specifically included on the chart, there would be no difficulty in placing such items (e.g., *heilagra manna sǫgur* 'saints' lives').

29. Cf., for example, Honko 1968, 61–62, and Ben-Amos 1976, xviii.

30. Cf. Kames's remark (1762, II, 219) that "literary compositions run into each other, precisely like colours: in their strong tints they are easily distinguished; but are susceptible of so much variety, and take on so many different forms, that we can never say where one species ends and another begins." Of course, the divisions suggested here are intended to be useful from a cognitive point of view; it is not difficult to imagine a text that would defy placement on one side or the other of the various boundaries.

Fabulous

fornaldarsǫgur	*Märchensagas,* or 'native *riddarasǫgur*'	*riddarasǫgur*
íslendingasǫgur	*konungasǫgur, biskupasǫgur*	*Sturlunga saga*

Factual

More traditional   Less traditional

ratives based on stereotyped heroic patterns and imbued with a sense of unreality (for example, the *fornaldarsǫgur*).[31]

(2) *Highly fabulous, moderately traditional* sagas would include those texts with a strong sense of unreality but whose heroes and narrative patterns are neither as continuous within the Nordic context nor as reliant on folkloric patterns as those in the preceding group (for example, the *Märchensagas,*[32] or the 'native *riddarasǫgur*'[33]).

(3) *Highly fabulous, weakly traditional* sagas would be romances of foreign origin, which, though they may be continuous in other cultural contexts, lack continuity in Scandinavia (for example, the translated *riddarasǫgur*).[34]

(4) *Highly traditional, highly factual* sagas are those which project an atmosphere of reality and are continuous within the Nordic context, but in which traditional motifs are common and a recurrent narrative pattern is to be found (for example, the *íslendingasǫgur*).[35]

31. Clearly there would be differences in the positioning of, for example, *Vǫlsunga saga* and the *fornaldarsǫgur* which have been called *Abenteuersagas* by Schier (1970, 77–78) and Naumann (1978).

32. On the *Märchensagas,* see Glauser (1983, 10–22), who defines them as a genre that began as a mixed form of *riddarasǫgur* and *fornaldarsǫgur*. This group and the native *riddarasǫgur* are largely, although not entirely, overlapping sets. See, for example, Schier 1970, 105.

33. On the native *riddarasǫgur*, see van Nahl 1981.

34. Cf. the introductory remarks in Halvorsen 1959.

35. On the *íslendingasǫgur* in relation to heroic poetry and legend, see Uecker 1980.

(5) *Highly factual, moderately traditional* sagas would include historical narratives with an air of reality, but in which traditional narrative and heroic patterns are occasionally discernible (for example, the *konungasǫgur* and *biskupasǫgur*).

(6) *Highly factual, weakly traditional* texts are those which are considered reliable and which are often highly individualized with regard to characterization and plot (for example, *Sturlunga saga* and parts of *Landnámabók*).

Such an apparently all-inclusive scheme would be incomplete without at least a few caveats. It is clear that some works (depending on how they are sectioned) will not fit neatly into a single category.[36] The position of *Ynglingasaga* will differ dramatically from the rest of *Heimskringla; Geirmundar þáttr*, with which *Sturlunga saga* opens, would be categorized quite differently from a more contemporary part of the collection, such as *Svínfellinga saga*. But this is obviously more a question of how we divide anthologies and seemingly encyclopedic works than a theoretical objection. After all, some of the *fornaldarsǫgur* (for example, *Helga þáttr Þórissonar*) exist only as embedded portions of larger works. Some texts, such as the traditional but foreign-influenced *Kjalnesinga saga,* tend to defy the system, although I believe *Kjalnesinga saga* would find a home somewhere along the border of the *íslendingasǫgur* and *fornaldarsǫgur*. The advantages of the system, on the other hand, are great, and it is not difficult to envision how we might continue to call *fornaldarsǫgur* two such very different texts as *Gríms saga loðinkinna* and *Yngvars saga víðfǫrla; Gríms saga* would clearly be positioned closer to the native *riddarasǫgur*, whereas *Yngvars saga* would be located near the *konungasǫgur*, given its relatively recent historical dimensions.

There is an implicit irony in the preceding discussion: it begins by questioning the validity of the prevailing system of literary taxonomy for Old Norse, but concludes by justifying it, a situation not unlike Vladimir Propp's criticism of Antti Aarne's division of tale types, in which he too ends up defending and justifying the very system to which he objected.[37] Nor is it unlike the conclusion that the genre

36. Cf. Lönnroth's comment (1964, 30–31) that "if one divides each saga up into smaller units, classification becomes considerably easier."

37. "He [Propp] found Aarne's classification untenable (at least from a theoretical point of view), then used it for his own purposes, showed that the tales numbered 300–749 in Aarne's index indeed form a remarkable unity of composition, and redefined the wondertale in his own terms [. . .] By doing so, he vindicated Aarne's division." Liberman 1984, xxxii–xxxiii.

system of Icelandic literature intuition has bequeathed us may not be all that far removed from the ethnic system.[38] The major objection to the standard classification of sagas which has been raised here (and elsewhere) rests not so much on its resulting division of materials, but rather on the unarticulated—and thereby potentially misleading—set of principles which forms its basis. With the basis for such a system of modes now established, it will be possible to refine the concept and scope of the *fornaldarsǫgur*.

In fact, early editors of the corpus of Old Norse literature took the initiative in viewing the *fornaldarsǫgur* as a distinct genre; especially influential was *Fornaldar Sögur Nordrlanda eptir gömlum handritum* 'Northern sagas of antiquity according to old manuscripts,' edited by Carl Christian Rafn and published in 1829, long the standard edition.[39] The rationale for grouping these texts together is presented both in this collection and in the introduction to the Danish translation, *Nordiske Fortids Sagaer*. This popular publication had been preceded by *Nordiske Kæmpe-Historier* 'Nordic heroic sagas' (*eller mythiske og romantiske Sagaer* 'or mythic and romantic sagas,' as Rafn was to add to the final volume).[40] In the prologue, Rafn writes that these sagas are those which treat events that took place in Scandinavia before the colonization of Iceland in the ninth century; he contrasts them to texts that contain reliable accounts. Thus, although the sagas are not held to be factually accurate, the motivation for the Icelandic term *fornaldarsǫgur* rests on their presumed historical perspective, however flawed. Rafn goes on to caution that the influence of native mythological and foreign romantic traditions will occasionally impinge on the usefulness of certain texts as historical sources. Whether or not these works possess any historical value from a modern critical vantage point, they do constitute a group whose protagonists generally "lived" (factually or fictionally) in the period before the historical Nordic period, both as we understand it and, more important, as the medieval Icelanders understood it.

Rafn's division of the sagas, although decisive in many respects for modern scholarship, was by no means original: Peter E. Müller's influential *Sagabibliothek* (1818), the second volume of which contains the

38. J. Harris 1975, 434–35.
39. The earliest collective edition of *fornaldarsǫgur* was Biörner's *Nordiska Kämpa Dater* (1737), a trilingual (Icelandic, Swedish, Latin) edition of over a dozen *fornaldarsǫgur* and *riddarasǫgur*.
40. *Nordiske Fortids Sagaer*, trans. Rafn, a 2d ed. of Rafn's *Nordiske Kæmpe-Historier*. On Rafn's contribution to Old Norse studies, see Widding 1964.

"romantic sagas," had already established the division of Old Norse texts into those considered more realistic and those which dealt with "the mythical time in Scandinavia."[41] Müller in turn subdivided this category into the following groups: material touching on the Vǫlsungs; material about Þiðrekr af Bern; miscellaneous mythological sagas; and three groups of romantic sagas. Müller's organization, like Sigurður Nordal's, depended to a great extent on the presumed date of writing: "The sagas in this volume, as in the first, are arranged according to their likely date of recording."[42]

The term *fornaldarsǫgur* is then a modern convention, although the concept might be said to have a pedigree of sorts in the Old Norse texts themselves. Although the modern term refers solely to the period in which the action of the saga purportedly takes place,[43] references in Icelandic texts to the presumed antiquity of the sagas themselves are common. Among the medieval terms, the phrase *fornar frásagnir* 'ancient accounts,' employed by Snorri Sturluson in the prologue to *Heimskringla*,[44] is perhaps the best-known example. The term *fornsaga* 'ancient, old saga' appears routinely in the Old Norse texts: when, for example, the author of *Heiðreks saga* praises the sword Týrfingr, he comments that *þetta suerd er frægt i ollum fǫrn sogum* 'that sword is famous in all the old sagas' (chap. 1); and when the compiler of *Vǫlsunga saga* wants to praise the hero's family, he claims that their prowess is well attested *i fornsaugum* 'in old sagas' (chap. 2). It must be borne in mind, however, that such citations by no means establish a traditional basis for modern usage, although they bear important testimony to the views the medieval Icelanders held toward the Viking age. Undoubtedly many terms, some of which we know (*lygisǫgur* 'lying sagas'; *skrǫk sǫgur* 'deceiving sagas'; *stjúpmæðra sǫgur* 'step-mother sagas'),[45] some of which can only be assumed to have existed, once designated narratives of the sort now regarded as *fornaldarsǫgur*. There

41. Müller 1817–20, II, vii. The three volumes that make up this work are arranged respectively as *íslendingasǫgur*, *fornaldarsǫgur*, and *konungasǫgur*.

42. Ibid., p. xi.

43. That is, where the term refers to anything *within*, as opposed to about, the saga; a number of the *fornaldarsǫgur* are essentially timeless, that is, lacking in any specific datable reference. Their designation as 'sagas of antiquity' has to do with the atmosphere the works conjure up.

44. In this instance, the term is almost certainly not in reference to what we know as *fornaldarsǫgur*, as Snorri is speaking specifically of the tales of the kings he includes in *Heimskringla* (although it is possible he may have lost *fornaldarsǫgur* about the Ynglings, for example, in mind).

45. The term *lygisǫgur* is used in *Þorgils saga ok Hafliða* (chap. 10) in reference to a *fornaldarsaga* (*Hrómundar saga Gripssonar*), although the term is sometimes used by modern critics to refer to the *riddarasǫgur* and other sagas.

is unfortunately no scholarly consensus as to what these terms designate: some critics, for instance, have used the term *lygisǫgur* to refer to the native romances; others have ʾapplied it to the entire corpus of indigenous romances and *fornaldarsǫgur;* still others have used the term to indicate a secondary development from the *fornaldarsǫgur* to another form.[46] Nor for that matter are the available terms limited: it has been suggested that all Old Norse 'romances' (including some of the texts in Rafn's edition) be called either *Fornaldarsǫgur Norðrlanda* 'northern romances' or *Fornaldarsǫgur Suðrlanda* 'southern romances.'[47]

That the medieval Icelanders who composed and told these tales understood that there existed important differences between the various saga genres is well illustrated in *Flóres saga konungs ok sona hans* (chap. 1) by an amusing—if somewhat defensive—writer, who divides the realm of saga literature into three groups. The first contains works about holy men (that is, hagiography), in which, he assures the reader, there is *lítil skemtun* 'little entertainment.' The second category consists of texts that deal with powerful kings from whom chivalric behavior might be learned, and the third is made up of the tales of kings who fall into adversity but are ultimately victorious by virtue of their strength and fierce weapons. Presumably the writer would have included the *fornaldarsǫgur* in this third category.

Commentary of this sort, indicating a recognition of thematic unity, is rare, but the notion that the *fornaldarsǫgur* represented a particular category of saga in the minds of medieval Icelanders is suggested by the codicological evidence, for the *fornaldarsǫgur* are frequently bound together in manuscripts in such a way as to prefigure the modern perception of them as a genre. These collections represent one of the few contemporary sources of information for the native scheme of saga classification.[48] In most instances, these collections of *fornaldarsǫgur* signal not the sense of a later binder, but the foliation of the medieval

46. Examples of the first type are Finnur Jónsson (1920–24, III, 98) and Schlauch (1934, 16); of the second, Lagerholm (1927, x) and de Vries (1941–42, II, 539); and of the third, Mogk (1901–9, 830–31, 845–46) and Einar Ólafur Sveinsson (1929, xxvi).

47. Kalinke 1985, 331–32. Cf. Gustaf Cederschiöld's anthology of Old Norse romances, *Fornsögur Suðrlanda* (1884). Kalinke (1985, 323–32) provides a review of scholarship on the technical nomenclature of the romances. On Kalinke's own plot structure approach, see Weber's objections (1986, 424–25).

48. Lönnroth (1965, 7) objects, "It also seems very difficult to justify these distinctions by pointing to certain more or less 'homogenous' 14th and 15th century manuscripts containing sagas now classified as belonging 'to the same genre.' When such manuscripts are analyzed, it is almost always found that the sagas are not grouped together because they belong to the same genre but because their historical content is related." J. Harris (1972, 24) rejects this assertion and argues that at least some manuscripts "imply a recognition" of genres.

producer. Three especially interesting collections from this point of view are AM 343a, 4to, AM 152, fol., and Gks 2845, 4to. Manuscript AM 343a, 4to consists entirely of fictional sagas of one sort or another, that is, ten *fornaldarsǫgur* and five romances.[49] AM 152, fol. displays the same sort of content, five *fornaldarsǫgur* and four romances, together with two of the most heroic of the *íslendingasǫgur* (*Grettis saga Ásmundarsonar* and *Þórðar saga hreðu*).[50] In the case of Gks 2845, 4to, there is only one realistic text in the current, admittedly defective, manuscript: *Bandamanna saga*.[51] Otherwise, it contains *Rauðúlfs þáttr*, with its heavy emphasis on dreams and Rauðúlfr's supernatural powers of interpretation, *Eiríks saga víðfǫrla*, a religious text showing clear affinities to the *fornaldarsǫgur*, and *Orms þáttr Stórólfssonar*, a text with substantial ties to the *fornaldarsǫgur*, and six *fornaldarsǫgur*.[52] Certainly there are manuscripts that do not reflect such organization, but one need only think of the elaborate editorial principle in effect in the Codex Regius manuscript (Gks 2365, 4to) of the *Poetic Edda* (eleven mythological poems followed by twenty heroic poems, each group with its various subdivisions and organization) to understand that such a concept was far from foreign to the medieval Icelanders.[53]

There are then indications that while the concept of a specific genre of Old Norse literature known as the *fornaldarsǫgur* may be a modern archival convenience in the strictest sense, the implicit ancestry of such a division precedes our era by many centuries, although admittedly in

---

49. *Fornaldarsǫgur: Ketils saga hœngs, Gríms saga loðinkinna, Ǫrvar-Odds saga, Áns saga bogsveigis, Egils saga ok Ásmundar, Hálfdanar saga Brǫnufóstra, Bósa saga, Yngvars saga víðfǫrla, Þorsteins saga bæjarmagns;* romances: *Samsons saga fagra, Flóres saga konungs ok sona hans, Saulus saga ok Nikanors, Vilhjálms saga sjóðs, Vilmundar saga viðutan.*

50. *Fornaldarsǫgur: Gautreks saga, Hrólfs saga Gautrekssonar, Gǫngu-Hrólfs saga, Hálfdanar saga Brǫnufóstra, Þorsteins saga Víkingssonar;* romances: *Mágus saga jarls, Hectors saga, Sigurðar saga þǫgla, Flóvents saga Frakkakonungs.* Lönnroth (1964, 23) cites AM 152, fol. as evidence of the heterogeneous nature of the Old Norse manuscripts. I agree that the manuscript implies that there were no absolute genre distinctions corresponding to the modern ones, but the manuscript does indicate that it was carefully organized and made up of sagas recognizably—then, as now—related to one another, and that something generally corresponding to our modern concepts of *fornaldarsǫgur* and *riddarasǫgur* existed. On the exact order of the materials, see *Katalog over Den arnamagnæanske Håndskriftsamling.*

51. But see Lönnroth's objection (1964, 24) that this collection too is evidence of the heterogeneous nature of the manuscripts.

52. *Norna-Gests þáttr, Hálfs saga ok Hálfsrekka, Gǫngu-Hrólfs saga, Yngvars saga, Hálfdanar saga Eysteinssonar,* and *Heiðreks saga.*

53. On the codicological testimony of the *Poetic Edda*, see Lindblad 1954, 1979, 1980. The placement of *Vǫlundarqviða*, and the reasons for it, are clearly open to interpretation.

a vaguer and less rigid sense than our modern categories suggest. As to what these sagas typically call themselves—for nowhere in the Old Norse corpus is the term *fornaldarsaga* used—their authors appear to take the distant and indifferent attitude to such discussions which characterizes traditional communities: when the *fornaldarsǫgur* are self-referential, as they often are, they tend to stick with the nebulous but effective terms *saga* and *frásagnir* 'accounts.'

The discipline of Old Norse studies has, virtually without exception, accepted the status of the *fornaldarsǫgur* as a distinct and legitimate division of Old Norse literature, yet modern scholars have been at a loss as to exactly what this category designates. Although many of the great names associated with the discipline have addressed themselves to this issue, none has satisfactorily defined what he or she means by a *fornaldarsaga*. Finnur Jónsson, for example, contents himself with what is ultimately a rather perplexing definition of the *fornaldarsǫgur:* they are, he states, a collection of sagas, the protagonists of which are generally Norwegians who are, or were felt to be, historical, although figures who are unhistorical might also be treated in this group.[54] Here Finnur has cast his net so wide that nothing, not even the *konungasǫgur* and *íslendingasǫgur,* could escape if we were to apply his description without prejudice to the entire corpus of Old Norse texts. Axel Olrik shows remarkable appreciation for the *fornaldarsǫgur* and the light they can shed on the literary world of the medieval Scandinavians, yet he never specifically identifies the qualities that comprise one; rather he accepts the division made by Rafn and clearly views the *fornaldarsǫgur* as a genre that begins as a kind of historical writing and slowly becomes increasingly folkloric (*æventyrlig*).[55]

Birger Nerman was one of the first to recognize the striking lacuna in our technical terminology with regard to the *fornaldarsǫgur.* In 1913 he pointed out that scholars had never specified what they meant by the term *fornaldarsaga* nor had anyone produced a clear definition of what this group consisted of. He concluded that no more specific characterization of the genre is likely than his own evolutionary formulation of them as Scandinavian prose romances, restructured from preexisting heroic poetry.[56] Other attempts to capture the essence of the genre

54. Finnur Jónsson 1920–24, II, 783.
55. Olrik 1892, 1–14.
56. Nerman 1913, 29–30. I do not disagree with the literary progression his characterization reflects, only with the adequacy of the diachronic phenomenon as the defining character of the genre, particularly where there are so many lacunae in our information.

have also been notably unsuccessful. Jón Helgason compares the *forn-aldarsǫgur* to the *íslendingasǫgur* and *konungasǫgur* and defines them as works that follow the patterns of these other genres, especially insofar as they are often biographies, but that are unlike these other works in that they are baroque and fantastic.[57] Helga Reuschel sees them as the artistic presentation of the Germanic heroic ideal, in contrast to the mundane realism of the *íslendingasǫgur*.[58] And one searches in vain in Margaret Schlauch's excellent discussion *Romance in Iceland* for a definition that would really distinguish between the various "non-historical" sagas.[59] Sigurður Nordal, despite the accuracy of some of his criticisms of the present system of genre organization in Old Norse, fares little better with his scheme for chronological nomenclature. According to his divisions, some of the *fornaldarsǫgur* would be classed as *fortidssagaer* 'early sagas,' others *oldtidssagaer* 'ancient sagas,' although he clearly intends the entire corpus to be included in the latter category.[60]

Continuity with the older poetic tradition is emphasized by Jan de Vries and Peter Buchholz. De Vries characterizes the *fornaldarsǫgur* as prose reworkings of old heroic lays, a perspective also adopted by Buchholz, who views them as the medieval manifestation of Scandinavian heroic legends.[61] Both writers emphasize an evolutionary approach in line with Nerman's characterization of the *fornaldarsǫgur*, which gives a sense of the main themes and figures one encounters in these texts but does little to validate the notion that, as a genre, the *fornaldarsǫgur* should be susceptible to description in terms of their formal features. Similarly, Kurt Schier describes the *fornaldarsǫgur* as embracing works that reproduce heroic materials from the Migration Era, as well as freely invented tales of the thirteenth and fourteenth

---

57. Jón Helgason 1934, 195.

58. "In the Icelandic Sagas we have realism [. . .] The *fornaldarsǫgur* are idealistic, they aspire to be heroic history (*Heldengeschichte*)" (Reuschel 1933, 8).

59. Schlauch 1934. Schlauch's book is primarily devoted to those *lygisǫgur* generally regarded as *riddarasǫgur* and *Märchensagas*. The closest she comes to a delineation of the *fornaldarsǫgur* is the following: "In the less historic or purely fictitious tales dealing with Icelandic characters, there is an increase in the use of strange, fantastic and supernatural motives. This second group, the *fornaldarsǫgur*, was regarded as fiction rather than history, although the chief characters were still supposed to be Icelanders [*sic*], and were in fact sometimes connected with eminent families" (1934, 12).

60. "*Sagas of Antiquity (oldtidssagaer)* are finally those sagas, which take place or are thought to take place in the time before 850. To this group belong all of the *forn-aldarsǫgur* and *riddarasǫgur* and certain episodes of other writings." Sigurður Nordal 1953, 181.

61. De Vries 1941–42, II, 464; Buchholz 1980, 16–19.

centuries.[62] In her discussion of recurrent structural features in the *fornaldarsǫgur*, Ruth Righter-Gould accepts the traditional corpus of sagas, but the features she proposes as distinctive for them are, as Kalinke rightly points out, also true of the *riddarasǫgur*.[63] Hermann Pálsson has called attention to the problem of the *fornaldarsǫgur* and what that concept does, or should, mean, although he appears to concede the impossibility of a definition,[64] apparently concurring with Åke Lagerholm when the latter writes that the heterogenous and multifaceted character of the group makes its description impossible.[65]

Those who have attempted definitions of the *fornaldarsǫgur* have typically contented themselves with characterizations that emphasize the origins of the sagas in another genre (for example, Birger Nerman, Jan de Vries, Peter Buchholz) or their supposed historicity (for example, Finnur Jónsson, Axel Olrik). A useful touchstone for the sort of distinction required in defining the genre was suggested by Knut Liestøl and A. Le Roy Andrews. Although Liestøl never provides a precise definition of the *fornaldarsǫgur*, the attributes he lists are among the most useful set of descriptive features to date: (1) the *fornaldarsǫgur* tend to resemble the historical sagas; (2) their subjects are often treated in a similar fashion to those of the *íslendingasǫgur*; (3) the action of the *fornaldarsǫgur* typically takes place outside of Iceland and before the

62. Schier 1970, 73. Significantly, he immediately adds: "It is difficult to establish truly sound criteria for such genre distinctions (*Gliederungskriterion*)." The extent to which some of the sagas can be considered "freely invented" is open to discussion; where there are no known antecedents, the sagas are usually based on folklore or other traditional patterns. Cf. Schier's definition for the *fornaldarsǫgur* (1971–), where he refers to them as a group of essentially unhistorical sagas that deal with the period before 850.

63. Righter-Gould 1980, Kalinke 1985, 326–27.

64. Hermann Pálsson 1979b. Hermann argues that "the formal treatment of those materials [i.e., the raw materials that went into the making of the sagas] and their relevance to the quality of human existence and ideals in early Iceland must also be taken into consideration." "Whatever the origins of the materials for the 'fornaldarsögur', it should be plain enough that most of them belong, formally at least, to the romance tradition of medieval Europe, and for that reason it would be a mistake to try to draw too sharp a dividing line between them [i.e., the *fornaldarsǫgur*] and the 'riddarasögur' and 'lygisögur' " (1979b, 16). See also Hermann Pálsson 1979a, in which he makes a number of valuable observations concerning the literary taxonomy of Old Norse texts. In his excellent introduction to the *fornaldarsǫgur* (1982a), Hermann attempts no definition of them as a group at all, giving instead a lengthy description of their prominent characteristics.

65. "An entirely adequate definition of the *fornaldarsaga* has not yet been given and as we are dealing here with an extraordinarily many-sided and heterogeneous genre, it is truly impossible to advance any such definition" (Lagerholm 1927, x).

colonization of it (all points about the *fornaldarsǫgur* made frequently by others as well); and (4) in neither their characters nor their events do the *fornaldarsǫgur* have what Liestøl calls an individual touch—they are "in the style of the folk-tales. In their general character, in fact, they rather resemble folk-tales or romances."[66]

This point of view had been voiced some fifteen years earlier by Andrews, who, in an attempt to distinguish the *fornaldarsǫgur* and *lygisǫgur,* on the one hand, from the other kinds of sagas, on the other, specifically remarks that *tradition* must be regarded as the key feature of such a distinction. Ultimately, he goes on, this same quality should be employed as a means of distinguishing between the *fornaldarsǫgur* and the *lygisǫgur* as well.[67] Employing this same criterion of traditionality in analyzing the saga genres has, in fact, made it possible to distinguish the *fornaldarsǫgur* from other genres of Old Norse literature. Folklore motifs, an obvious feature of this traditional quality, are especially common in the *fornaldarsǫgur,* and their combination with elements of learned lore helps indicate the degree to which the *fornaldarsǫgur* are something "more" than folklore, yet something "less" than wholly innovative works. They are, in fact, an unusual blend of inherited, borrowed, and individually crafted materials.

This fascinating, if problematic, relationship and the need for a critical response to it were underscored in the mid-1960s in the sagacious plea made by Francis Lee Utley that "in the light of great new advances in literary history and the study of folk-narrative, it is time for a renewed attempt to help these two disciplines join forces."[68] Mindful of these facts, we must undertake a characterization of the *fornaldarsǫgur* which not only details their formal features, but which also makes it clear that we cannot, for example, take to *Þorsteins þáttr bæjarmagns* the same critical apparatus we would use in analyzing *Njáls saga.* It is precisely the failure to realize this fact and to respond accordingly that has resulted in comments, and attitudes, of the kind reported above by Ker, Guðbrandur Vigfússon, and many other critics. Naturally, the appearance of a single folklore motif here or there in a narrative does not identify the saga as a *fornaldarsaga,* but where well-established *structural* similarities between modern folklore narratives and the Old Norse texts exist—especially where these similarities can be shown to date back for a considerable time—we should formulate a definition of

66. Liestøl 1930, 162–63.
67. Andrews 1914–16.
68. Utley 1965, 588.

the *fornaldarsǫgur* which takes this relationship to tradition into account. Likewise, the fabulous or unrealistic quality of the *fornaldarsǫgur* should be given appropriate place in such a definition, although it is well to be cognizant of the degree to which each text will display these two qualities in different measures. A definition of the *fornaldarsǫgur* which provides the *minimum* amount of information necessary to distinguish them from other kinds of sagas but does *not* attempt to include all the features shared by these sagas may then be proposed:

> *fornaldarsǫgur:* Old Icelandic prose narratives based on traditional heroic themes, whose numerous fabulous episodes and motifs create an atmosphere of unreality.

As we have seen above, one of the fundamental traits that distinguish the *fornaldarsǫgur* from other kinds of sagas is their grounding in traditional heroic themes, a characteristic that precludes such material as that borrowed from the Orient.[69] Although tales with foreign origins, such as *Friðþjófs saga ins frœkna* and *Hróa þáttr heimska,* often exhibit highly folkloric contents, they should not be confused with the indigenous *fornaldarsǫgur* whose materials display a lengthy continuity within the Nordic cultural context. The traditional component ensures that the corpus does not include the *riddarasǫgur,* which are based on Continental literature. Certain stylistic aspects of the *fornaldarsǫgur* which reflect the traditional character of the sagas and their connectedness to folklore are precisely those things that Ker decries so vehemently: repetitions, use of stock characters, and so forth. The proposed definition should perhaps further specify that the *fornaldarsǫgur* display *major* folkloric elements in their structure, in recognition of the fact that these texts are literary hybrids drawing on both popular and learned sources: where the inevitable compromise between the two has been in favor of the written culture, folklore elements will still appear but may be reduced to nothing more than the occasional motif. On the other hand, texts that remain closer to their traditional origins will tend to demonstrate a more fundamental indebtedness to folklore (one need only compare, for example, the indebtedness of the three sagas of the Hrafnistumenn to the so-called Bear's Son Tale for an instructive example of this process).[70]

The fabulous nature of the *fornaldarsǫgur* can only be judged from the

69. See, for example, Schlauch 1934, 69–94.
70. Pizarro 1976–77.

modern point of view, although there is little doubt that similar judgments would have been made by contemporary Icelanders as well.[71] The assessment is naturally a relative one, but one need only compare the soberness of the *íslendingasǫgur* with the time compressions, talking animals, metamorphoses, and supernatural beings of the *fornaldarsǫgur* to see how uncomplicated this decision is: even where the *íslendingasǫgur* treat such supernatural phenomena as premonitions and visions, they tend to do so for specific dramatic effect, unlike the comic and mystifying effect often generated in the *fornaldarsǫgur*.

The *fornaldarsǫgur* are also characteristically filled with verse. It is true that some of them do not contain large amounts of poetry, or in some cases, any poetry at all; however, most of them do, and if we look at those most often held up as the leading examples of this genre (*Ragnars saga loðbrókar, Hálfs saga ok Hálfsrekka, Ǫrvar-Odds saga, Hrólfs saga kraka*), we find that they often contain lengthy sections of narrative poetry, in addition to frequent *lausavísur* 'occasional poetry.' They are primarily prose works, however, unlike the completely versified *rímur*, Icelandic metrical romances that often deal with the same topics. A further characteristic of the poetry in the *fornaldarsǫgur* is that it is always in eddic, rather than skaldic, meter, unlike the *íslendingasǫgur* and *konungasǫgur*, in which the reverse is true. (Eddic poetry can be characterized as alliterative poetry with relatively simple diction and style, created by anonymous composers, and concerned with traditional themes; skaldic poetry, on the other hand, generally treated contemporary topics, was decidedly not anonymous, and displays highly elaborate rules of versification and use of metaphor.)

Temporally and spatially, the *fornaldarsǫgur* are unique among the sagas as well. Time is frequently treated in the *fornaldarsǫgur* in the same way as in folktales—it is simply ignored at the specific level. The time frame of the *fornaldarsǫgur* is either left unspecified or is said to be some remote period before the colonization of Iceland. In either case, time is of a completely different nature than the nearly ubiquitous opening *Þat var á dǫgum Haralds konungs ins hárfagra* 'It was in the days of King Haraldr Fair-Hair' and the like of the *íslendingasǫgur*. The treatment of geography in the *fornaldarsǫgur* is also reminiscent of folklore attitudes: although countries and cities are commonly named, they are merely ciphers for exotic settings, not carefully detailed locations. What they lack in precision, however, the *fornaldarsǫgur* make up

71. Cf., for example, the tension between the harsh critical perspective toward what one has not seen oneself and the more sympathetic cultural relativism inherent in the discussion between the father and son in the Old Norwegian *Konungsskuggsiá* (chap. 9).

in breadth, for the action of the sagas frequently occurs outside Scandinavia—France, Ireland, Russia, the Holy Land, and the Otherworld all figure in them. But here too there is an air of unreality about these sagas which derives from what may be called the undefined bleak landscape of the Teutonic epic;[72] such locations evoke a mood, but they do not detail a setting. Both features stand in stark contrast to the elaborate networks of temporal and spatial frames of reference in which the *íslendingasǫgur, konungasǫgur,* and *Sturlunga saga* delight.

Aside from these characteristics, though, there is little that can usefully be added: we cannot legitimately discuss such normal issues within literary purview as characterization because there is such a wide discrepancy between the standards to which the various compilers and editors of the *fornaldarsǫgur* subscribe, although there is certainly a strong tendency toward monodimensional figures.[73] Similarly, plots often revolve around quests, but this feature is no more characteristic of the *fornaldarsǫgur* than it is of many of the other Old Norse texts.[74] On the other hand, the features listed above are more than sufficient to delineate the *fornaldarsǫgur* as a separate genre and to reveal something of their special character.

There should be no mistake about the ramifications of this proposed definition: it does not merely ratify the collection of sagas in Rafn's edition from 1829, as has often been the case with previous descriptions (although most scholars would agree that Müller and Rafn were generally correct in their assessments). Rather than simply describing the sagas we have grown accustomed to calling *fornaldarsǫgur,* this definition demands that we rethink the traditional ascription of certain sagas to this genre and strains some of our standard perceptions about the sagas in general. It implies that some of the sagas long assumed to be safely ensconced within the corpus of the *fornaldarsǫgur,* such as *Friðþjófs saga,* actually belong elsewhere. Other sagas, including some we are accustomed to thinking of as *íslendingasǫgur,* ought to be considered in the light of the possibility that they are *fornaldarsǫgur,* or perhaps texts in the process of "moving" from the one genre to the other.[75]

72. Cf. Ker 1908, 20.
73. See, however, Hermann Pálsson and Paul Edwards 1971 for a thorough discussion of the *nature* of the hero of the *fornaldarsǫgur* vis-à-vis the environment and other men.
74. Cf. Kalinke 1985, 326–31.
75. A similar notion is rejected on a specific level (i.e., that of individual texts), but embraced on a more general level in Andersson 1967, 65–93; a theoretical presentation of the same idea as applied to traditional narrative genres is given in Littleton 1965.

An excellent example of such movement is offered by the case of *Grettis saga Ásmundarsonar:* although the saga certainly treats an historical figure (that is, its eponymous hero appears elsewhere in various supposedly reliable sources), the story has been heavily influenced by what one scholar has called its "obvious leanings in the direction of the *fornaldarsögur* and *lygisögur* ['lying sagas']" and by the traditional narrative elements commonly associated with the Bear's Son Tale.[76] In considering the possibility of such genre mutability, we should be troubled neither by the apparently historical nature of the hero nor by the appearance of some historical details about this person's life. The appearance of premonitions in *Njáls saga,* for example, does not convince us that it is somehow unrealistic in its basic tone and mood, nor does the apparently historical basis of the king who becomes the hero of *Ragnars saga loðbrókar* incline us to regard his saga as anything other than a *fornaldarsaga.* Neither should the apparent historicity of *Grettis saga* deter us from believing that its authors and redactors were influenced by the *fornaldarsaga* tradition in such a way that the saga reflects many of that genre's characteristic features. Viewing *Grettis saga* as one of the *íslendingasǫgur* moving toward the *fornaldarsǫgur* would also explain why it fits so poorly Andersson's description of the structure of the *íslendingasǫgur.*[77] It is for this reason that many of the most interesting and productive readings of the saga have based themselves on interpretations of folkloric elements in the saga.[78] Still, important features separate *Grettis saga* from the *fornaldarsǫgur:* most prominently, skaldic- rather than eddic-meter verses and characterization that is much more extensively developed in *Grettis saga* than is the case in any *fornaldarsaga.* In many respects, the saga consists of a number of historical and realistic surface features stretched over a structural frame of a traditional nature. It appears to be an example of a saga in transition, moving from one genre to another, increasingly following traditional heroic patterns over time; certainly the medieval editor responsible for the composition of AM 152, fol. seems to have been convinced that *Grettis saga* was in some way closely related to the *fornaldarsǫgur.*

76. Hume 1974, 470; R. Harris 1974. The complex now known as the Bear's Son Tale was formulated by Panzer 1910–12.

77. Andersson 1967.

78. E.g., Gering 1880, Pipping 1938, Arendt 1969, Motz 1973, Ciklamini 1966b, Hume 1974, R. Harris 1974, Óskar Halldórsson 1982, and Hastrup 1986. See also Watkins (1987, 297–98), who points out other ways in which the vocabulary of *Grettis saga* appears to respond to tradition.

This new definition will require rethinking the categorization of other texts as well: *Þiðreks saga,* for example, would not meet the criteria established for this genre.[79] The saga is cast in a form largely atypical of the Old Norse works envisioned in the definition of the *fornaldarsǫgur* proposed here. Because of its connections to indigenous themes, it has sometimes been viewed as a *fornaldarsaga,* despite the many differences of style and atmosphere which distinguish it from the *fornaldarsǫgur.* Recent work on the stylistics of the *fornaldarsǫgur* suggests too that there is no reason to place *Þiðreks saga* among them.[80] Neither *Friðþjófs saga ins frækna, Hjálmpérssaga ok Ǫlvis, Ála flekks saga,* nor a number of other sagas that display strong similarities to the *fornaldarsǫgur,* and are often included among them, is likely to be satisfactorily ascribed to the genre as it has been defined. A diagram of modes such as the one given above, however, makes these sagas' proximity to the genre immediately apparent.[81] Many of the texts culled from *Flateyjarbók* and other medieval collections because of their thematic relationship to the *fornaldarsǫgur* must also be considered outside the corpus of texts that actually constitute the genre. Although it is true that *Hversu Noregr byggðist, Sǫgubrot af fornkonungum,* and *Af Upplendinga konungum* have much to say that is of importance for our understanding of the traditional heroic material of Scandinavia, they are, of course, not *fornaldarsǫgur,* as their inclusion in editions implies. They are useful and relevant works, but for the most part they no more belong to the *fornaldarsǫgur* as a category of Old Norse *narrative* prose than the *ættartǫlur* 'genealogies' do to the *íslendingasǫgur.*

The proposed definition has thus helped pare away certain texts from the corpus of *fornaldarsǫgur.* It has also raised the possibility that other sagas should be considered as undergoing generic mutation. It is clear from the example of such liminal texts as *Grettis saga, Eiríks saga víðfǫrla,* and *Þiðreks saga* that although there are a variety of reasons for thinking of sagas as belonging to distinct genres, we also need to appreciate that these categories are neither widely separated nor inhospitable to influence from one another. The definition suggested for the *fornaldarsǫgur* allows us the best of both approaches to genre classifica-

---

79. *Þiðreks saga* has typically defied genre assignment according to the standard system: it is often regarded as a *riddarasaga,* but because it is based on Germanic, rather than British or French, sources it is sometimes included among the *fornaldarsǫgur.*

80. Hallberg 1982, 33.

81. On the untraditionality and other uncharacteristic features (for the *fornaldarsǫgur*) of such closely related texts, see, for example, Gould 1923 and R. Harris 1970a, v–vi.

tion: the description takes into account factors that are both analytic and ethnic,[82] insofar as the traditional axis reflects the relationship of the text to society. It is a viable working definition that captures the essence of the *fornaldarsǫgur* (that is, their relationship to tradition and reality), indicates the salient differences between them and other saga genres, and bases itself on their most distinctive formal features.

The *fornaldarsǫgur* and the Critics

The attitudes toward the *fornaldarsǫgur* which have been held during the past three centuries are intimately tied to the views held about the other saga genres and the Germanic heroic materials more generally.[83] To disengage the *fornaldarsǫgur* entirely from these perceptions would not only be an impossible task, but also a questionable undertaking. Within the wider framework of prevailing scholarly views, however, it is possible to discern distinct trends about the origins and nature of the *fornaldarsǫgur* which have helped shape current conceptions—and misconceptions—about these traditional, fabulous narratives. These perspectives conveniently fall into three categories concerning (1) the *fornaldarsǫgur* and history, (2) the reaction against the *fornaldarsǫgur* as history and as literature, and (3) the connection between the *fornaldarsǫgur* and folklore and mythology. It should be noted, however, that the attitudes represented by these divisions are neither mutually exclusive nor fully representative of the history of approaches to the *fornaldarsǫgur*.

Modern, non-Icelandic interest in the *fornaldarsǫgur* dates to the seventeenth century. The political rivalry between the Danish and Swedish kingdoms, and the resulting propaganda war, led to the systematic ransacking of older Scandinavian monuments, especially the Icelandic sagas. These texts, it was believed, offered testimony for the opposing claims of the two realms; questions concerning the possession of certain areas of Scandinavia, as well as issues of former glory and prestige,

---

82. See Ben-Amos 1969, 275–301. Cf. Dundes 1962 and Feleppa 1986.

83. The history of saga scholarship, especially with respect to the *íslendingasǫgur*, is covered in detail in Andersson 1964. Thorp 1940 discusses a number of intellectual and critical developments of importance to the *fornaldarsǫgur*, especially insofar as they relate to the Sigurðr-Siegfried tradition. For a review of the approaches to the Germanic *Heldensage*, see von See (1966; 1981a, 23–95 in particular), Uecker 1972, 6–17, and J. Harris 1985, 87–92.

were frequently debated on the basis of the saga evidence.[84] But the sagas were not valued for their role in political wrangling alone: their publication and enthusiastic popular reception were part of a burgeoning interest in such materials as reading matter in Scandinavia. Henrik Schück goes so far as to claim that the Old Norse sagas newly published in translation in the 1600s could be properly regarded as the equivalent of the Swedish novel of that era.[85] Although this view has not gone unchallenged,[86] it is certainly true that the Icelandic sagas held enormous fascination for the seventeenth century, and the *fornaldarsǫgur* were by no means least among the sagas in this regard. It is no mere coincidence that a Swedish edition of *Gautreks saga* and *Hrólfs saga Gautrekssonar* represents the first occasion on which *any* Icelandic saga was published in the original language (1664). The dual purposes—antiquarian (with its heavy political overtones) and literary—of the translation are made clear in the introduction:

> JAg hafwer i liuset framdraget twenne forna Götha Konungars Saga eller som man nu kallar Historia; nemligen K. Götriks och K. Rolfs: the thär mehr än för ett tusend åhr sedan then ene i Wester Göthland then andre och så här i Swerige regerat hafwer: hwilka fast the i tiocka hedendoms mörckret lefwat och icke heller ofmycket stort land haft hafwa att styra hafwa the doch warit stora och märkeliga Konungar: som af thenna theras saga nogsamt kan synias.[87]

> I have brought to light the sagas of two ancient Gautish kings, or, as one now says, histories; namely, those of King Gautrekr and King Hrólfr: they who ruled more than a thousand years ago, the one in West Götaland, the other here in Svealand: who, although they lived in the darkest heathendom and did not have control of large countries, were great and notable kings: which can easily be seen from their sagas.

84. There is a considerable body of literature on the rekindling of interest in the Nordic past and its impact on Scandinavian culture and letters. In addition to Andersson 1964, 1–3, see Gödel 1897; Löw 1908–10, I, 50–90; Blanck 1911; and Nordström 1934. On the "discovery" of Old Norse literature in this period, see Kålund 1900, iii–lxv.

85. Schück 1935, 101. A sense of the popularity these works enjoyed in the seventeenth and eighteenth centuries can be had from the following anecdote from the life of Sweden's youthful warrior-king, Charles XII. It is reported that the evening before the important—and disastrous—battle of Poltava (1709), the king relaxed by listening to the story of Hrólfr Gautreksson, in which the hero dispatches a *Russian* giant (according to the version told to him at least). See Guðbrandur Vigfússon 1878, cxcvi–cxcvii.

86. Nilsson (1954) disputes this claim.

87. *Gothrici et Rolfi Westrogothiæ regum historia lingua antiqua Gothica conscripta.* Uppsala: H. Curio, 1664.

Soon after the appearance of this edition followed the publication of *Bósa saga* (1666) and *Hervarar saga ok Heiðreks* (1672). Many of the remaining *fornaldarsǫgur* appeared during the last quarter of the century: *Þorsteins saga Víkingssonar* (1680); *Sǫrla þáttr, Helga þáttr Þórissonar,* and *Norna-Gests þáttr* (all three as part of the 1689 edition of *Saga Ólafs Tryggvasonar*); *Egils saga ok Ásmundar* (1693); *Sturlaugs saga starfsama* (1694); *Illuga saga Gríðarfóstra* (1695); *Ketils saga hœngs, Gríms saga loðinkinna,* and *Qrvar-Odds saga* (all 1697).[88] As part of the role the *fornaldarsǫgur* played in the propaganda war waged between Sweden and Denmark, the early printed editions brought out in Sweden incorporated the phrase "in old Gothic" (*Göthska*) into their titles.[89] The antiquarian spirit in which these works were published is further established in the prologue to *Bósa saga,* in which Olof Verelius decries the treatment such works receive from the unappreciative:

> Thär af äre the förra tijdars handlingar och bedrifter komne i förakt och glömska; thär medh äre the gamble och alwarsamme seder aflagde: på thet wijset är thet märkeliga wåra förfäders tungomål ödelagt [. . .] Förthenskull är thet så ringa och fattigt som wij hafwom quar af wåra förfäders stora och märkeliga gärningar.[90]

> Thereby do the events and achievements of former eras fall into contempt and oblivion; thereby are old and serious customs abandoned; in that way is the remarkable language of our forefathers destroyed [. . .] For that reason is what we have left of our forefathers' great and remarkable deeds so insignificant and poor.

After having thus raised the significance of the text due to its presumed rarity, Verelius evaluates the trustworthiness of the *fornaldarsǫgur* by discussing magic in *Bósa saga* and concludes that such supernatural elements do not impinge on the usefulness of the saga as an historical source.[91] This faith in the historicity of the *fornaldarsǫgur* held sway for many years.

88. For a complete list of editions, see Halldór Hermannsson 1912.

89. An historical relationship between the Scandinavians, especially the Swedes, and the Migration Era Goths was routinely assumed in the 1600s and has been the subject of much discussion since. See, for example, Svennung 1967 for an examination of the association of the concept of "Goths" and "Gothic" with Sweden; see Greenway 1977 and Mjöberg 1967–68 on the place of the Old Norse texts in this debate. For a more general treatment of the concept, see Haslag 1963.

90. *Herrauds och Bosa Saga Med en ny uttolkning iämpte Gambla Götskan.* Ed. Olaus Verelius. Uppsala: H. Curio, 1666, p. iii.

91. Ibid, p. v: *thenne Saga therföre ey må hållas för osann thär hon nogot om sådane förtälier* 'this saga may therefore not be considered untrue where it tells of such.'

The success, both popular and critical, that these Old Icelandic texts enjoyed in Sweden in the late seventeenth and early eighteenth centuries is not difficult to comprehend, given Sweden's sudden rise to the status of a great European power and its competition with Denmark for preeminence in northern Europe. The resulting chauvinistic view of the nation's history and character reached its zenith with Olaus Rudbeck's *Atland eller Manheim* (1675–89), a work that claimed for Sweden the honor of being nothing less than the lost Atlantis of Plato and the original home of man.[92] Rudbeck's theories about early Swedish history were based on a number of sources—and the imaginative interpretation of them—few of which played a more central role in his work than the sagas. If one desires to know something of that ancient world, he writes, *moste man fly till theßa witnen som äro först en SÄGN (traditio) eller berättelse hwilcken är grunden till the skrefna Sagor eller Historier* 'one must turn to the evidence which is first a legend (*traditio*) or account that forms the basis for the written sagas or histories.'[93] For their part, the Danes were certainly not immune to this sort of nationalism; they also pored over the *fornaldarsǫgur,* as well as the works of Saxo Grammaticus (which had been based at least partially on the traditions of the *fornaldarsǫgur*) for information that would allow them, in turn, to make claims about the glories of ancient Denmark.[94] Thus, the search for the ancient histories of the two kingdoms concentrated for the most part on the testimony of the *fornaldarsǫgur* and their related traditions.

The publication of an anthology of *fornaldarsǫgur* in 1737 by one of Rudbeck's students, Erik Biörner, ensured that they would continue to be one of the most popular and widely read saga genres; indeed, the edition soon became one of the most influential Scandinavian literary works of that century.[95] Yet in some ways, the collection also marks the end of the period of naive faith in the *fornaldarsǫgur* as sources of historical information, for soon the spirit of the Enlightenment would take its toll against the blind trust of the earlier Swedish and Danish antiquarians in the reliability of the sagas as historical documents. The 1730s may be conveniently regarded as something of a dividing line between the two views: in Denmark, the change is represented in the attacks of Ludvig Holberg, who possessed a very skeptical attitude

92. Olof Rudbe[c]k, *Atland eller Manheim.* Uppsala: H. Curio, 1675–89.
93. Rudbe[c]k, *Atland eller Manheim,* 2d ed. (1679), I, 1.
94. See especially Jørgensen 1940. For literature on Saxo, see the material listed in the entry by Skovgaard-Petersen 1956–78.
95. *Nordiska Kämpa Dater,* ed. Biörner.

toward the sagas; in Sweden, the witty and merciless parodies launched by Olof von Dalin on the enthusiastic views of the Rudbeckians likewise heralded the beginning of a new era.[96] Yet although the reaction against the *fornaldarsǫgur* had already set in, they continued to play an important role in the shaping of historical studies throughout the century, as important and influential histories of Sweden, Norway, and Denmark appeared which were based in part on the testimony of the *fornaldarsǫgur*.[97]

A new period of interest in, and scholarship on, the Icelandic sagas begins in Scandinavia in the early nineteenth century under the influence of German romanticism. This renewed fascination with the sagas is marked by the appearance of Peter Erasmus Müller's *Ueber den Ursprung und Verfall der isländischen Historiographie* (1813) and his subsequent *Sagabibliothek* (1817–20). The second volume of the *Sagabibliothek*, devoted entirely to the 'mythical and romantic sagas' (that is, both *fornaldarsǫgur* and *riddarasǫgur*), opens with an essay concerning how the reliability of these sagas could be determined. In this introduction, Müller provides a system whereby the *fornaldarsǫgur* are to be viewed as works of fantasy containing elements of historical truth.[98] Yet unlike Verelius in the seventeenth century, who sought to substantiate the historicity of the *fornaldarsǫgur*, Müller tempered his views with skepticism and a critical sensibility. The same position was adopted by Rafn in his influential editions and translations of the *fornaldarsǫgur*.[99] This reevaluation paralleled developments in Germany, where the idea gained favor that the heroic texts—the Nibelungen material in particular—contained elements of history, a concept fostered particularly by Karl Lachmann and the critical spirit (relatively speaking) of the *Liedertheorie*.[100]

The prevailing view throughout the nineteenth century was that the *fornaldarsǫgur* contained a core of factual material, a notion that reached its greatest blossoming in Scandinavia at the turn of the century with the writings of Axel Olrik in Denmark and Birger Nerman in Sweden.[101] Olrik's work treats the *Gesta Danorum* of Saxo Grammaticus, a

96. See Andersson 1964, 13–14, and Lamm 1908, 345–57.

97. See, for example, Göransson, *Svea Rikes Konungars Historia och Ättartal* (1749); Schøning, *Norges Riiges Historie* (1771); Suhm, *Historie af Danmark* (1782), all of which employ the *fornaldarsǫgur* as source materials.

98. Müller 1817–20, II, 10–32. Cf. J. Grimm 1813 and the tendency therein to emphasize the historical component of Germanic epic.

99. *Nordiske Kæmpe-Historier*, trans. Rafn (1821–26); *Fornaldar Sögur Nordrlanda*, ed. Rafn (1829–30); *Nordiske Fortids Sagaer*, trans. Rafn (1829–30).

100. See Thorp 1940, 13–44.

101. Olrik 1892, Nerman 1913.

text widely held to have been informed by early versions of the Icelandic tales. As part of his investigation, Olrik attempts to use the numerous *fornaldarsǫgur* that lay behind the Latin text as historical sources on pre-Christian Denmark. In particular, he hoped to distinguish two different groups of ancient legends (*Oldsagn*) in Saxo's work: a West Nordic group that reflected the *Weltanschauung* of the Viking period, and a Danish group.[102] To this end, he adopts a new approach to the *fornaldarsǫgur* and the kinds of material which can be deduced from them. In contrast to the early antiquarians, who had felt that these sagas reflected actual historical *facts*, Olrik takes the view that they reflect broad cultural information; that is, the world presented to us in these sagas may be reliable in general, rather than specific, terms. In much the same manner, Nerman examines the *fornaldarsǫgur* for information on pre-Christian Sweden, although he readily accepts their testimony on specific issues as well. An indication of Nerman's views on the relationship between literature and culture, as well as the faith he places in the *fornaldarsǫgur*, is provided in his book's opening gambit, which posits that a people's heroic poetry has a close relationship with its real history.[103]

The long and sustained reaction against the historicity of the *fornaldarsǫgur* begins with Holberg and von Dalin. The view that heroic legend should be regarded as a mixture of history and myth was disputed by Wilhelm Grimm and Svend Grundtvig.[104] Writing in 1832, the father of Svend Grundtvig, N. S. F. Grundtvig, shows the effects the attacks on the historicity of the *fornaldarsǫgur* have had on him; after discussing Holberg's arguments against their trustworthiness, he states: "I have written no Danish history, simply because I did not know what I should do with the ancient legends [*Old-Sagnene*], which I did not have the heart to leave out, could not manage and did not know how to handle."[105] In the early 1900s, Andreas Heusler analyzed the compositional materials of Germanic heroic legend and concluded that history was but one of four possible sources.[106] Heusler, whose views have dominated the study of heroic legend during much of this century, accepted the historical foundation or inspiration of such works as

---

102. See especially Olrik 1892, 134.
103. Nerman 1913, 3.
104. W. Grimm 1867, 345–47; S. Grundtvig 1863, 41–126, esp. 64–94.
105. N. F. S. Grundtvig 1832, 136–37. The much smaller first edition of *Nordens Mythologi* was published in 1808.
106. Heusler 1909b. The other three possible sources are the poet's imagination, private life, and available narrative materials (*Erzählgute*). Cf. Heusler 1905, as well as the reevaluation and renewal of Heusler's *Heldensage* theories in Haug 1975.

real, but also felt that such events were so thoroughly reworked by the individual poet as to be best regarded as literature. Thus, scholars have increasingly come to the conclusion that insofar as the *fornaldarsǫgur* reflect history at all, they contain historical information too garbled to be of importance in unraveling specific issues. At the same time, the testimony of the *fornaldarsǫgur* has often been examined for what these sagas can tell of cultural and social issues; thus, for instance, Otto Höfler has drawn on the heroic legendary materials for information concerning the sociocultic activities and beliefs of the Germanic peoples.[107] In his handbook on Germanic heroic materials Klaus von See takes a skeptical view of the "history" presented by them but accepts the possibility that such texts might reflect broad political and historical developments.[108]

Perhaps more than any other scholar, Hermann Schneider sought to disallow the more romantic ideas that had so often colored the study of Germanic heroic legend. A student of Heusler's, Schneider fought in his massive *Germanische Heldensage* (1929–34) against the analogical arguments that drew on the Greek case, with its heavy mythological connections. But his particular intellectual *bête noir* was the view that the heroic materials represented the expression of a "folk soul" (*Volksseele*), an idea Schneider dismissed. Individual artistic creativity, rather than the production of some amorphous mass, is for him the key to the development of our extant texts. Thus, the poetic materials surrounding the death of Hildibrandr in *Ásmundar saga kappabana* are not related to the ninth-century *Hildebrandslied* merely in some general way that might be explained by recourse to an understood shared tradition, but through the direct influence of an individual who knew the Old High German piece, as indicated by the repetition of a key phrase (*inn hári Hildibrandr*). Primacy in the development of heroic legend he gives to poetry, arguing that it is the individual who creates heroic poetry (and thereby heroic legend).[109] One result of Schneider's sensible emphasis on the individual poet working within a tradition was that it tended to return the study of Germanic heroic literature to the realm of literary history, an arena from which it had almost been banished.

---

107. Höfler 1941, 1952. Höfler (1959) has come closest to reading historical events into heroic legend.

108. "Of course, it may, in principle at least, be possible to interpret heroic legends as symbolically heightened reflections of political and military events or cultural-historical realities" (von See 1981a, 87). It should be noted, however, that von See cautions very strongly against any liberal application of such a principle.

109. Schneider 1928–34, I, 10.

In fact, the negative reaction to the *fornaldarsǫgur* as history had been mirrored by literary critics, who were generally little inclined to examine these sagas on their own terms. Thus, in the late nineteenth century Ker, Guðbrandur Vigfússon, and many others glibly maintained that the *fornaldarsǫgur* on the whole were without literary value, a view already expressed as early as 1818 by Müller.[110] Yet this dismissive attitude toward them was not uniform: a number of creative writers, the romantics in particular, had earlier turned to the *fornaldarsǫgur* and other nonrealistic modes of Icelandic literature for inspiration (for example, Esaias Tegnér, Erik Gustaf Geijer, Richard Wagner). But as European literary trends developed toward naturalism, the *fornaldarsǫgur* increasingly fell into disfavor, whereas the *íslendingasǫgur* loomed larger in literary circles.

The negative view of the *fornaldarsǫgur* has dominated the field for many years and stems, in part at least, from the belief that these sagas represent the decline of Icelandic literature from the brilliance of the thirteenth-century *íslendingasǫgur* and *konungasǫgur* to the abysmal cultural and literary low reflected in the subsequent century by the *fornaldarsǫgur* and other unrealistic genres. The historical reasons adduced for this intellectual and artistic retrogression vary. Sigurður Nordal suggests that it is due to the breakdown of the synthesis between two differing views of writing which he believes existed in the west of Iceland in the 1200s. The result of this breakdown is the subsequent demise of Icelandic letters into annals, on the one hand, and fantasy literature, that is the *fornaldarsǫgur* and native *riddarasǫgur*, on the other.[111] Bertha Phillpotts posits that in an age of social instability and deprivation the Icelanders needed a form of escape, and that this need, together with the Christian preference for characters with dramatic simplicity ("good" versus "evil"), led to a literature lacking in the subtlety and complexity associated with the *íslendingasǫgur*.[112] Peter Buchholz suggests that the aristocratic elite withdrew from saga production because they had already satisfied their entertainment needs with the manuscripts of the other genres of Icelandic literature (*íslendingasǫgur, konungasǫgur*, and *biskupasǫgur* in particular); this situation thus left only such works as the artless *fornaldarsǫgur* to the aesthetically disenfranchised peasants of the postclassical period.[113]

Indicative of this sense that the *fornaldarsǫgur* are an ignoble heir to

110. Müller 1817–20, II, 30, comments that the *fornaldarsǫgur* are of "little literary value."

111. See Sigurður Nordal 1953, 1933. Cf. Andersson 1964, 76.

112. Phillpotts 1931, 240–241.

113. Buchholz 1980, 52.

the *íslendingasǫgur* and other more realistic genres is the comment by Peter Hallberg in his introductory text on the Icelandic sagas in a chapter called, significantly, "The Decline of Saga Literature": "In spite of their seemingly popular style, the Sagas of the Icelanders [*íslendingasǫgur*] are an aristocratic art form, in comparison with which the *fornaldarsǫgur* and *rímur* ['metrical romances'] impress us as being a very plebeian kind of entertainment, not unlike the serial stories in our modern weekly and monthly magazines."[114] The basis for this perception of the *fornaldarsǫgur* rests on two factors: (1) the supposition that they can be compared to the other genres of Icelandic literature using the same critical apparatus and (2) an inherently romantic view of the history of Icelandic literature. Such a view posits a thirteenth-century Golden Age followed by an inevitable, irreversible decline. It has only been in recent years, particularly in Hermann Pálsson and Paul Edwards's monograph on the *fornaldarsǫgur,* that one begins to see a new attitude toward these texts, especially the attempt to apply modern critical methods to their study.[115]

The supernatural and mythological component of the *fornaldarsǫgur* has often been perceived as a significant, even defining, aspect of them, so much so that it is typically incorporated into our technical terminology for them, as in 'mythical-heroic sagas,' *mythiske sagaer* 'mythic sagas,' and so forth. Thus, Genzmer divides the traditional, non-historical sagas into *Heldensagas* and *Göttersagas,* which he describes as mythical narratives in saga form ("mythische Erzählungen in Saga-form").[116] Georges Dumézil explores the relationship between myth and legend in his work on Haddingus, one of the figures from Saxo's *Gesta Danorum.*[117] In fact, an entire "mythical school" has developed around the heroic materials: in addition to the previously cited works by Höfler, the studies by Karl Hauck and Franz Rolf Schröder, whose writings reflect a belief in the heroic legends as a profanization of myth, should be noted.[118] The connection between myth and the *fornaldarsǫgur* as a focus of study can boast deep roots: the nineteenth and early twentieth centuries regarded them as important sources of

114. Hallberg 1962, 145.
115. Hermann Pálsson and Paul Edwards 1971.
116. Genzmer 1948, 5.
117. Dumézil 1973a. Other works suggesting an Indo-European background to the heroic materials include de Vries 1963 and Gerschel 1960. Cf. the application of a modified comparative approach in Jones (1972), who takes up the case of *Hrólfs saga kraka.*
118. Hauck 1963, Schröder 1955, but see von See 1966 for a critique of the "mythical school."

information on pagan Scandinavian religion.[119] Indeed, there are good reasons for scholars to have done so, as in many cases the *fornaldarsǫgur* appear to bear vital testimony on issues reflected in the archaeological and mythological records. One of the best-known examples of this relationship is the death of Víkarr, prophesied in *Hálfs saga ok Hálfsrekka* and fulfilled in *Gautreks saga,* as part of a sacrifice to Óðinn. In fact, there are a number of reasons for believing that this sequence reflects "actual" practice, broadly defined, in pre-Christian Scandinavia. That the stories related in the two *fornaldarsǫgur* fit neatly into this pattern, both explaining and explained by the information from other sources, has helped confirm the belief that the *fornaldarsǫgur* do to some extent act as repositories of pagan practices.[120]

Closely affiliated with this position is the view that the *fornaldarsǫgur* bear a special relationship to folklore not evidenced, at least not to the same degree, in other categories of Icelandic narratives. This approach too is an old one. Sophus Bugge was one of its first major practitioners. In his attempts to prove the non-Icelandic origins of most extant Old Norse literature, Bugge often looked for international forms of folk literature in the *fornaldarsǫgur*.[121] What must surely be regarded as the seminal study of folklore and heroic legend is Friedrich Panzer's investigation of the Bear's Son Tale (*Studien zur germanischen Sagengeschichte*). In it Panzer seeks to demonstrate three basic biographical patterns found in numerous folktales throughout northern Europe which parallel many of the lives found in heroic legends, including those of Beowulf, Sigurðr, and Grettir. Panzer's work, although widely influential and still the inspirational source of many important con-

---

119. To name a few influential examples from a long list, N. F. S. Grundtvig 1832, Munch 1847, Bugge 1881–89, and Hermann 1903.

120. On Óðinn and sacrifices, see the discussion and bibliography in Turville-Petre 1964, 46–50. It should be noted that Turville-Petre (1964, 20) uses the *fornaldarsǫgur* with due caution: "They contain little history, but much of tradition, some of it ancient."

121. Stephens, who felt that his own theories had been abused by some of Bugge's ideas, described the "new mythology" and its technique in a public address (later published) in the following manner: "It is, in few words, that the Northern Mythology, properly so called, is for the *most* part or a *very large* part the result of accretions and imitations in the 9th and 10th centuries after Christ, the outcome of fragments and tales, Classical and Christian, pickt up chiefly in England and Ireland by Wiking adventurers, and gradually elaborated by them and their wise men and scalds at home or in their colonies." Stephens 1883, 5. In pursuit of this end, Bugge was one of the first to note systematically international parallels to Nordic texts, all of which he ascribed to Nordic borrowing. For a bibliography of Bugge's writings, see *Sprogelige og historiske Afhandlinger,* pp. 285–94.

tributions to our understanding of the concept of the hero,[122] has not been without its detractors. Perhaps Panzer's sharpest contemporary critic was the Swedish folklorist Carl von Sydow, who frequently used the *fornaldarsǫgur* in his own analyses of folklore growth and transmission.[123] Von Sydow's studies inevitably precipitated further attacks on those who would derive legendary figures from either historical events or mythological characters.[124]

Among the fullest treatments of heroic legend and its relationship to folklore are those by Hans Honti and Jan de Vries. Honti, following Wilhelm Wundt's theory that the similarity of motifs in folktale and legend is to be accounted for by the development of legend from *Märchen,* presses the historical relationship between the two beyond what most scholars would regard as the breaking point.[125] De Vries, on the other hand, suggests that it is heroic legend (and myth) that are transformed into folktale, and more particularly, that heroic legend possesses a sacral background.[126] Among the most important advances in the study of the *fornaldarsǫgur* and folklore must be reckoned the development of two indices, the first devoted to Icelandic folklore with relevant references to Old Norse texts, the second to Old Norse mythological material and the sagas, especially the *fornaldarsǫgur:* Einar Ólafur Sveinsson's *Verzeichnis isländischer Märchenvarianten* (1929) and Inger Boberg's *Motif-Index of Early Icelandic Literature* (1966). These works have greatly facilitated investigation of the *fornaldarsǫgur* and their relationship to folklore, helping place them in a more international perspective.[127]

In fact, the trend in the study of these sagas in this century has increasingly been toward exploration of their folkloric dimensions, especially the relationship between the Old Norse texts and other folklore traditions (particularly Celtic),[128] as well as the connection between the *fornaldarsǫgur* and modern Scandinavian folklore.[129] Attention has been focused in recent years, for example, on the structural

122. Recent studies that have built on Panzer's work include R. Harris 1974; Jorgensen 1975, 1986; and Pizarro 1976–77. See also below, Chap. 2.

123. See von Sydow 1911.

124. E.g., von Sydow 1918, 1927.

125. Honti 1935, Wundt 1908.

126. See especially de Vries 1954, 1963.

127. Cf. Thompson 1946, 420.

128. So, for example, Einar Ólafur Sveinsson 1932, 1957; Simpson 1963; and Almqvist 1965. That the nonhistorical sagas have more far-flung analogues and origins is the subject of a number of studies; of related interest, see Haug 1963 and Wikander 1964.

129. Liestøl 1915b, 1970; Einar Ólafur Sveinsson 1940, 63–75. Examples of folklore in specific *fornaldarsǫgur* include Ellis [Davidson] 1941, Simpson 1966, Ciklamini 1968.

dimensions of the *fornaldarsǫgur,* an approach whose theoretical foundations ultimately derive from folklore studies. Ruth Righter-Gould has attempted to demonstrate the structural unity of the genre according to two basic narrative patterns, while Rosemary Power has suggested a recurrent journey and marriage syntagm in several of the *fornaldarsǫgur.*[130] As part of the search for patterns within the genre, a tripartite division of the *fornaldarsǫgur* into heroic sagas, Viking sagas, and wonder sagas (*Heldensagas, Wikingersagas, Abenteuersagas,* the latter blending with the *Märchensagas*), has become a commonly accepted practice.[131] As a protagonist- and source-oriented categorization, such a division is a useful and logical approach, yet a simpler—and structurally more significant—subdivision of the genre is one according to which we recognize the more fundamental difference between tragic and comic *fornaldarsǫgur* (for example, the Hálfr episode of *Hálfs saga, Ragnars saga loðbrókar, Helga þáttr Þórissonar* versus *Gautreks saga, Bósa saga, Þorsteins þáttr bæjarmagns*).

Future Directions

The emphasis on the folkloric affinities of the *fornaldarsǫgur* in the definition of them as a genre has increased our awareness that these texts differ from the *íslendingasǫgur,* for example, in a way that is qualitatively different from the manner in which the *íslendingasǫgur* differ from the *biskupasǫgur.* Accordingly, the *fornaldarsǫgur* should be scrutinized by methods different from those used for these more realistic texts. The failure to appreciate this difference, *and* to act accordingly, has been fatal for the critical reception of the *fornaldarsǫgur* during much of the past century. And although folklore-influenced and -oriented studies have opened many new avenues for exploration, they themselves have often focused too narrowly on the possibility that the authors of the sagas used folklore as one of their sources and all too seldom examined the possibility that the folkloric influence is of a more fundamental and profound quality. Much of what follows is an exploration of this essential fact about the *fornaldarsǫgur:* they are a cultural hybrid, a constellation of (primarily) folkloric and traditional materials and of (secondarily) literary materials, the interpretation of which must depend on the methodological tools of both fields.

130. Righter-Gould 1975, 1980; Power 1984. Objections to such approaches have been strident; see, for example, U. Ebel 1982b.
131. E.g., Schier 1970.

CHAPTER 2

Origins and Influences

The characterization of the *fornaldarsǫgur* as "Old Icelandic prose narratives based on traditional heroic themes, whose numerous fabulous episodes and motifs create an atmosphere of unreality" emphasizes to a high degree the concept of tradition. This fact calls for an evolutionary perspective on the study of the genre, or a full appreciation, at least, of the nature of the background and compositional history of these late sagas. That continuity and tradition are thereby underscored, however, should not be taken to mean that the contents of these sagas are restricted exclusively to material inherited from earlier periods: although the extant *fornaldarsǫgur* are an essentially traditional genre, they are also acquisitive and highly eclectic. Thus, earlier mythological, folkloric, and native literary resources are fundamental to these narratives, as are indigenous non-narrative elements of popular tradition such as genealogical information; but they also draw on literary impulses from abroad. And in the case of the *fornaldarsǫgur* an ongoing cycle in which sagas were recomposed as metrical romances which were then reworked as prose sagas seems to have been quite common. A discussion of the origins of the *fornaldarsǫgur* should therefore not restrict itself to a discussion of probable dates of composition, at least not in an absolute sense, but rather, if anything, in a relative sense; rather than the reconstruction of hypothetical proto-sagas, the object of such studies should be an understanding of the inspirational (as well as direct) sources of the sagas, the processes by which they have come about, and the reasons for such a literary development.

With regard to the inspirational sources of these sagas, the idea of tradition, a mercurial concept at best, is of central importance. Although the term is much used, one may justifiably ask what it implies. If the term means anything in literary studies, 'tradition' must refer to the tendency of certain themes, characters, and plots to retain their essential distinguishing features through time in multiple existence, despite changes in the nature of their specific social and literary environments (= variation, continuity). American folklorists emphasize multiple existence and multiformity when they insist that the term be defined by the existence of recurrent forms, with change and variation an important and integral aspect.[1] Thus, it is clear that 'tradition' must mean more than what the nineteenth-century Anthropological School, typified by Edward B. Tylor and Andrew Lang, meant by a "survival."[2] The traditional components of the *fornaldarsǫgur* are not merely narrative fossils, for the continuity of these materials resides in their resilience, in their capacity to accept and merge with the innovative to the degree that they are dynamic and capable of alteration, but within the limitations that allow their forms to remain recognizable (= variation). Recurrence further implies that in a living tradition, such phenomena are shared by the members of the group concerned (= communality). Thus, the key concepts around which the idea of tradition centers are *continuity, variation,* and *communality.*

Among some writers, the notion of tradition is equated with the concept of culture itself, although for the most part recent trends have focused on the "consensus through time" of cultural institutions and their associated beliefs.[3] Other commentators, such as Lord Raglan, have attempted to focus on the nonmaterial aspects of tradition and have consequently dwelled on its verbal dimensions, but the emphasis thereby placed on oral transmission is unnecessarily restrictive, particularly in the case of a medieval genre in which all suggestions of orality are surmise.[4] The question of whether or not traditions must be em-

---

1. Cf. Richmond 1983, xi–xii. Georges and Dundes (1963, 117), for example, make the following remarks on tradition: "By *traditional* we mean that the expression is or was transmitted orally and that it has or had multiple existence. Multiple existence means that an expression is found at more than one period of time or in more than one place at any one given time. This multiple existence in time and/or space usually, though not necessarily, results in the occurrence of variation in the expression."

2. Cf. Tylor 1871 and Lang 1884.

3. Cf. Herskovits 1948, 17. Shils (1971, 123) writes: "The terms 'tradition' and 'traditional' are used to describe and explain the recurrence in approximately identical form of structures of conduct and patterns of belief over several generations of membership or over a long time within single societies." See also Shils 1978.

4. Thompson (1946, 4–5; 1970) also argues that orality is an impossible test for traditionality in medieval literature. Raglan (1933) stirred up a small storm on this topic when he delivered his Presidential Address, "What Is Tradition," to the Anthropology

pirically true is also a matter for consideration; that is, for something to be regarded as traditional, must it be a demonstrable and historically continuous phenomenon, or does it merely need to reflect an attitude on the part of later members of the community?[5] If we base our views solely on the interpretation of the later group, then there is very little that cannot be credited as being traditional; if, on the other hand, we demand some compliance on the part of the material with provable history, then we necessarily disallow much of our data from participation in the tradition, not because they are necessarily ahistorical, but because of our lack of knowledge. For the purpose of understanding the creative and aesthetic milieu that gave rise to the *fornaldarsǫgur,* it may be possible to have it both ways; that is, we can conclude that for certain texts it is possible to prove historical continuity through recourse to recurring forms and reliable evidence, whereas for others, it is sufficient to know that the authors have made use of material that gave the *appearance* of being traditional in order to evoke a particular mood and atmosphere and to tie their texts in with a specific desired ethos. Certainly such a position is in line with current thinking, which suggests that tradition is best conceived of as an *interpretation* of the past by present-day members of a society.

Vital as the role of tradition is in the case of the *fornaldarsǫgur,* they cannot be explained only by that which is traditional; a discussion of them, as of traditional or folk literature in the Middle Ages in general, must take advantage of the progress made in recent decades with regard to our understanding of oral literature and the relationship between folklore and learned lore.[6] Thus, such an examination should display an appreciation for the fact that those responsible for the *fornaldarsǫgur* were also familiar with a variety of narrative traditions, both native and foreign. Yet despite the vast complexity of the processes by which the *fornaldarsǫgur* have come about, we are occasion-

---

Section of the British Association for the Advancement of Science in 1933: in it, he maintained that tradition consisted of "anything that is handed down orally from age to age" and then went on to claim that all such traditional narratives were originally connected with the performance of rites and rituals. On the problem of identifying medieval literature as oral literature, see also Rosenberg 1977, 441–42. Cf. Kellog 1979. On tradition, continuity, and discontinuity more generally, see Brückner 1969, which contains an especially useful bibliography, and Ranke 1969.

5. On the various arguments concerning the "historicity of tradition," see the comments in Dorson 1961.

6. See especially Čistov 1976. Excellent reviews of work in this area are Davidson 1975 and Jón Hnefill Aðalsteinsson 1982. On the relationship between folklore and heroic texts, see Honti 1931, Ranke 1934, and de Vries 1954.

ally presented with a view of the medieval Icelandic saga writers as thirteenth- or fourteenth-century folklorists, faithfully recording oral tradition in the field. The fact of the matter is, they are more likely to have been medieval versions of Robert Burns, Sir Walter Scott, Poul Anderson, or Michael Creighton,[7] drawing heavily, but not slavishly, on the materials they had to hand. At the same time, it is equally inadequate and inappropriate to envision a writer isolated from the surrounding dynamic culture and essentially dependent on written models, as comparison of the manuscript variants quickly demonstrates (for example, the digressive accretions in the manuscripts of *Qrvar-Odds saga*). However much a *fornaldarsaga* may rely on traditional material or on individual innovation or on literary borrowing for its contents, it represents a meeting of, and compromise between, the oral (or popular) and written (or learned) cultures. In most important structural matters, the works with which we are concerned here tend—by definition—more toward the former category than the latter. Modern scholarship should be sufficiently respectful of the medieval Icelanders' narrative, creative, and antiquarian skills not to dismiss this literature, as did earlier generations of free-prosists and book-prosists, either as being so thoroughly indebted to oral tradition that the extant versions lack an independent existence or as being so thoroughly dominated by foreign literary influences and the creative impulses of the individual authors that the traditional culture fails to impart significant features to them.[8]

The benefits—both theoretical and practical—to be derived from abandoning the positions of such free-prose and book-prose "hardliners" as Andreas Heusler and Sigurður Nordal, as the tendency has in fact been in recent years,[9] are fairly obvious, but saga research need not be enervated in the process. A great many factors impinge upon the manner in which our extant sagas came into being: in addition to

7. Poul Anderson has published a number of popular texts that largely recount Old Norse sagas (e.g., *Ragnars saga loðbrókar*); Michael Creighton's book *Eaters of the Dead* combines elements of *Beowulf*, ibn Fadlan's encounter with Swedish Vikings on the Volga, and other medieval works.

8. The history of the debate between these two camps of scholarship on the Old Norse sagas is thoroughly covered in Andersson 1964. This review is updated by Hallberg 1972, Heinrichs 1976, Magerøy 1978, Vésteinn Ólason 1984, Byock 1984, and Clover 1985. Representative essays on the positions taken by the two schools of thought are conveniently collected in *Sagadebatt*, ed. Mundal, and *Die Isländersaga*, ed. Baetke. See also below, Chap. 3.

9. See, for example, Jónas Kristjánsson (1975) and his carefully worded attempt to place Björn M. Olsen in just this light.

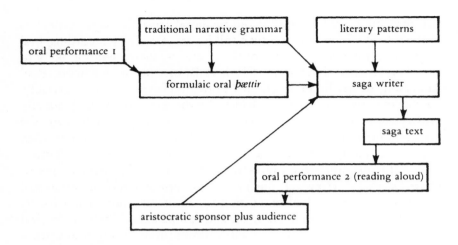

questions of source material may be added the important considerations of audience, presentation format, and sponsorship. As an example of the stimulating new direction in which saga research has moved as a result of such considerations, a model of "saga communications" was developed by Lars Lönnroth (diagram), articulated in detail in his *Njáls saga* study.[10] Although there are surely aspects of this model which discussion and debate will hone, this comprehensive graphic presentation of the creative process of *íslendingasǫgur* composition in the thirteenth and fourteenth centuries presents visually a number of the points to be examined further in this and later chapters, especially the relationship between tradition, innovation, literary borrowing, performance, sponsorship, and the creative process.[11] Lönnroth's model specifically addresses the *íslendingasǫgur,* but I can adduce no reason why it would not also work—with some modification—for the *fornaldarsǫgur.*

The nature of the traditional lore and learned lore that contribute to the extant *fornaldarsǫgur* is taken up in detail in the sections that follow. By exploring the primary factors that have helped form these sagas, I hope to indicate the complex nature of the relationship between the *fornaldarsǫgur* and tradition, as well as to provide a more precise sense of what tradition is in the Old Norse context and of the extent to which we must think of these works as belonging to the late Middle Ages, rather than earlier periods.[12]

10. Lönnroth 1980, 60; 1976. Diagram reprinted by permission of *Scandinavica.*
11. Lönnroth's model is implicitly endorsed—to the degree it supports the idea of "continual cross-fertilization between oral and literary tradition" in the Middle Ages—in Stefán Karlsson 1986.
12. The question of how the *fornaldarsǫgur* treat preexisting materials is also taken up in Ebel 1982a. Few areas of research on these sagas have been so thoroughly discussed as

Traditional Lore

To the modern mind the folklore and learned lore of the medieval period are often difficult to distinguish: from our more rational and scientific points of view, both are frequently characterized by an abundance of fabulous events in exotic settings with outlandish figures. To the writers of the late Nordic Middle Ages, however, the supernatural world they had heard about since childhood was a very different thing from the "Indíaland" they learned of through the medium of the written word.[13] Yet both kinds of lore represent fertile soil for literary horticulture, and frequently the results of such creative speciation are fascinating hybrids. But attempts to separate the two layers can be frustrating, especially for those who would explore the contribution of the native tradition to a given literary monument. It is a difficult thing indeed to prove that a medieval text has been influenced by a largely unrecorded popular tradition; it is almost always much easier to demonstrate, with the aid of linguistics and well-established and well-documented literary histories, that a particular motif or theme has come about by way of foreign models. The study of the interplay between the native oral and the written cultures is a treacherous course of investigation, for the pitfalls, both practical and theoretical, are many, as may be seen from more modern examples.[14]

Caution is then very much in order, but care, suspicion even, need

the question of sources and antecedents, whether they be foreign or native; thus, for example, Clover 1986, Gould 1923, Bjarni Guðnason 1969, Halvorsen 1951, Hughes 1976, Lukman 1976, Lönnroth 1975a, Milroy 1967–68, Power 1985b, Righter-Gould 1978–79, and de Vries 1928.

13. Cf., for example, the disbelief expressed toward the marvels of India (presumably in reference to a written version of the Prester John legend) in the Old Norwegian *Konungsskuggsjá* (chaps. 8–9). On the legend of Prester John in Scandinavia, see Toldberg 1961.

14. An excellent discussion of the complex affinities between Icelandic folklore of the nineteenth and twentieth centuries and the earlier written literature is provided in the epilogue in Schier 1983. An important mitigating factor in the relationship of folklore to saga literature is the fact that although Jón Árnason, the seminal figure in nineteenth-century Icelandic folklore collecting and founder of the study of modern Icelandic popular tradition, encouraged his collectors to refrain from tampering with the informants' style, the effect of saga popularity must still have been considerable. As Einar Ólafur Sveinsson writes in another context (1971, 429): "People were brought up on the narrative and stylistic genius of the ancient written sagas—both the story-tellers and the men who wrote down their stories—and this could not fail to have its effect on them." On the relationship of the Icelandic sagas and folklore, see also Dehmer 1927 and Einar Ólafur Sveinsson 1940. The oral traditions of Norway and Iceland have frequently been compared to the sagas (e.g., Guðni Jónsson 1940). On the complicated relationship between oral and written "folk tradition," see Mitchell 1991, which also treats *Auðunar þáttr vestfirzka* and the *Kjætten på Dovre* materials.

not deny the possibility that the *fornaldarsǫgur* have drawn much useful and substantive material and technique from the realm of Scandinavian folktales and legends. An example of how folkloric patterns have had an impact on the *fornaldarsǫgur* is readily seen in the short text known as *Helga þáttr Þórissonar*. The eponymous hero of the story is first seduced by a beautiful woman, Ingibjǫrg, who entices him to eat with her and her maidens and to share her bed. He is then given gifts at their parting and later abducted by her henchmen. Helgi's father appeals to King Óláfr, who promises to help if possible. At Christmas the king is visited by three men, one of whom is Helgi, who say that they have been sent by King Guðmundr of Glæsisvǫllr; they then present the king with two drinking horns. Óláfr has the horns blessed by the bishop and asks Guðmundr's men to drink from them first. Realizing that they have been deceived (in that the horns have been sung over by the bishop), they rush out of the hall, killing three men on their way. The following Christmas the three come before Óláfr again, and two of them leave the third there, saying, *her færum uit þer Gretti konungr ok er æigi uist, nærr þu færir af þer* 'Here we give to you "Gretti,"[15] king, and it's unknown when you'll get rid of it' (chap. 293). The figure is recognized as Helgi, who is blind. When the king asks him about his adventures, Helgi explains what had happened the previous year, tells them about the munificence of Guðmundr's halls, and says that King Óláfr's prayers have been directly responsible for his appearances again among men, both the previous year and this year. When the king asks why he is blind, Helgi says that Ingibjǫrg *græip ór mer bæde ǫgun þa er uid skildum ok sagde at konur j Noregi mundu min skamma stund niota* 'gouged out both my eyes when we parted and said that the women of Norway would only enjoy me for a little while' (chap. 293). Helgi dies exactly a year later, having spent his time entirely in the company of the king and his men; the reader is told that the drinking horns disappear with King Óláfr in his last battle.

Few themes are more common in the corpus of modern Scandinavian folklore, especially in Norwegian and Swedish legends, than that of the *bergtagning*, the abduction of a human by otherworldly creatures.[16] Such abductions are a regular feature of Icelandic folklore as

15. *Gretti* apparently refers to something wrinkled or shriveled up or (by extension) to a dragon. In their translation of the *þáttr*, Hermann Pálsson and Paul Edwards (1968, 146) suggest, "We've brought a skeleton for your feast." Simpson (1965, 178) comments in her translation, "The point of this remark is not clear; it is possible that 'to bring Grettir to someone' was a proverbial phrase for introducing an embarrassing or unwelcome visitor."

16. On the theme of otherworldly abductions in Nordic tradition, see Feilberg 1910. *Helga þáttr Þórissonar* is discussed in relation to the wider realm of migratory legends

well (indeed, a considerable number of such legends are recorded in Jón Árnason), and there seems little doubt that the tale we have in *Helga þáttr Þórissonar* is strongly influenced by such oral narratives, or perhaps represents yet another manifestation of this theme. In this case, however, it has been identified with a specific Norwegian locale and infused with a sense of history by the appearance of the missionary king Óláfr, a familiar figure in Scandinavian folklore (it should also be noted that this *fornaldarsaga* comes from the *Flateyjarbók* account of Óláfr's life). The similarity of themes and of their treatment between this *fornaldarsaga* and Scandinavian folklore invites inquiry, for which two Icelandic narratives collected in modern times are especially useful: *Barnið og álfkonan* 'The child and the elf-woman' and *Trunt, trunt og tröllin í fjöllunum* 'Trunt, trunt and the trolls in the mountains.'

Barnið og álfkonan relates how one night a certain woman goes out to her cowshed and when one of her children follows her, he is lured away by an elf-woman in the shape of the mother. The mother seeks assistance from a man rumored to be a magician, who agrees to help and sets to work cutting three triangular pieces out of the floorboard. As he works on the last one, a loud crash is heard. He assures the mother that everything is in order and when the woman returns home the next morning, she finds her son there. One of his cheeks has, however, turned black and blue, a blemish that never fades thereafter. The child says that he was treated well by the elf-woman, but that he refused to eat while in her home as everything looked red to him. When the magician had cut the pieces out of the floor, triangular stones had come rolling down from the mountain. After the last one came down, the elf-woman ran back to the house with the child and being very angry about this turn of events, she slapped him on the cheek before departing; this slap was the cause of the never-fading bruise. The child's name and something of his history are then given.

This tale belongs to the group of texts classed as 'Released from Fairyland' (ML 5086*) and contains many motifs common in such stories of otherworldly abductions: avoidance of food in the Other-

---

with which it shares this tale type (ML 5095 'Fairy woman pursues man') in Krappe 1930, 110–12. See also B. S. Benediktz 1973, and Steingrímur J. Þorsteinsson 1973. Power (1985b) points out that the opening scene of the *þáttr*, in which the hero encounters a woman who turns out to be the daughter of the king of a supernatural world, is closely paralleled in *Le Lai de Lanval*, which is known to have been translated into Old Norse; there is no particular reason to believe, however, that the *lai* itself could not have been inspired by such a folktale motif, albeit from Breton tradition. The few incidental (and functionally unimportant) embellishments that the *þáttr* has apparently taken from the realm of foreign romance provide an excellent example of the synthetic nature of the *fornaldarsǫgur*.

world (C211 'Tabu: eating in other world'), the assistance of a higher power (N845 'Magician as helper'), a lasting mark placed on the abductee (F362.4 'Fairy causes mutilation'). With its unexpected intrusion of the supernatural into the mundane life of peasants, this is a frightening tale, yet it is also a story that offers the hearer solace and psychological comfort in that it demonstrates the ability of higher powers in our world to countermand effectively the magic of the Otherworld. How unlike the *þáttr* the legend is in this regard, yet like *Helga þáttr þórissonar, Barnið og álfkonan* tells of how an otherworldly female possesses a human until she is forced to relinquish him; and like *Helga þáttr Þórissonar, Barnið og álfkonan* releases the abductee only after disfiguring him (in Helgi's case, by blinding [S165 'Mutilation: putting out eyes']). Of course, a whole host of differences separates the two texts— for example, lover versus "mother"; initial collusion of the victim versus his being deceived; eating otherworldly food versus refusing to eat; tragic versus felicitous conclusion—yet the saga shares with the folklore material the same fundamental theme in which a member of the human community is kidnapped by a member of the Otherworld.

Other legends that deal with this same story line evince a stronger— and one could easily believe, closer and possibly even historical— relationship to *Helga þáttr Þórissonar*. Such is the case with *Trunt, trunt og tröllin í fjöllunum*, a grotesque tale in which, as in *Barnið og álfkonan*, a human is abducted by an otherworldly female (here probably ML 5095 'Fairy woman pursues man'), but, as with the *þáttr*, the conclusion is more frightening than reassuring. According to the story, two men are out gathering moss. One night one of the men lies awake while the other sleeps. The one who is awake watches the sleeper get up and creep away. He follows, but however hard he runs, he cannot shorten the distance between them. He sees that the sleeper is heading straight for a giantess (*jökulgnýpa*) who is stretching out her hands in front of her and then bringing them up toward her breasts, thus magically drawing the man to her. When the man has run into her embrace, she runs off with him. The following year, people from his district are in the same area collecting moss, and he comes to them but is so taciturn and surly that it is difficult to get a word out of him. People ask him in whom he believes, and he answers that he believes in God. The year after that he comes to the same moss-gatherers and he is now so troll-like that he frightens them. He is asked in whom he believes, but does not respond. This time he does not dawdle with them as long as before. The third year he again comes to these people and he has now become very much a troll and a very ugly one at that. Someone finds the courage to ask him in whom he believes and he responds with the nonsensical "trunt, trunt and the trolls in the mountains" and then he disappears. He is never seen again after that and for some years afterward no one dares go gathering moss in that area.

Although the tales and the *þáttr* share the theme of abduction as their main concern, they treat it in very different manners. *Trunt, trunt og tröllin í fjöllunum* projects a sense of perverted eroticism lacking in *Barnið og álfkonan*, as well as a more frightening atmosphere, qualities that place it in close communion with *Helga þáttr Þórissonar*. In both the *þáttr* and *Trunt, trunt og tröllin í fjöllunum*, it is the motif of the 'Fairy mistress' (F302) which is paramount. Like the Old Norse tale, *Trunt, trunt og tröllin í fjöllunum* brings its forlorn "protagonist" back before us several times, so that we may observe the slow but inevitable decline to which he is subjected. Everything in *Trunt, trunt og tröllin í fjöllunum* occurs according to this tripartite structure: his religious convictions move from belief in God, to giving no answer when queried as to whom he believes in, to belief in "trunt, trunt and the trolls in the mountains"; his relationship to society moves from a time when he says little, to one where he stays an even shorter time with others, and finally to a point where he is never seen again; his bearing too goes from being taciturn and surly to that of a frightening troll-like figure to that of an actual troll. Similarly, the hero of *Helga þáttr Þórissonar* changes from a pleasant and talented young man to a near automaton after having been abducted by Ingibjǫrg and finally to a blind "Gretti." But whereas the legend is all dust and ashes, decay and terror, the *þáttr* positions itself halfway between the hopelessness of *Trunt, trunt og tröllin í fjöllunum* and the optimism of *Barnið og álfkonan*, for King Óláfr's prayers at least lead to Helgi's release.

Helga þáttr Þórissonar is more than a reflection of folkloric tradition— its author has a point of view and a purpose—but the similarity between it and the two narratives from oral tradition illustrates the extent to which the *fornaldarsǫgur* display themes, styles, and structures cognate with the rich material of Scandinavian folklore. One aspect of this style, evinced in these examples, is the tendency toward tripartition. Axel Olrik notes in his famous essay on the epic laws of folk narrative, "Nothing distinguishes the great bulk of folk narrative from modern literature and from reality as does the number three."[17] On the whole,

---

17. Olrik 1909, 133, an expanded version of which is found in Olrik 1921. Cf. Krappe 1930, 31, 86, 181–82, 215. On "superorganic" laws, see Pentikäinen 1978, 17–19.

such superorganic "laws" have been abandoned, but although the normative component of Olrik's formulation may no longer enjoy favor, tripling in European folk literature is nevertheless a common phenomenon. Such multiplication is a regular feature of the *fornaldarsǫgur* as well: Bósi has three lewd and bawdy adventures in *Bósa saga;* Egill and Ásmundr fight for three days in *Egils saga ok Ásmundar;* in his third adventure Þorsteinn and his three companions engage in three kinds of competition in *Þorsteins þáttr bæjarmagns;* Hjǫrleifr inn kvensami takes three wives in *Hálfs saga ok Hálfsrekka;* Oddr receives three special arrows (the *Gusisnautar* 'Gusir's Gifts') in *Ǫrvar-Odds saga;* Gǫngu-Hrólfr fights for three days against the forces of King Eiríkr in *Gǫngu-Hrólfs saga;* only on the third attempt does Reginn manage to forge Sigurðr's sword in *Vǫlsunga saga;* and so on. The examples could be multiplied many times. The *fornaldarsǫgur* abound in threes and although such a characteristic, Olrik's belief notwithstanding, cannot be granted the status of a folkloric litmus test, it unquestionably contributes to the traditional and stylized atmosphere of the narratives.

A folkloric quality also develops from the *fornaldarsǫgur*'s treatment of time, which is often handled in ways that would skew our reading of more realistic genres of Old Norse literature such as the *biskupasǫgur.* In the *fornaldarsǫgur,* two attitudes toward time are typically present in complementary distribution—either it is suspended in such a way as to catch our attention and underscore the theme of the text or else it is simply ignored as an unwanted and troublesome reminder of the outer frame of reference (that is, reality) with which these sagas seem unconcerned. Thus, in *Ǫrvar-Odds saga,* the hero is given a lifespan of three hundred years, but by doing so the author is not merely making an unusual hero available to himself; he is using the device to dramatic effect, making Oddr learn the same lessons over and over again.[18] At the opposite end of the spectrum from *Ǫrvar-Odds saga*—where time plays an important role in the structure and tone of the work—is the style of the *Märchen* ('fairy tales'), in which time is simply shunted aside.[19] Thus, for example, in *Gǫngu-Hrólfs saga* (chaps. 24–25), the hero has his feet cut off at dawn and wakes up again at dusk, but only general temporal references of this sort enter into the picture. When he eventually catches up with his missing feet, which have been kept alive through the application of herbs, they are magically reattached to his limbs; but we cannot say whether this reunion takes place the next day,

---

18. Cf. the excellent discussion of this device in Paul Edwards and Hermann Pálsson 1970, xiii.
19. Cf. Lüthi 1976, 44–45, 53.

that week, or a month later. The saga shows no interest in such details, which would only ensnare the tale in the leaden language of reality.

The *fornaldarsǫgur* often draw from the same cast of *dramatis personae* which populate Scandinavian folklore.[20] The nearly ubiquitous figure in modern Scandinavian folklore of the ashlad (*askeladden*, called *kolbítr* 'coal-biter' in Icelandic) is remarkably common among the *fornaldarsǫgur* as well.[21] Typical of such figures is Refr of *Gautreks saga*, who is described in this way:

> Þá er hann var ungr, lagðizt hann í elldaskála ok beit hrís ok bǫrk af trjám; hann var furðuliga mikill vexti; ekki færði hann saur af sér, ok til einkis rétti hann sínar hendr, svó at ǫðrum væri til gagns. Faðir hans var fjárorkumaðr mikill, ok líkaði honum illa óþrifnaðr sonar síns. Refr varð frægr mjǫk at ǫngum snotrleik né frama, helldr at því at hann gjǫrði sik athlægi annarra sinna hraustra frænda, ok þótti fǫður hans hann ólíkligr til nǫkkurs frama, sem ǫðrum ungum mǫnnum var þá títt. (chap. 6)

> When he was young, he used to lie about in the kitchen and chew twigs and tree bark; he was wonderfully large in size; he did not wash the dirt off himself and did not lend a hand to anyone, such that he might be of use to others. His father was a very wealthy man and his son's slothfulness was little to his liking. Refr became quite famous, although through neither wisdom nor courage, but rather because he made himself ridiculous among his valiant kinsmen; his father thought him unlikely to gain any of the fame that was common among other young men at that time.

Naturally enough (within the folkloric context), this same Refr proceeds through a series of events in which he is able to show off his true industriousness and which culminate in his winning a fair young princess to be his bride and his taking over a large earldom.

Something of this ashlad character is present in many of the heroes of the *fornaldarsǫgur*. It is in this fashion, for example, that Gǫngu-Hrólfr is presented to the audience of *Gǫngu-Hrólfs saga*. Although he is said to be tall and sturdy and the handsomest of men, he is also *meinlaus ok gagnlaus* 'inoffensive and useless' (chap. 4). His father tells him that he will never amount to much, and Hrólfr then sets out on the business of proving himself the very able man no one believes him to

20. On the hero of the *fornaldarsǫgur*, see especially Hermann Pálsson and Paul Edwards 1971, 36–68.

21. See Brunvand 1959. On the use of the ashlad figure in the *íslendingasǫgur* (with a discussion of the type in the *fornaldarsǫgur* and Scandinavian folklore), see Liestøl 1930, 166–69, as well as Dehmer 1927, 6–12, and Reuschel 1933, 106–9.

be, the typical hero of the folktale. This type of hero eventually becomes such a common figure in the *fornaldarsǫgur* that the author of the very late *Áns saga bogsvegis* sardonically writes: *Ekki lagðist Án í eldaskála, en þó var hann afglapi kallaðr af sumum mönnum* 'Án did not lay about in the fire, yet he was called a simpleton by some' (chap. 1).

Protagonists fashioned after a very different heroic template are also much in evidence in the *fornaldarsǫgur,* figures who do not develop through their actions in the manner of the ashlad. In fact, they do not develop at all; they are literally "born leaders." The image of the neonatal hero, a champion in everything but physical stature, is found at the birth of Sigurðr in *Vǫlsunga saga,* when the king comments that no one would be *líkan verda eda samiaðnan* 'like him or equal to him' (chap. 13). As often as not, these heroic figures spring nearly full grown into the saga; so, for example, when things seem to be at their worst for King Hertryggr of Russia, Ásmundr appears on the scene at sixteen years of age and the king tells him he has never seen a person of his age who looked more useful (*gildastan*) (*Egils saga ok Ásmundar,* chap. 2). In much the same style, Ragnarr is introduced to the audience as a large, handsome, witty fellow, generous to his men and grim to his enemies; his first act in the saga, at the age of fifteen, is to kill the serpent (*ormr*) that surrounds the earl's house (*Ragnars saga loðbrókar,* chap. 3). Not all the protagonists of the *fornaldarsǫgur* fit neatly into these categories (for example, Þorsteinn in *Þorsteins saga Víkingssonar* and Oddr in *Ǫrvar-Odds saga*), but certainly the large majority of the sagas draw their heroes from these two pools—one, the hero of *Märchen,* the other, the champion of heroic legend, figures that may be said to correspond loosely to the comic and tragic saga types.

In addition to themes, characters, and motifs that suggest a special relationship between the *fornaldarsǫgur* and folklore, the sagas' manner of presentation, especially in the form of the structural repetitions, often echoes the form of oral narratives. Although the writers of the *fornaldarsǫgur* may color episodes vividly, such motley coverings only thinly veil the (often) highly reduplicative skeletons beneath. The so-called *Gjafa-Refs saga* of *Gautreks saga* (chaps. 9–11 in the younger and longer version) illustrates this pattern well. The story's ashlad hero, Refr, leaves home with his father's prized ox and after presenting the beast to Earl Neri, manages, with the Earl's constant advice, to parlay this initial present into an ever escalating series of gifts which culminates in his gaining King Gautrekr's daughter and Neri's earldom. The story moves from one encounter with kings and earls to the other and tells how they assist Refr in acquiring his status as an accomplished

Refr's visit to:

	Gautrekr	Ælla	Hrólfr kraki	Óláfr	Gautrekr
1. Earl asks Refr about his plans		X	X	X	
2. Refr replies		X	X	X	
3. Earl gives Refr advice	X	X	X	X	X
4. Earl refers to ox		X		X	
5. Refr replies negatively		X		X	
6. Earl gives Refr advice	X	X	X	X	X
7. Refr follows Earl's advice	X	X	X	X	X
8. Refr offers a gift to the king	X	X	X	X	
9. History of the gifts told		X	X	X	
10. King comments on Gautrekr's generosity		X	X	X	
11. Refr is presented with a gift	X	X	X	X	X
12. Refr returns to the Earl	X	X	X	X	
13. Earl refers to the ox		X	X		X
14. Refr replies negatively		X			
15. Refr stays with the Earl	X	X	X		

hero. The structure of the story is represented graphically in the chart, where an *X* indicates that the action listed on the left occurred during Refr's visit to one of the various donor figures.

While this thematic roentgenogram gives only the barest version of the plot, which contains numerous other motifs, it does capture the *essential* structure, repeated episode after episode, as well as the basic narrative cohesion of the *þáttr*. In his work on the syntagmatic structure of certain Russian folktales, Vladimir Propp concludes that stripping away individualizing characteristics reveals the underlying continuity *between* fairy tales.[22] In this case, on the other hand, the recurring form exists *within* the individual saga, part of the "mechanical" quality of the *fornaldarsǫgur* to which critics so often object. Also apparent from this syntagmatic view of the Gjafa-Refr portion of *Gautreks saga* is its ring, or chaistic, structure, that is, it pattern of concentric mirrorlike actions.

22. Propp 1968, 23–24; see also the comments by Liberman (1984, ix–lxxxi). Propp's methodology has been applied to the Icelandic *Märchensagas* with good results in Glauser 1983, 145–61, and is implicit in Righter-Gould 1975. J. Harris (1972, 5) argues that the principal theoretical framework for Andersson 1967 derives from Proppian analysis as well, as does Harris's own study of the *þættir*. Cf. the application of Propp to the Old English epic *Beowulf* in Barnes 1970.

Here the ring is represented by Refr's encounters with, and gifts from, (1) Earl Neri, (2) King Gautrekr, (3) King Ælla, (4) Hrólfr kraki, (3) King Óláfr, (2) King Gautrekr, (1) Earl Neri. This so-called ring composition, the object of considerable study among Hellenists, is hardly a feature of oral literature alone, but appears to be a common feature of both written literature and the art of the raconteur.[23]

One of the most thorough investigations of the relationship between traditional literature and Germanic heroic materials is Friedrich Panzer's study of the Bear's Son Tale (*das Märchen vom Bärensohn*).[24] After careful analysis of over two hundred variants of this tale, Panzer adduces three fundamental patterns that typify the hero's early life. His is a monumental work that has created great admiration and equally great consternation among scholars of this century: almost immediately after its publication in 1910, the Swedish folklorist Carl von Sydow launched a stinging attack on Panzer's analysis, arguing that Panzer was really discussing the motifs of folk literature in general, which might be found in legend and myth as well as the folktale.[25] Detractors have continued to attack—or more often simply dismiss—the importance of the Bear's Son Tale since that time: in his handbook on Germanic heroic materials, Klaus von See, for example, waves Panzer's work aside.[26] Yet despite such objections, Panzer's analysis of the Bear's Son Tale has continued to generate much productive scholarship: since his original study, still other Old Norse texts have been shown to belong to the Bear's Son complex.[27] Among the Germanic texts often cited in connection with the Bear's Son Tale are *Beowulf*, *Grettis saga Ásmundarsonar*, *Hrólfs saga kraka*, and *Ormsþáttr Stórólfssonar*. That the figure of Bǫðvarr Bjarki in *Hrólfs saga kraka* can be understood as belonging to

23. For a description of ring composition in Homer, see, for example, Whitman 1958, 87–101, 249–84, 287–90, and the discussion in Niles 1983, 152–62, which contains an extensive bibliography. For a discussion of the phenomenon in the works of traditional oral poets, see Lord 1986 and Buchan 1972, 87–144.

24. Panzer 1910–12.

25. Von Sydow 1911.

26. Von See 1981a, 17: "It is not just students of heroic legend who today relegate Panzer's theories to the dustbin of history" ("Heute sind Panzers Theorien nicht nur von der Heldensagenforschung zu den Akten gelegt").

27. Already in the second volume of his study, Panzer points out that the German tale of Sigurðr preserved in the Old Norse *Þiðreks saga* (but not the hero of either the *Poetic Edda* or *Vǫlsunga saga*) subscribes to the basic pattern. It has been suggested that several of the romances were patterned after the Bear's Son Tale: W. W. Lawrence (1928, 181–91, 317–18) postulates such an influence on *Samsons saga fagra;* Schlauch (1930, 20–21) suggests the same for *Flores saga ok sona hans* and again (1934, 109–10) finds it in *Andra saga jarls*. See also Jorgensen's recent contributions (1975, 1986). Both R. Harris (1974) and Pizarro (1976–77) seek to apply the pattern in interesting new ways to additional Icelandic texts.

this group has long since been refuted,[28] but at the same time, many other texts have been interpreted as having drawn from the wellspring of folkloric inspiration, specifically that fed by the Bear's Son Tale.

The importance of Panzer's *Märchen vom Bärensohn* for the present discussion derives from the significance of so widespread an heroic template according to which many of the protagonists of the *fornaldarsǫgur*, and the events of their lives, are fashioned (whatever the exact nature by which such a pattern developed). Thus, in his excellent article on the use of the Bear's Son Tale by the author of *Grettis saga Ásmundarsonar*, Richard Harris demonstrates how each of Grettir's adventures—with Kárr, with the bear at the sea-cliff, with the trolls at Sandhaugr, and with Glámr—fits into this scheme, and how, most important, the author has used this same pattern in an inverted form at the conclusion of the saga and turned the tables on the protagonist: Grettir is now himself the monster and the land must be cleansed of him. The conscious efforts that the writers of the *fornaldarsǫgur* made in utilizing such traditional materials as the Bear's Son Tale are also made clear in Joaquín Martínez Pizarro's analysis of the use of elements of the tale in the three *fornaldarsǫgur* that deal with the men of Hrafnista, *Ketils saga hængs, Gríms saga loðinkinna*, and *Ǫrvar-Odds saga*. Pizarro concludes that in each of the *fornaldarsǫgur* the Bear's Son Tale has been altered for specific literary purposes, a poignant reminder of the synergism between tradition and innovation in this genre. After examining the appearances of such details in the various versions of *Ǫrvar-Odds saga*, he further concludes that the *fornaldarsǫgur* writers borrowed not only from each other, but also directly from folk narratives.[29]

That the writers of the *fornaldarsǫgur* were accustomed to borrowing from the realm of folklore allows us to understand why these sagas have so frequently run afoul of the critics. It is exactly this folkloric influence that has so often led to the negative literary assessments of the *fornaldarsǫgur*—the often repetitive and predictable events, the stock characters and themes in which they abound, in other words, those factors that seem so tired and tiring to modern audiences, accustomed as we are to the more varied character of realistic literature.[30]

Akin to this folkloric dimension of the *fornaldarsǫgur* is the special relationship they bear to the mythico-religious world of the pre-Christian Scandinavians and the degree to which the mythological

28. Olrik 1903–10, I, 134–37; O. Olson 1916, 59–60. Cf. Benson 1970, 18–19.
29. R. Harris 1974; Pizarro 1976–77, 281.
30. See, for example, Ker 1908, 282; Guðbrandur Vigfússon 1878, I, cxcvi; Schlauch 1934, 170.

details contained in these narratives reflect genuine historical practices and beliefs. An axiomatic part of our attitude toward the *fornaldarsǫgur* is that they are intimately tied to the mythological past: indeed, the view that the *fornaldarsǫgur* are heavily influenced by, and major repositories of, mythological materials goes far back in the scholarship on these sagas, as many of the commonly used terms for them indicate—mythical-heroic sagas, *mythiske sagaer* 'mythic sagas,' and so on. There are often good reasons for believing that such a relationship is evinced by these texts, for in addition to the obvious pagan theophanies in which the *fornaldarsǫgur* delight, they frequently suggest more subtle influences and echoes from pre-Christian mythology.

Unfortunately much of our data concerning ancient Nordic religious belief is highly suspect, since the textual sources for Old Norse religion are almost exclusively from the Christian period.[31] Whatever the historical accuracy of a text like Snorri's *Prose Edda,* it was a well-read work in medieval Iceland and thus surely exerted an influence on the creation of later texts, *whether or not* this impact was founded on an accurate reflection of ancient tradition. In the minds of the late medieval creators of the *fornaldarsǫgur,* and their audiences, these sagas were to be connected with the heathen past. And although scholars may well quibble now and in the future about the *reliability* of the myths and beliefs reported in the *fornaldarsǫgur,* there can be no question that the existence of such voluminous mythic materials (whether accurate or not) in the *fornaldarsǫgur* tells us a great deal about these literary works and the world they were intended to project. In fact, two kinds of "paganism" are to be found in the *fornaldarsǫgur:*[32] direct references to pagan deities and practices in the texts and the less obvious residue of the mythological tradition on saga literature. In the following section I examine the manner in which Óðinn functions in the sagas as the most prominent model of the first type, and *Þorsteins þáttr bæjarmagns* is discussed as an example of the second type.

The *fornaldarsǫgur* can make no exclusive claim to the Old Norse pantheon: there are frequent appearances in other saga genres of the chief god of the pagans, Óðinn. In these texts, as in some of the *fornaldarsǫgur,* he is presented as a devil. In the saga of one of the great missionary kings, *Ólafs saga Tryggvasonar en mesta* (chap. 198), for ex-

31. See, for example, R. Frank's (negative) reappraisal of Snorri's version of the acquisition of the Poetic Mead by Óðinn (1981).

32. By *paganism,* I mean here the conscious fostering and use of ancient heathen practice in a sense parallel to "folklorism" and revitalization. See Lord 1976 and Salmonsson 1984.

ample, he is called *fiandi* 'fiend.' Typical of these Old Norse the-ophanies is the scene in which the diabolical creature from the past focuses his attention on the possibility of snatching an apostate from among the faithful: disguised in a wide-brimmed hat, he engages the hero in conversation, regaling him with stories of bygone heroes. He then vanishes, but not before attempting the further perversion of the listener's faith by means of some physical object, such as a bit of meat, presumably from a sacrifice to the pagan gods (for example, *Óláfs saga Tryggvasonar*, chap. 64).[33]

One might reasonably expect the effects of *interpretatio christiana* on the Old Norse materials—the ascription of the old gods to the realm of demons and devils—to be commonplace in the *fornaldarsǫgur*, late as these texts are.[34] It is an interpretation expressed in connection with the ancient Scandinavian gods by Christian writers already in the ninth century (*Vita Anskarii*, chap. 19) and a regular feature of the Christian perspective on the old gods through at least the fifteenth century.[35] Yet despite this fact, revisionist interpretations of the old gods are generally far less common and less radical in the *fornaldarsǫgur* than elsewhere in saga literature: among those encountered in the *fornaldarsǫgur* are *jllur andi* 'evil spirit' (*Hrólfs saga kraka*, chap. 30); *raug uættir* 'cowardly being' (*Heiðreks saga*, chap. 10—*ill vættr ok ǫrm* in some manuscripts); and *hǫfðingja myrkranna* 'prince of darkness' (*Egils saga ok Ásmundar*, chap. 13).

Bǫðvarr Bjarki, in an apparent show of revisionist monotheistic attitudes, responds to the comment that the champions of Hrólfr kraki may spend the night in Valhǫll with the statement that he does not see Óðinn, but that if *þad jlla eyturkuykindi* 'that evil venomous creature' should appear, he would crush him (*Hrólfs saga kraka*, chap. 33). Close-ly connected to these references are the specific denials of Óðinn and his might made by some of the saga heroes such as Ketill hængr (chap. 5) and Ǫrvar-Oddr (chaps. 17, 29), although such denials as these and Bǫðvarr Bjarki's do not seem to be intimately tied to Christian views, but rather to the hero's belief in his own strength.[36] Yet these the-

33. The story, with accretions, is also told in *Ólafs saga Tryggvasonar en mesta* (chap. 198).

34. See Acterberg 1930 for a discussion of the history and nature of this missionary tool. See also Baetke 1951 and Addison 1936.

35. Paasche (1948, 17) mentions a case from Stockholm in 1484 in which a man confesses to having served "Odin" for seven years. Clearly he means Satan, but so thoroughly had the equation been made that even at this relatively late date the apparent warlock could substitute the name of the indigenous god.

36. See especially Weber 1981, as well as F. Ström 1948.

ologically salubrious views of Óðinn are rarely encountered in the *fornaldarsǫgur:* in these sagas we are more likely to meet an Óðinn who is very much in keeping with the deity as he might have appeared in some pre-Conversion prose version of the eddic poems. How is this situation to be interpreted and how does it relate to our understanding of the literature of fourteenth- and fifteenth-century Iceland; that is, what does it tell us about the literary ambitions and needs of this period? After all, many of Óðinn's appearances in the *fornaldarsǫgur* are late accretions; his deeds in the guise of Rauðgrani in *Qrvar-Odds saga,* for example, are part of the later manuscript tradition only.

Icelandic euhemerism is often expressed in the *fornaldarsǫgur,*[37] according to which the Æsir migrated to the north from Asia with Óðinn as their king, a belief expressed in the opening chapters of *Sǫrla þáttr, Sturlaugs saga Starfssama,* and *Bósa saga.* At other times, Óðinn is mentioned in ways that suggest phraseological, as opposed to narratological, significance, such as *gista Odin* 'to be the guest of Óðinn' (that is, 'to die') (for example, *Heiðreks saga,* chap. 3; *Hrómundar saga Gripssonar,* chap. 2). A smaller but still substantial number of references to Óðinn play on actual, or at least perceived, elements of the old religion. Among such allusions to Óðinn in the old faith are toasts (*Óðins minni* 'Óðinn's memorial cup' [*Bósa saga,* chap. 12; *Þorsteins þáttr bæjarmagns,* chap. 9]); the concept of hallowed ground (*hof eitt* [. . .] *helgat Þór ok Óðni, Frigg ok Freyju* 'a certain temple [. . .] dedicated to Þórr, Óðinn, Frigg, and Freyja' [*Sturlaugs saga starfsama,* chap. 17]); runes (*Vǫlsunga saga,* chap. 21); and magic (*Gǫngu-Hrólfs saga,* chap. 1; the C manuscript only). Most common are references to sacrifice, which occur in no fewer than five works (*Heiðreks saga,* chaps. 7, 9; *Hálfs saga ok Hálfsrekka,* chap. 1; *Qrvar-Odds saga,* chap. 29; *Egils saga ok Ásmundar,* chap. 8; *Gautreks saga,* chap. 7).

Odinic theophanies can also play a significant structural role in the *fornaldarsǫgur.* In these intrusions into the world of humans, Óðinn sometimes plays the part of the helper or donor figure, although at other times he is a much more suspicious character, whose actions appear to have solely malicious intent. Among his appearances as a donor figure are his offers of assistance to Hrólfr in *Hrólfs saga kraka* (chaps. 26, 30), his connections with the beginnings of the Vǫlsung lineage and his continued assistance to them (*Vǫlsunga saga,* chaps. 1, 2, 17, 18), the repetition of some of the same material in *Norna-Gests þáttr* (chap. 286), his somewhat useless assistance to Framarr in *Ketils*

---

37. For a discussion of this phenomenon, see Schomerus 1936, 20–48.

saga hœngs (chap. 5), his multiple forms of aid in various disguises to
Ǫrvar-Oddr (chaps. 19–24, 29) and his patronage and protection of
Starkaðr in *Gautreks saga* (chaps. 4, 7). Ǫðinn's less positive ap-
pearances in the *fornaldarsǫgur* include his withdrawal of support from
Sigmundr in *Vǫlsunga saga* (chap. 11), his manipulation of Freyja in
Sǫrla þáttr which results in the curse of the two armies (chaps. 228,
229, 234, 236), his appearance as Gestumblindi in *Heiðreks saga* (chap.
9), his activities in *Hálfs saga ok Hálfsrekka* which lead to the promise of
Víkarr as a future sacrifice (chap. 1), and the fulfillment of that same
promise in *Gautreks saga* (chap. 7).

There is little doubt that many of the references outlined above
derive from rekindled literary and antiquarian interest in the old pagan
gods, yet some of them may be genuine relics from the time of Scandinavian heathenism. Unlike their classical counterparts, the Germanic
gods were basically untouched by scholarly reinterpretations that
would view them as allegories or equate them physically with the stars
and planets. Thus, whereas the tradition of moral, physical, and historical reappraisal of the Graeco-Roman deities in the Middle Ages provided a moderating view of these gods,[38] the Scandinavian attitude
toward the pagan past is on the whole either "negative" (that is, the
gods are presented as devils, demons, deceptive sorcerers, and so on),
or "positive," in which case they are treated with an antiquarian's
dispassionate interest in the plots and motifs that (may) hark back to
pre-Christian Scandinavia.

It is tempting to assume, as many generations of past scholars have,
that all mythological components encountered in the *fornaldarsǫgur*
should be credited as authentic, that somehow the indigenous religious
tradition has maintained itself sufficiently well that we can rely on the
testimony of texts written down three and four hundred years after the
Conversion. This is a most unlikely prospect, yet warnings against
such a view of the religious testimony of the Germanic legendary texts
are still necessary.[39] The relationship between the literary uses of
Óðinn and the facts concerning the actual religious practices of the

38. On the various attitudes (Stoic, Neoplatonic, and so on) toward the classical gods
in the Middle Ages, see Seznec 1953, esp. 11–147. Faulkes (1983) suggests that the
prologue and subsequent portions of the *Prose Edda* represent an attempt to harmo-
nize—and exploit—common ground between Christianity and pagan beliefs.

39. See, for example, von See 1981a, 52. Caution is similarly advocated in the case of
the more realistic sagas in Boyer 1975. See also Martin 1973, Schach 1975, and Mc-
Creesh 1980. On the quality and extent of our knowledge of older Scandinavian beliefs,
see the review of source materials in Lindow 1985, 21–42.

pagan Scandinavians is convoluted and often misunderstood; interpretations have generally been predicated on consistent over- or underreliance on the *fornaldarsǫgur* as sources of reliable material.[40] With her usual acuteness, Margaret Schlauch comments that Christianity was no impediment to the Icelanders' curiosity about their ancestors' beliefs, but that such interest was antiquarian in nature.[41] A probable example of such an inherited belief is the insistence of the sagas on sacrifices to Óðinn. We are in a particularly advantageous position to credit this motif as a reflex of ancient practice, for in addition to literary evidence outside the *fornaldarsǫgur* for such a custom (for example, *Hávamál*, st. 138), there exists a substantial, and growing, amount of archæological support for the likelihood of such a practice, as in the findings from the bogs of northern Europe and the Gutnish picture stones.[42] And what would become of Starkaðr's tragic situation, in which he "mistakenly" sacrifices King Víkarr, if the Hǫttr character were reduced to just another Rumplestilzchen figure who deceitfully contracts with a mother for the life of her unborn child? Naturally Óðinn's part in *Hálfs saga ok Hálfsrekka* and *Gautreks saga* is based on this motif (S240 'Children unwittingly promised'), but the reduction of that role in these two sagas to something done by an elf, gnome, or dwarf would hardly give us the Starkaðr tale to which we are accustomed.

Not all mythological frames, or overlays, are as obvious as the references to Óðinn: it has been argued that the myths associated with pre-Christian Scandinavia played an important but not necessarily obvious or conscious part in the structure and theme of several Icelandic sagas.[43] An example of such influence from among the *fornaldarsǫgur* is *Þorsteins þáttr bæjarmagns*. The story concerns a young man of considerable strength (hence his cognomen, 'Strength of the Farm') who acquires several remarkable gifts on a series of journeys; in a third adventure he visits the halls of Geirrøðr, king of the giants, in the company of several huge companions led by Guðmundr, who renames Þorsteinn *bæjarbarn* 'Baby of the Farm.' In the course of their visit Þorsteinn

40. Cf., for example, the observations cited in Schomerus 1936, 58.
41. Schlauch 1934, 18.
42. On the question of the genuineness of such episodes vis-à-vis old Germanic religion, see, for example, Ranisch 1935, 121; de Vries 1956, I, 406–28; Turville-Petre 1964, 251–62; Å. Ström 1966; Simpson 1967; Milroy 1967–68; Beck 1970; and Mitchell 1985b. The question of Germanic sacrifice as an inheritance from Indo-European times is taken up in Sauvé 1970. Cf. the report in Adam of Bremen (IV, 27).
43. Cf. Harris 1976a, Bessason 1977, Lindow 1977, and McCreesh 1979–80. On reflexes of an archaic character in the sagas, see also Mitchell 1985c.

assists his newfound friends through the use of deception in various competitions, including wrestling and drinking. The Scandinavian lineage of the story has been seriously questioned by several writers, yet it seems likely that the Icelandic writer got his materials not from a Celtic source (at least not directly), but from a myth in which the god Þórr travels to the land of the giants in order to visit Útgarða-Loki and there encounters various deceits.[44] For by whatever fashion the story came to Scandinavia, by the time *Þorsteins þáttr bæjarmagns* was composed (1300s), the tale was regarded as traditional in the Old Norse world: trips to the Otherworld by Þórr are known from as early as the tenth century (Eilífr Goðrúnarson's *Þórsdrápa*) and are regularly met in accounts of Scandinavian mythology. Thus, for example, Saxo Grammaticus recounts Thorkillus's adventures with Guthmundus and Geruthus in the twelfth century (*Gesta Danorum* XIII), and the story is taken up again in Snorri Sturluson's *Edda* in the early thirteenth century (*Skáldskaparmál,* chap. 26). In a different part of this same work, the so-called *Glyfaginning* (chaps. 26–31), Snorri gives an account of a different tale in which Þórr also travels to the land of the giants, where he again experiences a series of deceptions and competitions, the trip to Útgarða-Loki.[45]

It is this adventure in Snorri's *Edda* which appears to have provided *þorsteins þáttr bæjarmagns* with its narrative material, given the closeness of the two texts. Among the related aspects of the narratives may be included the comments on the relative puniness of the texts' otherwise powerful hero made by his newfound traveling companion, the Otherworld journey theme, the reliance on companions, the use of deception, the nature of the competition, and the appearance of fire, drinking, and wrestling in both. Even such details as the thunder god's magic hammer, Mjǫllnir, a gift of the dwarves which always hits its target and then returns to the thrower, would seem to be mirrored in the *þáttr:* there a dwarf presents Þorsteinn with gifts (a magic marble and a point) which like Mjǫllnir always hit their targets when thrown and then return to the thrower. We do not need to imagine a conscious reflection of the one tale in the other, but it is likely that the author of

44. The foreign origins of this myth have been argued since at least the time of Bugge (1908, 210). The issue has been taken up in Simpson 1963 and Power 1985a. The relationship of these tales to the Middle English Gawain has also been noted by Speirs (1959, 204) and Taylor (1970).

45. For a discussion of the materials relating to Þórr's trip to the Otherworld, see Ciklamini 1968, which analyzes the differences between Saxo's story and *Þorsteins þáttr bæjarmagns,* and Ross 1981.

Þorsteins þáttr bæjarmagns had heard or read the story of Þórr's journey to Útgarða-Loki and was thus influenced, knowingly or not, in producing the *þáttr* as we have it.

Although the relationship between *Þorsteins þáttr bæjarmagns* and the Þórr myth may be unintentional, it is important to recall that the *fornaldarsǫgur* exhibit—and manifestly *want* to exhibit—a special relationship to the heathen Nordic past. In some cases the texts may indeed contain mythological residue, but in general they are not so much repositories of ancient pagan data as products of a renewed antiquarian interest in such material brought about by specific Icelandic conditions.

The saga writers were informed about Nordic mythology through many different conduits (for example, *Snorra Edda,* Icelandic 'learned history'), and one of these was surely eddic poetry. This traditional narrative verse was the vehicle by which heroic adventures were recounted before the existence of the extant *fornaldarsǫgur,* as in the case of Hálfr of *Hálfs saga ok Hálfsrekka* and Sigurðr of *Vǫlsunga saga.* For many of the heroes whose careers and adventures fill the Icelandic *fornaldarsǫgur,* origins can be postulated which stretch beyond the realm of the historical in even its most extended definition—where such a reference might indicate nothing more concrete than a postulated text—to a kind of inspiration which borders on the archetypal.[46] Before the written *fornaldarsǫgur* came into being, some, at least, of these heroic lives were recounted in verse,[47] which increasingly came to be embedded in a prose matrix, as in the case of *Vǫlsunga saga.* Here the compiler of the extant *fornaldarsaga* has employed the eddic poems that treat the lives of Sigurðr, Brynhildr, and Guðrún and from their

46. So, for example, de Vries (1963), who takes up several of the figures from the *fornaldarsǫgur.*

47. An older generation of scholars believed in the primacy of poetic forms of the *fornaldarsǫgur,* an idea which has been under much attack in recent years. Heusler (1955, 151), for example, maintains with reference to the Nibelung materials that what is usually called heroic legend (*Heldensage*) ought to be called heroic poetry (*Heldendichtung*), the product of a specific poet's labor. Schneider's dictum, that heroic legend *is* heroic poetry ("Heldensage ist Heldendichtung"), is implicit throughout his *Germanische Heldensage* (cf. de Boor 1929). It is a view that can boast fairly deep roots in literary interpretation. Ker 1908 divides the medieval world into an heroic age followed by an age of chivalry, with the parallel in literature of an age dominated by "epics" (e.g., *Beowulf*) followed by an age of romance. It is not difficult to imagine how the two came to be regarded as periods of poetic and prose composition respectively. Especially important in refuting this view have been Genzmer 1948 and Kuhn 1952. Genzmer and Kuhn argue against the idea that the majority of *fornaldarsǫgur* (and other Germanic heroic texts) are necessarily prose reworkings of earlier lays; thus, Kuhn maintains (1952, 276), "The sagas originated from widely known materials (*aus den bekannten Elementen*), although not necessarily in the form of lays (*Lieder*)."

testimony—and to some extent from quotations of this material—
formulated the most famous of the *fornaldarsǫgur*. Although such a
process accounts for the extant *Vǫlsunga saga* and probably for several
other works, it should not be assumed that the transition from poetry
to prose was ubiquitous.

What this process was like, how it began, and why it should have
taken place at all are difficult questions—and yet some propositions can
be offered. As a point of departure, we might well consider such
transitional texts, works moving between the poetic and prosaic categories by means of the gradual accretion of prose inquits, a kind of
process which describes several of the *fornaldarsǫgur*. Among the most
famous accounts of sagas being told is that in *Þorgils saga ok Hafliða*
(chap. 10), which reports how several sagas are delivered at a wedding
at Reykhólar in 1119: *Hrólfr af Skálmarnesi sagði sǫgu frá Hrǫngviði
víkingi ok frá Óláfi liðmannakonungi ok haugbroti Þráins berserks ok Hró-
mundi Gripssyni, ok margur vísur með* [. . .] *Þessa sǫgu hafði Hrólfr
sammansetta. Ingimundr prestr sagði sǫgu Orms Barreyjarskálds ok vísur
margar ok flokk góðan við enda sǫgunnar, er Ingimundr hafði ortan* 'Hrólfr
of Skálmarness told the saga about Hrǫngviðr the Viking and about
Óláfr the Warriors' King and the mound-breaking of Þráinn the Ber-
serkr and about Hrómundr Gripsson, together with many verses
[. . .] Hrólfr himself composed this saga. Ingimundr the priest told
the saga of Ormr Barreyjarskáld, including many verses and a good
poem (*flokkr*) at the end of the saga which Ingimundr had composed.'
Although we will never know with certainty what forms these texts
had, in trying to describe what such recitations might have been like
one scholar likens them to the eddic Helgi lays, that is, "verses set in a
simple narrative framework of prose."[48] Many of the *fornaldarsǫgur*
probably had beginnings of this sort. Such a compositional profile may
also imply that the poetry antedates the prose, and, to be sure, this
situation frequently obtains in the corpus (for example, the "Battle of
the Goths and Huns" in *Heiðreks saga,* which may be among the oldest
pieces of Old Norse heroic poetry).[49] Yet a relationship of this sort
between prose and poetry is far from standard in the *fornaldarsǫgur*:
some of the sagas contain poetry written in order to amplify and
comment on action not otherwise reflected in the text, as in *Hálfs saga
ok Hálfsrekka*.[50] In still other cases, the sagas contain paraphrases of the

48. *Þorgils saga ok Hafliða,* ed. Dronke, p. 75.
49. Tolkien 1955–56.
50. Cf. Genzmer 1948, 16, but see also Jón Helgason (1934, 203–4), who states that
the poetry is not particularly old, but older than the prose of the saga at any rate.

preexisting poetry, rather than the poems themselves; such is the situation in the famous case of the *Bjarkamál* of *Hrólfs saga kraka*.[51]

Something of this process of prose accretion may be observed in the case of *The Second Lay of Helgi Hundingsbani*, to which the scene in *Þorgils saga ok Hafliða* was compared.[52] The Helgi texts point toward the apparent growth of prose "connectors" between passages of poetry, at least one means by which some sections of the *fornaldarsǫgur* evolved. At certain junctures in *Helgaqviða Hundingsbana II*, for example, the events reported in poetry would make little sense without a mental dexterity that might tax even a knowledgeable audience familiar with the tradition. Even such an informed public might be confused when the stanzas of the extant poem move erratically from one scene to another, without any indication of the scene change. Such is the case, for example, following a conversation between Helgi and Sigrún in which she declares love for him and hatred for her betrothed, Hǫðbroddr. In the subsequent stanza (25) she states:

> "Muna þér Sigrún   frá Sefafiollom,
> Hǫðbroddr konungr,   hníga at armi;
> liðin er ævi — opt náir hrævi
> gránstóð gríðar — Granmars sona."

"Never, King Hǫðbroddr, shall you hold Sigrún of Sefafiall in your arms; that time is past; the gray steeds of the giantess [wolves] shall feast upon carrion—Granmarr's sons."

It is generally held that members of the audience were capable of making all the correct assumptions about the activity that intervenes between the two stanzas, as they were familiar with the plot of the story. Yet the collector of the *Edda* seems dissatisfied with such a presentation and consequently inserts a prose explanation in which he tells of the battle fought between Sigrún's aggrieved family and suitor and the forces Helgi commands, concluding it with the statement *Sigrún gecc í valinn oc hitti Hǫðbrodd at kominn dauða* 'Sigrún went out among the slain and found Hǫðbroddr near death' (p. 154). In this case, the prose insert forms a bridge between the units of versified dialogue and we may well ask whether or not at some earlier point in the poem's

---

51. Any discussion of *Bjarkamál* must begin with Olrik's daunting project (1903–10, I, 28–114), in which he bravely attempts to piece together the poem from the various medieval sources (Saxo, Snorri's *Heimskringla*, *Snorra Edda*, and *Hrólfs saga kraka*) and thereby provide a vernacular edition of the poem.

52. See the remarks and bibliography contained in J. Harris 1983.

existence, the same purpose was served by poetry in *Helgaqviða Hundingsbana II* (or **Vǫlsungaqviða in forna* 'The Old Lay of the Vǫlsungs,' the work to which the collector refers in the *Edda*).

At other points in the text, however, the redactor's asides function differently; they do not clarify the actions of the stanzas but merely serve to prepare the audience for that which could be inferred from the poetry itself. The prose and poetry are here no longer in complementary distribution, but instead amplify and enlarge, or simply duplicate, each other. Thus, when Helgi is later killed by Sigrún's brother and buried, the redactor tells us: *Ambót Sigrúnar gecc um aptan hiá haugi Helga oc sá, at Helgi reið til haugsins með marga menn* 'Sigrún's slave-woman went near Helgi's burial mound one evening and saw that Helgi rode to the mound with many men' (p. 159). The woman then speaks (st. 40):

> "Hvárt ero þat svic ein, er ec siá þicciomz,
> eða ragna rǫc, ríða menn dauðir?
> er ióa yðra oddom keyrit,
> eða er hildingom heimfor gefin?"

> "Is this a deception I seem to see, or the Fate of the Gods [end of the world]—do dead men ride? Do you with spurs urge your steeds; are heroes given leave to come home?"

Helgi responds to the servant, who runs off to report the news to Sigrún, including the fact that *up er haugr lokinn, / kominn er Helgi* 'the burial mound is open, Helgi has come' (st. 42). The dialogue given in verse relates the same information already amply provided in the prose of the collector, rendering the verse nearly redundant. Unlike the previous case, the redactor has here unnecessarily cluttered the text and added prose more or less for its own sake, perhaps as a means of exerting his own authorial presence on the preexisting materials. The effect is that the prose tends to impede the flow of the tale rather than to assist it. From the evidence of the *Helgaqviða Hundingsbana II*, it may be possible to see the process of prose accretion whereby traditional poetic texts become mixed prose and poetry narratives. At times such embellishments are useful, if somewhat overly ample, narrative bridges; at other times, they are little more than agrestic intrusions on the preexisting material.[53]

---

53. For parallel examples from other cultures, see Godzic and Kittay 1987.

The life of Helgi Hundingsbani is known not only from the eddic poems, but also from *Vǫlsunga saga,* the only *fornaldarsaga* in which the relationship between traditional eddic poetry and the prose form can be explored in some detail. Scholarship on the *Vǫlsunga saga,* and the rest of the corpus of texts dealing with the Nibelungs, is nothing less than voluminous, as are the theories that seek to account for the relationships between the several extant texts, to say nothing of the hypothetical works that have been inferred over the years.[54] In addition to the eddic poems and *Vǫlsunga saga,* medieval texts that treat the Sigurðr-Nibelung cycle include *Snorra Edda, Þiðreks saga,* and the Middle High German *Nibelungenlied.* The popularity of the tradition is further indicated by the wealth of supporting plastic representations of the tale throughout northern Europe (for example, the Ramsund petroglyph in Sweden, the wood-carvings in Norwegian stave churches, the petroglyph from the Isle of Man) and by the fact that the story of Sigurðr the dragon slayer appears among the literary traditions of other Germanic peoples, such as the reference to the story of Sigemund the dragon slayer in *Beowulf* (ll. 874–97).[55]

There are good indications too that Sigurð's youthful exploits and death were once the subject of their own prose saga. Just such a **Sigurðar saga Fáfnisbana* is mentioned in *Norna-Gests þáttr* (*sem segir j sǫgu Sigurdar Fafnisbana* 'as is related in the saga of Sigurðr the dragon slayer' [chap. 287]) and in *Snorra Edda* (*eptir Sigvrþar savgv* 'according to the saga of Sigurð' [p. 231]). Finnur Jónsson, after an exhaustive examination of the prose inquits in the early Sigurðr poems in the *Poetic Edda,* concludes that these inserts were in fact based on the redactor's knowledge of the **Sigurðar saga,* although this view has not been universally accepted.[56] It is reasonably assumed that the writer responsible for *Vǫlsunga saga* had access to the materials of the *Poetic Edda:* the citations from the texts testify to this fact.[57] At times, it seems that only the most meager discrepancies separate the prose of *Vǫlsunga saga*

---

54. For a comprehensive review of the scholarship in this area, see the discussion and bibliographic materials in Andersson 1980.

55. The many sources of plastic information on the Sigurðr cycle are covered in Margeson 1980 and *Sigurds saga i middelalderens billedkunst.* A convenient review of textual sources is provided in Andersson 1980, 20–22.

56. Finnur Jónsson (1917, 36) credits the lost prose story of Sigurðr's life with having been the basis for chaps. 1–8 of *Vǫlsunga saga.* In contrast, Heusler (1919, 47–48) feels that the Helgi material was an original contribution by the author of *Vǫlsunga saga.* Thus, both regard the Helgi material of chap. 9 as falling outside the scope of items encompassed by the lost saga.

57. Wieselgren 1935, 16–30.

and the poems of the *Edda*. Thus, for example, when Sinfjötli and Granmarr engage in a flyting in *Helgaqviða Hundingsbana I*, the text (sts. 37–42) closely mirrors the structure and essential contents of the eddic poems, as in the following example (st. 37):

> "Þú vart vǫlva   í Varinseyio,
> scollvís kona,   bartu scrǫc saman;
> qvaztu engi mann   eiga vilia,
> segg bryniaðan,   nema Sinfiotla."

> "You were a witch on the island of Varin, a deceitful woman, you created falsehoods, said that you wanted no other man, no mailed warrior, only Sinfjǫtli."

This passage may be compared to the corresponding section of *Vǫlsunga saga* (chap. 9), where the compiler writes: *Eigi mantu glokt muna nu, er þu vart volvann i Varinsey ok kvazt vilia mann eiga ok kaust mik til þess embęttis at vera þinn madr* 'You cannot now remember when you were a witch on the island of Varin and said that you wanted to have a man and chose me for the service of being your husband.' The same information is covered in the two narratives, but the results for the flyting as a whole are striking. The prose version no longer has the volume or range of invectives found in the poetry and loses much of the vigor contained in the abusive language of the original.

The difference in the resulting text—with its tendency to blunt the tale as given in the poetic original—is one exhibited throughout the saga. For example, using the two Atli poems of the *Edda*, which cover the same materials but in very different styles, the *Vǫlsunga saga* author attempts to mediate the differences between the two versions. The baroque and grotesque scene of the screaming thrall being chased about is retained, but lacks the deceit that justifies the motif in *Atlaqviða*; the consequence is that the episode in the saga merely dulls the heroic confrontation between Gunnar and Atli over the Niflung treasure and Hǫgni's fate (chap. 37). Yet despite this and other difficulties, it would be wrong to assume that the prose saga is consistently inferior to its originals. It is true that the saga does not in general possess the terseness characteristic of the eddic poems, preferring instead a more descriptive and reflective style; but as Wieselgren comments, the author is not nearly so bad as his reputation would seem to make him.[58]

58. Ibid., p. 14.

Wieselgren further points out that the degree of fidelity with which the *Vǫlsunga saga* author has held to the poetic materials of the *Edda* is highly variable: in some instances these texts are merely paraphrased, at other times, copied quite faithfully; at still others, lexical substitutions are common.[59] For unknown reasons, the author nowhere quotes the Helgi poems.

The conditions, considerations, and practical constraints under which the redactor of the *Edda* and the author of *Vǫlsunga saga* worked—and our inexact knowledge of these problems—should make us wary of using the example of the Helgi poems, and *Vǫlsunga saga* more generally, to draw conclusions as to how the authors of the *fornaldarsǫgur* made use of traditional eddic poetry. Yet certain points of comparison—especially with regard to a growing preference for prose narration—help us understand how traditional poetic material often gave rise to long prose sagas, or was taken wholesale as the basis for saga composition. In the case of *Vǫlsunga saga* (at least), the process appears to have been something very much like Heusler's characterization of the book-prose theory, when he writes that the saga author's main source was tradition, supplemented by the poetic heritage and by written works.[60] It is unlikely that any single method will ever account for the entire body of *fornaldarsǫgur*, and certainly there is no reason to believe that every one of the extant *fornaldarsǫgur* was preceded by an elaborate set of poems. Still, this process—the transformation of traditional poetic materials into basically prose sagas—is no doubt the historical and technical reason the *fornaldarsǫgur* display a uniform preference for eddic, as opposed to skaldic, poetry. Skaldic verse accommodates occasional poetry, whereas it is to the various eddic forms of poetry, such as *málaháttr, ljóðaháttr,* and *fornyrðislag,* that all early lengthy narrative poetry in Scandinavia looks. Where poetry was composed for the express purpose of accompanying a *fornaldarsaga* text, it always imitated one of these verse forms, since the connection between eddic poetry—and the world conjured up by the poems of the *Edda,* with their legendary heroic figures and mythological characters—and

59. Ibid., p. 12. See also Finch (1962–65), who carefully reassesses the contributions and techniques of the compiler, as well as his more recent study (1981), which regards the saga as a synoptic prose version of the poems. The general question of the relationship between prose and poetry in the *fornaldarsǫgur* has been addressed by Daviδ Erlingsson (1987).

60. Heusler 1909a, 445. Basing his remarks on the writing of Finnur Jónsson and others, Heusler characterizes the view with the "oft-used formulation." "The author's main source was tradition [. . .] an important further source consisted of verses or the 'poetic tradition'; a third consisted of written works."

the topics of the *fornaldarsǫgur* must already by an early point have been very strong.

Learned Lore

Our popular image of Scandinavian relations with the rest of Europe in the Middle Ages tends to be the very picture that the *fornaldarsǫgur* themselves sought in part to preserve and glorify, namely, that of the brutish barbarian sea-kings who descended upon hapless Continental Christians in search of booty. Of course this view was also held in the early Middle Ages as well, when western Europeans interpreted the appearance of the Vikings as the fulfillment of the prophecy in Jeremiah I:14, "Out of the north an evil shall break forth on all the inhabitants of the land." It was an image that only slowly faded, in part because of the inclination of some writers, such as Dudo and Saxo, to glorify this past. However true this vision may once have been, certainly much had changed during the intervening centuries. By the thirteenth and fourteenth centuries the flow of Norsemen to the rest of Europe had an entirely different intent than the plundering and quick riches uppermost in the minds of the Vikings—these later Scandinavians continued to travel at a steady pace to western Europe, but now for much more peaceful purposes. Students and pilgrims, traders and clerics, they provided a constant medium for intercourse and cultural exchange between the Nordic area and the rest of Europe.[61] Natives of England, France, and Germany likewise traveled to, and often stayed in, the north, typically through marriages or as clerics or as members of the retinues of leading men.[62] The image of an extraordinarily busy twelfth-century intellectual center at Hólar is certainly drawn in *Jóns saga helga eptir Gunnlaug múnk* (chap. 27): to the newly formed school

61. On Norwegian relations with England, see Leach 1921, 25–113, Helle 1968 for the period to ca. 1290, Tuck 1972 for the late 1400s. See Glauser 1983, 50–60, on Anglo-Icelandic relations ca. 1400–1535; on Nordic contacts with Europe more generally, especially French and German influences, see Lindroth 1975–81, I, 33–64.

62. Einar Ólafur Sveinsson 1953, 162, lists several of the influential foreigners resident in Iceland in the twelfth and thirteenth centuries: Rikini, a teacher at Hólar; Ljúfvini and Gunnfarðr, priests in the West of Iceland (and probably English); and Herburt, a German in Snorri Sturluson's company. One of the most famous foreign residents of Scandinavia, at least in saga literature, is Tyrkir, apparently a German and a member of Leifr Eiríksson's household in *Grœnlendinga saga* (chaps. 3 and 4). Iceland was a fairly constant host to foreign travellers, not infrequently there on church-related business. Cf. Magnús Már Lárusson 1960.

are brought foreigners well versed in *grammatica* in order to teach the Icelanders; among their students is a young woman named Ingunn whose "book-learning" allows her to listen to Latin books being read as she sits and embroiders.

Although still remote from the mainstream of European culture by comparison with many other areas, Scandinavia was anything but isolated from the great kingdoms to the south; in fact, so strong were the ties between the Scandinavian cultural region and the Continent by the 1200s that the courts of Norway and Sweden set about the business of intentionally copying the chivalric institutions of their southern counterparts.[63] Yet despite these facts, given both the *apparent* geographical isolation of Iceland and the plethora of native literary monuments it produced in this period, it is all too easy to dismiss the extent to which it too participated in the European culture of the Latin Middle Ages.[64]

Intellectually and aesthetically, the Icelanders of the later Middle Ages looked to the past for sources of inspiration, but they also looked outward to the rest of the world. Often the two frames not only existed simultaneously, but were held to validate one another. Thus, for example, in *Leiðarvísur* (also called *Landafræði*), Nikulás Bergsson, the first abbot of the Þverá monastery, provides his countrymen with a guidebook to the various sites they would pass on a pilgrimage to the Holy Land. Although the current manuscript dates itself to the year 1387, there is every reason to believe that it faithfully reproduces the contents of the twelfth-century original.[65] Nikulás indicates that his compatriots are as apt to be interested in the monuments to their history and traditions as they are in those of a more Christian nature, when he points out sites in Europe connected with some of the *fornaldarsǫgur*.

---

63. On the influence of Continental manners and institutions on Scandinavian courts, especially on the Norwegian situation, see Löfqvist 1935, 112–52.

64. This essential point—that the Icelandic sagas ought to be viewed more in the context of their relationship to general European writing than had hitherto been the case—was the thrust of several articles by Lönnroth in the 1960s (1963–64, 1964, 1965–69, 1965). A similar spirit imbues the contributions to *Norrøn Fortællekunst*. Cf. Tveitane 1969. For an overview of knowledge of Latin and the classics in the Old Norse period, see Berulfsen 1948, Dronke 1971, Walter 1971, and Skard 1980, 26–50. An earlier review with a number of enduring original contributions is T. Frank 1909.

65. In its account of the history of the world (*Heimsaldrar*), the manuscript states: *Enn þa er þetta var skrifat, var lidith fra hingat-burdinum M.CCC.LXXXVII vetr* 'But when this was written, 1387 years had passed since the birth of Christ' (p. 54), a date Kålund seems inclined to accept (p. ii). Einar Ólafur Sveinsson (1953, 36) indicates in another context (on the first appearance in Icelandic of the word *kurteisi* 'courtesy') his belief that this later manuscript faithfully reproduces the contents of the original twelfth-century text. On Bishop Nikulás and his pilgrimage works, see Magoun 1943, 1944.

Vǫlsunga saga, for example, is represented near Mainz: *þar er Gnita-heidr, er Sigurdr va ath Fabni* 'there lies Gnita-heath, where Sigurðr fought against Fáfnir' (p. 13). Luna in northern Italy is mentioned in connection with an *ormgard, er Gunnar var i settr* 'a snake-pit, into which Gunnar [Gjúkason] was placed' (p. 16), and in Switzerland one may see "Vivilsborg" (either Avenches or Wifilsburg) about which he says: *hon var mikil, adr Lodbrok[ar]-synir brutu hana, enn nu er hon litil* 'it was a great city before the sons of [Ragnar] loðbrók destroyed it; now it is little' (pp. 14–15), an event related in both *Ragnars saga loðbrókar* (chap. 13) and *Norna-Gests þáttr* (chap. 289). Other sections of the manuscript in which Nikulás's *Leiðarvísur* is to be found (AM 194, 8vo, known as *Alfrœði íslenzk*) complement the picture of the Icelanders' familiarity with didactic and encyclopedic literature: here are discussions and descriptions, for example, of the five great church councils (*Stórþing*), of the monstrous races in India and Africa (*Rísaþjóðir*), of dragons (*Ormar*), of gems (*Merking steina*), and of medicine (*Læknisfrœði*).

Although *Alfrœði íslenzk* is a unique compilation, neither its connectedness to Continental learning nor its tendency to tie that learning to the Nordic past is unique. Occasionally, one encounters attempts to meld the two cultures, the one traditionally Nordic and the other borrowed and Roman-derived, and smooth out differences. Thus the Old Norse *Trójumanna saga* 'Saga of the Trojans' is no mere literal translation of Darius Phrygius, but represents a translation at the broadest possible level,[66] in which the Old Norse pagan gods are substituted for their classical counterparts, a trait also found, for example, in *Rómverja saga* 'Saga of the Romans.' Such equations were fairly common: the *Rímbeygla* 'Calendar' of AM 625, 4to (also known as *Blannda*), for example, equates Mars with Týr, Mercury with Óðinn, Jupiter with Þórr, and Venus with Freyja (p. 63).

Familiarity with classical writings and beliefs is evinced not only by obvious translations, such as *Rómverja saga,* an Icelandic rendering of Sallust and Lucan, and equally conscious equations of Nordic and classical figures (for example, the equation of Vǫlundr, the Nordic smith, with Daedalus in *Kirialax saga*), but also by more subtle interweavings of classical culture into the fabric of Old Norse literature, including the *fornaldarsǫgur.* Two examples of such appropriation *may* be the images of Meleager and Polyphemus, although the likelihood that these are typological parallels, and not borrowings, cannot be

66. See Eldevik 1987.

discounted. When Norna-Gestr explains his immense life span, he says that it is because at his birth a Norn tied his life to the continued existence of a little candle he carries about on his person. It has been widely supposed that this idea has its origin in the legend of Meleager related by Ovid in *Metamorphoses* (VIII). In Ovid's account, the Fates declare at Meleager's birth that his life will last no longer than a particular faggot, which is thrown into the fire but taken out and saved by his mother.

Similarly, when *Hrólfs saga Gautrekssonar* (chaps. 22–23) tells of how its eponymous hero meets and outsmarts a giant, the influence of the Polyphemus episode of the *Odyssey,* or of one of the several other similar tales current in medieval literature, is generally suspected.[67] Hrólfr's ship is blown to an island by a gale and when he and his men explore it, they are trapped inside a giant's home. The giant, named Grímnir, returns, discover them, impales several of Hrólfr's men on a two-pronged fork, and throws them into the fire as a demonstration, threatening to do far worse with Hrólfr the next day. With a companion, Hrólfr dispatches the sleeping giant in a manner that combines aspects of both the Polyphemus tale and the Bear's Son Tale: Hrólfr runs the giant through with the beast's own sword (which they had earlier removed from its scabbard against the wall), while the lieutenant

---

67. It is not clear in what form the works of Homer were known in medieval Iceland. Certainly his was a name well known there as elsewhere in the Latin West (cf. the attribution of *Vilhjálms saga sjóðs* to Homer), but whether the Polyphemus episode appears as a result of Virgil's *Aeneid* (Book III, 613–81), one of the Virgilean commentaries, or some other source, including an indigenous folklore parallel, is impossible to say. A possible source for this Polyphemus episode in the Old Norse context is *Dolopathos sive de rege de septem sapientibus,* written ca. 1184, and quickly translated into the metrical *Roman de sept sages de Rome* (ca. 1222–26). The story told in *Dolopathos* is especially interesting in the case of the Old Norse episode in *Egils saga ok Ásmundar* in that they give parallel treatments of the giant's eye(s). According to both tales, the hero strikes a bargain with his captor regarding the treatment of the giant's eyes and then blinds his cooperative enemy. A further Old Norse variant appears in *Maríu saga* (chap. 217). On this tale and its appearances in European folk tradition, see, for example, Hackman 1904; van Gennep 1908; Frazer 1921, 404–55; Röhrich 1962; and Vajda 1975. On the Old Norse context, see the extensive discussions and bibliographies in Fry 1977 and Naumann 1979. Fry rules out direct knowledge of the *Odyssey* by the saga writer and concludes that both the folkloric analogues and indirect (written) transmission of the Homeric materials are possible sources, inclining toward a combination of the two. Naumann rules out any direct transfer from the Latin *Seven Sages* tradition in favor of a probable knowledge of the Old French version. It should be noted, however, that Calame (1986, 124, 145, 150–51) concludes that the Polyphemus episode in the *Odyssey* itself is but one variant among many, not the archetype for which it is usually taken: Hackman's view (1904, 42–44) that the Old Norse episodes are reflexes of indigenous oral variants of the tale type (AT 1137) may, after all, be the correct one.

heats the fork in the fire, with which he puts out the giant's eyes. Hrólfr tricks the giant by throwing a log toward the door; when Grímnir rushes to the sound in the hope of crushing them as they try to escape, he collapses from the severity of his wounds and dies.

A parallel story line is followed in *Egils saga ok Ásmundar* (chaps. 9 and 10), with Egill escaping the dim-witted giant when, after convincing him that he can replace his eyes with gold ones, Egill ties his captor to a column and gouges them out. The similarity here to the *Odyssey* is much closer, as Egill cannot immediately dispatch the giant, and so they spend the night together in the cave. Egill attempts to escape by dressing himself in the skin of one of the giant's goats, but his ruse fails and he escapes only by cutting off the giant's right hand. In neither *Hrólfs saga Gautrekssonar* nor *Egils saga ok Ásmundar* are the supernatural adversaries really much more than giants of the native tradition; the authors go out of their way to tell the reader about the *járngaddi miklum ok var klofinn í endann annan, sem tveir væri mjök hvassir* 'great iron spike [which] was cloven at one end so that the two [points] were very sharp' (chap. 22) and about the *tvíangaðan flein* 'two-pronged rod' (chap. 10) the heroes use to put out the giants' *two* eyes. Yet, as the section on exotic races in *Alfræði íslenzk* amply demonstrates, learned Icelanders were aware of the race of cyclopes, who appear elsewhere in the *fornaldarsǫgur* (*Yngvars saga víðfǫrla*, p. 34).

Specific allusions to the classical world, and its heroic legacy, are also to be found in the *fornaldarsǫgur*. When, for example, in *Sǫrla saga sterka* the old woman Mána is about to present the hero with armor and a sword, she provides these objects with an awe-inspiring heritage by declaring that they had once been borne by *hinn mikli kappi Pantíparus, sem eptir Agamemnon keisara stýrði Grikklandi* 'the great champion Pantíparus [Pandaros of the *Iliad*], who ruled Greece after Emperor Agamemnon' (chap. 6). Much of the borrowed material came from the Latin West, although Margaret Schlauch, among others, has argued forcefully for the possibility of medieval Greek romances having been important *direct* sources for aspects of the *lygisǫgur*. She cites the frequently mentioned journeys of Scandinavians to Byzantium to serve in the Varangian guards and the ample opportunity these men would have had to become acquainted with the plots and style of the popular Greek romances, which, like their Nordic counterparts, often drew on *Märchen* and folklore.[68]

68. Schlauch 1934, 55–68, 161–63. See also Leach (1921, 165–66, 268–88), who argues for Byzantine sources of some of the *riddarasǫgur*, as well as Strömbäck (1963b,

In addition to influences from the classical and Byzantine world, European literature was increasingly available and popular in Scandinavia.[69] Anglo-Norman and German cultural contacts were particularly important and these influences came, for the most part, not directly to Iceland, but rather through the intermediary of the thirteenth-century Norwegian court at Bergen, especially the court of Hákon Hákonarson, at which foreign literature was heavily promoted and subsidized in the form of translations. The receptiveness of the Norwegian court to foreign literary works is documented in Old Norse translations of foreign romances which state that the work was carried out under the sponsorship of Hákon. The king greatly prized learning and literature, a fact underscored by Hákon's biographer, who has the monarch listening first to Latin books and then vernacular saints' lives and konungasǫgur on his deathbed.[70] During his reign, many of the great works of Continental literature appeared in Old Norwegian translations, from which they traveled west to Iceland and east to Sweden and to Denmark: the stories of Tristan, Arthur, and Charlemagne and the lais of Marie de France became popular forms of entertainment in Scandinavian translation.[71] Tristrams saga states that the work was translated by Brother Robert in 1226, at which time the interchange—in religious, diplomatic, and commercial realms—between England and Norway was at its zenith.[72]

1970), who argues cogently for an ultimately oriental origin of Hróa þáttr heimska, generally regarded as one of the Märchensagas. Amory's argument (1984) against the direct written influence of the Byzantine materials is based largely on the Scandinavians' lack of sufficient erudition in the language of the written medieval Greek romances. Cf. Davidson 1976.

69. Cf. Turville-Petre 1953, esp. chaps. 5 and 6.

70. Í sóttinni lét hann fyrst lesa sér Latínu-bækr [. . .] Lét hann þá lesa fyrir sér Norænu-bækr, nætr ok daga; fyrst Heilagra-mannasögur; ok er þær þraut, lét hann lesa sér Konungatal frá Hálfdani Svarta, ok síðan frá öllum Noregs-konungum, hverjum eptir annan 'In his illness, he had Latin books read to him first [. . .] Then he had Norse books read to him, night and day; first, Saints' Lives; and when they came to an end, he had the "Konungatal" about Hálfdan the Black read, and later about all the Norwegian kings, the one after the other' (Hákonar saga Hákonarsonar, chap. 329).

71. A large body of literature is devoted to the Scandinavian versions of these widely known European narratives. For a full bibliography, see Kalinke and Mitchell 1985.

72. Tristrams saga (p. 3) states: Var þa liðeð fra hingaðburðe Chri. 1226 Aar, er þesze Saga var a Norrænu Skrifuð, Efter befalningu ok Skipan Virðuglegz herra Hakonar Kongz. En Broðer Robert efnaðe og Uppskrifaðe epter Sine kunattu '1226 years had passed since the birth of Christ when this saga was written in Norse by order of the worthy king Hákon; Brother Robert prepared and wrote it according to his knowledge.' It should be noted, however, that this prefatory remark—as the state of the language in which it is written makes abundantly clear—is preserved in a later paper manuscript (AM 543, 4to) from the seventeenth century, and its testimony is somewhat suspect. On the age of the

By the end of the century German materials—brought to Scandinavian in part through the cultural intercourse that resulted from the Hanseatic League—were popular, 'as in the case of *Þiðreks saga*. The tradition of royal sponsorship of translations continued well into the fourteenth century, for as *Victors saga ok Blávus* states, Hákon Magnússon, king of Norway (1299–1315), *hiellt mikit gaman at fogrum fra sogum. ok hann liet venda morgum ᴿiddara sogum j norænu uᴿ girzsku ok franzeisku mali* 'took great pleasure in beautiful stories and he had many *riddarasǫgur* translated into Norwegian from Greek and French' (chap. 1). *Blómstrvalla saga* claims to have been brought to Scandinavia in the middle of the thirteenth century, when a Norwegian emissary heard it read in German (*lesit í þýzku máli*) at a wedding feast in Spain and brought the story back to the king (chap. 1).

Although the great workshop for translations was Norway, few of these texts survive in Old Norwegian originals, and, as is so often the case, much of our knowledge of medieval Scandinavian literature comes from Iceland, where these foreign romances became enormously popular. Although manuscript testimony from the Icelandic thirteenth century to the vitality of this foreign literature is virtually nonexistent, other factors indicate the early hold these texts had in Iceland. Thus, already by the mid-1200s the rather strictly observed anthroponymic customs of Icelandic society begin to erode under the influence of foreign romances when such names as Karlamagnús and Þiðrekr begin to be used.[73]

The loss of political independence in 1262–63 altered Icelandic society on many different fronts: more and more of the Icelandic ruling elite, for example, became the Norwegian king's liegemen, and consequently relatively large numbers of Icelanders were knighted in the period 1277 to 1300.[74] Many of these leading men spent nearly half

---

Old Norse *Tristrams saga* (and the authenticity of this comment in particular), see Sverrir Tómasson (1977), who concludes that it is reliable. It has been suggested, although not widely accepted, that Icelandic saga writing in general received its initial impetus from this translation. See Rubow 1936, 21, but see also Einar Ólafur Sveinsson's comment (1958, 84) that "there is really no evidence for such an assertion." The subject of *Tristrams saga* and its influence on medieval Scandinavian literature is taken up in Bjarni Einarsson 1961; Schach 1957–59, 1964, 1969; and Hallberg 1973. On the relations between Norway and England in this period, see Leach 1921, 25–113 and especially the detailed comments on 181–82, and Helle 1968.

73. Einar Ólafur Sveinsson 1953, 39. Einar Ólafur (1936) closely documents the changes in name-giving in the twelfth and thirteenth centuries among the Oddaverjar.

74. Einar Ólafur Sveinsson 1953, 163. Einar Ólafur lists some fifteen Icelanders who were knighted in this period according to the annals and the *biskupasǫgur*, although he states that the list is by no means exhaustive.

their adult lives at the Norwegian court, providing a conduit for the transplantation of Continental tastes to Iceland. This transplantation was all the more thorough because this court was no longer the haven for skalds it had been earlier, when poets could declaim their elaborate *dróttkvætt* 'praise poetry' and receive a munificent token of the monarch's gratitude, the sort of image portrayed in the *konungasǫgur*. Although such exchanges continued to take place until the end of the thirteenth century, the practice must already have been seen as something of a relic, for, as Einar Ólafur Sveinsson maintains, the traditional court poetry had ceased to have meaning for the court.[75] A monumental change in literary tastes at the Scandinavian courts was under way, but the effects of this change were apparently never so sweeping in Iceland as they were in the rest of the Nordic cultural region. Icelandic literary sensibilities remained unrepentantly traditional to a surprising degree, yet they were sufficiently eclectic to accommodate new literary material.

The effect of this new brand of literature on the *fornaldarsǫgur* ranges from the addition of merely ornamental information to fairly significant alterations in the heroic ethos. Among the most striking of the former is the familiarity with the non-Scandinavian world evinced in the *fornaldarsǫgur*. Certainly the wide-ranging geography of the *fornaldarsǫgur* owes much to the many sites actually visited by Nordic tradesmen and pirates of earlier centuries, yet surely some of their geographical knowledge also springs from book-learning.[76] Thus, Ǫrvar-Oddr manages to cover much of the known world of northern Europe and the Mediterranean in his saga, including a pilgrimage to the Holy Land; the author of *Yngvars saga* makes references to Citopolis (p. 29) and Hieliopolis (pp. 17, 25); India plays a significant part in *Þorsteins saga Víkingssonar* and adds an exotic element to one of the figures Þorsteinn bæjarmagn sees in his journeys (chap. 2). Asia and Arabia both figure in the *fornaldarsǫgur* (for example, *Sǫrla þáttr*, chap. 228; *Bósa saga*, chap. 1; *Sǫrla saga sterka*, chap. 4), and references to Greece and Greek cities abound (for example, *Vǫlsunga saga*, chap. 23; *Sǫrla þáttr*, chap. 232; *Yngvars saga*, p. 31; *Hálfdanar saga Brǫnufóstra*,

---

75. According to *Lǫgmannsannáll*, Guðmundr evidently received the governorship of the North Quarter of Iceland in 1296 for a poem so delivered at court: *Jtem skipadr Nordlendinga fiordungr Gudmunde skalldstikle* 'Item the North Firthing was assigned to Guðmundr (for the sake of?) a skaldic poem' (p. 261). See Einar Ólafur Sveinsson 1953, 41.

76. A comprehensive discussion of geography in the *fornaldarsǫgur* is given in Simek 1986.

chap. 17). Surprisingly, such references do not necessarily multiply over time as one might expect—in the older *Qrvar-Odds saga* (chap. 33), for example, Greece is the site for significant action in the tale, yet it does not appear at all in the younger version of the saga.

The races of beings encountered in these locations and at home also testify to the influence of learned lore on the *fornaldarsǫgur*, for many strange beasts and different kinds of people have entered the narratives from the world of learned lore. As we have seen, the Polyphemus story may have made an important contribution to the adventures encountered by the saga heroes, yet even though cyclopes are relatively common in the late medieval Icelandic romances,[77] of the *fornaldarsǫgur*, only *Yngvars saga* makes specific reference to them (*þess kyns lyd kalla menn cikoples* 'this race of people is called the cyclopes' [p. 34]). Again in *Yngvars saga*, a great flying dragon, *iakulus*, guards a treasure (pp. 14, 42); this same "Iaculus" is prominently included among the various dragons listed in a learned account of such beasts called *Ormar* (p. 39). Likewise the *blámenn* 'blacks' encountered in *Sǫrla saga sterka* (chap. 2) are more likely to be the products of a medieval Icelander's book-learning than of encounters with black Africans, although the latter situation is not unthinkable. And when Sturlaugr and his companions encounter Cenocefali (called *Hundingjar* in the saga), the description almost assures us that it was derived from written reports of this race: *stóðu menn í dyrum, ok var haka þeirra gróin í bringuna. Þeir gjǫlltu sem hundar* 'men stood in the doors and their jaws grew into their chests. They barked like dogs' (chap. 17). These beasts are also described in *Risa þjóðir*, an enumeration of fantastic beings in *Alfrœði íslenzk: Þeir ero enn, er haka er groin vid bringu, þeir heita Hundingiar* 'There is a [race] whose jaws grow to their chests; they are called Hundingiar' (p. 36).

One suspects that the awful *hjasi* of *Egils saga ok Ásmundar* (chap. 1), although not identified in any extant work of learning, had a similar textual origin, largely unparalleled as it is in native tradition.[78] Just how such a remarkably unnordic beast as the lion, *leo*, of the younger *Hrólfs saga Gautrekssonar* (chap. 24)—with its powerful if unreal tail, capable of pulling trees up by their roots—enters the world of the *fornaldarsǫgur* is impossible to say (a slightly different version is given in the older *Hrólfs saga Gautrekssonar*, chaps. 30–31); but one can well imagine it entering the Scandinavian literary world through the influ-

77. Cf. Schlauch 1934, 44–45.
78. The only other occurrence of the *hjasi* is in *Gibbons saga* (chap. 14): *Litlo sidar sa þeir fram koma einn hiasa med storum eyrum* 'A little later they saw a *hiasi* with large ears approach.'

ence of the Old Testament, Chrétien's *Yvain,* or the Icelandic translation of the *Physiologus.*[79] And in *Gǫngu-Hrólfs saga* the author describes
the wonderful steed Dúlcefal as a special breed of horse *af kyni dróm-
edaríórum* 'related to the dromedary' (chap. 1).

Cultural elements that would surely have been out of place in the
Viking age and that we can ascribe to the compilers' familiarity with
learned lore also abound. When Húnvǫr, in desperate need of help,
sends a servant to Víkingr in *Þorsteins saga Víkingssonar* (chap. 2), he
does not repeat a message from the princess, but rather delivers a *bréf*
'letter' which he throws into Víkingr's lap. After reading it, Víkingr
passes it over to his father for his inspection—hardly a scene imagin-
able in pagan Scandinavian. Likewise, the courtly world projected in
the feasting scene of *Gǫngu-Hrólfs saga* (chap. 37)—with its lavishly
prepared dishes of peacocks, boars, and geese; its ale, English mead,
and claret; and its diverse musical entertainment, including harps, fid-
dles, lyres, and psalteries—has much more to do with continental
Europe in the later Middle Ages than it does with Iceland or pre-
Christian Scandinavia.

More important than the trappings of learning and courtly culture
such details reflect is the fact that certain characters, or aspects of
characters, in the *fornaldarsǫgur* periodically strike the reader as "modern." The texts are often peopled with men and women who espouse
cultural norms not even remotely a part of the long-gone Viking
world. Perhaps the most famous incident of this sort occurs in *Ǫrvar-
Odds saga* (chap. 17), when Hjálmarr explains to Oddr his "Viking
laws," which amount to a creed very much at odds with the picture
usually associated with that age and that calling. Among the rules
according to which Hjálmarr says he has always lived and to which
Oddr binds himself are insistence on cooked meat, refusal to rob wom-
en, and respect for a woman's person. Also anachronistic are some of
the romantic touches of the *fornaldarsǫgur:* although he is one of the
greatest Vikings of his age and fights Ǫrvar-Oddr to a standstill, this
same Hjálmarr later sends a poem and a bracelet back to Sweden with
Oddr with the instruction that he should give it to Ingibjǫrg and "tell
her that I sent the ring to her on my dying day" (chap. 29). When Oddr
presents the bracelet and the news of Hjálmarr's death to Ingibjǫrg, she

79. On the question of Yvain and his lion in Iceland, and a possible plastic represen-
tation of it, see R. Harris 1970. The Icelandic *Physiologus* is extant in two fragmentary
manuscripts, neither of which refers to the lion, although the second fragment of AM
673a, 4to contains "panthera," which encompasses panthers, leopards, and cheetahs.

falls over dead and the bodies of the two lovers are buried together, an episode also recounted in part in *Heiðreks saga* (chap. 3).

This shift to a more romantic tone in saga writing is perhaps nowhere more pronounced than in the *fornaldarsǫgur*'s treatment of women. In contrast to the *íslendingasǫgur*, where direct comment on the female figures beyond saying that they are accomplished is rare, the *fornaldarsǫgur* are effusive in praise of their women. The recurrent *Hún var prýdd ǫllum kvenligum listum* 'She was gifted [literally, adorned] with all feminine skills' is frequently elaborated at great lengths. When in *Hrólfs saga Gautrekssonar* (AM 590, 4to) the masculine Þórbergr is defeated and turns to more feminine pursuits, for example, the author describes the transformation in the following manner:

> Eptir þat gekk hún til skemmu, en gaf í vald Eireki konúngi vápn þau, er hún hafði borit; settist hún til sauma með móður sinni, ok var hún hvǫrri mey fegri ok fríðari ok kurteisari, svá at engi fannst jafn fríð í Norðrhálfu heimsins; hún var vitr ok vinsæl, málsnjǫll ok spakráðug ok ríklynd. (chap. 13)

> After that she went to the bower and gave the weapons she had borne into the keeping of King Eirekr; she began sewing with her mother and she was the most lovely of maidens, beautiful and courteous, so that no one could find an equal to her in the northern world; she was intelligent and popular, eloquent and wise in advice and imperious.

Likewise, the concept of *kurteisi* 'courtesy' figures prominently in the world of the Icelandic Middle Ages, a world much altered since the days of the Nordic heroic age. A fair measure of the extent to which the Continental sense of *courtois* retained its meaning in the Nordic context is provided by *Konungsskuggsjá*, a Norwegian *Fürstenspiegel* 'prince's mirror' of the thirteenth century. Here in a discussion of the term (chap. 55), the father explains to his son the rules of court: what one must know of eloquence and polite speech, of deportment and attitude, and of table manners and dress. Although cultural and economic conditions in Iceland would hardly have allowed for the wholesale transplantation of such norms to the island nation, there is no doubt that conduct and attitudes in line with Continental values were actively fostered at the Norwegian court, of which Iceland's leading citizens were frequently important members. And in literature, if not in everyday reality, these notions of decent bearing and behavior certainly made themselves felt, with the result that values associated with *kurteisi* and the world of chivalry color several of the major figures of the *fornaldarsǫgur*.

The effects are occasionally a bit jarring on literary sensibilities as Viking heroes are imbued with late medieval court refinement. The Sigurðr of *Vǫlsunga saga*, for example, is no longer the uncomplicated hero of action to be found in the eddic poems; in the saga's retelling of the story, he has been endowed with *kurteise* 'courtesy' and *hǽfersku* 'good manners' beyond other men (chap. 23). The author of *Áns saga bogsveigis* uses the new concept to good effect when he portrays Án as an ashlad figure and explains that this characterization is due in part to the fact that he grows neither in intelligence nor courtesy (*hvorki* [. . .] *vit né kurteisi* [chap. 2]). And although his adventures include such events as beheading trolls (chap. 4), few men are "more courteous" than Hálfdan Brǫnufóstri (chap. 10). The *Helga þáttr* of *Hrólfs saga kraka* (chaps. 5–13) begins its hero's perversely erotic tale of woe with an exchange between Queen Ólǫf and Helgi in which she too tells him that no other man is *kurteisligri enn þu* 'more courteous than you' (chap. 6). The term appears in many of the *fornaldarsǫgur* and its spirit is certainly present throughout the genre, even among the most heroic pieces (for example, *Vǫlsunga saga*, *Hálfs saga ok Hálfsrekka*, *Hrólfs saga kraka*). That spirit is easily discernible: although the villainous, if foppish, Vilhjálmr is primarily a foil for the eponymous hero of *Gǫngu-Hrólfs saga*, the audience would have placed considerable value on the virtues he claims to possess: *eigi vantar mik skotfimi ok vopnfimi, sund eðr tafl ok burtreiðir, vizku ok málsnild, ok öngva missi ek þá, er karlmann má prýða* 'I'm not lacking [in skill] when it comes to shooting or using weapons, swimming or chess or [jousting at] tilts, wisdom or eloquence; I want for nothing that might adorn a man' (chap. 14).

Other aspects of the world of chivalry frequently find a place in the *fornaldarsǫgur* too: Gǫngu-Hrólfr, although incapable of riding a horse all day because of his size, can still *fara í skotbakka* 'practice at butts' and *vera at burtreiðum* 'ride at tilts' (chap. 4). In fact, the *fornaldarsǫgur* are filled with terms appropriated from the world of chivalry and tournaments which would hardly have belonged to the Viking age: *burtreið* 'tilts' (*Hálfdanar saga Brǫnufóstra*, chap. 11; *Gǫngu-Hrólfs saga*, chaps. 3, 16, 21; *Sǫrla þáttr*, chap. 23); *burtstǫng* 'tilting lance' (*Hálfdanar saga Brǫnufóstra*, chap. 12; *Gǫngu-Hrólfs saga*, chaps. 1, 3, 16, 20, 21); *skotbakka* 'butts' (*Sǫrla þáttr*, chap. 233; *Hálfdanar saga Eysteinssonar*, chap. 7). Numerous other lexical appropriations from "the sphere of chivalry," as Peter Hallberg terms it in his fascinating study of the language of the *fornaldarsǫgur*,[80] hint too at the inroads the vocabulary of romance made into the *fornaldarsǫgur*.

Important facets of this imported culture are the titles by which its leading men and women are known, and these linguistic artifacts too appear in the *fornaldarsǫgur*, such as *jungfrú* 'princess, lady,' a foreign designation for high-born women found in a number of the sagas (*Sturlaugs saga starfsama*, chap. 26; *Hálfdanar saga Eysteinssonar*, chap. 19; *Bósa saga*, chap. 13; *Gǫngu-Hrólfs saga*, chaps. 21, 37).[81] However much at odds such designations are with the world of the Viking age, in the fourteenth- and fifteenth-century accounts of the *fornaldarsǫgur* we encounter *hofmaðr* 'courtiers' (*Egils saga ok Ásmundar*, chaps. 2, 17), *skemmumær* 'lady's maids' (*Gǫngu-Hrólfs saga*, chap. 21; *Hálfdanar saga Brǫnufóstra*, chaps. 1, 14), *burgeisar* 'burgesses' (*Gǫngu-Hrólfs saga*, chap. 37), *riddarar* 'knights' (*Hrólfs saga kraka*, chap. 27; *Vǫlsunga saga*, chap. 40; *Gǫngu-Hrólfs saga*, chap. 30), and *riddaralid* 'band of knights' (*Ragnars saga loðbrókar*, chap. 12). The most striking appearance of these late medieval figures must be the wedding feast in *Gǫngu-Hrólfs saga* mentioned above, where we find in attendance *kurteisir júnkerar ok hæverskir hofmenn* 'courteous young lords and polite courtiers' (chap. 37). As often as not, it seems we meet these anachronistic figures in *kastalar* 'castles,' a term that again appears not only in the more obviously recent literary products, but also in those texts long cherished as representing truly ancient traditions (for example, *Ragnars saga loðbrókar*, chap. 14; *Hrólfs saga kraka*, chap. 23).

In addition to a general acquaintance with foreign cultural norms, specific texts from abroad sometimes influenced individual episodes in the sagas. Literary works from a wide spectrum of countries have been suggested as the source material for parts of the *fornaldarsǫgur*, and certainly foreign literary and didactic works helped form the *fornaldarsǫgur* as we have them.[82] This fact, as well as the authors' awareness of it, is nowhere more evident than in *Gǫngu-Hrólfs saga*, easily one of the most self-absorbed of all the *fornaldarsǫgur*. In an attempt to justify the fact that the hero's feet have just been reunited

80. Hallberg 1982.
81. The items cited here are not intended as a complete catalogue of all such occurrences. For more complete information, see the convenient chart at the conclusion of Hallberg 1982. CREST's computer-generated concordances of the *fornaldarsǫgur* (based on the Guðni Jónsson edition) were used in locating a number of these references.
82. E.g., Leach 1921, 241; Schlauch 1934, 63–64; Mundt 1971; Lukman 1976, 1977; McTurk 1977; and Davið Erlingsson 1980.

with the rest of his body—the probability of which the author obviously views with deep suspicion—the audience is told (chap. 25): *Nú þótt mönnum þiki slíkir hlutir ótrúligir, þá verðr þat þó hverr at segja, er hann hefir séð eðr heyrt. Þar er ok vant móti at mæla, er hinir fyrri fræðimenn hafa samsett* 'Now although people may believe such things incredible, it is still up to everyone to say what they have seen or heard. It is difficult to difficult to speak against what has been composed in the past by learned men.' To this observation, one manuscript (AM 589f, 4to) adds the following fascinating expansion:

> Hefði þeir þat vel mátt segja, at á annan veg hefði atborizt, ef þeir vildi; hafa þeir ok sumir spekingar verit, er mjök hafa talat í fígúru um suma hluti, svá sem meistari Galterus í Alexandrí sögu eðr Umeris skáld í Trójumanna sögu, ok hafa eptirkomandi meistarar þat heldr til sanninda fært, enn í móti mælt, at svá mætti vera; þarf ok engi meira trúnað á at leggja, en hafa þó gleði af, á meðan hann heyrir.

> Had they so wished, they might well have told a different story; they were wise men who were much given to speaking figuratively about such things—men such as Master Gualterus in *Alexander's saga* and the poet Homer in *Trójumanna saga* ['The Saga of the Trojans']—and subsequent masters have held that [which they wrote] to be true and have not denied that things might have been so; one can still enjoy listening [to such things] without believing in them.

The author here appeals to the higher authority of Homer and Phillipe Gautier de Chatillon in order to bolster his views; we can certainly infer that he expects at least a part of his audience to be swayed by his use of these two learned figures in his argument.

In the realistic saga genres no great emphasis is placed on this kind of documentation by reference to other texts. It is true that cross-references to other sagas appear in the *íslendingasǫgur*, for example, and that in the prologue to his *Heimskringla*, Snorri comments specifically on the historical accuracy and general validity of skaldic verse, which he then employs throughout his history of the Norwegian kings as both source material and a sort of running footnote. Yet the fact remains that the references to other sagas in the *íslendingasǫgur* occur largely by way of explaining why the author has not gone into a given story at that point and as a sort of "see also" for the benefit of the audience; in other words, they rarely assist the writer in "proving" the truthfulness of any statement. Quite the opposite situation obtains in the *fornaldarsǫgur*, where the numerous references to other literary works have the common mission of bolstering the writer's position, either as in the case cited above from *Gǫngu-Hrólfs saga*, where the author discusses the notion of speaking figuratively, or as in those instances where the author employs well-respected texts (for example, *Landnámabók*) in order to add weight to his comments. A good example of the latter situation is given in *Hálfdanar saga Eysteinssonar*, where the author links the genealogy of one character to an historical figure *er getr í Landnámabók á Íslandi* 'who is mentioned in the *Book of Settlements* on Iceland'; another character is connected to a figure who *er getr í sǫgu Ragnars konungs loðbrókar* 'is mentioned in *Ragnars saga loðbrókar*' (chap. 2). The author of *Yngvars saga* likewise makes reference to both learned lore and popular tradition in providing the story with appropriate credentials: according to some, the author states, Yngvarr was the son of Eymundr Óláfsson, because they deem it more honorable to make him the son of a king. In subsequently explaining the tradition behind *Yngvars saga*, the redactor concludes the story with a colophon detailing its sources and admonishing those who do not like the current version to rework it for themselves. The self-consciousness of the author of *Yngvars saga*—the attempted documentation of authenticity, the admonition, and so forth—is typical of many *fornaldarsǫgur*, although certainly not all.

A characteristic of so-called saga style in the realistic genres is its tendency toward objectivity, at least as regards direct editorializing.[83] The *íslendingasǫgur* rarely go much further than the occasional *ok er hann nú ór sǫgunni* 'and now he is out of the saga.' But dotting the landscape of Old Norse legendary fiction are frequent disclaimers that demonstrate the authors' discomfort with the lack of verisimilitude of the *fornaldarsǫgur*. The self-conscious authorship that results begins to invade the narrative art itself: the author of *Bósa saga*, for example, writes that when the hero's foster mother offers to teach him black magic, Bósi states his unwillingness, as he does not want *at þat væri skrifat í sǫgu hans* 'it to be written in his saga' (chap. 2) that he had had to rely on magic rather than his own manliness. In *Hrólfs saga Gautrekssonar*, the writer concludes his tale with an explanation of why certain events in the saga might strike a "modern" audience as incredible and comments that although it had not previously been written down, wise men had long preserved it in their memories; *hvárt sem satt*

83. Cf. Lönnroth 1976, 84–101, and the bibliography it contains.

er, eða eigi, þá hafi sá gaman af, er þat má afverða, en hinn leiti annars, þess er meira gaman verðr at 'whether it is true or not, may those enjoy it who can, but he should look elsewhere where more enjoyment is to be had' (chap. 46). This kind of self-consciousness is eclipsed among the *fornaldarsǫgur* only by *Gǫngu-Hrólfs saga,* which both begins and ends with similar statements as to how the text should be interpreted: how it is that ancient tales come to be recorded and then expanded upon, that individuals will be familiar with different aspects of the same event, that old stories ought to be interpreted figuratively and as entertainment rather than as truth, and so on.

Few appearances of authorial intrusion in the *fornaldarsǫgur* are as obvious as those of *Hrólfs saga Gautrekssonar* and *Gǫngu-Hrólfs saga,* yet the tendency is present in many of them. This self-consciousness must result from both a disinclination to believe in that which one has not witnessed, as well as from the influence of a more book-oriented saga compiler. Yet despite their frequent appearances in the *fornaldarsǫgur,* such courtly and foreign elements as those taken up here are generally narrative bagatelles when viewed in the broad perspective; they impart far less of import to the sagas than does, say, folklore (excepting perhaps only the case of the self-consciousness peculiar to these authors). The main characters and essential plots of the *fornaldarsǫgur* derive from the unrecorded literary histories of Scandinavia. Presumably it is only in their current forms that these late sagas are thus adorned with motifs, characters, and episodes drawn from the much larger inspirational spring of Christian learning, the classical world, and Continental culture.

Forging Traditions

This discussion of the influences on the *fornaldarsǫgur* focuses primarily on the factors that account for the final legendary texts the modern period has inherited from the late Middle Ages in Iceland. Analysis of these factors inevitably hints at origins, that is to say, at the various components that have been brought together in the extant texts, and suggests something of the manner in which this process may have taken place. Given the scope of the current work, it is axiomatic that the study of the *fornaldarsǫgur* should be primarily directed to the period from which we possess solid evidence of the formation of the current texts—the fourteenth and fifteenth centuries—and not to the uncertain prehistories in which the traditions began to form, the focus of an earlier generation of scholars.[84]

It may be objected that it is misleading to generalize from specific cases to the entire genre. After all, the extant *fornaldarsǫgur* are the products of *individual* shapings of tradition, and it is important to bear in mind that no two sagas will have undergone the same process of accretion, deletion, and editing: *Vǫlsunga saga* depends more heavily on known preexisting poetic materials than do other *fornaldarsǫgur; Gǫngu-Hrólfs saga* is among those texts most heavily influenced by aspects of foreign culture; *Yngvars saga* reflects a considerably greater familiarity with medieval encyclopedic literature than do most of the sagas; *Helga þáttr Þórissonar* bears a closer relation to genuine folkloric materials than do other tales; and so on. Nevertheless, from the individual texts that constitute the genre a larger, collective picture begins to emerge, especially in relation to other saga genres: to a trunk of traditional texts that were drawn, no doubt, from oral tradition and from earlier collected anthologies such as the *Poetic Edda,* later authors have grafted elements of the literary culture with which they were familiar, both native and foreign.

The process was undoubtedly highly varied, as are too the extant results. In *Yngvars saga,* we possess one account of the transmutation of tradition into recorded literature which gives us an excellent idea of what that process was like in at least some instances:

Enn þessa sogu hofum uer heyrt ok ritat epter forsaung þeirar bækr, at Oddur munkur hinn frodi hafdi giora latit at forsaugn frodra manna, þeira er hann seger sialfur j brefi sinu, þui er hann sendi Joni Lofzssyni ok Gizuri Hallsyni. Enn þeir er uita þiciazt innuirduligar, auki uid, þar sem nu þiker a skorta. Þessa sogu segizt Oddr munkur heyrt hafa segia þann prest, er Isleifur hiet, ok annann Glum Þorgeirsson, ok hinn þridi hefer Þorer heitit. Af þeira frasaugn hafdi hann þat, er honum þotti merkiligazt. En Isleifur sagdizt heyrt hafa Ynguars sogu af einum kaup[manni], enn sa kuezt hafa numit hana j hird Suiakongs. Glumur hafdi numit at fodur sinum. Enn Þorer hafdi numit af Klaukku Samssyni, en Klacka hafdi heyrt segia hina fyrri frændur sina. (pp. 48–49)

This saga we have heard told, but have written [it] according to the authority of that book which the monk Oddr the Wise caused to have

---

84. An excellent review of the scholarship on the heroic legends is provided in J. Harris 1985, 87–92. On this point, cf. Schneider's apparent "conversion" (1955) and Haug's review (1975) of Heusler's theory of heroic legend.

done based on the authority of wise men, whom he mentions himself in the letter he sent to Jón Loftsson and Gizurr Hallsson. And they who consider themselves wiser may increase it where it now seems wanting. Oddr the monk declared that he heard this saga told by the priest who was named Ísleifr, and again by Glúmr Þorgeirsson and the third was named Þórir. From their accounts he took that which he thought most remarkable. Ísleifr declared that he had heard *Yngvars saga* from a merchant, who said he had learned it from the retinue of the Swedish King. Glúmr had learned it from his father, but Þórir had learned it from Klakka Sámsson, and Klakka had heard it told by his kinsmen.

The prehistory of *Yngvars saga víðfǫrla* as provided by the writer is one of traditional oral accounts of the saga being recorded and then rewritten from the recorded version. The degree to which this scenario is specifically accurate to that saga is uncertain,[85] but the *general* image it presents is one that accounts very well for our corpus. It is not difficult to imagine that the cultural picture *Yngvars saga* provides of the intersection of tradition and learning lies behind each of the extant *fornaldarsǫgur*. The impetus for creating the written *fornaldarsǫgur* and the factors that impinged upon the execution of this task form the topic of the next chapter.

85. On the discussion surrounding the authenticity of the compiler's comments in *Yngvars saga* and the background of the material, see especially Hofmann 1981, 1984.

CHAPTER 3

Uses and Functions

Although the beginnings of the *fornaldarsǫgur* stretch far back into the narrative history of northern Europe, the tales about which we know anything in the modern period tend, almost without exception, to be products of the later Middle Ages; that is, even for those sagas that were quite certainly written down already by the thirteenth century, the extant manuscripts date from the later periods. Pretenses as to the interpretation of such cultural documents will therefore necessarily be quite uneasy: should analysis of the *fornaldarsǫgur* regard them as the products of the long-gone Viking era or of the later Middle Ages? There are certainly attractive aspects to the former view—not least the possibility of learning more about this most famous period of Scandinavian cultural history—but such a line of investigation is fraught with serious difficulties, in particular determining the extent to which the extant texts reflect the sagas as they would have been told centuries earlier.[1] Thus, while the main events of the "same" saga as it existed in the different eras might be essentially unaltered, certainly substantial amounts of information-laden cultural elements, fundamental to the correct interpretation of the tales, would have changed. We are, in short, in a much better position to make claims as to the meaning and purpose of the *fornaldarsǫgur* in the later Middle Ages than for any preceding period. With recognition of this fact, the present chapter takes up several major aspects of these sagas in the Icelandic thirteenth, fourteenth, and fifteenth centuries, specifically, their use as entertain-

---

1. The view that the Germanic heroic materials are best interpreted in the context of much earlier periods, such as the Migration Era, is still routinely bruited about. For examples, see the bibliography and discussion in Uecker 1972, 17–18.

ment, their literary value, and the role the *fornaldarsǫgur* had in Icelandic society.

Sagnaskemtan and the Aesthetic Dimension

Despite the fanciful and unrealistic contents of the *fornaldarsǫgur*, there can be little doubt as to their ability to delight and entertain their audiences. Yet despite the fact that the circumstances under which such entertainment took place have been subjected to much debate, little is really understood about the exact manner in which the *fornaldarsǫgur* formed a component of Icelandic artistic and diverting life. Much of the discussion concerning *sagnaskemtan* 'saga entertainment' and the question of how sagas were transmitted and delivered has centered on the *íslendingasǫgur*, despite the fact that the evidence from the Old Norse period largely relates to the *fornaldarsǫgur* and other legendary materials.[2] That our understanding of these references to 'saga entertainment' has remained largely disputed and inconclusive is due, it seems, to the tendency of much previous research to approach the evidence with a particular framework relating to the free-prose/book-prose controversy (and its successors) in mind, into which the texts are then forced. The results have been unfortunate. No account of *sagnaskemtan* has been more closely scrutinized than that of the wedding at Reykjahólar in 1119 related in *Þorgils saga ok Hafliða* (chap. 10), with its report of how several sagas and some verses are told. It has been exhumed time after time, subjected to one inquest after another, and then put to rest until its next meeting with scholarly coroners, and yet almost always, interpretations of the episode with regard to saga entertainment vary according to the intellectual orientation of the researcher involved.[3] The following examination of references to *sagnaskemtan* and the use of the *fornaldarsǫgur* for entertainment has no prescribed orientation and accepts as its framework two facts only: that some of the *fornaldarsǫgur* (at least) existed in Scandinavia before the widespread vernacular use of the Latin alphabet and that the versions we possess are themselves written accounts and must be treated accordingly.

2. The most extensive treatment of *sagnaskemtan* is to be found in Hermann Pálsson 1962. A useful review of the conditions for oral literature in medieval Iceland is given in Sørensen 1977, 87–125. Buchholz (1976, 1980) argues the orality of the *fornaldarsǫgur*.
3. See, for example, Heusler 1909a, 403–8; Liestøl 1945; Brown [Dronke] 1947–48 and in her edition of *Þorgils saga ok Hafliða*, pp. 75–76; Foote 1955–56; Lönnroth 1976, 170–72; von See 1981b.

A discussion of the diverting value of the *fornaldarsǫgur* might well begin with the simple question, in what manner were these tales used for entertainment in the Middle Ages, that is, in what fashion were these narratives transmitted to their audiences? Three possible methods—by no means mutually exclusive in the aesthetic and cultural progression of Norse society—for the delivery of the *fornaldarsǫgur* and their traditions suggest themselves: (1) telling the sagas without the aid of manuscripts (the so-called composition-in-performance style), (2) reading aloud from manuscripts for the entertainment of others (perhaps including some extemporizing),[4] and (3) employing the manuscripts as we typically use a book today, that is, reading to oneself. Although we possess only a few references to an individual relating a story to an audience without the use of a manuscript, we have even less testimony to reading aloud or reading in a more modern sense. Of these two forms, performative readings from manuscripts are better attested in Old Norse texts; silent reading is, of course, a natural conclusion but only poorly documented. Yet despite the apparent *relative* wealth of information concerning the composition-in-performance style of narration, two peculiar—and suspicious—aspects of such testimony should be noted at the outset. In two cases, *Norna-Gests þáttr* and *Tóka þáttr*, the vision of the composing performer is clouded by the fact that the stories told by the 'oral narrators' are based on written texts. Adding to these suspicions, in most of the remaining cases we are presented with performances of texts not otherwise preserved (**Huldar saga, *Vatnars saga*). The degree to which these facts impinge on the cultural image projected in the texts may be slight, yet it is worth noting that we nowhere have a full explanation—complete with documented texts—of how such performances took place.

There is, however, a fair amount of circumstantial evidence to support the notion that the sagas were narrated or read aloud: most prominent in the case of the former are such standard repeated phrases as *svá er sagt* 'as is said,' *nú er at segja* 'now it is to be told,' and *er frá var sagt* 'as was told earlier.' But these frequently encountered phrases can hardly be credited as the remnants of an underlying oral stage, the status earlier researchers such as Knut Liestøl gave them.[5] Tempting though

---

4. With respect to reading aloud, I have suggested (Mitchell 1987) that saga manuscripts may have been used as a kind of promptbook for extemporized performative readings. See Zumthor (1972, 286–338, 405–28; 1987, 245–68) and his idea of recreations of oral performances. The concept of the "double-scene," developed in Lönnroth 1971, 1978 has applications here as well.

5. Liestøl 1930, 33–34.

such readings may be, no one seriously considers them in this light today, at least not uniformly so, especially in the face of evidence that suggests that these phrases were essentially interchangeable with similar items referring to written composition. Stylistic devices of this sort probably served a real purpose (for example, they may have validated the written text by putting it on a par with the narrated tradition),[6] but they do not necessarily provide a solid foundation for the idea that the sagas were orally narrated. One important study concludes, however, that roughly a fourth of these references in the *íslendingasǫgur* should be regarded as genuine.[7]

The much-touted references to reading aloud found in the *riddarasǫgur* are somewhat more promising. The writers of *Elis saga ok Rósamundu* and *Rémundar saga keisarasonar*, for example, admonish their audiences with such opening and closing phrases as *Hæyrit, horskir menn, æina fagra saugu* 'Hear, wise men, a lovely tale' (*Elis saga*, chap. 1); *Nu lyðit goðgæfliga! betra er fogr frǫðe en kuiðar fylli; þo scal við saugu súpa, en æi ofmikit drecka; sœmð er saugu at segia, ef hæyrendr til lyða, en tapat starfi, at hafna at hæyra* 'Now listen well! A fair story is better than a full belly; although one should sip during a saga, one should not drink too much. It is an honor to tell a tale, if the audience listens, but a lost labor when listening is abandoned' (*Elis saga*, chap. 15); and *Hafi sá þǫkk, er las, ok sá, er skrifaði, ok allir þeir, (er) til hlýða* 'Let him have thanks who read, him who wrote, and all those who listened' (*Rémundar saga*, chap. 72).[8] Similar phrases are to be found occasionally among the *lygisǫgur* and *fornaldarsǫgur* as well, for example, *hafi þeir þǫkk, er hlýddu, en hinir skǫmm, er óhljóð gerðu* 'let them have thanks who listened, but shame to those who made a racket' in *Ála flekks saga* (chap. 19). In *Bósa saga* (chap. 16), the author asks a blessing for those *sem hér hafa til hlýtt lesit ok skrifat* 'who have listened, read, and written.'

Such authorial exhortations indicate an awareness of the practice of reading aloud, although they do not tell us how frequently or with which texts such practices were followed. But just as similar references

6. Baetke 1956, 29–31. This idea was anticipated already in Sigurður Nordal 1940; the concept of saga style imitating oral style is given a full treatment in Allen 1971, 23–25.

7. Andersson 1966.

8. Glauser (1983, 78–100) concludes that these phrases reflect genuine practice (i.e., that the *Märchensagas* [at least] were intended for public, oral presentation, not private reading). See his discussion for a complete inventory of such phrases in the native romances. The probable continuity of Icelandic culture in this regard has played an important role in allowing adherents of the "reading aloud" theory to cite the more recent practice of reading sagas aloud as evidence for such a custom during the Middle Ages. See Magnús Gíslason 1977.

to the use of manuscripts and to specific points of origin in the Faroese ballads must be taken lightly, as when the opening verse in the *Hálfs saga* reflexes maintains that the ballad was composed in France (*Álvur kongur*, st. 1), these casual references to reading aloud do not themselves provide evidence that public readings were common in medieval Iceland. That the Icelanders of that period were aware of such practices, as the references most definitely demonstrate, however, orients our thinking in that direction, an interpretation bolstered by the fact that instances of such deliveries are presented in the sagas themselves. When the hero of *Þorgils saga skarða* is asked by his host what he would like for his amusement, Þorgill asks what sagas there are to select from and chooses *Tómas saga erkibyskups* because he loves Thomas more than all other holy men. There can be little doubt but that he has been told what manuscripts were available and has elected to have the one about Thomas Becket read to him.[9] A similar scene unfolds in *Hákonar saga Hákonarsonar* (chap. 329), where King Hákon apparently has had a variety of manuscripts brought with him to Scotland and has both hagiographic and secular materials read aloud to him in Latin and Norse. It is of some value to note, however, that in almost all instances in which the practice of reading aloud is documented, the texts involved are either religious texts or translations of foreign originals.[10]

Nor can the practice of reading silently to oneself be disregarded:[11] indications of it are especially prominent in religious writings, although materials thus used were not always restricted to religious topics. When, for example, in *Jóns saga helga hin elzta* (chap. 13) Bishop Jón discovers that Klængr Þorsteinsson, later Bishop of Skálholt, *las bók þá er köllut er Ovidius epistolarum* 'read the book that is called *Ovidius epistolarum*,' he forbids him to read books of that sort (*at lesa þesskonar bækr*). On the other hand, the testimony of this episode is

9. *Honum var kostr á boðinn, hvat til gamans skyldi hafa, sǫgur eða danz, um kveldit. Hann spurði, hverjar sǫgur í vali væri. Honum var sagt, at til væri saga Tómás erkibiskups, ok kaus hann hana* [. . .] *Var þá lesin sagan* 'He was asked whether he would prefer sagas or dance [*danz*] for entertainment in the evening. He asked what sagas there were from which to choose. He was told that among them was *Tómas saga erkibyskups*, and he chose that one [. . .] The saga was then read' (II, 295).

10. E.g., *Blómstrvalla saga, Elis saga ok Rosamundu, Pættir ur Miðsögu Guðmundar byskups, Húngrvaka, Jóns saga helga, Laurentius saga byskups, Rémundar saga keisarasonar, Þorgils saga skarða.*

11. On the question of reading Old Icelandic texts in the modern sense, see especially Clover 1982, 188–204. The case for a reading public (in this individual sense) of the late medieval German rhymed epic (*aventiurehaft*) is outlined in Heinzle 1978, 56–98. The question of the medieval audience and its mode of textual interaction has in fact been much bandied about in recent years. See, for example, Bäuml 1980, Batts 1981, Scholz (1975; 1980, 1–34; 1984), and Walker 1971; on the Old Norse situation, see Schier 1977.

brought into question by another version of Jón's life, *Jóns saga helga eptir Gunnlaug múnk*, which says that when Bishop Jón sees and realizes (*sá ok undirstóð*) that Klængr is reading (*las*) Ovid, he forbids him to *hear* (*heyra*) such books (chap. 24), a comment that challenges our modern concept of what it meant to "hear" or "read" a text in the Middle Ages.[12] Few of the references to such individual interaction with "books" occur outside the walls of the cloister; however, one such example is documented in *Orkneyinga saga* (chap. 58), when Earl Rǫgnvaldr composes a verse in which he claims, *týnik trauðla rúnum, / tíð er mér bók ok smíðir* 'I rarely ruin runes, I occupy myself with books and works of skill.'[13] Yet apart from this reference, one is hard pressed to find any solid evidence of nonclerics engaged in the use of books in anything like the modern sense. Education was, however, more or less continuously available in Iceland from the early eleventh century through the Reformation,[14] and the degree of literacy among laity and clergy alike presumably allows us to infer such a practice.[15] By the early fourteenth century—at least—reading aloud and reading silently had sufficiently established themselves as complementary treatments of written materials that phrases of the sort *Ollum monnum þeim sem þetta bref sea edr heyra* 'To all those men who see or hear this letter' become nearly ubiquitous in the corpus of the Icelandic diplomas.[16]

12. On the question of the semantic fields of *lesa* and *heyra*—and their possible synonymy—see Bjarni Guðnason 1977.

13. In all occurrences of *bók* in the *Poetic Edda*, as Joseph Harris has pointed out to me, the word means 'tapestry.' The Earl's comment would, if this were the sense here, also complement the sense of *smíðir* in the verse.

14. For an overview of education in Iceland, see Halldór Hermannsson 1958, ix–xxiv. On foreign study trips made by Icelanders during the Middle Ages, see Jónas Gíslason 1981, as well as Jakob Benediktsson 1956–78b.

15. See especially Einar Ólafur Sveinsson 1944, 1956a, and Stefán Karlsson 1970. But cf. Lönnroth's more pessimistic appraisal of literacy in the Icelandic Middle Ages (1976, 166–70). It is commonly suggested that much of the substantial Icelandic production of saga manuscripts was intended for export to Norway, but Stefán Karlsson (1979) concludes that the linguistic differences between the two areas were sufficiently great by the end of the fourteenth century that such activity must have been increasingly intended for the home market. The questions of widespread literacy, manuscript production, and intended audience in Iceland are addressed in Sigurður Nordal 1952.

16. Thus the opening of the oldest dated letter (1311) written in Icelandic and preserved in the original, *Islandske originaldiplomer*, p. 7 (see also Stefán Karlsson's comments, p. xvii), an invocation quite common among surviving epistles of this sort. The phrase already enjoyed currency in Norway, as demonstrated by *Diplomatarium islandicum* (II, 330 et passim). Of particular interest for this discussion is a letter sent by Árni Laurentíusson with a copy of *Dunstanus saga erkibiskups* in which he sends a greeting to good men and those who will hear or read through the saga (*[A]wllum godum monnum oc rettruavndum eda þenna bækling heyravndum oc yfirlesavndum*) and includes an exhortation for them to listen with humility and patience (*bidr ec alla ydr oc*

Discussions of *sagnaskemtan* are frequently dominated by a single narrow view as to what saga entertainment meant, but it is not difficult to imagine that all three forms of *skemtan* were used during the thirteenth century, no doubt in varying degrees in different subcultural settings within the broad spectrum of Norse society. That is, it is highly likely that manuscripts had different uses and that saga entertainment had different forms in monasteries, Icelandic farm houses, and the Nordic courts. An evolution from the strictly oral saga to the written saga that was popularly "read" with the ear rather than the eye, to use Ruth Crosby's famous formulation,[17] is a natural development for us to imagine and the evidence from contemporary documents supports a course of this sort.

Certainly one factor that favors such an evolution in the case of the *fornaldarsǫgur* is the fact that we possess substantial evidence of them in preliterary settings. Yet even as Norse society moves toward increased literacy, the sagas remain unwritten and thus outside the realm of this important cultural innovation for some time; when, for example, the author of *The First Grammatical Treatise* states in the mid-twelfth century that he has worked out an alphabet that will make it easier to read and write laws and genealogies and religious commentaries, the sagas are conspicuously and significantly absent from his list (par. 84, 90).[18] Yet already by the twelfth century the Icelanders enjoyed a reputation among the other Scandinavians for their exceptional narrative abilities. Writing in about 1180, the monk Theodoricus states in the prologue to his *Historia de antiquitate regum Norwagiensum* that the Icelanders have been especially good at preserving traditions in their old poetry (*antiquis carminibus*). Somewhat later, Saxo Grammaticus claims in the preface to his *Gesta Danorum* that he has employed the Icelanders' treasure of ancient material in assembling his own work and comments at length on the interest they display in recounting famous deeds.[19] In the fourteenth book of his history (XIV:36:2), Saxo recounts the story of

---

sierhveria. at þier hlydit til eftir farannda efnis med godfvsv litilæte. oc bætit vm med þolinmædi. þo at min orda tiltæki se nockvd suo. atfynndilig eda leidindafullt. edur eigi svo listuligt sem þessv agæta efne til heyrir [II, 493]).

17. Crosby 1933.

18. But see Hreinn Bendiktsson's pessimistic appraisal of the usefulness of the remark in this regard, *The First Grammatical Treatise*, 181–88. See also Bekker-Nielsen 1986 on the First Grammarian's remark.

19. The question of Theodoricus's and Saxo's sources, and whether they were written or oral, or written but based on oral sources (the current prevailing view), has been the subject of intense scrutiny. See the discussion and bibliography in Andersson 1985b, 209–11.

Arnoldus Tylensis (presumably the Icelandic skald Arnaldr Þor-valdsson), who was an experienced and clever storyteller.

The sort of *sagnaskemtan* envisioned by both clerics is probably accurately captured in such episodes as the wedding at Reykjahólar portrayed in *Þorgils saga ok Hafliða* (chap. 10), in which sagas are told together with verses, and throughout *Norna-Gests þáttr*, a text preserved first in the late fourteenth-century *Flateyjarbók* but dating from a somewhat earlier period.[20] In the *þáttr*, we see Norna-Gestr take up his harp on one occasion after the other and sing lays about various heroes connected with the Vǫlsung tradition. The same scene, in which a monarch interviews a traveling stranger and entices narratives out of him, is repeated frequently in the sagas. Such is the case in *Tóka þáttr Tókasonar*, also from the *Flateyjarbók* manuscript, where the old stranger tells the court of his experiences with the legendary heroes Hálfr and Hrólfr kraki. From small queries by King Óláfr the Saint, the visitor spins narratives, with the predictable result that the king finds the stranger's speech to be *hin mesta skemtan* 'the best entertainment' (chap. 107).

These scenes are clearly literary fabrications, but episodes of this type are by no means limited to the *fornaldarsǫgur:* one of the best-known testimonies to oral saga telling fits the same pattern, the so-called *útferðarsaga* of Haraldr harðráði from the *Morkinskinna* manuscript, also a relatively late source. In this episode, an Icelander grows despondent after having entertained the court with tales over a period of several months. The king discerns the reason and finally the saga teller admits that his bad humor derives from the fact that the only saga he has left in his repertoire is the king's own saga. Haraldr asks him to tell it during the thirteen evenings of Christmas, and the Icelander complies. The king thanks him at the conclusion for a tale that is both accurate and well told, and the Icelander explains that he learned part of the saga each summer at the Alþingi from Halldór Snorrason. From this episode it has been adduced that saga tellers had special repertoires of materials, that these narratives could be of some length, and that the position of saga teller was semiprofessional.[21]

One of the most important episodes in which the Norwegian court is entertained by the narrative sensibilities of an Icelander is found in *Sturlu þáttr*, part of the late thirteenth-century *Sturlunga saga*. The im-

---

20. *Norna-Gests þáttr* is found in three manuscripts, the oldest of which is *Flateyjarbók*. On the date of the manuscript (ca. 1390), see Finnur Jónsson 1927.

21. On the significance of this passage for the free-prose position, see especially Heusler 1943, 205.

portance of this scene derives partly from the fact that the events are recorded only some thirty-five years after they took place and fewer than twenty years after the death of the scene's main character, providing us with relatively firm ground for believing in the authenticity of the events as they are narrated. The story tells of how Sturla Þórðarson goes to Norway in the hope of ingratiating himself with the king, to whom he has been slandered. King Magnús takes a cautious approach to the Icelander, neither accepting him nor allowing him to speak, but he does permit Sturla to accompany him and the queen as they sail southward down the coast. As Sturla prepares to sleep that night on board the ship, the following scene ensues:

> En er menn lǫgðuz til svefns, þá spurði stafnbúi konungs, hverr skemta skyldi. Flestir létu hljótt yfir því. Þá mælti hann: "Sturla inn íslenzki, viltu skemta?"
>
> "Ráð þú," segir Sturla. Sagði hann þá Huldar sǫgu, betr ok fróðligarr en nǫkkurr þeira hafði fyrr heyrt, er þar váru.
>
> Þrøngðuz þá margir fram á þiljurnar ok vildu heyra sem gerst, varð þar þrǫng mikil.
>
> Drottning spurði: "hvat þrǫng er þar fram á þiljunum?"
>
> Maðr segir: "þar vilja menn heyra til sǫgu, er hann Íslendingrinn segir."
>
> Hon mælti: "hvat sǫgu er þat?"
>
> Hann svaraði: "þat er frá trǫllkonu mikilli, ok er góð sagan, enda er vel frá sagt."
>
> Konungr bað hana gefa at þessu engan gaum ok sofa. Hon mælti: "þat ætla ek, at Íslendingr þessi muni vera góðr drengr ok sakaðr minnr en flutt hefir verit."
>
> Konungr þagði. Sváfu menn þá af nóttina. En um morguninn eptir var engi byrr, ok lá konungr í sama lægi. En er menn sátu at drykk um daginn, sendi konungr Sturlu sendingar af borði. Mǫtunautar Sturlu urðu við þetta glaðir, "ok hlýz betra af þér en vér hugðum, ef slíkt venz opt á."
>
> En er menn váru mettir, sendi drottning eptir Sturlu, bað hann koma til sín ok hafa með sér trǫllkonu-sǫguna. Gekk þá Sturla aptr í lyptingina ok kvaddi konung ok drottningina. Konungr tók kveðju hans lágt, en drottning vel ok léttiliga. Bað drottning hann segja þá sǫmu sǫgu, er hann hafði sagt um kveldit. Hann gerði svá, ok sagði mikinn hluta dags sǫgu. En er hann hafði sagt, þakkaði drottning honum ok margir aðrir, ok þóttuz skilja, at hann var fróðr maðr ok vitr. (II, 325–26)

And when men lay down to sleep, the king's forecastle-man asked who should entertain them. Most remained silent at this. Then he asked: "Sturla the Icelander, will you entertain [us]?"

"You decide," says Sturla. Then he told (*sagði*) **Huldar saga,* better and more cleverly than any of them who were there had heard (*heyrt*) before.

Many thronged forward on the deck and wanted to hear (*heyra*) it clearly, so that there was a great throng there.

The queen asked, "What is that crowd of men on the foredeck?"

A man says, "The men there want to hear (*heyra*) the saga that the Icelander is telling (*segir*)."

She said, "What saga is that?"

He replied, "It's about a great troll-woman, and it is a good story, and it is being well told (*vel frá sagt*)."

The king told her to pay no heed to this but to sleep. She said, "I think this Icelander must be a good man and much less to blame than he is reported to be."

The king remained silent. People went to sleep for the night. The following morning there was no wind, and the king['s ship] was in the same place. When the men were sitting at table during the day the king sent to Sturla some dishes from his table. Sturla's messmates were pleased at this, and [said], "Things look better with you here than we thought, if this sort of thing goes on."

When the men had eaten, the queen sent a message to Sturla asking him to come to her and have with him the saga about the troll-woman (*bað hann koma til sín ok hafa með sér trǫllkonu-sǫguna*). Sturla went aft to the quarterdeck then and greeted the king and queen. The king received his greeting shortly but the queen received it well and easily. The queen then asked him tell that same story (*segja þá sama sǫgu*) that he had told in the evening. He did so, and told the saga for much of the day (*sagði mikinn hluta dags sǫgu*). When he had told [it] (*hafði sagt*), the queen and many others thanked him and understood that he was a knowledgeable and wise man.

Having thus established himself as a raconteur of some skill, Sturla then requests a hearing for the poem he has composed about King Magnús. The poem is declaimed and well received, and the following day Sturla recites a poem he has made up about Magnús's father, King Hákon. This piece too is well received and the poet becomes a favorite of the court, so much so that he is commissioned to write the saga of King Hákon, a task, as the author reminds us, of great responsibility.[22]

The phrase used by the queen, "and have with him the saga about the troll-woman," has been taken to indicate that Sturla is not relying on his narrative skills alone, but rather has a manuscript with him, a

22. The *þáttr* here bears a striking similarity to Egill's predicament at the court in York before Eiríkr Blood-Axe. On the narrative stance of the saga see Ciklamini 1984.

view that has been widely accepted.[23] Dissenting from this interpretation, Dietrich Hofmann points out that the saga states explicitly that
Sturla leaves Iceland with nearly no possessions, a scenario into which
a manuscript whose telling requires most of the day would fit very
poorly.[24] Thus, the phrase "have the saga with him" must be interpreted as meaning something on the order of "be prepared to tell the
saga," a view dictated by the rest of the episode.

Both points of view can be made to appear quite reasonable, despite
the fact that they are diametrically opposed. The phrase "have the saga
with him" surely does presume the presence of a manuscript, yet every
other bit of evidence in the episode points toward an oral recounting of
*Huldar saga. These two views are incompatible, however, only if one
assumes that the writer has portrayed only one form of sagnaskemtan.
Quite the opposite, I suspect, is in fact the case, for the differences in
the various forms of sagnaskemtan presented in Sturlu þáttr underscore
important themes in the narrative. The point of Sturla telling *Huldar
saga is that the act ingratiates him to the king, who allows him to recite
his poems; furthermore, it lays the groundwork for his being asked to
compose Hákonar saga. Surely a manuscript reading, however elegant,
would be inadequate to such tasks. Thus the þáttr emphasizes that
Sturla comes to the court essentially naked of everything but the narrative skills he will employ in reestablishing his position at court and in
composing one of his most enduring literary monuments. The dispari-
ty of his position vis-à-vis that of the royal couple is therefore emphasized by the queen's request that he bring along his manuscript—a
natural assumption for a member of the royal Norwegian court, where
so many foreign romances have been translated—and is thus an important element in the tale. In some ways it parallels the fact that Sturla
does not even bring his own provisions along, but instead receives food
from the royal table after he entertains the crew. When Sturla tells the
saga to the crew and again later to the royal couple, he does so orally,
but when the queen requests him to entertain them, she assumes a
form of "saga telling" which had already become common at court,
expected even—reading aloud from a manuscript.

Thus in Sturla's life and works, we catch a glimpse of Old Norse
society at a liminal moment, or of several strata of it at any rate. Sturla

23. Hermann Pálsson 1962, 52; Lönnroth 1976, 172. Lönnroth states that the language of the text does not make the situation absolutely clear, but concludes that
Hermann is "probably right."
24. Hofmann 1971. Note that Stefán Einarsson (1957, 158) attempts to balance the
obvious discontinuity of the account: "It seems that [Sturla] had the story Huldar saga
with him in manuscript, though he is said to have told—not read—it."

is surely one of the last Icelanders to receive substantial benefit from the declaiming of skaldic poetry; he narrates a *fornaldarsaga orally;* and he is engaged by King Magnús to *write Hákonar saga Hákonarsonar.*[25] The chain of events which ultimately leads Sturla from disgrace and poverty to royal favor and what was surely one of the great literary commissions of the thirteenth century thus begins with a humble *fornaldarsaga* well and intelligently told, *"better* and *more cleverly* than any of them who were there had heard before," the comparative forms themselves indicating too that no fixed form of the tale could be the object of such praise.

We possess no medieval **Huldar saga,*[26] but the image of an orally narrated *fornaldarsaga* projected in *Sturlu þáttr* must have still been a frequent occurrence in the thirteenth century; in the case of some of the *fornaldarsǫgur,* such performances probably led directly to the writing down of the texts, as indicated at the conclusion of *Yngvars saga víðfǫrla.* An enduring, and perhaps insoluble, question arises in this context: if narratives already existed in good and entertaining oral forms and if individuals equipped to tell them abounded, as seems to have been the case with the *fornaldarsǫgur,* why were such tales written down? What were the forces at work in society which promoted the recording—and elaboration—of a narrative whose natural cultural setting was in the hands—or mouth—of a storyteller?

Recourse to written—and hence authoritative and legitimizing—texts was no doubt promulgated by the conventions of the church, whose huge inventories of *altarisbækr* 'altar books,' *aspisiens bækr* 'breviaries,' *lesbækr* 'lectionaries,' *messubækr* 'missals,' and similar materials were read aloud in the course of the Mass and other celebrations.[27] The routine employment of such manuscripts over the centuries helped create a climate in which written texts were imbued with an aura of reliability and authority not accorded unwritten materials. An illustra-

---

25. See Chap. 2 on the demise of skaldic poetry. Curshman (1984, 149) proposes the ultimate transitional moment, when he suggests that saga entertainment might consist of reading out loud followed by saga telling after nightfall. I have suggested (Mitchell 1987) that the transition from a completely oral culture to a reading and "verbal" culture may have promoted saga texts that were partially read aloud, partially told in the traditional manner. On the decline of the oral tradition and the rise of saga reading, see Lönnroth 1976, 211–13.

26. There does exist a late eighteenth-century piece (in three recensions) with a similar protagonist and title, *Sagan af Huldi hinni miklu og fjölkunnugu trölldrotningu,* but Halldór Hermannsson (1912, 72) comments that "it probably has no connection with the old saga."

27. For a systematic review of the manuscripts held by various churches in Iceland, see Olesen 1957, 1959, 1960, and Olmer's important study (1902).

tion of this point is to be found in Gunnlaugr's version of *Jóns saga helga*, the saga of the bishop of Hólar from 1106 to 1121, where the story of the *val bóklærðan ok hinn snjallasta túlk guðligra ritnínga* 'very book-wise and most excellent interpreter of divine writings' Gísli Finnsson is given (chap. 23). Gísli taught Latin at Hólar and the saga says that when he spoke the word of God before the people, he did not speak without books very often nor did he trust much in his memory, but rather explained the writings of the Holy Fathers according to a book that lay before him on the lectern. He did so, the saga continues, because *hann var úngr at aldri, þætti þeim meira um vert, er til lýddi, at þeir sæi þat, at hann tæki sínar kenníngar af helgum bókum ok merkiligum, en eigi af einu saman brjóstmegni ok hugviti* 'he was young, [and] they who listened might believe it more valuable if they could see that he took his lessons from holy and distinguished books and not from his strength of mind and cleverness alone.' This view is no doubt an important, and nearly ubiquitous, development throughout medieval Christian societies, one which combined a sense of *auctoritas* with the fear of losing knowledge—*Hungrvaka* (chap. 1), for example, claims that the work has been composed in order that the accounts narrated therein might not fall out of the author's memory. In other words, we must begin to understand and reassess such references within the "grammar of context" and the dialectic of speech act theory.[28] Ultimately these references depict authority, but whereas at one point authority resided in "performed," "winged," or "heavy" words (as indicated by the widespread use of the "as is said" phrases), by the later Middle Ages it was the written word that was supreme.

The thirteenth century was subject to a wide array of cultural changes in Scandinavia, not least among them the growth of Continental conventions and an increased interest in the literature of the Continent at the Norwegian court. Along with this fascination for translated—and therefore untraditional—romances came a linked reliance on the use of manuscripts in such secular contexts, a practice that must have underscored and paralleled the image of the authoritative written word projected by the church. Perhaps this image was even promoted by the church, which controlled access to literacy: can it be mere coincidence that in the image of oral saga telling in *Þorgils saga ok Hafliða* (chap. 10) the lay teller relates a story that is held up to ridicule as demonstrably false and historically inaccurate, whereas Ingimundr *the Priest* tells a saga that "wise men" hold to be true? It is a natural

---

28. See R. Martin 1989, especially 4–10.

practice in all forms of narration and history to lay claim to true and verifiable sources, whether the medium of narration is written or oral. Such is certainly the case with a work like Snorri's massive *Heimskringla*, the introduction to which carefully sets out the various sources of information which have been employed in compiling it, such as skaldic poetry and the accounts of wise men. The author of *Yngvars saga* feels the same need when he carefully delineates a legitimizing pedigree for his text. Mere recounting is no longer sufficient; "telling the tale" gives way to "telling the correct version of the tale"; documentation—being able to "prove" that one has the right version of a tale—becomes an important element in its narration.[29]

A combination of these factors, as well as the influence of the written *íslendingasǫgur* and *konungasǫgur*, is surely responsible for the preservation of the *fornaldarsǫgur*. But it would be inaccurate to portray all the extant versions of the *fornaldarsǫgur* as dictations taken from oral performances: that fact is emphasized by numerous comments in the sagas to the effect that dissatisfied readers may augment the stories as they see fit. Yet the care with which some—at least—of the *fornaldarsǫgur* set out their sources (for example, *Yngvars saga*) lends credence to the possibility that the preservation of these fabulous tales resulted from the reliance religious and foreign writings placed on manuscripts. The process by which these entertaining sagas came to be written down was no doubt a gradual one, for although we cannot say with any certainty which *fornaldarsaga* was the first to be recorded or worked out extensively in a written format, it is reasonable to assume that this honor may belong to the oral *fornaldarsǫgur* that contributed to Saxo's *Gesta Danorum* and Snorri's *Ynglingasaga*, as well as to *Skjǫldunga saga*.[30] Indeed, it is not unthinkable that acquaintance with these essentially historical works inspired those who recorded the *fornaldarsǫgur* on the large scale we encounter in the high Middle Ages.

By whatever means the *fornaldarsǫgur* were used in the Middle Ages, modern scholars have been quick to dismiss them as literature. That is to say, by modern standards they simply do not favorably withstand

29. On the attitude of the medieval writers toward the legitimacy of their sources for the *konungasǫgur*, see Andersson 1985b, 209–11.

30. Although we no longer possess *Skjǫldunga saga*, a number of works presumed to be part of, or derived from, it are extant. For a discussion of them, see Bjarni Guðnason 1982, xix–lxx, as well as his earlier detailed study (1963). It is Bjarni's view that *Skjǫldunga saga* must be contemporary with Saxo Grammaticus and Theodoricus, that is, approximately 1180–1200. He accepts the theory first proposed by Einar Ólafur Sveinsson (1937) that the saga was composed in Oddi in connection with the family of the Oddaverjar. Among those texts indebted to *Skjǫldunga saga* are *Snorra Edda*, *Ynglinga saga*, and *Þáttr af Ragnars sonum*, as well as *Ólafs saga Tryggvasonar hin mesta*.

comparison to more realistic narratives with tragic modes such as *Njáls saga* and *Laxdœla saga;* one need only think of the frequent description of the *fornaldarsǫgur* as "worthless" and so on to appreciate how sweeping the judgments have been. Yet our contemporary notions of what constitutes a "good saga," or "good" literature of any sort, are for that matter no more enduring than the apparent shifts in genre popularity one notes in the history of saga writing. Modern audiences, for example, are willing to forgive *Vǫlsunga saga* its blemishes because of its relationship to the Nibelung materials and to Wagner's *Ring* cycle, but despite extensive modern interest in the text, the popularity in medieval Iceland of that specific text (although not the tradition itself) must have been rather limited if we may use the vagaries of manuscript preservation as an indication, for only one vellum manuscript of it has come down to us.[31] The "fossil record" provided by manuscript survival is indeed telling: whereas we possess only single medieval copies of such landmarks of Western literature as *Beowulf* and *Vǫlsunga saga,* texts such as *Bósa saga* and *Egils saga ok Ásmundar* are attested in numerous vellum manuscripts. Codicological details of this sort are clearly no indication of literary value, but certainly they suggest that tastes change over time and that for reasons that may wholly escape modern readers, the audiences of the late Middle Ages found the *fornaldarsǫgur* to be exceptionally enjoyable.

Yet enduring literary merit and the ability to entertain are occasionally only partially overlapping sets, and it is worth remembering, after all, that medieval Icelanders were more likely to question the *historical* worth of a saga than they were to comment on such *literary* traits as style and manner of characterization. The comments made in *Þorgils saga ok Hafliða* questioning the genealogical reliability of the **Hrómundar saga Gripssonar* told at the wedding at Reykjahólar indicate what qualities were of central importance to Icelandic audiences (chap. 10).[32] In many cases where sagas are lauded for being "good" and the like, emphasis tends to fall on the *narrative process* rather than on specific

---

31. Nks 1824b, 4to is the only extant medieval version of *Vǫlsunga saga,* although later paper manuscripts of it exist. A case can certainly be made for the saga having once been part of AM 147, 4to as well. See Olsen's remarks in his edition of *Vǫlsunga saga ok Ragnars saga loðbrókar* (pp. lxxxvi, 180), as well as McTurk 1975, 45. A token of the popularity of this text in the Anglo-American world, for example, is the fact that though a number of *fornaldarsǫgur* (e.g., *Ketils saga hœngs*) have never appeared in English, there have been no fewer than five English translations of *Vǫlsunga saga* to date.

32. After having described how the lost **Hrómundar saga Gripssonar* was delivered, the author of *Þorgils saga ok Hafliða* (chap. 10) goes on to comment, *Ok þó kunnu menn at telja ættir sínar til Hrómundar Gripssonar* 'And yet men know how to recount their genealogies back to Hrómundr Gripsson.'

aspects of the text itself. The example above of *Sturlu þáttr* may be taken as a case in point, where at least some of the praise is directed toward delivery; the saga says that Sturla *tells* the story better than anyone had heard before. A notable exception to this point is provided by the views of King Sverrir reported in *Þorgils saga ok Hafliða* (chap. 10), in which he declares the *lygisǫgur* to be the *skemtiligastar* 'most entertaining,' apparently referring to their contents at least as much as to their presentation.[33]

The various terms applied by the Icelanders to these unrealistic texts—*lygisǫgur* 'lying sagas,' *skrǫksǫgur* 'deceiving sagas,' *stjup-mæðrasǫgur* 'step-mother sagas'—undoubtedly derived from their lack of historical verisimilitude vis-à-vis other saga genres. Yet modern readers often assume that these tags necessarily reflect negative judgments in other ways as well.[34] The evidence, codicological and otherwise, refutes such an interpretation. Yet scholarship on the literary dimensions of the *fornaldarsǫgur* has only slowly replaced the "motif-hunting" that characterizes most of the early research in the area. From the time of the nascent literary interpretations of the *fornaldarsǫgur,* which really only chipped away at the periphery of the well-established core of studies focused exclusively on issues of interpolation and motif, a deeper appreciation for the aesthetic qualities of the *fornaldarsǫgur* has developed through the twentieth century.[35] In the preceding chapter I pointed out that we must read the *fornaldarsǫgur* with a proper appreciation for their affinities to folklore; the same may be said with regard to the influence of romance. Although his is in most respects a remarkable treatment of Old Norse literature, W. P. Ker could still state the following in his introduction to a discussion of the postclassical sagas:

> The history of the Sturlungs is the last great work of the classical age of Icelandic literature and after it the end comes pretty sharply, as far as masterpieces are concerned. There is, however, a continuation of the old literature in a lower degree and in degenerate forms, which if not intrinsically valuable, are yet significant, as bringing out by exaggeration some of the features and qualities of the older school, and also as show-

33. *En þessarri sǫgu var skemt Sverri konungi, ok kallaði hann slíkar lygisǫgur skem-tiligastar* 'This saga was [used to] entertain King Sverrir and he called such *lygisǫgur* the most entertaining' (chap. 10).

34. Thus, for example, Sigurður Nordal (1957, 26) states that when medieval Icelanders called a text "a 'lying saga' [it] was the same thing as to denounce it as a bad Saga, poor literature."

35. Van Sweringen 1909, 1915, Reuschel 1933, Schlauch 1934, Hermann Pálsson and Paul Edwards 1971, Ciklamini 1966a, and Righter-Gould 1975, 1980.

ing in a peculiar way the encroachments of new "romantic" ideas and formulas.[36]

Certainly it is true that elements of medieval romance are to be found in the *fornaldarsǫgur*. Indeed, throughout the genre, one senses an odd mixture of popular and courtly elements, a polymorphic blend of traditional heroic material and incongruent ideals and scenarios. Thus we find sensitive and chivalric codes of behavior in the mouths of Vikings (for example, *Ǫrvar-Odds saga*, chap. 17); undying emotional love among people whose marriage norms undoubtedly followed political and economic expediencies more often than personal inclinations (for example, *Vǫlsunga saga*, chap. 22); and tournaments and elaborate banquets where charcoal-burning and various forms of dried fish more exactly typified daily activity and diet (for example, *Gǫngu-Hrólfs saga*, chaps. 20–21, 37).

Many aspects of the *fornaldarsǫgur* allow us to think of them as having been influenced by the romance tradition.[37] Among the characteristics usually associated with medieval romance are a self-conscious fictionality (recognized by author and audience alike), elaborate descriptions, frequent use of the supernatural, and an emphatic adherence to an idealized code of behavior.[38] In varying degrees of distribution, all of these points are realized in the *fornaldarsǫgur*: there is unusual—by earlier Icelandic standards—narrative self-consciousness, interest in depiction, reliance on magic, and commentary on ethics.[39] A further characteristic feature of medieval romance is the tendency toward cycles of romances centered on materials associated with a certain location or figure (for example, "The Matter of Britain," "The Matter of France"); even this quality finds apparent imitation among the *fornaldarsǫgur*, which might be said to form "The Matter of Hrafnista" (*Ketils saga hængs, Gríms saga loðinkinna, Ǫrvar-Odds saga*, and *Áns saga bogsveigis*), "The Matter of Gautland" (*Gautreks saga, Hrólfs saga Gautrekssonar*, and *Bósa saga*), and so on.[40] And if there is a single feature nearly everywhere connected with the romance, it is the con-

---

36. Ker 1908, 275.

37. See Hermann Pálsson and Paul Edwards 1971, in which they apply to the *fornaldarsǫgur* the classificatory scheme Northrop Frye (1957) outlines in "Historical Criticism: Theory of Modes."

38. On the medieval romance, see, for example, Jackson 1960, 67–70, 80–159.

39. On the use of magic in a wide range of later Icelandic sagas, see Schlauch 1934, 119–48.

40. Cf. Leach's comment (1921, 162) that the *fornaldarsǫgur* "correspond to the Arthurian cycle in Britain, and the Carolingian in France, and may be said to constitute the Matter of the North."

cept of the quest carried out over wide-ranging geography, a commonplace in the *fornaldarsǫgur*—usually with a woman or women as the goal.[41] But such quests in the *fornaldarsǫgur* are an almost serendipitous parallel, an imitation of chivalric material lacking, for the most part, chivalry. It is likely, however, that some Nordic quests are ultimately derived from foreign models: in *Eireks saga víðfǫrla*, a work that tends to defy neat classification but is related to the *fornaldarsǫgur* in some ways, Eirekr struggles to find the Earthly Paradise, Ódáinsakr, in apparent imitation of Parzival's search for the Grail Castle.

These sagas are indeed hybrids, surprising and often pleasing concatenations of traditional heroic and folkloric materials, but texts that also display the surface influence of foreign romance. It is with an appreciation for these variegated traditions and their irregular combination that the *fornaldarsǫgur* must be read, a difficult mission in that it has become commonplace in studies of medieval literature, whether clearly articulated or not, to accept Ker's dictum that heroic poetry should be associated with a warrior society ("the heroic age"), whereas romances belong to the "age of chivalry."[42] The Icelandic *fornaldarsǫgur*—and the whole of Icelandic literature for that matter—stand outside of this generalization. The closest brush with chivalry experienced by any Icelander would have been either a visit to a foreign court, including the Scandinavian ones where Continental courtly fashions were eagerly imitated in the thirteenth century, or on encounter with translated romances, such as the Arthurian materials. Yet the *fornaldarsǫgur* show traces of the romance legacy, in both form and incident, as well as touches of artistic embellishment which build over time. In short, one finds in the *fornaldarsǫgur* texts whose skeletal frames consist of an heroic legacy occasionally clothed in the wardrobe of chivalry; the results are sometimes charming, sometimes laughable, sometimes stirring.

It is largely as a consequence of this heterogenous, and often stereotyped, quality that such concepts as artistry and literary design are rarely connected with the *fornaldarsǫgur*, but this circumstance does not mean that they should not receive such critical attention. Indeed, although a reliance on traditional protagonists and their supposed ancient deeds and the resulting unreal atmosphere help bind the *fornaldarsǫgur* together as a group, these texts nonetheless exhibit nearly all the literary forms and modes associated with more sober, or at least

41. On the geography of the *fornaldarsǫgur*, see Simek 1986. With regard to the bridal quest, see Kalinke 1985, 327–31; Kalinke 1990; and, especially, Andersson 1985a.
42. Ker 1908, 3–5.

more seriously regarded, genres of narration. Thus, for example, the disastrous reliance Ragnarr loðbrók places on his own abilities leads to his death in proper tragic form; the macabre scene of Hervǫr coaxing the sword from her dead father Angantýr in his grave in *Heiðreks saga* is worthy of any Gothic novel; and the delightfully bawdy treatment given three items closely associated with the life of a warrior—sword, steed, and ship—as sexual metaphors in Bósi's amorous escapades is perfect burlesque. Nor are the *fornaldarsǫgur* incapable of charming characterizations and delicate touches: when, for example, the author of *Ragnars saga loðbrókar* returns again and again to Gríma's suggestion to her husband and others that the beautiful "Kráka" *could* be her daughter despite her own ugliness, since she too might have been beautiful in youth, a wonderfully humorous touch of vanity graces this otherwise loathsome creature. Yet clearly these are rare moments, for the preference is for more or less stock characters, devoid of such individual qualities.

The development of *Ǫrvar-Odds saga,* one of the longest and oldest of the *fornaldarsǫgur,* provides an excellent example of the degree to which these sagas were reworked in the interest of arriving at ever more pleasing and aesthetically refined texts. Among the *fornaldarsǫgur,* *Ǫrvar-Odds saga* is a tale best known for its haunting beauty and deep mystery, a saga in which the hero endures life for three centuries before returning to die, as prophesied, at his childhood home. During these exceptional lifetimes, Oddr's travels cover much of the known world, but each of the saga's episodes, despite an almost picaresque structure, contributes toward the final trip home to the protagonist's long overdue death. The relationship of the saga's manuscripts has been suggested in a stemma, in which the two main manuscripts, Sthlm Perg. 7, 4to and AM 344a, 4to (referred to as S and M), are usually assigned respectively to the early and late fourteenth centuries, while the various other manuscripts (A, B, C, E) range in age from the fifteenth to the seventeenth centuries.[43]

A central point in all the accounts of Oddr's preternaturally long career is his conversion from heathendom to Christianity; the manner in which this change of faith is presented differs widely in the manu-

---

43. The stemma is given in Boer's edition (p. xxxiv). There is general agreement on the date of the manuscripts. In addition to Boer's edition, pp. i–iv, see Cederschiöld's remarks in his *Fornsögur Suðrlanda,* p. xlix, and Gödel's comments in *Katalog öfver kongliga bibliotekets fornisländska och fornnorska handskrifter,* p. 45. This discussion assumes, of course, that S is closer in taste and form, as well as in age, to the *y manuscript than is M. With respect to the background of the saga, I find myself very much in line with Bandle 1988.

scripts and allows us an exceptional perspective on the literary variations and aesthetic growth of these sagas. The earliest text (S) describes
the event as follows:

> Þenna vetr eptir sótti Oddr með liði sínu út á Grikkland, ok þar fekk
> hann sér skip ok sigldi út undir Sikiley, þar var þá kristit. Sá ábóti réð þar
> fyrir einu klaustri, er Hugi hét, hann var inn mesti ágætismaðr; hann
> fekk spurn af, at þar váru heiðnir menn komnir norðan ór heimi; fór
> þessi inn góði ábóti þá til fundar við þá ok tók tal við Odd, sagði ábóti
> honum marga hluti frá dýrð guðs; lét Oddr sér þat alt vel skiljaz. Ábóti
> bað þá Odd at láta skíraz, en hann kvez mundu sjá fyrst siðu þeira. Oddr
> ferr nú einn dag til kirkju með sínum mǫnnum; heyrðu þeir þar kluk-
> knahljóð ok fagran sǫng. Ábóti fór þá enn tils tals við Odd ok spurði,
> hversu þeim gætiz at sið þeira. Oddr lét vel yfir: "munu vér nú" segir
> hann "sitja hér í vetr með yðru lofi." Ábóti kvað svá vera skyldu. Sem
> Oddr hafði þar setit fram um jól, lágu illgørðamenn úti ok herjuðu á
> Sikiley. Hugi ábóti átti þá tal við Odd ok bað hann frelsa land þeira af
> illþýði. Oddr játar því, býr hann nú her sinn. Þenna vetr fór hann víða
> um Grikklands eyjar ok herjaði ok vann stór verk ok fekk auð fjár. Þar
> kom hann fremst, er heitir Akvitanaland; þar réðu fyrir fjórir hǫfðingjar,
> ok þar átti Oddr orrostu mikla ok feldi þar alla þessa hǫfðingja ok mikit
> fólk annat ok fekk þar øróf fjár. Þar um kvað hann þessa vísu:
>
> > "Þar kvamk útarst,   es Akvitana
> > bragna kinder   borgom réþo;
> > þar létk fjóra   fallna liggja
> > hrausta drange,   nú 'mk hér komenn."
>
> Eptir þat heldr Oddr aptr til Sikileyjar ok dvalðiz þar um hrið. Var Oddr
> þá skírðr af Huga ábóta ok allr herr hans. (pp. 113–17)

The following winter, Oddr and his men went to Greece, and there he
got himself a ship and sailed out to Sicily, which was then Christian. An
abbot named Hugi was in charge of a certain cloister there and was a
very fine man; he had tidings that heathens had come there from the
north; this good abbot went to meet them and began to speak with
Oddr, telling him many things about the glory of God; Oddr allowed
himself to be convinced. The abbot then bade Oddr to allow himself to
be baptized, but he said that he first wanted to see their customs. On a
certain day, Oddr goes to church with his men [and] they hear there the
ringing of bells and beautiful music. The abbot again engages Oddr and
asks what they think of their customs. Oddr expressed approval: "We
could now," he says, "stay here throughout the winter with your permission." The abbot said that it should be so. When Oddr had been there
until after Christmas, evil-doers set out and harried in Sicily. Abbot
Hugi spoke with Oddr and asked him to save their country from the

rabble. Oddr agrees and gets his army ready. That winter he traveled widely among the Greek islands and harried and accomplished great deeds and gained great wealth. He came as far as the place called Aquitaine; four chieftains ruled there and Oddr fought a great battle and killed all those chieftains and many other people and acquired immense wealth. About this he made this verse:

> "Farthest out I came there, where in Aquitaine
> sons of men ruled over strongholds;
> there I caused four valiant warriors to fall,
> now I have arrived."

After that Oddr returned to Sicily and stayed there for a while. Then Oddr and all his army were baptized by Abbot Hugi.

In this the oldest version, Oddr merely expresses reluctance about being baptized without first knowing something of Christian faith and customs (*siðr*); after having witnessed a Mass during his stay, Oddr gives his approval. The process is rather conventional, unmarked by any special attention to the aspects of Christian worship which impress Oddr and his men, other than the mention of the bells pealing and the music they hear. This same episode is handled quite differently in the next generation of manuscripts (M), where the redactor focuses on the humor latent in S. In this description of Oddr's conversion, the potential of naive pagans encountering church services is fully exploited as the redactor toys with his audience, slowly allowing them to realize that the strange building Oddr and his men have discovered is a church:

Nú búa þeir skip x ór landi, ok halda nú suðr fyrir land, þvíat Oddr hafði þar sízt komit. Ok herja þeir nú suðr um Valland ok Frakkland, ok nú er ekki frá sagt, fyrr en þeir koma suðr í land, þar sem grunnsævi var, ok svá lýkr um, at þeir brjóta skipin við eitthvert land. Þar ganga þeir upp með lið sitt, ok er þeir koma á landit, þá sjá þeir þar hús eitt fyrir sér, þat var nǫkkut með ǫðrum hætti, en þeir hefði fyrr sét. Þangat ganga þeir til hússins, ok var þat opit ok af steini gørt. Þá spyrr Oddr Sigurð, hvat húsi þat mundi vera. "Eigi veit ek þat," segir hann. "Þat veit ek," segir Oddr, "at menn munu búa í húsinu ok vitja hússins, skulu vér því eigi inn ganga." Ok þeir setjaz niðr úti hjá húsinu, en vánu bráðara drífa menn at húsinu, ok þat fylgir, at þar koma upp þau læti, er þeir hǫfðu aldri fyrr heyrt. "Þat ætla ek," segir Oddr, "at hér sé allkynligr háttr á þessu landi, en hér skal bíða til þess, er menn koma út ór húsinu." Þat ferr eptir því sem Oddr gat, at menn drífa braut frá húsinu, ok þangat gengr einn af liði þeira landsmanna ok spyrr, hverir þar væri komnir, en Oddr spyrr, hvat landa þat væri. Sá segir, at þat heitir Akvitanialand, en Oddr spyrr, hvat hús þat táknaði. "Þetta kǫllu vér kirkju." "En hvat látum er þat, er þér hafið látit hér?" "Þat kǫllu vér tíðagørð. Hvernig er til farit um ráð yðart," segir þessi maðr, "eru þér heiðnir menn til lykta?" "Vér vitum ekki til annarrar trúar," segir Oddr, "en vér trúm á mátt várn ok á megin, en hverja trú hafi þér?" segir Oddr. "Vér trúum á þann, er sól hefir skapat ok himin ok jǫrð." "Sá mun mikill vera, er þat hefir skapat." Nú er þeim Oddi fylgt til herbergis; þar eru þeir viku ok eiga mál við landsfólkit; taka þeir þar við trú Guðmundr ok Sigurðr. Oddr tók ok við trú, ok vildi sjálfr þó ráða hǫgum sínum, sem honum líkaði. (chap. 33)

They made ready ten ships from the country and steered southward, for Oddr had been there least. And they harry south through Normandy and France [literally, *Valland ok Frakkland*, both usually glossed as 'France'], and now nothing is related before they come to the south where there were shallows and it ends such that they break the ships on a certain coast. There they go ashore with their troops and when they come up [from the beach], then they see there a certain house before them, which was of a different sort than they had seen before. They went thence to the house and it was open and made of stone. Then Oddr asks Sigurðr what kind of house this one might be. "I don't know," he says. "I know this," says Oddr, "that men live in the house and will return to it, and therefore we should not go in." And they sit down outside next to the house, and sooner than expected, men throng to the house, and it follows that such noise comes up as they had never heard before. "I think," says Oddr, "that there are all sorts of fashions here in this land, and [we] shall wait until men come out of the house." Everything happens as Oddr guessed, [and] men flock out of the house and one of the group of the local people goes thence and asks who it is who has come, but Oddr asks what country they are in. The one [who had come over] says that it is called Aquitaine, and Oddr asks what the house is used for. "We call that a church." "And what was the noise you made here?" "We call that a Mass. How about yourselves," says this man, "are you truly heathens?' "We know no other belief," says Oddr, "than that we believe in our might and main, but what do you believe?" "We believe in him who fashioned the sun and the heavens and the earth." "That one must be great who fashioned that." Oddr and the others are taken to [their] quarters; they are there for a week and speak with the people of the country; Guðmundr and Sigurðr accept their religion. Oddr also accepted their religion, but wanted to decide his affairs himself as he liked.

This later manuscript exhibits a great deal of humor, carefully wrought. Not only does the later author take the "raw material" exhibited in the S manuscript and play up its burlesque qualities, but he does so in a skillfully sustained manner, building first on the discovery of the strange structure, then on the arrival of many people all at once, and finally on the noise emanating from the building, a pattern repeated in Oddr's questions to the local. Thus, the M redactor has developed the rather humdrum conversion scene of S into a wonderfully reworked comic episode that emphasizes the self-confidence and pagan qualities of the hero and his followers, as well as their total ignorance of Christian customs. The two episodes do not differ greatly in their plots—after all, they both suggest that Oddr's conversion included a brush with the Christian Mass which impressed him—but the tone they take and the subsequent effects on the atmospheres of the two versions differ substantially.

Nor are such alterations and accretions infrequent in the histories of the *fornaldarsǫgur* in the Nordic Middle Ages: following Oddr's conversion in S, he goes directly to the Holy Land; in M and the other manuscripts he witnesses and avenges a bishop's murder. In the later manuscripts (A, B, E), there follow substantial interpolations concerning Oddr's humorously amorous adventures among the giants and his dealings with Rauðgrani. In essence, there is no single *Ǫrvar-Odds saga,* but rather several, each reworked by succeeding generations apparently building on the foundations left by earlier editors, or in any event by different writers with differing tastes. Both oral tradition and the literary sensibility of the individual writer undoubtedly played a role in these accretions. And in all such cases, attention is certainly paid to the literary effects of the changes, whether or not we as modern readers prefer this rather than that version. Interpolations and other changes are, of course, characteristic of manuscript traditions among all the saga genres, but they tend to be especially pronounced among the *fornaldarsǫgur,* paralleling the situation that prevails in oral traditions. Within the traditional community there may be a sense of "the story," but there exists no archetypal "Story," only multiforms of it. Thus, even though *fornaldarsǫgur* authors may have wanted their versions to appear authoritative, nothing seems to have prevented them from playing freely with the materials.

Literary analysis of the *íslendingasǫgur* did not begin until relatively late in the nineteenth century.[44] With so many realistic sagas—and their seemingly accurate reflections of early Icelandic life—to occupy researchers, it is perhaps forgivable that the *fornaldarsǫgur,* as fancy-filled latecomers to the Nordic literary scene, were relegated by scholars to a low position. To be sure some of them were held worthy of

44. See Andersson 1964, 50–52.

note, but these tended to be *fornaldarsǫgur* connected with the Sigurðr and Ragnarr loðbrók materials.[45] It is obvious that the Icelanders of the post-Sturlung age found the *fornaldarsǫgur* pleasing and entertaining, and, as the preceding section suggests, there were a variety of reasons why this was so; certainly, one of the tasks of contemporary scholarship must now be to explore further the belletristic dimensions of a group of texts which inspired the literary consciousness of an entire nation for several centuries.

The Heroic Age and the Social Dimension

It is perhaps not so surprising that when in the spring of 1840 Thomas Carlyle gave his famous lectures on heroes and the heroic in history, he devoted the first talk in the series to Scandinavian mythology and the figure of Óðinn.[46] Carlyle crystalizes what, for him at least, is the fundamental precept on which the Old Norse religion was founded when he says that Óðinn, "speaking with a Hero's voice and heart, as with an impressiveness out of Heaven, told his people the infinite importance of Valour, how man thereby became a god."[47] This consecration of valor, as he later calls it, might well stand as the underlying ethical principle of the *fornaldarsǫgur*, whose protagonists may be thought of collectively as *den egna kraftens män* 'self-might men,' to borrow Folke Ström's useful phrase.[48] The implicit—and often explicit—heroic ideal of the Icelandic sagas and the effects of the older Germanic heroic ethos on them have long been the subject of scholarly discussion, which initially focused on the parallels between the sagas and other Germanic texts, the best-known case being the analogues between *Grettis saga* and *Beowulf*.[49] Those who in more recent years have examined the *íslendingasǫgur* from the point of view of heroic ideals and conduct have tended to underscore the influence of heroic

45. Cf. Guðbrandur Vigfússon 1878, I, cxciv–cxcvi.
46. Carlyle n.d., 3–52.
47. Ibid., p. 40.
48. F. Ström 1948. Ström's study, while including some figures from the *fornaldarsǫgur*, focuses primarily on characters from the *íslendingasǫgur*.
49. Examples from the discussion: Fors 1904; Kochs 1911; Heusler 1926, 1934; Gehl 1937; van den Toorn 1955, 1964; Davíð Erlingsson 1970; van der Westhuizen 1973; and Thompson 1977. For a review of the early literature, see Andersson 1967, 65–74. In a series of works (e.g., 1971, 1974, 1982b), Hermann Pálsson has eschewed the study of "Old Norse" concepts such as luck and fate, and maintained that only by examining the Christian theology that dominated the society can we expect to understand the ethical considerations of the saga writers.

poetry and the changing nature of the heroic concept in the sagas.[50] M. C. van den Toorn, however, argues for the presence of three ethical strata and insists that since the three—the pagan ethics reflected in the eddic poem "Hávamál," heroic ethics, and Christian conduct—could coexist, they should not be interpreted as periods.[51]

Attempts to find periods or strata of heroism and ethical frames are long-cherished components of literary criticism, especially where traditional literature is concerned: Cecil M. Bowra suggests, for example, a distinction between primitive, proletarian, and aristocratic types of heroic outlook; Gertrude R. Levy likewise believes in three fundamental heroic types and opines that they can be determined by the degree of freedom and independence allowed the hero.[52] Useful as such commentaries are in general terms, application of them to specific texts must certainly be approached with caution, for it is unlikely that any two individuals would hold the same views on interpretation. It is valuable in this regard to recall the rapidly changing and fundamentally opposing views of *Beowulf*'s world and values which have been offered during the past century. To the nineteenth-century scholar, it was perfectly natural to think of Beowulf as the quintessential Germanic warrior-king cleansing the land of dangerous monsters and to believe that although the poem may have been written down after the conversion of the Anglo-Saxons, "no Christian vestment was thrown over the epic hero," as one influential literary historian put it. In 1911, at the height of foreign emigration to the United States, it seemed sensible and surprisingly easy to discuss the "melting pot" background of the poem and its presentation of a "democratic aristocracy." Amid the political and social ferment of the 1960s, it was argued—unsurprisingly in retrospect and entirely consonant with the times—that "the poem presents a criticism of the essential weakness of the society it portrays"; and now there are even those who, in a complete abandonment of the traditionalist perspective, would argue that in nearly every detail *Beowulf* is a thoroughly Christian work.[53] Such a comparison of views says little about the poem itself, which, aside from some progressive manuscript decay, has not changed at all; it speaks reams, however, about the nature of scholarship and its relationship to prevailing intellectual and cultural developments. The search for value systems and heroic ideals in a medieval text may then ultimately be more a

---

50. E.g., Bandle 1969, Gehl 1937, Andersson 1970.
51. Van den Toorn 1955, esp. 135–38.
52. Bowra 1952, 476–80; Levy n.d., esp. 216–18.
53. Ten Brink 1889, 27; Lawrence 1911, esp. 52; Leyerle 1965; Huppé 1984.

commentary on the sociohistorical context of the critic than of the work itself. Despite such inherent pitfalls, research into the intriguing area of heroic standards and behavior need not be enervated—a cautious description of the hero, of heroic action, and of heroic values in the *fornaldarsǫgur* remains a desideratum.

Although attention has generally been focused on the more realistic *íslendingasǫgur*, the *fornaldarsǫgur* have certainly not been ignored in discussions of heroic values.[54] Helga Reuschel attempts to use Saxo's *Gesta Danorum* as a standard by which to judge the heroic conventions of the later sagas, but the influence of the earlier forms of the *fornaldarsǫgur* on Saxo so thoroughly clouds the issue that separating the two may be impossible.[55] Van den Toorn applies to the *fornaldarsǫgur* his threefold division of ethics, and by comparing these ethical layers to those of the *íslendingasǫgur*, concludes that ethical outlook—as exemplified in the treatment of such topics as cruelty and friendship—may be a useful means of distinguishing the two groups; the differences between the older and younger ethical strata he attributes to the influence of foreign narratives.[56] A comprehensive treatment of the hero in selected *fornaldarsǫgur* is given by Hermann Pálsson and Paul Edwards, who demonstrate the dominance of the hero's character over the saga, insofar as it dictates the form the story takes, and the necessity in works like *Ǫrvar-Odds saga* and *Gǫngu-Hrólfs saga* of the protean enemy who keeps the hero's success and pride in check.[57]

The background against which the *fornaldarsǫgur*'s heroic presentation must be judged is ultimately that of the "heroic age," a concept promulgated in the influential writings of W. P. Ker and H. M. Chadwick.[58] Characteristic of the period is the fact that it is a world of epic, as opposed to romance; a world in which characters are motivated by such goals as a thirst for fame, or revenge, or material gain; a world in

54. It is difficult to extricate a discussion of the *fornaldarsǫgur* in this regard from other areas of Old Norse literature, the heroic poetry in particular, and from the concept of the centuries-older Vikings. Among studies that take up the *fornaldarsǫgur*, or are relevant to such a discussion, are Vedel 1903, 160–95; Heusler 1926; Kuhn 1938; de Vries 1963; Wax 1969; Pörtner 1971, 93–116. Particular emphasis has been placed on the concepts of luck and fate in the heroic life: e.g., Weber 1969. Cf. Hermann Pálsson 1975 and Boyer 1986.

55. Reuschel 1933.

56. Van den Toorn 1964.

57. Hermann Pálsson and Paul Edwards 1971, esp. 36–68. Cf. Hume (1974), who applies some of the same ideas to *Grettis saga*.

58. Ker 1908, 3–15; Chadwick 1912. See also the summary of the latter's views in Chadwick and Chadwick 1933. A review and critique of the Chadwicks' views on the heroic age is provided in Finnegan 1977, 246–50. On the concepts of the hero, heroism, and the heroic age, see also Curtius 1973, 167–70.

which the heroes are real men, not allegories; a world in which the narrative gaze is steadily focused on the individual, even in the midst of large pitched battles; a world with a limited and essentially integrated social hierarchy that does not prevent the interaction of men of different stations; a world in which a man's stature as a hero comes about not because he possesses powers of an entirely different order than those of other men, but because he is much better at what everyone knows and does.[59] Although the extant *fornaldarsǫgur* are centuries younger than the Nordic heroic age, they focus on it and are generally preoccupied with it; to a very great extent, it is this world the *fornaldarsǫgur* present—or hope to present in any event.[60]

Perhaps the most thoroughly interwoven aspect of the heroic age in the *fornaldarsǫgur* is that of honor and *drengskapr* 'courage, highmindedness.'[61] Like its Latin counterpart *virtūs* 'manliness, courage, worth' (modern English 'virtue'), the word derives from a sense of what it means to be a man, to do what is of value to society (‹ *vir* 'man,' *drengr* 'bold or noble-hearted man'). Yet as important as the concepts of honor and bravery are to the *fornaldarsǫgur*, they are rarely, if ever, mentioned: neither *drengskapr* nor the thirteenth-century loanword *æra* 'honor' appears at all in such works as *Áns saga bogsveigis*, *Bósa saga*, *Hálfdanar saga Brǫnufóstra*, *Hálfs saga ok Hálfsrekka*, and *Yngvars saga*, but the idea itself is indispensable to them.[62] The most succinct and best-known articulation of the principle of honor in Scandinavian sources is to be found in *Hávamál* 77, namely, that although the body will perish one day, fame lives on:

Deyr fé, deyia frœnder,	Cattle die, kinsmen die,
deyr siálfr it sama;	you will die yourself;
ec veit einn, at aldri deyr:	one thing I know which never dies:
dómr um dauðan hvern.	a dead man's fame.

59. Cf. Frye 1957.

60. But cf. Ker (1908, 15), who specifically denies that such is the case for the epic. Writing at a time when confidence in the fidelity of the heroic tradition as an unmuted, continuous entity was higher, he comments, "They [i.e., epics] are not separated widely from the matters of which they treat; they are not antiquarian revivals of past forms, nor traditional vestiges of things utterly remote and separate from the actual world."

61. On this concept, see especially Grønbech 1955, 57–107; Kuhn 1938; and Heusler 1926; but see van den Toorn's sensible objections to its generalization to all of Old Norse literature and culture (1955, 12–13 et passim).

62. Based on *A Concordance to Five Legendary Sagas*, part of a pilot project of computer-generated concordances begun in 1975 by CREST (Computer Research in Early Scandinavian Texts), which reflects the vocabulary of the Guðni Jónsson edition of the *fornaldarsǫgur*.

This concept, which brings with it a uniquely Germanic view of death, tends to flourish in the face of overwhelming odds; Byrhtwold's famous response as he and the other men in the English force grimly steel themselves against the onslaught of the Vikings in *The Battle of Maldon* provides what many would regard as the most perfect expression of the consecration of valor in Germanic poetry: *Hige sceal þe heardra, heorte þe cenre, / mod sceal þe mare, þe ure mægen lytlað* 'Our minds shall be stronger, our hearts braver, our courage greater, as our numbers diminish' (ll. 312–13). That relatively few utterances of this sort are to be found in the Icelandic *fornaldarsǫgur* is explained in part by the unsurpassed physical prowess that so many of its heroes possess; they are never defeated, or if so, only temporarily (as the audiences were surely aware, as in the case of *Gǫngu-Hrólfs saga*). Comparison of the Old English *Battle of Brunnanburh,* in which the victorious English army sweeps the field of its Scottish and Nordic enemies, with the tragic and moving *Battle of Maldon* exemplifies the difference—important as they are politically, military victories make much worse foundations for literature in the early Germanic world than do defeats, for they yield no occasion for tragic situations with their attendant heroic utterances. A further parallel may be drawn to *Egils saga Skalla-grímssonar,* whose protagonist almost alone of the *íslendingasǫgur* heroes is allowed to live on to advanced years. He is in essence *too* much the perfect warrior; rather than dying gloriously in a pitched, desperate battle of the sort that concludes so many heroic careers in the sagas (for example, Gísli in *Gísla saga Súrssonar,* Gunnarr in *Njáls saga*), Egill outlives his heroic status, becoming an infirm old man bullied about in the kitchen by the serving maids.

In the more tragic *fornaldarsǫgur,* however, the Germanic warrior ethos shines through brightly. Thus in *Hálfs saga* (chap. 7), when Hálfr wakes his men and tells them to break through the walls in order to fight the enemy who have set fire to the hall, Innsteinn composes the following verses:

Hrindum heiler	Throw down
hallar bíorí	the walls;
nu taka sulur	now the pillars
j sundr þoka	begin to burst;
æ man uppi	always will be remembered—
med⟨an⟩ aulld lifer	while men live—
Halfs ʀeka faur	the journey of Hálfr's warriors
til hertuga	to this king.

hartt skulum ganga	Sternly shall we go
ok hlida ecki uid	and not give way;
verdr uísis líd	a king's band
at uega med sauxum	shall slay with swords;
þeir skulu sialfer	they too should
a síer bera	receive
blodgar beniar	bloody wounds
adr braki letti.	before the din eases.

Snuízt snarlíga	Turn sharply,
snyrti dreinger	keen warriors,
utt or elldi	out of the fire
med audbrota	with your king;
eingín er yta	no one on earth
sa er ǽ lifuer	lives forever,
mun ecki baug broti	the ring-breaker will not
uid bana kuida.	at death feel fear.

If *drengskapr* provides the *means* for a hero to defend his life or reputation in the *fornaldarsǫgur,* the concept of honor can be an almost ruthless force with a will of its own. When, for instance, Sǫrli sees King Hálfdan's magnificent ship, *rann j hiarta hans æigingirnnd mikil sua at hann uillde drekann æiga* 'there flowed in his heart a great selfishness such that he must have the ship' (*Sǫrla þáttr,* chap. 231). There is no prehistory here, no theme of revenge, not even a covetousness that derives from material avarice; rather the ship presents Sǫrli with the opportunity to measure his own greatness against that of a noble king. When one of his men attempts to dissuade Sǫrli by saying that Hálfdan is a most famous man and has two sons who will surely avenge him, this argument only serves to egg Sǫrli on. Similarly, in *Ásmundar saga kappabana* when Ásmundr challenges Hildibrandr's courage by asking why he will not fight him, Hildibrandr can no longer put off the fight with his half-brother—a fact of which he is apparently aware, although it is not explicitly stated (chap. 7). The famous encounter of King Hrólfr with King Aðils and his berserkers comes about as the result of the king's idle speculation on his own greatness: in the midst of a lavish feast, Hrólfr looks out over his men and domain and asks of Bǫðvarr Bjarki *huǫrt hann vissi nǫckurn kong slijkan sem hann og styri slijkum kǫppum* 'whether he knew of any king who was his equal or who had such warriors' (*Hrólfs saga kraka,* chap. 25). When it develops that Hrólfr's greatness suffers because of his unresolved dispute with the Swedish king, Hrólfr mounts an expedition to Uppsala from which he and his men only barely return. Yet even though Hrólfr does not accomplish his objective, within the framework established by such texts the journey must be judged a success, as *vrdu þeir storliga frægir af þessari ferd* 'they became exceedingly famous from this trip' (chap. 30).

The concepts of honor and valor, especially as proved in single combat (H1561.2 and H1561.2.1), lie then at the very heart of the heroic outlook implicit in the *fornaldarsǫgur*. Closely allied with these themes, despite the general emphasis on individualism in the sagas, is the ideal of faithfulness and loyalty, a reflex of the Germanic *comitatus*. Thus *Hálfs saga*, a text particularly devoted to the concepts of faithfulness and treachery, tells of how the king's men, the *Hálfsrekkar*, eagerly vie with one another in jumping overboard in order to save the ship in a storm, thereby demonstrating not only their devotion to their companions but also their bravery (chap. 6). This devotion is played out in the succeeding chapters as the *Hálfsrekkar* follow their doomed chief to the hall of the treacherous King Ásmundr, despite the warnings of Hálfr's lieutenants that they will die. And one need only recall the extent to which Qrvar-Oddr's career consists of a succession of sworn brothers who die in his service or because of his actions to gain a sense of the importance placed on faithfulness. In brief, the *fornaldarsǫgur* are rich in examples of heroes swearing brotherhood to one another and then performing nobly on behalf of the other (cf. P310–12.3).

Royal largess (the 'Munificent monarch' motif, W11.2) is likewise a much admired characteristic in the *fornaldarsǫgur* and an idea intimately tied to the notion of an heroic age. Thus, *Norna-Gests þáttr* (chap. 4) and *Vǫlsunga saga* (chap. 22) list Sigurðr's generosity among his virtues; in praising its hero, *Hrólfs saga kraka* maintains that he was *myklu milldare af fie* 'much more generous with money' (chap. 16) than other kings; likewise *Hálfs saga* lauds Hjǫrleifr's generosity (chap. 2). Although a regular feature of the monarchs of the heroic age, the motif of the generous lord, which appears in most of the *fornaldarsǫgur*, must also have served the useful purpose of reminding the text's sponsor in not so subtle terms of the virtues of openhandedness.

Pagan religion features prominently in the *fornaldarsǫgur*'s retrospective on the heroic age: the gods are largely untouched by Christian attitudes, but the heroes themselves are rarely allowed to be genuine pagans, as a number of scholars have reminded us.[63] The authors of the *fornaldarsǫgur* had a sense of propriety; they did not allow their protagonists to become strangely anachronistic Christians but they did

---

63. F. Ström 1948, Lönnroth 1969, Weber 1981.

attempt to put them in the best possible light, usually without any fixed religious views at all. The figure of Hrólfr kraki, for example, for whom there is no religion, stands in stark contrast to that of the evil King Aðils who is consistently portrayed as an active heathen.

The heroic age—or perceptions of it—had its darker sides as well, in particular the grim fascination the Icelanders of the later Middle Ages took in recounting horrible mutilations. Perhaps the grisliest such scene in the *fornaldarsǫgur* comes when Hálfdan Brǫnufóstri meets up with the man who has lied about him to the king. Not satisfied with merely slaying him, Hálfdan cuts off his nose, puts out his eyes, chops off his ears, castrates him, breaks his legs, and further mutilates his feet; only then does he send him back to the king draped across his horse (*Hálfdanar saga Brǫnufóstra,* chap. 15). In a similar fashion, Án bogsveigir is not content merely to defeat the men King Ingjaldr sends after him; he must instead mutilate them by, for example, shaving, tarring, and feathering them before sending them back to their lord (*Áns saga bogsveigis,* chap. 4).

All of these incidents lack the moderation that the characteristic verisimilitude of the *íslendingasǫgur* and *konungasǫgur* would provide: when a *fornaldarsaga* states that the hero is the greatest champion or the finest warrior in the north, this is not mere formulaic hyperbolic praise; the author means it and writes the saga accordingly. The protagonist's virtues and talents are inevitably superlative and it is hardly surprising that the qualities of his world should be likewise intensified and extreme. Those who crafted the *fornaldarsǫgur* and their audiences were peering back at an heroic age when anything was possible, just as modern fantasy literature employs the primeval hyperborean world or its opposite, the world of the future, as the setting for its inventive characters and plots.

The failure to understand the *fornaldarsǫgur* within their *actual* social and historical context, rather than that of the *projected* world just examined, has often led critics astray. Highly consistent with the view that the *fornaldarsǫgur* represent a literary fall from the thirteenth century is the recent suggestion that the "artless" quality of these sagas may derive from a scenario of the following sort: having sufficiently supplied its entertainment needs with manuscripts of the *íslendingasǫgur* and *konungasǫgur,* the aristocracy withdrew from saga production, leaving the creation and preservation of the *fornaldarsǫgur* to the lower classes.[64] There are several factors that argue against such an interpreta-

---

64. Buchholz 1980, chap. 3, sec. 2, esp. p. 52. Cf. Holtsmark's remark (1965, 14) that "what we call *fornaldarsögur* are properly heroic literature designed for a wider public."

tion, in particular the high cost of saga production (both in direct pecuniary terms and in terms of lost labor), the extent to which the clergy were engaged in producing and preserving *fornaldarsǫgur*, and the substantial role learned lore and foreign literary models played in the writing of these sagas. The proposition does, however, invite investigation as to the relationship these texts would have borne to the leading families of the thirteenth, fourteenth, and fifteenth centuries, especially in light of Jürg Glauser's suggestion that the indigenous romances were in fact a sponsored literature reflecting the values of their wealthy patrons.[65]

In 1937 Einar Ólafur Sveinsson carefully outlined the probable connection between *Skjǫldunga saga* and the Oddaverjar, who could claim direct descent from the Danish royal house; his view has been widely subscribed to.[66] Einar Ólafur argues carefully and sensibly that this prominent family had both the motivation and the means to promote and sponsor the writing of *Skjǫldunga saga*. It is not difficult to imagine that similar motivations and filiations lie behind other *fornaldarsǫgur* as well—that the descendants of Egill Skallagrímsson, for instance, would have had particular interest in *Ketils saga hœngs*, *Gríms saga loðinkinna*, *Áns saga bogsvegis*, and *Qrvar-Odds saga*—yet such an approach to the *fornaldarsǫgur* has never been well developed.[67] It has, however, been argued that *Hervarar saga ok Heiðreks* came about as the result of a specific (although much-delayed) attempt by the Swedish royal house to set its ancestry in the best possible light, a commission presumably given to the Icelanders by King Philippus.[68]

---

65. Glauser 1983, 219–33. Cf. the application of the same principle in Lönnroth 1976, 174–88. The social dimensions of saga writing have been much emphasized in recent years, especially by native Icelanders (e.g., Vésteinn Ólason, Sverrir Tómasson, Njörður Njarvik). The rise of a substantial middle class of well-to-do farmers (*stórbœndir*) in the thirteenth century challenged the traditional authority and power of the chieftains (*goðar*). It has been regularly suggested that many of the *íslendingasǫgur* represent the point of view of one group or the other in the conflict. For a review of the discussion, see Clover 1985, 267–68. The question of the function of legend in Germanic society has been underscored by Hauck 1963.

66. Einar Ólafur Sveinsson 1937. See Bjarni Guðnason 1963, 153–62, 254–91; 1982, lxx. It should be noted, however, that Bjarni is inclined to see *Skjǫldunga saga* as unique in this regard. Already Craigie (1913, 93–94) had noted the connections between *fornaldarsǫgur* and Icelandic genealogical tradition.

67. See, however, the list in Stefán Einarsson 1966, as well as Ciklamini 1975. Hollander 1913 makes a similar argument concerning the composition of *Hrólfs saga Gautrekssonar*. With regard to the descendants of Egill Skallagrímsson and their claims to a relationship with Ketill hœngr, see Bjarni Einarsson 1975, 66–72.

68. Pritsak 1981, 220–25.

Without necessarily ascribing to them responsibility for the production or preservation of particular sagas, I find it instructive in this regard to examine the case of a prominent Icelandic couple who lived exactly at the point when the writing down of *fornaldarsǫgur* must have been reaching its zenith, Haukr Erlendsson and his wife Steinunn Óladóttir.[69] In addition to sponsoring the compilation of *Hauksbók* (part of which he apparently wrote himself), Haukr was an active figure in Icelandic and Norwegian affairs in the late thirteenth and early fourteenth centuries. He was, for example, *lǫgmaðr* 'lawman' in Iceland in 1294–95, in Oslo in 1302, and for a long time in Gulating, and although much debate has been generated over the question of his residence, it appears that with the exception of the years 1306–8 and 1331–32, which he is known to have spent in Iceland, Haukr may have lived much of his later life in Norway.[70] Coming as both did from leading families, Haukr and Steinunn would have had direct family connections to such *fornaldarsǫgur* as *Ketils saga hœngs, Gautreks saga, Hálfs saga ok Hálfsrekka, Ragnars saga loðbrókar, Þáttr af Ragnars sonum, Vǫlsunga saga,* and **Skjǫldunga saga,* as well as more general associations with such figures of legendary history as Starkaðr inn gamli.

The ties between this couple and such texts were strong: both were, for example, direct descendants of the kings of Rogaland and Hǫrðaland who dominate *Hálfs saga*—Haukr from Hjǫrleifr and Hildr (the king's second and faithful wife) and Steinunn from Hjǫrleifr and Æsa (his first and treacherous wife). These lines of descent are specifically mentioned in the saga: *Sonur Híorleifs ok Æsu uar Oblǫðr fader Otrygs fader Haugna híns huíta faudur Ulfs híns skíalga er Reyknesíngar eru fra komner* 'The son of Hjǫrleifr and Æsa was Óblauðr, the father of Ótryggr, the father of Hǫgni the White, the father of Úlfr the Squinter from whom the Reyknesings are descended' (chap. 3); *Þorer a Espiholi uar son Hamundar þadan eru kom⟨n⟩er Espelíngar* 'Þórir of Espihóll was the son of Hámundr, from whom are descended the Espilings' (chap. 11). The connection with Hjǫrleifr would also have tied the couple to the story of King Víkarr, whose tragic fate is set in *Hálfs saga* and fulfilled in *Gautreks saga.* Similarly, both Haukr and Steinunn were direct descendants of Ketill Trout (*hœngr*) ór Hrafnistu and would therefore have enjoyed a special relationship to his saga, and presum-

69. Similar reasoning has led to Haukr's nomination as the author of several other sagas. See, for example, Berger 1980.

70. See the discussions in Eiríkur Jónsson and Finnur Jónsson 1892–96, i–v; Jón Helgason 1960, vi–vii, xx–xxii; and Jakob Benediktsson 1956–78a.

ably to those of his legendary progeny (*Gríms saga loðinkinna*, *Áns saga bogsvegis*, and *Qrvar-Odds saga*). Both Steinunn and Haukr could claim descent from Haraldr War-Tooth (*hilditǫnn*) and the Skjǫldung dynasty, and Haukr could also trace his family (through his maternal grandmother) to Ragnarr Hairy Breeks (*loðbrók*). Both Haukr's and Steinunn's families went back to Qlvir Children's Friend (*barnakarl*), whose history as an Icelandic pioneer was much intertwined with the story of Geirmundr Hell-Skin (*heljarskinn*), the twin brother of Hámundr, Haukr's ancestor, of *Hálfs saga ok Hálfsrekka*, *Sturlunga saga*, and *Landnámabók*.[71]

Above and beyond whatever pleasure the couple might have derived from the stories as entertainment, it is likely that such relations would have been a valuable political and social asset to Haukr and Steinunn in Norway and in Iceland. Certainly someone seems to have gone to some lengths to ventilate such an ancestry in *Hauksbók:* in chapter 175 of its *Landnámabók*, Haukr's family is specifically traced from Ragnarr loðbrók to Valgerðr *moðvr* herra *Erlenz sterka* 'the mother of Sir Erlendr the Strong,' Haukr's own father, a claim also made in the *Eiríks saga rauða* of *Hauksbók* (chaps. 7, 14). Significantly, this information is *not* contained in other versions of *Landnámabók*, a fact that strengthens the view that Haukr (or someone working on his behalf) was engaged here in a kind of personal promotion.

Similarly grand filiations to other royal and illustrious ancestors are outlined in *Landnámabók* (chaps. 326, 348) and *Eiríks saga rauða* (chap. 7) and in the genealogies at the conclusion of *Hauksbók*, in which Haukr's and Steinunn's lines are traced not merely back to Haraldr hilditǫnn, but also to a vast array of legendary heroes and kings.[72] Haukr's relationship to Ragnarr loðbrók comes through Bjǫrn járnsiða, Ragnarr's son with Aslaug, the daughter of Sigurðr Fáfnisbani and Brynhildr Buðladóttir. This union, in turn, ties Haukr to such kings as Haraldr hárfagri and Óláfr Tryggvason.

Thus according to the genealogical information of *Hauksbók*, Haukr would have been related to the Norwegian and the Danish royal houses, some of the greatest figures from the world of legendary heroes, and a significant portion of the outstanding *íslendingasǫgur* heroes, such as Egill Skallagrímsson and Víga-Glúmr. Such a lineage—especially for someone who may well have been a bastard—was un-

---

71. Cf. Tables X, XVIIa and XXXIIIb in the ÍF edition of *Landnámabók*.

72. The genealogies are from a paper manuscript, AM 115, 8o (ca. 1638), by Björn Jónsson of Skarðsá, but Finnur Jónsson (1892–96, vi) regards them as genuine excerpts from the original *Hauksbók*.

doubtedly of significant value in the political maneuverings of the Norwegian court, an activity at which Haukr showed no mean skill, to judge by his lengthy and successful career.[73]

Comparable, although perhaps less extensive, connections to other *fornaldarsǫgur* were probably common among other aristocratic families in Iceland. The impulse is not difficult to understand and may be discerned in the *ættartala* 'genealogy' of a work like *Íslendingabók* of Ari fróði, who traces his own lineage back through Ragnarr loðbrók, Freyr, and Njǫrðr to Yngvi Tyrkjakonungr. Indeed, one may even say that the same motivation lies behind the very concept of *Landnámabók*, as expressed in a late manuscript (*Þórðarbók*) of the *Melabók* tradition (although it may well go back to **Styrmisbók* or even Ari's original):

> Það er margra manna mál ad það sie uskilldur frodleikur ad rita land-
> nam. Enn uier þikiunst helldur suara kunna utlendum monnum. þa er
> þeir bregda oz þui, ad uier sieum komner af þrælum eda illmennum, ef
> vier vitum vijst vorar kynferdir sannar. Suo og þeim monnum er vita
> vilia fornn fræde eda redia ættartolur, ad taka helldur ad uphafi til enn
> högguast i mitt mal. enda eru suo allar vitrar þioder ad vita uilia uphaf
> sinna landzbygda eda huers huerge tilhefiast eda kynsloder. (*Melabók*,
> chap. 335)

> It is said by many people that writing about the settlement is improper
> learning, but we think we can better answer the criticism of foreigners
> when they accuse us of coming from slaves or rogues, if we know for
> certain the truth about our ancestry. For those who want to know an-
> cient lore or how to trace genealogies, it is better to start at the beginning
> than to come in at the middle. All wise people want to know the begin-
> nings of their own society and of their own kindred.

Such fears are frequently addressed in the *fornaldarsǫgur*, which provide their heroes' Icelandic progeny with an ancient, noble, and admired heritage—one might compare the Icelanders' zest for such lineages to the delight the average Euramerican takes in crests and other symbolic paraphernalia of the nobility in the country of his or her family's origin. Such claims to the reflected glory of heroic figures are documented outside of Iceland as well, as when the thirteenth-century *Fornsvenska legendariet* (p. 758) asserts that the founder of the Norman

---

73. See especially the details on Haukr's career in Finnur Jónsson's introductory comments (1892–96, i–vi). Literature in the service of political maneuvering has a lengthy history in Scandinavia. In addition to the possible function of the *íslendingasǫgur* in this regard, see the cases for similar activity in Norway in F. Ström 1981 and, in Denmark, in Skovgaard-Petersen 1985.

dynasty in France, Gǫngu-Hrólfr, was a Swede (*en swænskir herra*). The search for connectedness to the old, established world has an inherent and indefinable appeal, as well as a specific value in social and political terms, especially in a country that had only recently been integrated into the Norwegian kingdom. Whether or not Haukr and Steinunn actually sponsored the writing of *fornaldarsǫgur* (although one notes in passing that *Þáttr af Ragnars sonum* to which both have such ties is known only from *Hauksbók*), they undoubtedly benefited from them and were eager to trade on such connections, as the genealogical materials from *Hauksbók* indicate. It seems highly likely, as Stefán Einarsson suggests, that the preservation of these traditions was frequently connected to the leading families at Reykholt, Oddi, and Reykhólar, families with the resources and the motivation to undertake such a task.[74] This possibility is strengthened by evidence from the post-Reformation period which indicates that just such familial connections to certain saga heroes accounted for the texts' popularity.[75]

Attempts to explain the popularity the *fornaldarsǫgur* enjoyed in the postclassical saga world have, in general, stressed their entertainment value. This view is largely a reaction to the reverence the seventeenth and eighteenth centuries showed these sagas as the supposed bearers of history. In subsequent periods, the pendulum has swung to the opposite extreme, and scholars have almost universally abandoned this social and historical perspective on the *fornaldarsǫgur* in favor of the view that they are entertainment pure and simple, a sort of fantasy literature with which Icelanders of the thirteenth to fifteenth centuries, and presumably long before as well, could escape their cares.[76] Taken

74. Stefán Einarsson 1966. Although this article is no more than a list of the probable points of origin (or schools) of selected *fornaldarsǫgur* and *riddarasǫgur*, it is clear that Stefán has used genealogical connections as an important factor in sorting them out.

75. Jakob Benediktsson 1981, esp. 169–70. In an as-yet-unpublished study of marginalia in AM 152, fol., I have found that the same situation prevails. Not only is ownership directly related to genealogy (the manuscript evidently passed, for example, from Ari Jónsson [d. 1550] to his daughter Helga to her daughter Elín to her son Magnús to his daughter Helga to her daughter Elín to her son Vigfús), but "readership" likewise evinces kin group networks (cf. the signatures of three fathers-in-law whose children intermarried: Sigmundur Guðmundsson [40v, 104r], Magnús Jónsson [51r], and Einar Eiríksson [186v]).

76. Two cases in point: With specific reference to the *rímur*, but in the context of discussing the *fornaldarsǫgur, rímur,* and the decline of saga literature, Hallberg (1962, 145) states, "They seem to have served as a kind of asylum in which one could seek refuge, as a fantasy world in which one could forget the poverty and national isolation and humiliation which followed the fall of the Commonwealth. The feeling of impotence, the consciousness of no longer being able to cope with the problems of life, destroyed the appreciation and the acceptance of reality which are revealed in the great sagas." Beyer (1956, 56) comments that the *fornaldarsǫgur* "correspond to the wish of the people for pleasant, escapist entertainment." Cf. Kalinke 1985, 319.

as a partial explanation for the popular reception of the *fornaldarsǫgur,* such a reading has its merits—indeed the following discussion partially supports this view—but both the *fornaldarsǫgur* and medieval Icelandic society are ill served if we fail to probe the texts for a deeper level of meaning, for these narratives are as worthy of analysis as are other forms of folklore and literature. It is doubtful that any of the *fornaldarsǫgur* have a conscious "point" or moral, but the concerns they reflect, the themes they treat, and the world view they project can provide insights into the cultural and psychological dilemmas of their audiences.

The escapist interpretation of later Icelandic literature, or 'Verfall Theory' as it has come to be known, has paradoxically been overplayed and underexamined, for although it is indeed a meritorious interpretation of the cultural setting that gave rise to the popularity of the *fornaldarsǫgur,* no one has fully explored just what it means to say that this literature is escapist. It is worth noting as well that the tendency to regard the *fornaldarsǫgur* in strictly evolutionary terms—that is, as the result of decline in Icelandic culture and therefore a literature of diverting fantasy—implies a false scenario; after all, fourteenth-century Icelanders were as likely to have read eddic material and *konungasǫgur* or *íslendingasǫgur* as they were to have been entertained by *fornaldarsǫgur.* *Hauksbók* may be taken as the outstanding example of a fourteenth-century "gentleman's library," a *summa literarum* with selections from the corpus of eddic texts (*Vǫluspá*), historical literature (*Landnámabók*), *íslendingasǫgur* (*Fóstbrœðra saga*), translated pseudohistories (*Breta sǫgur*), religious writing (*Elucidarius*), and *fornaldarsǫgur* (*Heiðreks saga*). It is true that this encyclopedic manuscript is an exceptionally eclectic work, but the scope of its contents underscores the fact that although the *fornaldarsǫgur* may have been *one* of the genres that reached the zenith of their popularity in the postclassical saga period, they were not the only sort of literature Icelanders read at that time. It is, then, an erroneous dismissal of the less realistic sagas to suggest that they are merely the most obvious manifestation of decline in Icelandic letters. In reaction to the Verfall Theory, Jürg Glauser proposes a very different interpretation in the case of the *Märchensagas,* namely, that they are not escapist literature at all, but rather serve to promote a feudal ideology convivial to their late medieval sponsors.[77] His documentation of a significant wealthy class able and willing to underwrite the costs of producing such literature is a major advance in our understanding of the social context of the postclassical sagas. In addition to such specific

77. Glauser 1983, 229–33. Cf. Weber 1978, 490–92; 1981; 1986.

sponsorship, the popularity these works enjoyed must also be understood as a response to the historical setting in which they flourished.

Icelandic history in the later Middle Ages—the cultural milieu for
the great popularity of the *fornaldarsǫgur*—is generally regarded as a
period of decline and retrogression.[78] Following the years 1262–64,
which mark the formal domination of Iceland by the Norwegian
crown, a number of political, ecclesiastical, commercial, geological,
meteorological, and epidemiological developments alter the world
generally associated with Icelandic saga writing. Politically, the loss of
independence which marks the end of the commonwealth is followed
by a new law code (*Jónsbók*) that does away with the traditional chief-
tainships and replaces them with representatives of the Norwegian
king.[79] Yet the nation was only a minor player within the Norwegian
kingdom, and by mid-century (1349), the governorship of Iceland was
routinely sold to the highest bidder, who might then gain whatever
economic benefit he could above and beyond the state's own requirements, a system that invited abuse and led to severe taxation and
economic oppression. With the domination of Denmark over Norway-
Iceland (1380) came a concomitant increase in the Danish presence on
the island, although it has been argued that Norway continued to be
the primary foreign connection of the Icelanders until the sixteenth
century.[80] Changes within the Icelandic church were no less dramatic
and no less hostile to the inherited system:[81] the institution was
brought ever more into line with the dictates of Rome and away from
the traditional native organization during the 1300s. Thus, for example, celibacy (or at least a ban on marriage) for priests became the
official norm. With the division between secular and sacred authority,
which the previous religious order had tended to obscure, the church
was brought more and more into conflict with large and wealthy

78. In addition to Glauser 1983, 29–100, see Björn Þorsteinsson 1978, 183–348, and,
on the earlier period, Hastrup 1985, 158–77. Byock 1988 provides an excellent description of the internal political system during the commonwealth.

79. For an overview of political developments leading up to this event, see Gunnar
Karlsson 1974–78 and Björn Þorsteinsson 1978, 153–82. It should be noted that
Hastrup (1982) argues that the concept of the Icelanders as a nation and as a people
separate from the other Scandinavians was a fairly late (i.e., twelfth-century) development; the demise of the Freestate in the thirteenth century would therefore have been all
the more tragic for many of the Icelanders.

80. Vésteinn Ólason 1978c, 71–72.

81. Detailed accounts of the Icelandic church at this time are given in Jón Helgason
1925 and Magnús Stefánsson 1974; a summary of the primary changes is taken up in
Hood 1946. See also Byock's interesting and provocative comments (1985).

members of the Icelandic aristocracy. The result of such confrontations generally meant augmented landholdings by the church.

Trade too experienced a decline throughout the period: early in the post-Sturlung age commerce was dominated by Norwegian merchants, but with the catastrophe of the Black Death, which killed a third of the kingdom's population at mid-century, ships from Bergen and other Norwegian ports ceased to come to Iceland.[82] Danish vessels replaced them to some extent, but brisk trade does not seem to be the norm again until the early fifteenth century, when commercial ties to England—particularly the export of dried stockfish—become increasingly important.[83] These ties eventually slacken in favor of trade with German cities, Hamburg especially, despite the efforts of the Danish crown to parcel out the Icelandic economy to the merchants of other countries, Holland in particular.[84] Nor was Iceland granted favorable physical conditions in the fourteenth and fifteenth centuries: cycles of volcanic devastation, earthquakes, harsh weather, failed crops, and plague took their toll, although as has been pointed out, these catastrophic elements must always have been a part of Icelandic life.[85]

The domination of such disasters in the Icelandic annals of the fourteenth and early fifteenth centuries, however, is striking. It is only natural that these records should focus on dramatic and tragic events. Yet though this prejudice may compromise the annals' virtues as historical sources, it also underscores how medieval Icelanders themselves understood their situation and brings an immediacy and vitality to the question of Icelandic conditions in the late Middle Ages which no analysis or description can equal. A few selected entries from the annals of the early fourteenth (*Lǫgmannsannáll*) and fifteenth (*Nýi annáll*) centuries will suffice as examples:

1300 Elldz vpp kuama j Heklufelle med sua miklu afle at fiallit rifnade sua at siaz mun megha medal [!] Island er bygdt.

1308 Landskialfte fyrir sunnan land sua mich[ell ad o]fuan fellu .xviij. beiir.

---

82. See Gelsinger 1981.

83. See especially Björn Þorsteinsson 1970, esp. 23–57; 1956–78a.

84. The trade relations between the German cities and Iceland are reviewed in Björn Þorsteinsson 1957, 1956–78b. See also E. Ebel 1977.

85. The history of disease and famine in Iceland is thoroughly treated in the collected essays by Jón Steffensen (1975, 275–425). For a review of estimates on the population of medieval Iceland, see Ólafur Láruson 1936; on meterological deterioration, see the brief list in Wallen 1970.

1321   oaaran michit aa Jslande *ok* doo men*n* vida af sullte.
1323   Vet*r* allhardr.
1327   Skiplaust aa Isl*a*nde.

1300   An eruption at Hekla with so much power that the mountain split, as will be seen as long as Iceland is inhabited.
1308   An earthquake in the south, so great that eighteen farms were destroyed.
1321   A very bad season in Iceland, and men died far and wide from starvation.
1323   A very hard winter.
1327   No ships came to Iceland.

1420   Vet*ur* þen*n*a for mikel sott yf*ir* allar sveit*ir*.
1421   Deydi þen*n*a vet*ur* m*a*rgt hraust folk.
1424   Vet*ur* langur oc h*a*rdur fyrir uedrattv sak*ir*. fiskia*r* litid m*i*ckit man-*na* tion oc skipa.

1420   This winter a great illness went through every district.
1421   This winter many hearty folk died.
1424   A long and hard winter due to the weather. A poor year for fishing. A great loss of men and ships.

An appreciation for these severe conditions lies behind the standard explanation of late, nonrealistic Icelandic literature as mere escapism; such a tag is indeed a convenient and straightforward interpretation of the literary phenomenon supported by the history of the culture. It may also be considered the most ancient explanation for Icelandic literary activity, since its foundation was laid already in the twelfth century when Saxo commented in the preface to his *Gesta Danorum* that the Icelanders compensate for their neediness with their wit (*inopiam ingenio pensat*). Yet the mechanism by which the *fornaldarsǫgur* provided relief is worth examining in some detail, for when employed too glibly, the escapist explanation implies that relief derived solely from diversion during the actual moment of entertainment. In fact, "how traditional literature does what it does," to paraphrase Gertrude Stein's famous comment on English literature,[86] is more subtle and more effective than the fleeting amusement of the moment.

Examples are common among oppressed societies of folktales and other forms of folk literature which allow real problems to be ad-

86. "What does literature do and how does it do it. And what does English literature do and how does it do it. And what ways does it use to do what it does." Stein 1935, 14.

dressed fictionally in a way they are rarely treated in reality; tales of such dimensions provide a psychological buffer between the oppressed minority and the larger dominating society. An excellent example of this mechanism is found in the folklore of black America, where it is employed in the "John tales," many of which relate how the ex-slave outwits his former master. Similarly, this function is carried out by the figure of Sen'deh among the Kiowa Indians. A frequent hero of Kiowan tales who has been characterized by Elsie Clews Parsons as "our human prototype,"[87] Sen'deh can often be regarded as the Kiowan alter ego, especially in a tale like "Sen'deh Cheats the White Man," in which Sen'deh meets a "mule man." After many protests from Sen'deh that he has left his medicine at home and cannot possibly cheat the white man, the hero manages to persuade the gullible mule man to lend him his horse, hat, coat, blanket, and whip, one after another. The white man is completely fooled by Sen'deh and thereby loses his belongings according to their wager. In the history of Kiowan-Euramerican relations, events have inevitably taken the opposite course, one in which the Kiowa have lost political, economic, and geographical territory to whites;[88] in its own way, the tale provides an outlet for frustration and a forum for regaining some of history's lost ground.

In fact, such historical inversions are commonplace in cultures dominated by larger and mightier societies. Much the same pattern, for example, is reflected in the oral traditions concerned with the Benin Kingdom and its neighbors in western Africa.[89] In Welsh tradition, the idea of a revival and a coming of the *Mab Darogan* 'the prophesied son,' who would lead the Welsh to victory over the English, developed into an important aspect of epic literature. And not infrequently it was believed that this messianic figure would be one of the great heroes of the past.[90] A similar case of inversion, and one clearly closer to home,

87. Parsons 1929, xvi.
88. Following the failure of their alliance with other Southern Plains Indians in 1840 to hold back the encroachments of Euramericans, the Kiowa signed a treaty (whose ramifications they may not entirely have understood) which moved them to a reservation in 1868. Decreases in already insufficient game reserves and a lack of promised government supplies led to sporadic raids on the Indians' part, to which the government responded by attacking the Kiowas on the reservation. By 1875, the old nomadic Kiowa culture was essentially a thing of the past. Although the treaty had promised 2,968,893 acres for the Kiowas and their allies, in 1892 the U.S., in defiance of the tribes' wishes, allotted 160 acres to each person and opened the "surplus" land to white settlement. Collected in the 1920s, the Kiowa tales were thus easily within living memory of such abuses. On the Kiowa, see Debo 1970 and Newcomb 1961, 360–62.
89. See Okpewho 1987.
90. See the account in Gwyndaf 1987.

is that of the white (and gray) magicians who flourished in Icelandic folklore in the seventeenth and eighteenth centuries.[91] Their rise to folkloric prominence provides a fascinating model of the function the *fornaldarsǫgur* probably had in post-Sturlung Iceland which accounts for their great popularity in that period. Stories parallel to "Sen'deh Cheats the White Man" are to be met in the legendary careers of the Icelandic magicians Halla, Eiríkur, and Dísa, all of whom cheat the hated Danish merchants in such a way that the oppressors end up, like the mule man, looking quite foolish, while the protagonists come away with victory and honor, as well as the material goods. Typical of such stories is one in which Halla goes to trade with the foreign merchants, who only later discover that the major transactions of sheep, butter, and tallow she has conducted with them have, thanks to her power of illusion, in reality yielded nothing more than mice and stones; it is a choice example of folklore's capacity for allowing the situations and relationships that obtain in reality to be refashioned and inverted within the fictional framework.

Although such interpretations are appropriate to later Icelandic folklore and fit neatly with the prevailing cultural-historical context, a difficulty immediately arises when we try to apply to the *fornaldarsǫgur* the same "esoteric-exoteric" factor,[92] namely, the fact that the important distinction between Icelander and non-Icelander is not made in the *fornaldarsǫgur*.[93] This circumstance is due in part, of course, to the attempt at historical verisimilitude, but other factors may also play a role. One aspect of the *fornaldarsǫgur* which led to their exceptional popularity in the later Middle Ages was their connectedness to the Viking age, the "great" period of Scandinavian history, with for the most part *Norwegian, Danish,* and *Swedish* pirates and adventurers freely looting much of Europe, establishing kingdoms right and left, and the most accomplished of men marrying the most skilled and beautiful of women—or at least so the era is often interpreted in the popular imagination, then as now.

The antiquarian interest in the indigenous heroic tradition displayed in the *fornaldarsǫgur* might then appropriately be termed folklorism and

---

91. The figure of the Icelandic magician is surveyed in B. S. Benedikz 1964–65.
92. Cf. Jansen 1959.
93. Iceland figures very little in the *fornaldarsǫgur*, except for the various genealogical connections that tie specific sagas to Icelandic families (e.g., the Skjǫldung material and the Oddaverjar). On the question of "us" versus "them" as a typical component of folk literature, see Eleazar Meletinsky et al. 1974, 94; with respect to the appearance of the same theme in Old Norse, see Mitchell 1983.

cultural revitalization.[94] One of the hallmarks of these sagas is the more or less deliberate exploitation of Nordic cultural heritage, from which traditional characters, events, and plots are appropriated; of particular interest are those stories concerning pagan gods, whose relevance to then-current religious life must have been nearly nil. In many of the most famous revitalization movements (for example, the Ghost Dance of the Plains Indians, the Vailala Madness) there is an explicit renunciation of alien values and a call for a return to traditional ways, so-called nativism. Nothing along these lines seems to have been the case in Iceland, where an actual reversion to older ways and beliefs would not have distinguished Iceland from the "offending" societies, Norway and Denmark. Compounding the odd state of affairs in Iceland, one of the single most obvious representatives of non-native culture, the church, appears not only to have tolerated the *fornaldarsǫgur*, but even to have fostered them, insofar as many of them were no doubt written by clerics and demonstrably formed part of church libraries.[95] It would be wrong to think of the popularity of the *fornaldarsǫgur* in the thirteenth through fifteenth centuries as a revitalization *movement*, which has been defined as "a *deliberate, organized, conscious* effort by members of a society to construct a more satisfying culture."[96] An organized effort was certainly not under way, but Icelandic conditions display important elements of the processual stages usually attached to such movements, including an origin in the increase of psychological and physical stress.

In classic movements of this sort, a prophetic figure usually emerges to formulate and organize a drive to better the existing culture and to

94. On these topics, see, for example, Wallace 1956, 1968; Moser 1962; Lord 1976; and Köstlin 1982. An essay with interesting points of contact is Hobsbawm 1982. In the Nordic context, see Velure 1977, Bringéus 1982, Salmonsson 1984, as well as Hastrup 1982.

95. There is evidence for the monastic settings some sagas claim for themselves, at least to the extent that *fornaldarsǫgur* formed part of church libraries. An inventory from Mǫðruvellir (1461) claims the following *fornaldarsǫgur* among its possessions: *hrolfs saga kraka*, *skioldungha saga*, *volsaunga saga*, and *hrolfs saga gautrekssonar* (*Diplomatarium Islandica*, V, 290).

96. Wallace 1956, 265 (emphasis added). Recent writers have, however, been less strict in their application of the term. For example, Salmonsson (1984, 34) defines revitalization as "the resumption of abandoned, older cultural traits or the retention of such cultural features without any visible, material reason" and continues, "Some scholars mean that there has to be a revitalization of some cultural traits before a folklorism situation will arise; that the term folklorism mostly would represent the cultural situation short[ly] after a revitalization. Other scholars use the two terms more or less synonymously. In my opinion the disorder has gone so far that there is no more reason to separate them."

develop a code of behavior or belief which specifically addresses the ills of the society and the ways in which a return to, or renewal of, the departed culture would improve the lot of the people. In Iceland, the relative deprivation of the postclassical period led only to the wide-spread, but unorganized, popularity of tales extolling the virtues of primarily pre-Christian heroes, whose progeny more often than not had settled in Iceland. A sense of the delight these audiences took in such materials and of the role the *fornaldarsǫgur* played in this regard may be garnered from the fact that the ancient pagan gods actually *increase,* rather than diminish, in appearances in the *fornaldarsǫgur.* Thus, the extensive role played by Rauðgrani (Óðinn in disguise) in *Qrvar-Odds saga* exists only in the late paper manuscripts—the oldest texts simply have nothing corresponding to it. A parallel example may be the treatment of the so-called blood-eagle during the Middle Ages. The idea seems to have begun as a fairly straightforward "beasts of battle" image but became, in one scholar's words, "more lurid, pagan and time-consuming with each passing century [. . . .] Medieval men of letters, like their modern counterparts, were sometimes overeager to recover the colorful rites and leafy folk beliefs of their pagan an-cestors."[97] And therein lies the story, for the Icelanders of the late Middle Ages were also looking backward, albeit at not so great a distance as we do today, at a Scandinavian "Golden Age" in which they could take much pride and in which they could, perhaps, place their hope of a better future society.

Much has been made in recent years of the Germanic heroic tradition as a source of inspiration for different periods of modern Scandinavian literary history. Thus, for example, Jöran Mjöberg, John Greenway, and others have commented extensively on the influence of early Scan-dinavian materials on later Nordic literary consciousness.[98] Although these developments were particularly prominent in Norway, Den-mark, and Sweden, cultural appropriation and exploitation of just this type also occurred in the Icelandic nineteenth century.[99] For that mat-ter, something of the same sort took place earlier in this century.[100] It is not difficult to envision a scenario in which the same process took place six and seven hundred, as well as a mere one hundred, years ago. Just as

97. R. Frank 1985, 170–72. Lukman (1976, 7) likewise maintains that "medieval Scandinavia formed its own picture of the Viking Age." Cf. Strömbäck (1963a, 22–23), who recounts some of the closeness of the pagan world to the thirteenth century.

98. Mjöberg 1967–68; Greenway 1977. See also the essays in *Medieval Legacy,* ed. Haarder et al.

99. Cf. Hallfreður Örn Eiríksson 1980.

100. Cf. the Introduction above.

the Swedish intellectual establishment exploited the nation's "Gothic past" during the age of the Empire, so too did Icelandic saga writers of the later periods take advantage of the grand Germanic legendary traditions in putting together their texts, although the motivations could not have been more dissimilar; for the Swedes, such a move provided an opportunity to explain and legitimize their rapid rise to power in the seventeenth century; for the Icelanders, it provided an opportunity to intertwine the miserable fate of the Icelandic fourteenth and fifteenth centuries with the glorious Nordic past.[101]

It has been suggested with regard to economically deprived areas that folklorism functions as a compensatory factor for these conditions;[102] it seems probable that something very much along these lines happened in the Icelandic Middle Ages. In opposition to the grim realism so characteristic of the *íslendingasǫgur* and much of *Sturlunga saga,* and especially to the actual tormented world reflected in the chronicles, the later *fornaldarsǫgur* brought their audiences a measure of relief—psychological and emotional on a national scale, not merely momentarily diverting—and instead of the past as it was, told them of a past as it might have been, of that Teutonic "Golden Age" that has haunted northern Europe since Tacitus's *Germania.* Just as it has been suggested that in our modern world science fiction presents a justification for the future, so in traditional societies such a function resided in heroic myth: in the vision of the past lay also a vision of the future and a justification for the present.

The Value of Tradition

The role of the *fornaldarsǫgur* in medieval Icelandic society as entertainment and therapy is then hardly the facile escapism that has been suggested time after time, that is, a literature interesting only as the diminished, exhausted remnant of a once great heroic tradition with broader Germanic affinities. That the *fornaldarsǫgur* amused their listening audiences is beyond dispute, but that fact does not mean they were impervious to literary refinement once they entered the realm of written literature, nor does the fantastic element by which they are partially

101. This observation clearly holds best for the *fornaldarsǫgur* that had independent existence (that is, were separate from *konungasǫgur*) and include genealogies that lead to Icelandic families; it is less relevant to such works as *Norna-Gests þáttr* and *Tóka þáttr Tókasonar.*
102. Korff 1980.

defined mean that they did not fulfill a significant and meaningful role in later Icelandic society. Their historical setting may be the Viking age, but the focal point for the interpretation of their popularity must surely be the Icelandic Middle Ages.

Just what sort of joy and wonder these sagas and their traditions must have engendered among Icelanders, as well as the extent of their popularity, may be gauged from *Nýi Annáll*.[103] In the entry for 1405, Árni Ólafsson is said to have seen a variety of religious relics in "Affrica," including, for example, articles of clothing associated with the Virgin Mary and John the Baptist. But pride of place is reserved for what are treated as even more impressive relics: *hiallted af sverdi Sigurdar Fofnes bana* 'the boss [or guard] from Sigurðr Fáfnisbani's sword' and—as another hand has added—*taunn er sogd var ur Starkadi gamla* 'a tooth that was said to have been from Starkaðr the Old.' In contrast to the religious relics, which are merely mentioned in passing, each of the heroic items is described in detail.[104] It is highly unlikely that the scribes who added these touches to the annals believed in the existence of such items, but their placement on a par with the relics of John the Baptist and the Virgin Mary certainly underscores the important place the *fornaldarsǫgur* must have held in Icelandic consciousness.

103. Although the manuscript is dated ca. 1550, it is generally agreed to be a direct copy of the original manuscript. See Storm 1888, xxii–xxiii, as well as the entry in *Katalog over Den arnamagnæanske Håndskriftsamling*.

104. It should be noted that a number of circumstantial details tend to tie the *fornaldarsǫgur* to the church: some are specifically said to have been held in church libraries; Abbot Nikulás goes out of his way to include references to heroic legends in his pilgrim's guide; and the citation quoted here likewise ties religious relics to heroic tradition. In a personal communication, Lars Lönnroth has suggested that the role of the church in the production and promotion of the *fornaldarsǫgur* for the "pilgrim trade" deserves further scrutiny.

CHAPTER 4

The Legacy Renewed

Perhaps the most astonishing feature of the Nordic heroic legacy is its longevity. Whatever the exact form the narratives take, they constitute a literary continuum spanning much of the history of Scandinavia itself, from the Dark Ages up to and including the modern period, during which ballads and *rímur* (sg. *ríma* 'Icelandic metrical romance') connected with the *fornaldarsǫgur* and their traditions have continued to be actively sung and composed. Both ballads and *rímur* emerge as new literary forms in the later Middle Ages, and this fact has given rise to the view that a sort of literary speciation took place, according to which *fornaldarsǫgur* themselves necessarily evolved or were consciously recast as *rímur* and ballads. But the relationship between the *fornaldarsǫgur* and the versified texts cannot be characterized by transmutation in a single direction only; indeed a surprising degree of movement between the genres has occurred, a symbiosis exemplified by the fact that a now lost **Hrómundar saga Gripssonar* formed the basis for a *rímur*, a text which in turn gave rise to the extant *Hrómundar saga Gripssonar*.[1] In fact, some of what we generally regard as *fornaldarsǫgur* are simply prose reworkings of *rímur*.

Rather than thinking of translations and transfers from one genre to another as the only means by which these tales were interconnected, however, we should envision texts coming about by several means. In some cases, a substantial pool of traditional legendary material was directly and independently transmuted into *fornaldarsǫgur*, ballads, and

1. See the discussion and bibliography surrounding the saga's relationship to the other genres in Jesch 1984. See also Weber's rejection (1986, 419–20) of linear developments in Old Norse literature.

rímur. In others, a preexisting *text* (not simply a tradition, but an actual work of literature), typically a *fornaldarsaga,* provided the direct source materials for another type of work, usually a ballad or one of the *rímur*. The difference between the story in general (its characters and events lacking specific literary form, that is, what members of a traditional community already know before hearing or reading a given multiform) and its individual manifestations over time as prose and poetic texts (i.e., between discourse and monument) is thus not an idle distinction. Moreover, the popularity of these new genres did not bring about the demise of the prose *fornaldarsǫgur*—they continued to be written and copied and circulated side by side with the *rímur* for centuries in Iceland. Indeed, the impact of the new literary modes seems to have been, if anything, to reinvigorate the traditions associated with the *fornaldarsǫgur*.

With the understandable desire of scholarship to distinguish neat diachronic developments, we naturally welcome the sense that the ballads and *rímur* evolved from preexisting literary forms. But the relationship of these versified traditions of the *fornaldarsǫgur* materials to the medieval *fornaldarsǫgur* little resembles the inverted branching tree to which manuscript stemmata accustom us; the filiation is instead like a complex net of interrelationships based on both direct and indirect influences. In paleontological and anthropological circles of the 1950s, debate frequently concerned whether the course of human evolution should be described in terms of "trees" or "nets" or some combination thereof.[2] That question parallels the situation of the *fornaldarsǫgur* and their related texts—how are the various treatments of the same heroic materials in different literary contexts connected? The resolution of this issue vis-à-vis the *fornaldarsǫgur* may well be thought of in terms of what Lars Lönnroth calls "saga communications."[3] The sort of model that would account for the relationship between the *fornaldarsǫgur,* ballads, and *rímur* is then the subject of this chapter, as is the issue of what these later uses of the traditions of the *fornaldarsǫgur* can tell us about the medieval texts and about the Nordic heroic legacy more generally.

Establishing the relationship between the various genres is a highly complex undertaking, due in no small way to the fact that both oral and written versions of the texts have influenced subsequent multiforms. Where we have been fortunate enough in the modern period to

2. In the technical terminology of the biological sciences, the discussion revolved around the question of divergent versus divergent plus reticulate patterns of phylogenetic descent. Cf. Wiley 1981, 37.
3. Lönnroth 1980.

observe the processes at work, good evidence abounds of oral traditional composition—or at least of verbal ballads in David Buchan's sense[4]—as well as of written composition in the most literal sense. Examples of the former include many of the heroic ballads of the Faroe Islands and of the latter, such modern *rímur* as those of *Áns saga bogsveigis* whose nineteenth-century authors are well known.[5] But what of the medieval period itself? The circumstantial evidence certainly lends credence to the possibility of direct manuscript inspiration of the versified versions—or reflexes—of the *fornaldarsǫgur*,[6] yet the histories that connect the various texts are exceedingly complex, and it is likely that oral variants too were important factors in the treatment of the legendary materials. Thus before turning to the difficult question of the general relationship between the genres, I review the histories of the ballad and *rímur* in Scandinavia and examine their connectedness to selected individual *fornaldarsǫgur*.

Scandinavian Balladry

Few issues have so dogged the study of medieval Scandinavian literature as has the enigmatic question of when the ballad entered the Nordic cultural region.[7] Although much discussed, the topic is as impervious to solution now as it has been since the mid-nineteenth century, when it was brought to prominence by Svend Grundtvig who argued for a very early date of introduction, the twelfth century.[8] A

4. Buchan (1972, 2) equates "oral" with the narrative traditions of preliterate peoples and "verbal" with "the word-of-mouth tradition of a literate culture."

5. Cf. "*Áns rímur bogsveigis*," ed. Hughes. Older *rímur* versions of *Áns saga bogsveigis*, probably dating from the fifteenth century, are discussed and presented in *Áns rímur bogsveigis*, ed. Ólafur Halldórsson.

6. This material is extensively reviewed in Einar Ólafur Sveinsson 1956b.

7. The Scandinavian medieval ballad is characterized by B. R. Jonsson (1967, 855) as "a *genre* of orally transmitted song that is defined by its form (two-lined stanza with one or two burdens, four-lined stanzas with one burden), its narrative content and its objective style, the latter characterized not least by the frequent use of formulaic expressions and so-called commonplaces."

8. Grundtvig argues in *DgF* III, xiii–xiv (vol. III is devoted to historical ballads) in favor of an early date for the arrival of the ballad in Scandinavia—the twelfth century. It was Grundtvig's view that the ballad had existed everywhere in Scandinavia and through time had, due to literary preferences and historical peculiarities, come to be identified with particular living traditions. As he puts it with regard to the Germanic world more generally in a letter (dated August 25, 1877) to Francis Child, "Now there is no doubt that the ballad poetry of the Gothic nations is upon the whole contemporary and of a homogeneous character both with regard to its contents, treatment, style of poetry and form of verse, but nevertheless each department has its own peculiarities and

number of other scholars (for example, Axel Olrik, Knut Liestøl, Sverker Ek) have likewise attempted to place the beginnings of the Scandinavian ballad relatively early, by the thirteenth century at any rate, although few have been inclined to place it as early as had Grundtvig.[9] The references most often cited in favor of the existence of a ballad form in Iceland at an early period are the two apparent dance stanzas from the thirteenth-century *Sturlunga saga: Loptr er i eyiom, / bitr lvnda bein, / Sæmunðr er aa heiðvm / ok etr berin ein* 'Loftr is in the islands gnawing puffin bones, Sæmundr is on the heath and eats berries alone' (I, 348), one of many *dansa* 'dance-verses' with which Loftr was lampooned; and *Mínar eru sorgir þungar sem blý* 'My sorrows are heavy, as heavy as lead' (II, 316). Moreover, Gunnlaugr's *Jóns saga helga* (chap. 24) reports on a kind of antiphonal verse exchange between men and women which was so scurrilous that the bishop forbade it. These data need not, however, be read as confirmation that the *narrative* ballad was an established genre in Scandinavia at such an early date. Indeed, a number of scholars have concluded that such a form was introduced later. Vésteinn Ólason, for example, after a conservative review of the evidence, contends that there is no *proof* that the narrative ballad—as

---

also there is a great difference between the Scandinavian and the Anglo-Scottish, for instance, with regard to what parts of the whole body, the entire ballad stock, have been preserved and further developed in the different literatures." Quoted in Hustvedt 1930, 276. Grundtvig sets this principle out in *DgF* I, x–xi, where he maintains not only that the ballad is an ancient Scandinavian form, but also that the songs from which the ballads were fashioned prefigure and form the basis for the eddic lays. See also his comments in a polemical review article (1866, esp. 547) on N. M. Petersen's *Bidrag til den oldnordiske Litteraturs Historie* and R. Keyser's *Nordmændens Videnskablighed og Literatur i Middelalderen*.

9. Reviews of the development of the various opinions are treated in Dal 1956, 227–40, and, as the debate relates to Iceland, in Vésteinn Ólason 1982, 83–103. One of the few twentieth-century researchers to follow Grundtvig in his early dating of the Scandinavian ballad is Ek (1921, 7), who accepts that a type of "ballad" existed already in Denmark in the 1100s, although Ek has in mind the single-stanza dance verses such as those taken up in Steffen 1898. As regards the heroic ballad, Ek (1921, 69) suggests for the East Norse region an entry from the western Scandinavian area ca. 1400. Metzner (1972), however, concludes that the Kölbigk verse demonstrates the ballad form in northern Germany already by the early eleventh century. The question of dating the ballad thus seems far from over. It was something of an article of faith to assume the widespread existence of the ballad in northern Europe by the thirteenth century; thus, for instance, Krenn (1940, 23–24), without adducing any evidence (of which for the Faroes there can be none before the seventeenth century), states with confidence that the ballad ("Lieder [. . .] mit dem Tanze") had established itself in the Faroes by the 1200s. On the earliest *datable* evidence of Faroese ballad texts, see Jón Helgason 1924a and the reviews in Thuren 1908, 14–18, and Grüner-Nielsen 1945, 13–16. B. R. Jonsson (1989) has taken up the question of the oldest historical topics in Swedish balladry.

opposed to verses of the sort illustrated in *Sturlunga saga*—existed in Iceland before 1450.[10]

It is true that there is remarkably little by way of actual medieval evidence of the ballad in Scandinavia, and no complete medieval ballads,[11] but research into the language of the ballads by Peter Skautrup, Johannes Brøndum-Nielsen, Elias Wessén, Valter Jansson, and others demonstrates that the ballads contain linguistic forms that must be dated to the medieval period and, further, that the ballads and their special idiom had a perceptible influence on other documents of medieval literature.[12] Exactly when narrative ballads, as opposed to dance and lyrical verses, were sung in Scandinavia will remain a mystery, yet there seems little reason to doubt that the genre existed there on a fairly large scale by the fourteenth century and perhaps earlier still. It is useful in this context to recall, as Bengt R. Jonsson points out, that certain features associated with the ballad, such as end rhyme, were anticipated in Nordic literature outside the genre by several centuries.[13]

It is, then, quite probable that the ballad *form* existed in Scandinavia, including Iceland, at a time contemporary with the period in which the

10. Togeby (1961–70, II, 300; 1971–74) has expressed the view, for instance, that the Scandinavian ballad is no older than the beginning of the fifteenth century, having in his opinion come to the north in 1406 with the retinue of the English princess Philippa who was to be married to Erik of Pomerania. Togeby's suggestion has been specifically rejected by B. R. Jonsson (1978). Arguing for an even more recent date, Sønderholm (1978) maintains that the Nordic ballad is an essentially post-Reformation phenomenon. Using an entirely different course of reasoning (i.e., the lack of verifiable evidence), Vésteinn Ólason has in a series of publications (1978a; 1978c; 1982, esp. 109) maintained that we cannot *demonstrate* ballads in Iceland before mid-fifteenth century. As he comments (1978c, 74), "There is no evidence that enables us to trace the Icelandic ballad farther than, at best, 1450. On the other hand, however, there is nothing that positively excludes a longer prehistory for the Icelandic ballad." Cf. the view expressed simultaneously by Schück (1891, 290) and Steenstrup (1891, 129) that the philological "rule of thumb" must be to assume no date older than the first preserved version of a text, unless it can be specifically established by other means.

11. A convenient review of the Danish materials is given in Dal's popular *Danske viser*, pp. 243–45, 288–91. See also Steenstrup 1918. On the early evidence for the Swedish ballad, see the discussions and bibliographies in Hildeman 1958a, 1958b.

12. Linguistic approaches have been an especially interesting, if sometimes controversial, means of dating the ballad in Scandinavia, particularly in the East Scandinavian cultural region. The Danish ballads have been examined in Brøndum-Nielsen 1910 and Skautrup 1944–70, II, 73–80. Wessén (1928) concludes that the ballad idiom was to some extent fixed already by the 1200s. Traces of Swedish balladry have been found in the early fourteenth-century *Eufemiavisor*, on which see Frandsen 1935, Sawicki 1939, and Jansson 1945, but cf. Hildeman 1958b, 161. Finnur Jónsson's view (1914) that the Icelandic *fornkvæði* retain Old Icelandic syllabic quantity and are therefore relatively old has been specifically rejected by Einar Ólafur Sveinsson (1960) and Vésteinn Ólason (1982, 100–103).

13. B. R. Jonsson 1978, 13–14.

fornaldarsǫgur flourished. It was formerly believed that the "oldest" Nordic materials—those associated with the *Eddas* and ancient Germanic heroes—should have been converted rather quickly into items of this new genre, the so-called heroic ballads (*kæmpeviser*), with the other ballad groups (for example, the more romantic ballads of chivalry) following thereafter.[14] Against this model, which was particularly favored by Grundtvig, there has emerged during the past century or so a different view according to which Scandinavia consists of two separate ballad areas. These regions mirror the linguistic division of northern Europe into an East Norse zone (Denmark and Sweden) and a West Norse zone (Norway, the Faroes, and Iceland).[15] Not only do these two areas differ with regard to the history of the introduction of the ballad, which was held to have come at an earlier point in the east, but also as concerns fundamental characteristics of the ballad (*folkevise, kvæði*). The East Norse area is typified by the courtly chivalric ballads, usually treated mono-episodically, whereas the western region, the Faroes in particular, displays a tendency toward lengthier ballads concerned with indigenous heroic themes and often demonstrating a marked fondness for alliteration. Insofar as the heroic ballads are encountered in the East Norse corpus, they are generally derived from the west.[16]

This perspective on the overall development of the Nordic ballad has won general acceptance. The question of which *country* acted as the epicenter for the *kæmpeviser* within the West Norse area has been somewhat less easily answered, however. For Liestøl there is little doubt that these ballads hark back to Norwegian *fornaldarsǫgur;* these traditions would then have spread east and south to Sweden and Denmark, and west to Iceland and the Faroe Islands.[17] The heroic ballads are pre-

14. Cf. the organization of *DgF,* whose volumes, arranged as heroic ballads, magical ballads, chivalric ballads, and so on, are intended to reflect the chronological development of the genre. See also Grundtvig's remarks in *DgF* I, v–vi, and in his "Plan til en ny Udgave af Danmarks gamle Folkeviser" (1847).

15. In many respects, the first statement to this effect came in Olrik 1898, the author's response to Steenstrup's unfavorable review of his study of Saxo's sources. Olrik (1898, 83–84) enumerates the West Norse characteristics of certain East Scandinavian ballads and thereby sets the stage for the subsequent discussion of the West-East Norse ballad regions in von der Recke 1907; Liestøl 1915b, 1921, 1936; Ek 1921; and Solheim 1970. A review of some of the East and West Norse ballad characteristics is provided in Vésteinn Ólason 1982, 79.

16. See, for example, Mitchell 1985a.

17. "Such ballads as *Hjálmar og Angantýr, Álvur kongur* and *Brúsajøkils kvæði,* which are common to the Faroes and Sweden or Denmark, must, as discussed above, be of Norwegian origin. From Norway they have migrated to the east and west." Liestøl 1915b, 229. Liestøl elsewhere (1915a) accords this prominent position to Norway and argues for the key role of Norway in the transfer of ballads between Denmark and Iceland.

served in especially rich numbers in the Faroe Islands, and Liestøl regarded the *fornaldarsǫgur* that inspired these ballads as having come to the Faroes by way of Iceland, often in manuscript form, but having derived ultimately from oral Norwegian sagas.[18] It was the great achievement of Liestøl's early work, especially his dissertation from 1915, to argue for the existence of a Norwegian *fornaldarsaga* tradition and to demonstrate the dependence of many of the ballads on Norse sagas, especially the *fornaldarsǫgur*. Among the evidence he marshals in favor of the origin of these heroic ballads on the West Scandinavian mainland are the style and attitude of the ballads which he judges to be especially Norwegian.[19] The relationship of the Norwegian ballads to the *fornaldarsǫgur* is a case he strengthens in his posthumously published *Den norrøne arven* 'The Old Norse Heritage.'[20] Still incomplete at the time of his death in 1952, this survey was intended as the introductory matter to a planned scientific edition of the Norwegian ballads; in it Liestøl sets out point by point the indebtedness of specific heroic ballads from the Faroese and other Nordic traditions to *written* sagas and eddic poetry. He carefully builds the individual cases for such a relationship, but nowhere in the work does he provide a general statement of the ballads' indebtedness to the written Icelandic sagas.[21]

In a sense, this work, only published eighteen years after its author's death, is supplemented by Einar Ólafur Sveinsson's important article on West Norse cultural contacts and the ballad, apparently written without knowledge of Liestøl's manuscript.[22] Einar Ólafur enumerates the following points as evidence for his belief that the transmission of the *kæmpeviser* was based on a series of *essentially* written, but in all events Icelandic, contacts: (1) Icelandic scribes often carried out their

18. Liestøl 1915b, 239: "If there existed in Norway a rich tradition with *fornaldarsǫgur* topics, then it is not impossible that the saga form which lies behind the [Faroese] ballads could have come in a manuscript from Iceland." It is clear, however, that Liestøl prefers to believe first and foremost in *munnlærde sogor* 'oral sagas' from Norway. Grüner-Nielsen (1945, 18) summarizes the view at mid-century by stating, "After saga-influenced ballad composition [from Norway] had established itself on the Faroes, presumably in the fourteenth century, it developed independently on the islands under the continuous fresh influence of written Icelandic sagas."

19. Cf. Liestøl 1931.

20. Cf. ibid., pp. 234–35, for example, as well as Liestøl 1970. On the history of this work, see Blom 1982, 18. Many of Liestøl's comments were anticipated in print in the overview provided in Koch 1964–65.

21. Although Liestøl's research on the Old Icelandic sagas tends to identify him with the free-prosists, he by no means limits himself to a monolithic view of the means of communication. He argues, for example, for the composition of the Faroese ballad directly from a manuscript of *Þorsteins þáttr uxafóts*, one of the *þættir* of *Óláfs saga Tryggvasonar* (1916), while his discussion of the Norwegian ballad *Steinfinn Fefinnson* (1915b, 60–91) assumes an oral basis for the dissemination of the material.

22. Einar Ólafur Sveinsson 1956b.

work in Norway, (2) contemporary sources refer to extensive communication links (or possibilities thereof) between Iceland and the Faroes, (3) later Faroese sources refer to written texts from Iceland, and (4) many of the Faroese ballads derive from extant Icelandic texts. Einar Ólafur makes no exclusive claim to literate transmission in the sense of a scribe having a manuscript in front of him; at several junctures he suggests the possibility of ballad composers recreating texts that they had earlier heard read aloud, a situation paralleled—and documented—in living traditional communities.[23] In general, however, he inclines toward the view that written Icelandic sagas have been the *ultimate* source of the individual ballads.

Several views of the dissemination of the *kæmpeviser* have thus developed through the twentieth century. Liestøl's 1915 model was one in which Swedish and Danish heroic ballads derived from a Norwegian "heartland," the region that also gave rise to the oral sagas fundamental to the Icelandic texts. These Icelandic texts, together with further direct impulses from Norway, would then lie behind the Faroese ballads.[24] In his work from the early 1950s, which deals nearly exclusively with the heroic ballads, Liestøl seems to have altered this view somewhat. In it he acknowledges the possibility that Norway, while still the ultimate point of origin for the Icelandic texts, might have received secondary influences from the Faroes. Einar Ólafur Sveinsson's analysis from 1956 is not unlike Liesøl's later model, save only that Einar Ólafur accords primacy to Iceland and suggests a two-pronged route to Norway for these Icelandic materials: the one direct by way of Icelandic scribes working in Norway (as well as other undiluted cultural contacts between the two countries); the other, through the Faroes.

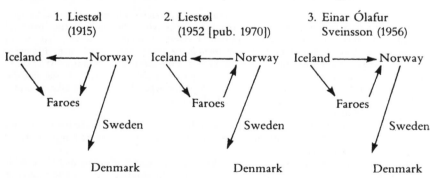

| 1. Liestøl (1915) | 2. Liestøl (1952 [pub. 1970]) | 3. Einar Ólafur Sveinsson (1956) |

23. Cf. ibid., p. 64. On the relationship between a modern illiterate singer of epics and written texts read aloud to him, see Lord 1974, 24–27.
24. Liestøl 1915b, 229. See also Ek 1921.

Whatever the *means* of survival and diffusion then, the fundamental picture that thus emerges from these studies substantiates the West Norse origins of the heroic ballads and the key role the Icelandic *fornaldarsǫgur* and their materials played in the formation of them. As to the specific point of origin of the heroic ballads, preparation of *The Types of the Scandinavian Medieval Ballad* occasioned statistical validation of the importance—and probable originality—of the Faroese tradition in the history of the Nordic *kœmpevise*. According to Svante Solheim, twenty-seven types of the heroic ballad exist among the Norwegian ballad corpus, yet there are 115 types among the Faroese texts. He concludes from this fact that the Faroese tradition, as the most productive not only in terms of length of texts or numbers of variants, but also of types, was more likely to have been the generative center for many of the *kœmpeviser*. The prevailing view today, much like the one presented by von der Recke in 1907, with the Faroes and Denmark as the respective centers of the West and East Norse ballad traditions, has been challenged by Bengt Jonsson, who believes Norway to have been the balladic epicenter.[25]

Study of the items in the Nordic ballad repertoire with analogues among the *fornaldarsǫgur*—numerous with regard to the *Sjúrðar kvæði*, those ballads relating to Sigurðr and *Vǫlsunga saga*,[26] yet rather scarce elsewhere—yields fascinating, if occasionally surprising, results. Among the *kvæði* collected in the eighteenth and nineteenth centuries from Faroes oral tradition are, for example, such pieces as *Sniolvs kvæði*, *Ragnarskvæði*, *Gátu ríma*, and *Álvur kongur* (corresponding to parts of *Ásmundar saga kappabana*, *Ragnars saga loðbrókar*, *Heiðreks saga*, and *Hálfs saga ok Hálfsrekka*), items that occasionally display additional reflexes in the store of Norwegian, Swedish, and Danish balladry.[27] In fact, *Ásmundar saga kappabana*, *Hálfs saga ok Hálfsrekka*, *Heiðreks saga*, *Hrólfs saga Gautrekssonar*, *Illuga saga Gríðarfóstra*, *Ketils saga hœngs*, *Norna-Gests þáttr*, *Ǫrvar-Odds saga*, *Ragnars saga loðbrókar*, *Sǫrla saga sterka*, and *Vǫlsunga saga* are all paralleled by material in the corpus of traditional Scandinavian ballads. Interestingly, nowhere is the tradition represented in the sagas reflected fully in any individual ballad, even in the

25. Solheim 1970, 301. A brief review of evidence on the Faroese ballad is given in Nolsøe 1987, but the whole question has recently been reappraised by B. R. Jonsson (1991), who concludes that "the Scandinavian ballad originated in circles close to the Norwegian court."

26. E.g., de Vries 1915, de Boor 1918.

27. Cf. the list in Olrik 1890. On the *Hálfs saga* reflexes in modern Faroese and Swedish ballad traditions, see Mitchell 1985a.

case of short sagas. Rather the ballads take up only brief episodes, scenes that naturally fit the scope of the ballad more readily.

It should be stressed that the legacy of the *fornaldarsǫgur* in the Nordic ballad tradition is highly varied: the many different forms of saga-ballad communications which undoubtedly existed preclude the possibility of our sketching a scenario that could accurately capture *all* the complexities of the relationship. Still, a general description of the interplay between the traditions behind the *fornaldarsǫgur*, the written *fornaldarsǫgur* themselves, and Nordic balladry is a highly desirable goal; toward this end I consider below the specific cases of the complexes tied to *Norna-Gests þáttr, Illuga saga Gríðarfóstra,* and *Heiðreks saga.*

An excellent illustration of the simplest sort of relationship between the Icelandic *fornaldarsǫgur* and the Faroese ballad tradition is provided by *Norna-Gests þáttr* and *Nornagests ríma.* Limited as the story is to manifestations in only these two works, this dyad is a particularly good point of departure because there are fewer obfuscating factors than is usually the case. *Norna-Gests þáttr* is generally believed to have been written ca. 1300, or perhaps somewhat earlier, and is preserved in three Icelandic manuscripts from the late fourteenth and early fifteenth centuries—Gks 1005, fol. (*Flateyjarbók*); Gks 2845, 4to; and AM 62, fol.[28] As part of the legendary materials of *Óláfs saga Tryggvasonar en mesta,* the *þáttr* was among the first *fornaldarsǫgur* to appear in print in the seventeenth century (1689) and was also included in Biörner's influential *Nordiska Kämpa Dater* (1737).[29] The *kvæði* were collected on several occasions in the early nineteenth century (first in 1818) but about the story's earlier history in the Faroes nothing is known.[30] Although the Gestr complex thus presents a relatively less complicated scenario than do most Old Norse texts with reflexes in Scandinavian balladry, the

---

28. A date of about 1300 for *Norna-Gests þáttr* enjoys widespread currency. See, for example, Halldór Hermannsson 1912, 32, and Sauer 1971, 6789. *Norna-Gests þáttr* is perhaps best known for its direct reference to the differences between the Nordic and German versions of Sigurðr's (Siegfried's) death; cf. chap. 9 of the *þáttr* and Aventiure 16 of *Das Nibelungenlied.* Scholarship on *Norna-Gests þáttr* has primarily focused on its relationship to other literary and folklore types, such as Meleager, Óðinn, and the Wandering Jew. For discussions of such items, see Bugge 1881–89, II, 95–103; Hollander 1916; and Panzer 1925.

29. *Saga þess haloflega herra Olafs Tryggvasonar Noregs Kongs,* ed. Jón Snorrason (Skalholt: n.p., 1689), II, 132–46; *Nordiska Kämpa Dater,* ed. Biörner (1737), pp. 1–34 (separately paginated; *Norna-Gests þáttr* is item 16).

30. On the circumstances and informants of the Faroese materials, see S. Grundtvig 1882 and [Schrøter] 1951–53, x–xviii. The figure of Nornagestur is not restricted to this ballad, but has become a fairly common ancillary character in other Faroese ballads (e.g., *CCF* 10).

case of *Nornagests ríma* is difficult enough, presenting, for instance, such questions as whether the Faroese ballads derive from a shared oral tradition concerning Gestr, or from a knowledge of the written Icelandic *þáttr* tradition, or from acquaintance with the seventeenth- and eighteenth-century printed materials, or from some combination of these factors.

With the exception of the introductory matter of the AM 62, fol. version,[31] the three medieval Icelandic manuscripts display an impressive degree of verbal correspondence, so much so that anything other than the work of copyists would be unthinkable. The situation with regard to the Faroese texts and their relationship to the extant *þættir* is quite different, however. Although the titles of the texts suggest a high degree of conformity between the traditions, varying perhaps only as regards the technical differences inherent in their forms, the stories themselves actually diverge in several important respects. The hero's name, the general frame story, and Nornagestr's association with Sigurðr Fáfnisbani (Sjúrður in Faroese) are all present, yet there are significant differences as well. That the Faroese text casts the tale in ballad form and tells a simpler version of it cannot alone account for the disparities between the traditions. Rather than the complex scenario that brings about Gestr's loquaciousness in *Norna-Gests þáttr*, for example, the ballad motivates his reminiscences by having him fail to praise the king (identified as Ólavur only in later versions) when the monarch strikes off the head of twelve oxen in a single stroke.[32] The reduction inherent in the ballad form is also felt in the scope of what Gestur tells as well, as he now no longer includes Starkaðr and focuses exclusively on materials from the Vǫlsung tradition. In addition, the ballad relates an episode not found in *Norna-Gests þáttr*, which contains lengthy citations from eddic poetry (*Reginsmál* and *Helreið Brynhildar*); in the ballad, Sjúrður's exploits with Fávnir are related in a few verses. The focus of the ballad narrative is on Gestur's service to Sjúrður after the hero has arrived home with Høgni and Gunnar following a particularly messy ride through a bog. Nor does the treatment of the pro-

31. AM 62, fol. begins with a story in which Gestr's *fylgja* 'guardian spirit' apparently visits King Óláfr prior to Gestr's arrival. After the introductory matter, the tales are similar, although there are minor differences.

32. Liestøl (1970, 84) suggests that this motif may represent a literary borrowing from *Egils saga Skallagrímssonar*, chap. 38, in which Skalla-Grímr cuts off the heads of two steers with one slice. I think this interpretation somewhat strained: K1951.1 'Boastful fly-killer: "seven at a blow"' is a motif encountered widely in folk literature (in, for instance, North America, India, Oceania, and Europe). The Faroese ballad simply seems to be, like the occurrence in *Egils saga*, one more appearance of it. See the entry in Thompson 1932–36 for examples.

tagonist's death in *Nornagests ríma* parallel the texts from the late fourteenth and early fifteenth centuries other than in a general way—some
of the specifics are now quite different.

In short, apart from the general frame story concerned with an
ancient hero who reminisces about Sjúrður and then dies peacefully
after baptism as his life's candle burns out, there is little by way of
specific evidence to connect the Faroese ballad directly to the Icelandic
tradition. Nothing about the current text demands that it be interpreted as anything other than a ballad that *could* have come about as a
result of familiarity with the seventeenth- and eighteenth-century published versions that fed into the living tradition of ballad singing in the
Faroes in those centuries. The lack of correspondence between the *þáttr*
and the ballad, however, indicates that any such relationship was quite
remote and that the printed versions failed to exercise any corrective
power over the Faroese multiforms. But it is equally true that there is
nothing to prevent us from believing that *Nornagests ríma* might have
much more ancient roots in the Faroese ballad tradition, based on a
knowledge, either direct or indirect, of the manuscripts or of an oral
version. Certainly there are cases, such as that of *Hálfs saga ok Hálfsrekka* and *Álvur kongur* (*CCF* 14), where we can be confident that the
Faroese ballad, although not collected until the nineteenth century,
antedated all published versions of the Old Norse text, since East
Scandinavian multiforms—clearly dependent on the Faroese—were recorded already by the seventeenth century.[33] Whatever the nature of
the historical relationship between *þáttr* and *kvæði,* the Faroese tradition has in no way been bound by the *fornaldarsaga*—if it is indeed the
ultimate inspiration for the ballad—and develops the tale along very
independent lines. Gone are most of the allusions to the great heroic
events of Sigurðr's and Starkaðr's lives and in their place is the much
more humble story of the ride through the swamp, which culminates
in Gestur washing Sjúrður's horse, providing him with the opportunity to praise Grani's long legs and other equine attributes.

A very different situation obtains in the case of *Illuga saga Gríðarfóstra*
and the ballads connected to it; not only is the distribution of this tale
much greater, with related items in Faroese, Norwegian, and Danish
ballad traditions (*CCF* 18, Ldsd 2, *DgF* 44), but the materials themselves are less heroic and more intensely folkloric (insofar as they dwell
on human interaction with trolls) than those of *Norna-Gests þáttr.*[34]

33. Mitchell 1985a.
34. On this motif, frequently encountered in the *fornaldarsǫgur*, see Davidson 1941.

The general contents of both the *kvæði* and the saga are aptly described by the ballad type E140 'Man saves princess from ogress to marry her.' The saga relates how a certain king unwittingly takes to wife a troll woman, who curses her stepdaughter, Gríðr, such that she must live as an ogress up in the fells. Gríðr's own daughter, who retains her natural beauty, stays with her, and the curse demands that every man who sees the daughter should fall in love with her, only to be murdered by her mother.

The hero, Illugi, who is on an expedition in the company of another king's son, goes in search of fire when his group is driven off course by bad weather. Encountering the ogress and her daughter, Illugi asks Gríðr for fire. She responds that he may have it only after telling her three truths; if he can accomplish this feat, he may then sleep with her daughter. Illugi, having seen and fallen in love with Hildr, her daughter, then says the following truths: that he has never seen a larger or stronger house than hers; that he has never seen a more grotesque (*meira skrípi*) creature than the one before him, as black as she is and with such a huge nose; and that her daughter is the most beautiful woman he has ever seen. The bargain fulfilled, Illugi and Hildr go to bed, but their pleasures are interrupted three times by the ogress, who pulls Illugi to the edge of the bed by his hair, holds a knife to his throat, and threatens to kill him for daring to violate her daughter. Each time Illugi responds that he has never known fear and that no man dies more than once, a rejoinder that temporarily halts her onslaught. On the third occasion, Gríðr says that he is not like other men and grants him her daughter. The hero's fearless behavior breaks the spell on Gríðr and she then goes on to tell her life's story. The saga concludes with the marital arrangements of Illugi to Hildr and Sigurðr, the king's son, to Gríðr, who has now assumed her normal shape.

As with the case of *Norna-Gests þáttr* and *Nornagests ríma*, there exists a published seventeenth-century version of the saga (1695),[35] a fact that might cast suspicion on the traditionality or authenticity of the nineteenth-century Faroese and Norwegian versions; however, the known history of this saga and the ballads connected to it is unique insofar as the oldest recording of one of the Danish ballads (ca. 1583) actually antedates the oldest extant manuscript of the saga (ca. 1600).[36]

---

35. *Sagan af Illuga Grydar fostra eller Illuge Grydar fostres Historia, fordom på gammal Göthiska skrifwen, och nu på Swenska uttålkad,* trans. Gudmund Olofsson (Uppsala: n.p., 1695).

36. Although the saga is generally dated to the fourteenth century—but cf. Finnur Jónsson (1920–24, II, 821) who dates it to the thirteenth—the oldest surviving manu-

For Grundtvig, the relationship between the various multiforms fits neatly with his overall view of the development of sagas and ballads: an ancient poem gave rise to the Icelandic saga and that same poem had been the basis for the three ballad traditions as well.[37] In a series of articles and books, Liestøl developed the following views on the texts: that there existed a direct relationship between the saga and the ballads; that only one Ur-ballad lay behind the three national traditions; that the kvæði did not manage to convert the saga material entirely into ballad form; and that the original ballad was of Norwegian provenance.[38] Einar Ólafur Sveinsson concurs with many of Liestøl's conclusions, which he regards as relatively uncontroversial, especially that the ballad author had read or heard the written saga (las eða heyrði söguna á bók) and that the Icelandic text therefore formed the basis for the ballads.[39]

An entirely new perspective on the relationship of the saga and the ballads has been forwarded by Davið Erlingsson.[40] In a detailed analysis of Illuga saga, the ballads, and a version of the story reflected in Saxo's Gesta Danorum, Davið argues that the ballad forms are much closer to the original legend, which must have been built on two folktale motifs, the search for fire including the three truths (H505.1 'Test of cleverness: uttering three truths') and the rescue of a princess from a giantess (H1385.1 'Quest for stolen princess'). To this fundamental story, the author has added a frame story based on another motif (M411.1.1 'Curse by stepmother'). This elaboration, along with several other features of the prose work (for example, the sworn brothers, the evil counselor), must, he maintains, be expansions of the origi-

script of it, AM 123, 80, is from ca. 1600, according to Katalog over Den arnamagnæanske Håndskriftsamling (II, 403); it should be noted, however, that Fornaldar Sögur Nordrlanda, ed. Rafn, III, xv, the only edition from the manuscript, ascribes it to the late fifteenth century. The oldest of the Danish ballad manuscripts, that by Karen Brahe, is usually dated to 1583; the other collections containing variants of "Herr Hylleland henter sin Jomfru" date from the late sixteenth century to ca. 1641. On the dates of the Danish ballad manuscripts, see Danske Viser fra Adelsvisebøger og Flyveblad 1530–1630, VI, 199–223.

37. There is some ambiguity in Grundtvig's statement; he writes that Illuga saga Gríðarfóstra utvivlsomt grunder sig paa en gammel Vise, der vel i Sagaen kan være bleven noget udvidet og udsmykket, men som vi dog kjende igjen baade i denne vor danske Vise, i en færøisk og i en norsk 'is undoubtedly built on an old song [Vise], which could certainly have been somewhat enlarged and embellished in the saga, but which we recognize in our Danish ballad [Vise], and in a Faroese and in a Norwegian' (DgF II, 94). Einar Ólafur Sveinsson (1956b, 71) interprets the sentence to mean that the poem gave rise to both the saga and the ballad.

38. Liestøl 1910; 1915b, 92–109; 1936; 1970, 61–62.

39. Einar Ólafur Sveinsson 1956b, 72.

40. Davið Erlingsson 1975.

nal story, rather than the reverse. In other words, if there is a direct relationship between the saga and the ballads, a knowledge of the ballad would have to have led to the composition of the saga and not the other way around: the ballads cannot have been derived from the saga. Davið concludes, however, that there is no proof that the ballad complex contributed to the saga and leaves open the question as to whether *Illuga saga* came about in this fashion or by drawing from a common tradition about Illugi which it shared with the ballads.

Certainly there is a great deal about these multiforms that properly connects them: the general story in which the hero saves a princess and marries her, the names, certain events (for example, the interruption of coitus), and the landscape projected in the various accounts all correspond to a high degree and lend credence to the view that there is a very specific—and possibly even immediate—connection between the multiforms. On the other hand, the continuity between the four national traditions has been stressed to such a level over the years that important differences between the texts (for example, the theft of the princess by an ogress versus the stepmother's curse in the saga) have tended to be ignored, a fact of which Davið Erlingsson's work reminds us. Essential elements of the plots are similar, but as with so many other saga-ballad complexes, the tale related in the *fornaldarsaga* is lengthier and more complicated than that given in the ballads. The difference is in itself unsurprising, but its consequences for the tale are significant. The ogress of the *kvæði* is no bewitched princess; she really is an ogress and as such, her fate is not to be saved from evil enchantment and married to a prince, but rather to be tricked and abandoned, or even slain. The manner in which the hero deals with his adversary, and vice versa, the focal point of all the multiforms, bears consideration in depth, for in it we find one of the central distinguishing characteristics of the various traditions.

In the saga, the ogress makes a demand for three truths, a motif (H505.1 'Test of cleverness: uttering three truths') specifically Scandinavian, appearing already in Saxo's *Gesta Danorum* (VII:15:6) and enduring into nineteenth-century folktales.[41] Due to the essential distinction in the scope and course of the ballads, however, this motif does not appear in the Faroese *kvæði* (CCF 18), *Kappin Illhugi*. In these

---

41. See Boberg 1966, 153, and the references cited there, as well as the corresponding section in Thompson 1932–36. Saxo's use of the motif seems to be more than casually related to the appearance of H505.1 in *Illuga saga Griðarfóstra*, in that in both cases the motif is associated with quests for fire and two of the three truths comment on the nose and the home of the interlocutor.

ballads, Illhugi and Hilda dress up a wooden image (*træbtílæti*) which the ogress attempts to kill in the morning. The couple laugh at her mistake and she winds up giving them costly gifts! In the Norwegian ballad, *Kappen Illhugin,* on the other hand, the motif of the three truths appears, although in a somewhat altered form. When the troll woman comes in the morning, Illhugin dispatches her and her family.[42] In the Danish texts, *Herr Hylleland henter sin Jomfru,* the 'Test of cleverness' appears in more or less the same form and with the same function to be found in the saga, but Hyllde-land (that is, Illugi) now resorts to the use of runic magic in order to frustrate the ogress's attempt on his life. So potent are these runes, in fact, that he not only forestalls her attack, but manages to change her mind as well, so that she grants Hyllde-land and his *iomfru* 'maid' (for Hildr has lost her identity in the Danish ballads and become little more than a cipher for a woman) peace and good gifts before they leave.

In the case of the saga-ballad complex relating to Illugi Gríðarfóstri, then—even if, as both Liestøl and Einar Ólafur Sveinsson believe, the ballads are based on an earlier written version of the *fornaldarsaga*—the various national *kæmpeviser* traditions must be regarded as highly independent keepers of the tale. If, as Davið Erlingsson's work suggests, the prose and verse multiforms have drawn more or less independently from a common wellspring of legendary material, then the fact that there are such widely varying versions of the Illugi tale becomes much more comprehensible. Liestøl points out that the ballads frequently make little sense without a knowledge of the Icelandic tradition, but it should be borne in mind that the singer and audiences of the ballads knew enough about the tradition for it to be a complete tale from their point of view; not everything about the story would necessarily have to find a place in the ballads. Due to the restricted manuscript history of *Illuga saga Gríðarfóstra,* we know far too little about the possible means

42. This section of the ballad presents serious difficulties, although such problems may be resolved with the appearance of the volume of *Troll- og kjempeviser* in the ongoing edition of Norwegian ballads. Liestøl 1915b, 92, lists recordings of this ballad in the collections of Jørgen Moe, Sophus Bugge, and Moltke Moe, in addition to that of Landstad. It would be of obvious interest to know how this section is treated in the different recordings. In the version he prints, Liestøl, apparently following a recording by Jørgen Moe in 1847, has Iddugjen calling to "Jorunn Joklekaapa"; likewise, Landstad has him call to "Jorun Joklekapa." In the multiform in *Norsk folkediktning* I, 125, the hero wishes for *Tor* 'Thor.' The notes to the passage (p. 282) do not comment on how Tor entered into it, only that his appearance does not really fit well into the context as it now is, and that this passage is remarkable testimony to ancient tradition. The parallel—if that is indeed what it is—between the ballad and similar situations in *Snorra Edda* is then drawn. For an example of how popular translations of Old Norse material were reintroduced into oral tradition in the nineteenth century, see Mitchell 1991.

by which an Icelandic version of the story might have been converted into the ballads according to the view held by Liestøl and Einar Ólafur Sveinsson, but surely such a transmutation would have to have been under way for some time in order for such an independent multiform as *DgF* 44 to have been recorded by 1583. Indeed, the question of a direct and written transmission of the saga from Iceland to other parts of Scandinavia, where it would then have been recast as a ballad, seems to be very much in doubt. We may well ask in line with Davið Erlingsson what aspects of the extant texts compel us to believe that such was the case, rather than the possibility that the story—not necessarily a written *Illuga saga,* but simply the outlines of a plot concerning a young hero, an ogress, and the rescue of a princess—made its way orally by the communication links so carefully identified by Einar Ólafur and others from Iceland to the Faroes, Norway, and Denmark (or in the reverse direction), where it was taken up in the prevailing popular form of entertainment, the ballad? In Iceland itself, a written *Illuga saga* might have been simultaneously elaborated such that it resulted in the basic story reflected in the ballads plus the frame story of the *álǫg* 'spell.'

Representative in many respects of the full range of complexities which surrounds *fornaldarsaga*-ballad relationships are those items connected with *Hervarar saga ok Heiðreks konungs* (hereafter *Heiðreks saga*). The oldest of the three manuscript traditions is from ca. 1325 (*Hauksbók*), but it is generally agreed that the saga as we know it dates to about the middle of the thirteenth century and that much of its poetry existed long before. Evidence for such an independent existence is provided by several parallel items in Saxo (Book V).[43] A popular work among copyists, *Heiðreks saga* also had a special appeal in the early modern period because of its apparent relevance to Scandinavian history; it was among the very earliest published Old Norse sagas (1672) and was reedited and printed again in the eighteenth century (1782).[44] Even within so agglutinative a genre as the *fornaldarsǫgur,* *Heiðreks saga* is a notably eclectic and heterogenous work. It consists of

43. On the manuscript relations, see Jón Helgason 1924b, i–xlviii. The material from Saxo Book V—also found in *Qrvar-Odds saga*—relates to the battle on Sámsey and certainly underscores the popularity of the scene in the thirteenth, and perhaps even the twelfth, centuries. See, for example, Olrik 1894, 59–62.

44. *Hervarar saga på Gammal Götska,* ed. and trans. Olaus Verelius (Uppsala: Henrik Curio, 1672); *Hervarar saga ok Heiðreks kongs,* ed. and trans. Stefán Björnsson (Copenhagen: P. F. Suhm, 1785). A thorough treatment of the vellum and paper manuscript traditions is provided in Jón Helgason's criticial edition, pp. i–lxxxvi. The composition of *Heiðreks saga* and its treatment of preliterary source materials is taken up in U. Ebel 1982a.

at least four discrete sections dealing variously with the battle on Sámsey, Hervǫr's retrieval of the sword Týrfingr, the riddle contest between Gestumblindi (Óðinn in disguise) and King Heiðrekr, and the battle between the Goths and the Huns. Although this latter section is regarded by some as one of the oldest surviving examples of Nordic poetry,[45] the episode has given rise to no known ballad group. Each of the other three sections, however, has, and the range of ballads connected with the materials of Heiðreks saga extends from Iceland in the west to Sweden in the east and Denmark in the south.

Ballads relating to the fornaldarsǫgur have been recorded almost exclusively in the modern period, but not so in the case of Heiðreks saga. In fact, one of the Danish items is the oldest datable evidence of a Scandinavian ballad (ca. 1425).[46] This and other pre-Vedelian texts of Angelfyr og Helmer Kamp (DgF 19A-D) secure the place of the Heiðreks saga ballads as part of a well-established set of kæmpeviser in East Scandinavia long before published versions of the materials could possibly have been a factor.[47] Related to the fifteenth-century verse is a later Swedish ballad (Kung Speleman) collected ca. 1700, believed to have independent value in establishing the relationship of the ballads.[48] In addition, there exist eighteenth- and nineteenth-century Faroese kvæði, CCF 16 (A:58–113; B:1–59; C II), known as Arngríms synir, and CCF 15, known as Hjálmar og Angantýr. These parts of the Faroese ballads are, like the Swedish Kung Speleman and the Danish ballads, concerned with the battle on Sámsey. The other parts of the Faroese ballads, CCF 16 (A:1–56; B:60–95), take up Hervǫr's discourse with her dead father. CCF 17, a fragmentary ballad called Gátu ríma, deals with the riddle contest.

In addition, several ancillary texts relate to the primary tradition. Liestøl in particular emphasizes the relationship between the Týrfingr ballads and the Norwegian ballad known as Ormaalen unge (together

45. See the discussion and bibliography in Tolkien 1955–56.

46. In the preparation of a map of northern Europe, the Danish cartographer Claudius Clavus Svart gave each of the features of Greenland a name that largely corresponded to the successive words of the first verse of DgF 19D, Angelfyr og Helmer Kamp, making it the oldest—and most oddly preserved—ballad text from Scandinavia. On the map and the ballad verse, see Axel Olrik (1904), who regards the verse as inauthentic, perhaps even a travesty of a ballad, and especially Bjørnbo and Petersen 1909, 85–90, 224–27, as well as DgF X, 15–16. Although it has been assigned to DgF 19D, there is nothing to connect it to this variant; it could as well have been called DgF 19E.

47. DgF 19B and DgF 19C, both from Rentzel's manuscript, date to ca. 1570, several decades before Vedel's published collection of one hundred Danish ballads (1591).

48. B. R. Jonsson (1967, 291–98) discusses the collection from which the text comes and concludes that this and other ballads in the manuscript have "independent source-value."

with its Danish and Swedish multiforms) and the Icelandic *Ormars rímur,* concluding that "Hervarar saga is thus the primary source for the Ormarr materials, but one also finds connections with other and younger *fornaldarsǫgur*."[49] Here Liestøl has in mind *Sturlaugs saga starfsama,* which he sees as the most significant of the other, younger, and written *fornaldarsǫgur* that have influenced, in his view, a lost **Ormars saga,* from which the *rímur* and Ormarr ballads derive.[50] Although the major motifs of the Ormarr group—such as the retrieval of a famous sword from the grave mound of a dead father (in the Danish ballads, also for the purpose of avenging his death)—show clear affinities to *Heiðreks saga* and may well have further promoted the popularity of the tale in northern Europe, these ballads are not central to the current discussion. The Ormarr ballads may have had a secondary role in furthering familiarity with the underlying motifs, but it is not clear that they have any direct, or generative, relevance to the other ballads.

One striking fact about the texts that constitute the core of the *Heiðreks saga* complex is that in general, the further back in time we go, the *slighter* the similarity between texts. Thus, if we compare the saga to the 'S group' (the Swedish *Kung Speleman* and the Claudius Clavus Svart verse), known in full from the late seventeenth century but which must already have had some currency in eastern Scandinavia early in the 1400s, it is easy to see that despite important points of contact between the saga and these ballads, there is relatively little that suggests a direct and conscious imitation of the one in the other.[51] The Swedish

49. Liestøl 1915b, 132. The possible relation of the Týrfingr portion of *Heiðreks saga* and the Ormarr ballads had previously been noted by Landstad in his *Norske Folkeviser* (pp. 99–102) and by Grundtvig (*DgF* IV, 705), who takes exception to some of Landstad's remarks. On the Ormarr texts, see E 132 in *TSB.*

50. Liestøl (1915b, 133) suggests that *Heiðreks saga* was the source for "Arngríms synir" and for another text (x), which in turn formed the basis for both the Icelandic *Ormars rímur* and the non-insular Ormarr ballads. Einar Ólafur Sveinsson (1956b, 71) agrees with much of what Liestøl concludes regarding the development of the various texts, but differs somewhat in how he interprets the lineage for our understanding of the sources and their transmission through Scandinavia: "Out in Iceland a now-lost *fornaldarsaga, Ormars saga,* was written, but as may be seen from the *rímur,* the material was used (*sótt*) in other written *fornaldarsǫgur.* The saga was apparently from the fourteenth century. A manuscript of the saga was taken to Norway and from it was composed the ballad *Ormaalen unge,* which was then taken to Denmark and Sweden. As to what the links (*milliðir*) were between the manuscript and the poet, I make no assertions."

51. The unique similarity between the two items convinces me that something very much like the Swedish ballad must have been familiar to Claudius Clavus Svart. The two texts show a remarkable degree of cross-cultural fertilization: as Bjørnbo and Petersen (1909, 87) demonstrate (despite Olrik's objection [1904, 212]), the Danish ballad fragment gives its protagonist, Spieldebedh, a name that must have Swedish origins, while the Swedish ballad localizes the events to Helsingbo[r]g, a Danish city until the seventeenth century.

ballad has impressively—and typically—condensed the events leading up to the battle on Sámsey (the villain's demand for Kung Speleman's daughter) as well as its outcome (the deaths of the villain's eleven sons and of Kung Speleman) to a mere thirteen verses, while at the same time maintaining the essence of the plot. In addition to the broad sweep of the action, several specifics suggest a direct connection to *Heiðreks saga*. The ballad calls the father (Arngrímr in the saga) Tyre, a name no doubt derived from the saga's name for his sword (Týrfingr).[52] Moreover, the emphasis the ballad places on the companion's connection with silk, mentioned three times (sts. 8, 10, 11—for example, *du skal icke slita valmaret grå,* / *om Silke fins uti lande* 'you should not wear out gray homespun, if there is silk in the country'), probably derives from the magical *silki skyrta* 'silk shirt' that protects Qrvar-Oddr in the saga.[53]

Yet despite such indications of a specific connection between saga and ballad, in how many more ways the ballads differ from the saga! Not a single other name seems to derive from the saga; the protagonist in the fight against the brutish warrior is no longer the secret admirer Hjálmarr, but rather the suited maiden's father, Kung Speleman; the locations are completely different and no longer is the trip to Uppsala a central motif; the outcome of the fight—with Otte avenging his king's death by pulling up an oak tree and using it as a weapon—has apparently drawn on several sources, but certainly not the saga.[54] In some ways, the S group significantly modifies, curtails, and condenses the "original" tale as we know it from the saga, whereas in others, it clings tenaciously to the fundamental plot of the saga.

Even more radically different are the Danish materials: *DgF* 19A–D (exclusive of the previously discussed fragment; hereafter the *DgF* ballads) were all collected (or published) between ca. 1570 and 1616.[55] The key component that serves to differentiate this group from all the other texts within the *Heiðreks saga* orbit is the inversion of relationships between the main players. Whereas the S group significantly

52. The form *Tyre* (from Týrfingr) may have been influenced by the native **Tyri* (*Tyry*), a name attested in eastern Småland in the sixteenth century. See Modéer 1957, 68.

53. The R and U traditions read *eN silki skyrta Odds uar suo traust, ecki uópn festi a* 'and Oddr's silk shirt was so strong that no weapon could cleave it' (*Heiðreks saga*, p. 11). There may also be a connection with Oddr's benefactor, Silkisif, as well. It should be noted, however, that "silken" clothing is a commonplace in the Nordic ballads.

54. See Boberg 1966: F614.2 'Strong man uproots tree and uses it as a weapon.'

55. Note that S. Grundtvig (*DgF* I, 250) calls the ballad printed in Vedel a very awkward (*uheldig*) composite of the A and B versions.

prunes the action related in the saga by making the father the maiden's champion against Tyre, the *DgF* ballads produce a more tragic and quintessentially balladlike plot by making *brothers* of the two antagonists. In *Angelfyr og Helmer Kamp* (*DgF* 19), the combatants are both sons of a certain man (Offue or Alff), who is able to find his progeny only after one has killed the other; he then feels compelled to slay his surviving offspring himself. Neither the romantic tale of the saga nor the heroic action it portrays survives in the *DgF* ballads; rather they tell of family mayhem at a level rivaled only by such works as *Ebbe Skammelson* (*DgF* 354). The fratricidal motif may, however, have been introduced from the saga itself, in which Heiðrekr kills his brother Angantýr, the grandson of the Angantýr in the ballads.[56] An indication that the restructuring of the tale as we know it elsewhere had not yet been completed at the moment the Danish ballads were "frozen" by their recording and publication is the fact that the maiden chooses Angelfyr's brother Helmer. She then proceeds to say that she would not marry Angelfyr, who, like *the rest* of his family, is half a troll (I cite the A version, st. 11):

"Ieg will icke haffue Anngelfyr,   "I do not want Angelfyr,
och hand ere halff en throld: for he is half a troll:
saa ere hans fader, saa ere hans moeder, so is his father, so is his mother,
saa ere hans slecttning alle"   so is his family all"

Despite the fact that her comments are contradictory, fidelity in other areas indicates a close relationship between these ballads and the other materials.

That already a version of this ballad group had appeared in Vedel's edition (1591) calls for a healthy degree of skepticism about later texts, not least the Faroese *kvæði* connected to these ballads, known as *Arngríms synir* (*CCF* 16).[57] Yet if these heroic ballads are influenced by, or even based on, Vedel, they must also have had additional sources. In keeping with the tendency of the West Scandinavian ballads to be multiepisodic, only portions of *CCF* 16 (A:58–113; B:1–59; C II) actually deal with this episode. Already the oldest of the Faroese ballad texts, collected in 1781–82 by Svabo, shows clear filiation with the Danish ballads, especially with regard to the tragic innovation of brother fighting and slaying brother (*hann kleyv Angantýr, bróður sin, /*

---

56. Cf. Mudrak 1943, 335–52.
57. Note that Matras (1969) points out that the rhyme scheme of these ballads indicates that they must in general be relatively old.

sundur í lutir tvá 'he clove Angantýr, his brother, asunder into two pieces' [*CCF* 16A, st. 102]), as well as the therefore incongruous accusation that Angantýr's family is made up of trolls. At the same time, this Faroese work corresponds more closely to the saga than do the Danish ballads: the father's name is now Arngímur; the maiden is again Ingibjørg; Oddur (Ǫrvar-Oddr) is again a central figure in the plot; the singer's focus is much more obviously on the battle itself than is the case in the *DgF* ballads, a fight into which the father now no longer enters. And rather than the Danish conclusion, in which the father stands between the bodies of his slain sons, the Faroese ballad ends in the manner of the saga episode, with Ingibjørg dying *av harmi* 'from sorrow' when she hears of Hjálmar's death.

This similarity to the published versions of *Heiðreks saga* is even more pronounced in the later recordings of *CCF* 16: in the B version (from 1851), for example, Angantýr's antagonist is no longer his brother, but has again become 'the Swedish warrior Hjálmar' (*av Svitjóðum*) (st. 23).[58] Moreover, their fight once more takes place specifically on Samsoy. And because this variant places the Týrfingr episode after the battle on Samsoy, it does not need to develop and distinguish between Ørvaroddur, on whom Hervik (the saga's Hervǫr) avenges her father's death, and the Oddur who subsequently assists Hjálmar, as is the case in A; instead it follows the plot of the saga. In short, the similarities between the saga and the Faroese ballads have become so close by the middle of the nineteenth century that it is difficult to believe that a printed—or paper manuscript—version of *Heiðreks saga* has not had an important impact on the later *kvæði*. But the sort of "corrective" influence such a comment envisions should not be confused with inspiration. Indeed, further evidence supports the traditional nature of this ballad within the West Scandinavian context, in the form of a refrain from an Icelandic *vikivakakvæði* recorded in the late seventeenth century, concerning "Angantýr og Hjálmar."[59]

Very similar to the *Arngríms synir* ballads is *CCF* 15, *Hjálmar og Angantýr,* although more restricted in scope. It sets the episode in the everyday world (kings become farmers, for example) and focuses like the S and *DgF* groups exclusively on the attempts to gain the maiden's hand and the subsequent fight. The refrain of the B variant—*Arngríms*

58. *CCF* 16 A:85 refers to him as "Hjálmar kappi av Upplondum."

59. *Íslenzk fornkvæði: Islandske folkeviser,* ed. Jón Helgason, VIII, 127. The comment with which Jón precedes this example is certainly thought-provoking in this context: "If one goes through the *vikivakakvæði* refrains [. . .] one often finds items which appear to bear the stamp of an older tradition than the poems in which they have survived, and the question then inevitably arises, have they not come from lost ancient ballads."

synir av Blálondum / berjast á Samsoy 'The sons of Arngrímur of Bláland fight each other on Samsoy'—suggests the central tragedy of this version. In this variant, however, the father does not exact revenge on the surviving son and instead it is Angantýr and Hjálmar who kill one another.

A further portion of *Heiðreks saga* is reflected in the Faroese ballad tradition (*CCF* 16 A:1–57 and B:60–95) in which the sword Týrfingr is retrieved from Angantýr's burial mound for use in avenging the father's death (cf. E373.2 'Sword received from summoned dead father'). Were it not for the similar motif in the texts of the E132 group (generally believed to have developed from the lost *Ormars saga* which in turn is held to have derived much of its material from *Heiðreks saga*), it might be possible to dimiss these appearances of the Týrfingr sequence in the Faroese corpus as constructs taken from the modern published material. Although the E132 texts do not provide absolute proof of the continuity of the tradition, they certainly strengthen the possibility. Likewise, Hervík's brutality against her playmates, her confrontation with her mother about her father's killer, and her trip to find the slayer are filled with commonplaces from the Faroese ballad tradition, a fact that, together with the unique form of her name, suggests a lengthy existence within the tradition.[60]

A final ballad text belongs to the *Heiðreks saga* group: *CCF* 17, *Gátu ríma*. A great deal about this riddling contest in rhyme is reminiscent of the verbal duel between Gestumblindi (Óðinn in disguise) and Heiðrekr in the saga. Indeed, the epic form of the confrontation is preserved in the ballad, although some details have changed. Thus, for example, whereas the frame story in the saga has the protagonist make a sacrifice to Óðinn, the old man in the ballad helps him for twelve marks of silver, and whereas Heiðrekr is killed by his slaves in the saga, he is "burned in" in the *kvæði*. Such alterations are truly minor, however, compared to the fact that Óðinn turns himself into a bird at the end of the contest and flies away. The riddles themselves, however, are another matter: there are thirty-seven riddles in the saga, but only ten in the ballad. Of these ten, only a few (four or five) are the same in the saga and in the ballad; and in the last three "riddles" in the *kvæði*, no

---

60. Oral tradition concerning the cursed sword Týrfingr appears to be quite strong; in addition to these ballads, there are, for example, several Icelandic riddles that play on the name, one of which specifically identifies the answer as being the same as what Hervör sought in the mound on Sámsey. See "Týrfingr Riddles." The inspiration for these riddles has undoubtedly been the written tradition of *Heiðreks saga* in Iceland. On the use of commonplaces in the composition of Faroese ballads, see Conroy 1974, 1980, and O'Neil 1970.

actual riddling transpires, but rather solutions to unspoken riddles are given. The topics taken up in the ballad riddles—thunder as a drum, thoughts going through a door, streams of water in an ocean, a man's beard as a forest cut down on holy days—are of a common enough sort, and suggest substitution of popular items for the sometimes more esoteric materials of the saga riddles.

What then is the relationship between the various medieval, modern, oral, written, and printed aspects of the *Heiðreks saga* tradition? What picture of legendary material communications does the *Heiðreks saga* group provide? It seems quite probable from the complex texts in evidence here that all sorts of channels, both written and oral, must have been in use, with no one school of thought, either that represented by Liestøl or that of Einar Ólafur Sveinsson, being entirely correct. The main texts related to the *Heiðreks saga* group can all be accounted for by the stemma given here, which seeks to place the extant works (and fragments) into their appropriate relationships.[61]

This postulated genesis of the extant *Heiðreks saga* complex attempts to account for the prevailing modern situation by recourse to a minimum number of hypothetical texts; moreover, it restricts the discussion to *texts,* although the impact of the oral tradition might have been introduced at any point in the process. Other configurations are conceivable, of course: Saxo may have derived his material from earlier versions of the poems contained in *Heiðreks saga;* the hypothetical ballads may have been derived directly from the saga or from the traditional legendary material itself; the influence of *Heiðreks saga* on *Ormars saga* remains an unknown and unknowable factor; the possible role of *Ǫrvar-Odds saga* must be borne in mind; and so on. Despite these caveats, however, certain conclusions are possible; especially noteworthy is the influence the published Danish ballads and the written saga itself have exerted on the Faroese *kvæði.* The increased "correctness" (that is, adherence to the saga form) of the Faroese ballads over time suggests that a synergistic relationship exists between oral and written texts within the tradition; it is a dynamic that deserves to be underscored, for at one point it seemed almost completely lost from discussions of balladry.

Nowhere has this fact been more prominent than in discussions concerning the Scandinavian ballads relating to the *Nibelungenlied.* The appropriateness of Hermann Schneider's observation that only three

61. In this proposed schema, I have concentrated on the relationship of the ballad reflexes and reduced the manuscript stemma to a single descent, obviously an infelicitous presentation of the actual situation.

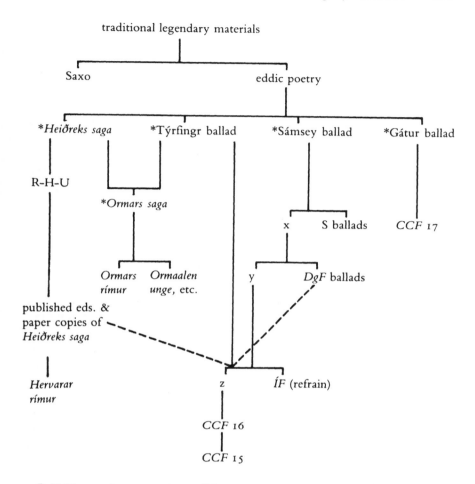

R-H-U = main manuscript traditions
S ballads = *Kung Speleman*, Claudius Clavus Svart verse
ÍF = *Íslenzk Fornkvæði*
CCF = *Corpus Carminum Faeroensium*
DgF = *Danmarks gamle Folkeviser*
x, y, z = hypothetical lost texts

basic views on the Nordic Sigurðr ballads exist has not been diminished over the years, although more than fifty have passed since he
made it.[62] One group, consisting of Svend Grundtvig, Axel Olrik, and
to some extent, Gustav Neckel, sees the Faroese and other ballads

62. Schneider 1928–34, I, 153–57.

connected with the Nibelungs as having derived from (oral) German songs ("aus deutscher Liedquelle stammen"). The other extreme is the one taken by R. C. Boer and Jan de Vries, who regard the *fornaldarsǫgur* and eddic poems in manuscript form as the only conceivable sources. Even the attempt by Knut Liestøl, which clearly wins Schneider's own approval, to propose a moderating third alternative according to which the materials are introduced into Scandinavia in a written format, taken up in popular tradition, and then reworked orally in the Faroes, fails to take into account the possibility that there existed an *ongoing* interplay between written and verbal forms of the tradition. For the most part, the question of the *Sjurðar kvæði* and the other Scandinavian Sigurðr ballads has only been discussed as a small part of the much larger question of the evolution of the *Nibelungenlied;* many questions about the Nordic ballad texts and their growth and development remain to be answered.

This discussion of selected saga-ballad complexes leads to certain hypotheses concerning what Lönnroth terms 'saga communications.' But where he addresses a situation with a relatively limited time frame and geography, the generalizations suggested here must apply to works that cover a considerable temporal and spatial range. It is clear from the fragmentary but nevertheless compelling testimony of the earliest recorded ballad texts that a tradition of ballads based on legendary themes, motifs, and characters was well established by the end of the medieval period. These texts cannot possibly have been inspired or influenced by the printed versions of the sagas and ballads, since they antedate them, although the possible role of manuscript copies remains an unknown factor. Even in situations where the inspiration for a ballad may have been a saga manuscript (for example, *Nornagests rímur* ⟨ *Norna-Gests þáttr*), the significant divergences from the original, the use of ballad commonplaces, and the full expression of the story in ballad idiom suggest that once a story was taken into the ballad repertoire, the resulting *kvæði* behaved as any other orally transmitted traditional ballad.[63]

It is likewise clear that in general, the more recent a ballad recording, the greater the likelihood that it has been "corrected" by knowledge of authoritative printed versions, as in the case of the *Heiðreks saga* multi-

---

63. On the relationship of the oral and written cultures with respect to the ballads, see Buchan 1977 and Nolsøe 1976. A similar appreciation for the two cultures and their interaction is shown in Lord 1967, where the many types and degrees of effect such a text can have on the oral tradition are discussed. Cf. Stefán Karlsson 1986.

forms, which, when viewed historically, display an almost consistent movement in content and treatment *toward* the saga version. Finally, like Lönnroth's model (and the biologist's concept of phylogenetic descent with reticulates), the relationship among traditional legendary material, *fornaldarsaga,* and ballad does *not* consist solely of a series of constantly branching binaries. Indeed, the relationship is much more one of dynamic reticulation, that is, frequent exchange between the various multiforms and their genres. The system of saga-ballad communications which thus begins to emerge, relevant both synchronically and diachronically, is one in which transmission (or 'communication') takes place through both oral *and* written channels, the latter consisting of printed as well as of scribal copies, not on one occasion only but also over time. Furthermore, literary activity concerning a given tradition is by no means confined within a specific genre, but can instead undergo relatively easy and surprisingly frequent transmutations from one literary form to another.

Icelandic *rímur*

Unlike the other Nordic cultures, Iceland did not develop a tradition of heroic ballads. Yet another innovation in narrative verse gripped the creative imagination of the country for over five hundred years and thereby continued the traditions of the *fornaldarsǫgur* in a new form, although it is important to remember that the popularity of the *fornaldarsǫgur* themselves never waned very much and that they were constantly being reworked over time. This new form of literature is the *rímur.*[64] Scholarly opinion concerning the origins of this uniquely Icelandic form of metrical romance has undergone dramatic revision in the past decade or so. For many years, the prevailing view of this lengthy narrative poetry, with its divisions into fits (*rímnaflokkar*), typically held the genre to be an outgrowth on the one hand of the indige-

---

64. The source of the term *rímur,* most often used in the plural because of the cantos or fits of which they consist, must ultimately be Old French. But whether it entered Icelandic through Middle Low German (and Middle Dutch?) or Middle English, where it appears fairly often in the sense of "poem," or "ballad," is unclear, although the latter view is favored by Craigie (1952, I, 283) and Nolsøe (1978). For reviews of literature on *rímur,* see Stefán Einarsson 1955 and Hughes 1980; introductions to the genre, in addition to Craigie's bilingual (English and Icelandic) prefaces to the *Sýnisbók* volumes (1955), are Davið Erlingsson 1987, Ólafur Halldórsson 1956–78, and, particularly as regards melodies, Hallfreður Örn Eiríksson 1975.

nous skaldic poetry and on the other of the dance (*danzleikr*) and the ballad.[65] From the native poetic tradition, it was believed, came the *rímur*'s celebrated love of alliteration, consonance, assonance, and metaphoric language, whereas its metrical form and (assumed) association with ring dances harked back to the dance strophes and ballads.[66] This explanation of the aesthetic background that gave rise to the *rímur* has undergone considerable scrutiny and revision in recent years, especially at the hands of Vésteinn Ólason, who, together with Shaun F. D. Hughes, has challenged the evidence and rationale associated with the view that the *rímur* came about as a synergism of the two preexisting poetic forms; indeed, Vésteinn Ólason even goes so far as to claim that "it would be more appropriate to say that the West-Nordic ballad has its origins in *rímur* than vice versa."[67] Vésteinn connects the development of the *rímur* to the Norwegian trading center of Bergen, where Icelanders could have easily come into contact with other European traditions (especially German), in which he finds early evidence for the *rímur* meters; Hughes, on the other hand, links the development of the *rímur* to an evolution of the existing eddic meters.[68]

Our knowledge of the early stages of the genre is negligible and it is almost by chance that the oldest known specimen, *Óláfs ríma Haraldssonar* (written prior to 1370) by Einar Gilsson, came to be included in the late fourteenth-century *Flateyjarbók*.[69] It is already a fully developed work, although it lacks what becomes one of the characteristic features of the later *rímur,* the *mansǫngvar,* that is, introductions to each fit in the tradition of medieval courtly love songs. Originally addressed

65. This view has been subscribed to by many of the most influential figures in the field—e.g., Björn K. Þórólfsson (1934, 35–51; 1950), Craigie (1952, I, 281–91), Sigurður Nordal (1953, 272)—although the possible derivation of *rímur* meters from those of the ballad was questioned already by Jón Þorkelsson 1888, 123–24. The first systematic refutation of the idea is Vésteinn Ólason 1976. The older view on the relationship between dance, ballad, and *rímur* is well represented in Einar Ólafur Sveinsson 1935 and Stefán Einarsson 1949; see also Konráð Gíslason 1897.

66. The belief in an eventual link between the ring dance and the *rímur* is founded on implicit references in the romances themselves and on later cultural practices, but the notion of a derivation from, or an original association with, the dance has been attacked in Rokkjær 1964. On the florid language of the *rímur,* see Davið Erlingsson 1974.

67. Vésteinn Ólason 1978a, 33.

68. Vésteinn Ólason 1976; Hughes 1978. With regard to the variety of meters, Síra Helgi Sigurðsson (1891) distinguishes twenty-three metrical "families" or branches (*bragættir*), with over two thousand different specific meters. The oldest and most common is the *ferskeytt,* which can be described as a four-lined meter with two alliterating elements in the even lines and one in the odd and having the rhyme scheme *a b a b.*

69. On *Óláfs ríma Haraldssonar er Einar Gilsson kvað,* see Björn K. Þórólfsson 1934, 298–99.

to a woman, in later works these were often simply lyrical prefaces in which the author might list famous personages, dedicate the work to a patron, or offer excuses for his or her limited talents.[70] Although the *rímur* are an originally medieval genre, they have continued to be created well into modern times, including the present century; given this lengthy history, it is not surprising that every *fornaldarsaga* has been reworked into *rímur*.[71] Most of these metrical romances have been based on late paper manuscripts and published versions of sagas, especially the texts contained in Biörner's *Nordiska Kämpa Dater* (1737) and Rafn's *Fornaldar sögur Nordrlanda* (1829–30), but the *fornaldarsǫgur* are also well represented among what are thought of as the traditional *rímur*, those from before 1600.[72] Indeed, nearly one-third of all the works from this period have *fornaldarsǫgur* materials as their topics, with another third coming from the *riddarasǫgur*, and the final third being more or less evenly divided between the *konungasǫgur* and *þjóðsögur* 'popular traditions' (legends and so on). In addition, a few are based on eddic materials.

Certainly the *rímur* became an essentially written phenomenon,[73] although the suggestion has been made that they may have begun as an orally composed form and become increasingly literary over time. This belief is based in part on the evidence of *rímur* transcriptions made from oral tradition during the late seventeenth and early eighteenth centuries.[74] In addition, there are some *rímur* for which no corresponding saga exists (for example, *Illuga rímur eldhússgoða*) and others that, if they are indeed to be regarded as closely based on written versions,

70. On the evidence for a separate origin for the *mansǫngvar*, see Hughes 1978, 39–40.

71. Cf. Finnur Sigmundsson 1966.

72. This date—about fifty years after the Icelandic Reformation—has served to demark the more traditional *rímur* from the more literary works since at least Jón Þorkelsson (1888) and is routinely employed in such standard works as Björn K. Þórólfsson 1934 and Finnur Sigmundsson 1966.

73. Vésteinn Ólason 1978a, 29: "They seem to have been written from the very first, rather than passed on orally. Even if a few were memorized, and the texts later recorded from oral—or as Buchan would say 'verbal'—tradition, the genre is basically a literary one. Everyone agrees on this, and it fits very well with the fact that the stories told in *rímur* come mostly from written sagas."

74. Jón Þorkelsson (1888, 116) expresses the view that some of them at least must have lived on in oral tradition, since in 1700 Árni Magnússon recorded (or had recorded) a number of them from performances. Craigie (1952, I, 283, 285) suggests that the *rímur* probably had a popular origin "of purely oral composition" (by which he means initial creation without writing, followed by subsequent memorization), but became increasingly literary over time.

must have had as their models radically different multiforms than those now extant (for example, *Bjarkarímur*). In general, however, the early *rímur* texts can be linked to known manuscript traditions and therefore are no doubt best considered an essentially literary phenomenon. Certainly the authors of the *rímur* were often learned individuals, in touch with the wide range of literature current in late medieval Iceland. Nearly every sort of literary work was recast in the *rímur* form, including foreign texts and the Bible, but in those metrical romances based on *fornaldarsǫgur* one is still occasionally surprised to see the incorporation of extensive lists of figures from other traditions. Thus, for example, *Bósarímur* (ca. 1500), composed from a now lost manuscript of *Bósa saga* closely related to the extant AM 510, 4to manuscript, mentions, as one would expect, such figures, places, and races from the old pagan tradition as Þórr, Nóatún, and the Æsir. But references to classical (Ovidius, Príamus í Tróju), biblical (Samsón), and foreign (Bévus, Rémundur keisarason, Blávus, Tristram) literature appear in such abundance and so thoroughly lack relevance to the tale itself as to indicate a sheer joy in the opportunity to list such personages.[75]

The transferral of the prosimetrical *fornaldarsǫgur* (or their traditions at any rate) into the multimetered *rímur* dictates not only the expansion of the existing text at one juncture and its contraction elsewhere, but also a new style of narration and the introduction of completely new material.[76] As examples of the results of these processes, the cases of *Bósarímur* and *Bjarkarímur* are instructive. Bósi, as the hero of the saga, has three sexual escapades in which he seduces his hosts' daughters with witty and only thinly veiled sexual references. As each of the maidens asks in turn why he has come to her bed, he answers: *Ek vil herða jarl minn hjá þér* 'I want to harden my warrior with you' (chap. 7); *Ek vil brynna fola minn í vínkeldu þinni* 'I want to water my foal in your wine-spring' (chap. 11); *hann bað hand hólka stúfa sínn* 'he asked her to encircle his stump' (chap. 13). In the case of the *rímur*, Bósi's concupiscent adventures now number only two. And whereas the saga builds toward the third episode in that each of the hero's conversations with his paramours becomes increasingly salacious, the *rímur* elaborates the initial encounter, thereby deemphasizing the second. In the first scene,

75. See Ólafur Halldórsson 1974, 21, concerning the date of the *rímur;* 1974, 21–23, concerning the relationship of the extant and lost manuscripts to one another.
76. An excellent examination of the differences in style and narrative technique of the *rímur,* ballads, and sagas is found in Vésteinn Ólason 1983, 1985. See also Hughes 1978. Kölbing (1876) maintains that the *rímur* authors generally followed their models with almost slavish exactness. For an example of a poet who in fact exercises substantial control over contents, see Krijn 1925.

one stanza after the next robustly relates the dialogue between Bósi and his lover, with little left to the imagination.[77] In the second encounter (IX, 21–27), the narrator recounts the events and retains the equine metaphor of the saga, but places nothing into direct speech.

A further difference between the saga and the *rímur* lies in the fact that the narrator of the metrical romance uses the episodes as an opportunity to tweak the audience's sensibilities through his asides:

Allar *kenna ungar frur	All young women know
yndis bragdit þetta	that trick of charm,
leikinn *þenna er liek hann nu	that game, which he now played,
liufur uid sprundit setta:	beloved, with the seated woman.

(IX, 27)

These remarks to the audience underscore a further difference between the *rímur* and other genres: whereas the classical saga writers, those of the *íslendingasǫgur*, and to a lesser degree, the ballad singers, display an impersonal relationship toward their stories, the *rímur* narrators are frequently intrusive. Even the *fornaldarsǫgur*, which are among the most self-referential of the saga genres, can hardly compete with the *rímur* on this point. Phrases of the sort *fré eg* 'I hear' are common in the *rímur* undoubtedly because they so conveniently fill out lines in the highly syllable-conscious meters in which the *rímur* are written, but authorial presence is not limited to such short phrases only. Entire lines, and even stanzas, are systematically devoted to commentary of this sort: *hef eg það lagt í minni* 'This I have committed to memory' (*Bjarkarímur*, VIII, 13); *FARA skal en hin fimta nv* 'Now the fifth ríma will begin' (*Vǫlsungsrímur*, V, 1); *Nú má hverr, er heyrir til, / hafa að sér ið fjórða spil* 'Now all those who listen, have the fourth fit' (*Griplur*, IV, 64); *TIME er at rima vm travsta menn, / tel ec nv uel at giordizt enn, / smidazt uida saga med brag, / sueitir leita tons uid lag* 'It is time to "rhyme" about mighty men, I say that they conducted themselves manfully, fashioned great sagas in verse, seek the tone that fits best' (*Sǫrlarímur*, VI, 1).[78] Such lengthy asides are almost without exception part of the openings and closings of *rímnaflokkar* and bear comparison to what Lars Lönnroth terms "the double-scene."[79] Indeed, they are at times even "treble-scened," insofar as they occasionally refer not only to the events of the story and the circumstances of the narration, but

---

77. For example: *Drag þu ott at drosinn kuad / dreingur j afli minum / spara skal ecki sprundit þad / at spektar radum þinum* (VI, 32).

78. The translation of *Sǫrlarímur* follows Finnur Jónsson's reading.

79. Lönnroth 1978, as well as 1971.

also to the actual labor of transforming *fornaldarsǫgur* into *rímur*, as when the author of *Bósarímur* (X, 19) refers to his model: *seigir bokin min* 'says my book.'

The creative independence of the *rímur* authors is further evinced in *Bjarkarímur*, one of the best-known *rímur* (to non-Icelanders at least) due to the important role it has played in discussions of Nordic analogues to *Beowulf*.[80] The part of the tale which treats the arrival of Bǫðvarr Bjarki ('Battle Bjarki') at King Hrólfr's court and the subsequent slaying of a monster there provides an excellent example of the freedom *rímur* authors must have felt in treating their sources. In the *Bjarkaþáttr* of *Hrólfs saga kraka*, Bjarki's arrival at Hleiðargarðr is marked only by the relative emptiness of the hall and the manner in which he tethers his horse. In *Bjarkarímur*, the poet elaborates the scene considerably: the gates to the hall are guarded by two dogs, which the hero manages to dispatch only because his hostess on the previous night has forewarned him and provided him with the means for killing them. Bjarki no longer enters the hall quietly but instead comes in and, in order to make room for himself on the benches, kills two of Hrólfr's men. On the other hand, the saga and the *rímur* agree on the essentials as to how Bjarki saves Hǫttr (Hjalti later in the saga and throughout the *rímur*) from his fate as an object of derision and persecution behind the bone-pile at the court. The climax of *Bjarkaþáttr* comes when Bjarki slays a winged dragon that year after year has terrorized the kingdom at Yuletime. After he has killed it, the hero forces his cowardly companion Hǫttr to drink some of its blood, which gives him both strength and a brave disposition, and sets up the carcass in such a way that Hǫttr can "kill" the beast the next day in full view of the king and his retinue.[81] In the *rímur*, on the other hand, this scene is elaborated such that Bjarki and Hjalti fight not a single adversary, but two, a she-wolf (*ylgr*) and a gray bear (*grábjǫrn*):

Flestir ǫmuðu Hetti heldr,	Most [of the men] vexed Hjalti,
hann var ekki í máli sneldr,	he was not quick in speech,
einn dag fóru þeir út af hǫll,	one day they left the hall,
svó ekki vissi hirðin ǫll.	such that the company did not know it.

80. The extensive early literature on this topic is reviewed in Olson 1916, 7–12, and further in Caldwell 1939. Björn K. Þórólfsson (1934) assigns *Bjarkarímur* to no specific date, but places it among the "oldest *rímur*"; Finnur Jónsson (1904, xxx) sets the date to approximately 1400.

81. Cf. Dumézil (1973b, 69–70), who suggests that Hǫttr's "slaying" of the dead monster may be analogous to Þjalfi's victory over the giants' effigy in the story of Þórr's battle with Hrungnir, both recalling the initiation of a young warrior.

Hjalti talar er felmtinn fær,
"fǫrum við ekki skógi nær,
hér er sú ylgr sem etr upp menn,
okkr drepr hún báða senn."

Hjalti, who was afraid, spoke,
"Let us not approach this forest,
a she-wolf is here who devours men,
she will soon kill us both."

Ylgrin hljóp úr einum runn,
ógurlig með gapanda munn,
hǫrmuligt varð Hjalta viðr,
á honum skalf bæði leggr og liðr.

The she-wolf sprang from the bushes,
frightful with gaping mouth,
Hjalti was distressed at this,
he shook in leg and limb.

Ótæpt Bjarki að henni gengr,
ekki dvelr hann við það lengr,
hǫggur svó að í hamri stóð,
hljóp úr henni ferligt blóð.

Bravely Bjarki goes to her,
he does not dally longer at this,
[he gives] such a stroke through the
    skin,
that hideous blood sprang forth from
    her.

"Kjóstu Hjalti um kosti tvó,"
kappinn Bǫðvar talaði svó,
"drekk nú blóð eða drep eg þig hér,
dugrinn líz mér engi í þér."

"Choose, Hjalti, between two
    choices,"
so spoke Bǫðvarr the champion,
"drink now the blood or I'll kill you
    here,
courage does not seem to me to be in
    you."

Ansar Hjalti af ærnum móð,
"ekki þori eg að drekka blóð,
nýtir flest ef nauðigr skal,
nú er ekki á betra val."

Hjalti answers wearily,
"I dare not drink the blood,
best to do so if I must,
there is no better choice."

Hjalti gjǫrir sem Bǫðvar biðr,
að blóði frá eg hann lagðist niðr,
drekkur síðan drykki þrjá,
duga mun honum við einn að rjá.

Hjalti does as Bǫðvarr asks,
at the blood—I hear—he lay down,
drinks then three drafts,
sufficient for him to fight one [man].

Hugrinn óx en miklast máttr,
minst var honum í litlu dráttr,
raunmjǫg sterkr og ramr sem trǫll,
rifnuðu af honum klæðin ǫll.

Courage grew and strength waxed,
he gained much, [became]
tremendously strong and mighty as a
    troll,
from him burst all his clothes.

Svó er hann orðinn harðr í hug,
hann hræðist ekki járna flug,
burtu er nú bleyðinafn,
Bǫðvari var hann að hreysti jafn.

Thus is he made courageous,
he did not fear battle ('flight of iron'),
gone is now the coward's tag,
he was Bǫðvarr's equal in valor.

[Four non-narrative verses from the end of the fourth and the beginning of the fifth
fits deleted]

Hann hefr fengið hjartað snjalt
af hǫrðum móði,
fekk hann huginn og aflið alt
af ylgjar blóði.

He has received a valiant heart
in a great wrath,
he got courage and might
from the blood of the she-wolf.

Í grindur vandist grábjǫrn einn
í garðinn Hleiðar,
var sá margur vargrinn beinn
og víða sveiðar.

A certain bear troubled the pens
of Hleiðargarðr,
many a beast was there
and traipsed widely about.

Bjarka er kent, að hjarðarhunda
hafi hann drepna,
ekki er hónum allvel hent
við ýta kepna.

Bjarki is informed that the herder's
        dog
he has slain,
he is not very suited
to contend with men.

Hrólfur býst og hirð hans ǫll
að húna stýri,
"sá skal mestr í minni hǫll
er mætir dýri."

Hrólfr and all his retinue prepared
to hunt the bear,
"he shall be greatest in my hall
who attacks the beast."

Beljandi hljóp bjǫrninn framm
úr bóli krukku,
veifar sínum vónda hramm,
svó virðar hrukku.

Roaring, the bear sprang forth
from its den,
shook its evil paws,
so that men retreated.

Hjalti sér og horfir þá á,
er hafin er róma,
hafði hann ekki í hǫndum þá
nema hnefana tóma.

Hjalti watches,
as the battle begins,
he had nothing in his hand,
save only an empty fist.

Hrólfur fleygði að Hjalta þá
þeim hildar vendi
kappinn móti krummu brá
og klótið hendi.

Hrólfr threw to Hjalti then
his sword ('battle wand'),
the champion shot forth his hand
and caught the sword-hilt.

Lagði hann síðan bjǫrninn brátt
við bóginn hægra,
bessi fell í brúðar átt
og bar sig lægra.

Then he soon laid into the bear,
at its right shoulder,
the he-bear fell to earth
and gave up its life.

Vann hann það til frægða fyst	With that he first won renown
og fleira síðar,	and several times since,
hans var lundin lǫngum byst	his heart was long brave
í leiki gríðar.	in battle ('play of axes').

(IV, 58–66; V, 4–12)

It is undoubtedly the case, as many researchers have concluded, that the original story had but one monster, as reflected in Saxo and the saga, and that *Bjarkarímur* has taken the notion of the second encounter with that beast and developed it into a second slaying. Yet Finnur Jónsson deems the *rímur* more logical and closer to the original on several other points of organization and order.[82]

Whether or not Finnur is correct on this point, it is certainly true that the *rímur* can be an invaluable aid in understanding saga texts. The information in *Bjarkarímur* concerning the ring that dominates the episodes about King Hrólfr's father, uncle, and cousin, for instance, is decisive for apprehending the item's character and importance, a significance overlooked in the surviving manuscripts of *Hrólfs saga kraka* (chaps. 7–9). Moreover, we are indebted to the *rímur* for our knowledge of otherwise lost saga traditions, as in the cases of *Gríms rímur og Hjálmars*, *Haralds rímur Hringsbana*, *Ormarsrímur*, and *Þóris rímur háleggs*. The *rímur* also flesh out our understanding of extant saga texts; the authors of these poems had the opportunity to examine saga manuscripts now lost or damaged, and they may have known aspects of the tradition which were not incorporated into the sagas.

An element of the *rímur*'s narrative style which indicates a departure from previous modes of narration is their tendency to divide the plot into fits at what seem, to the modern reader at least, odd junctures. Whereas eddic poems and ballads—and even the chapter divisions of saga manuscripts—are organized around specific actions and themes, the *rímur* do not balk at leaving off their stories in the middle of the action, digressing in the close of that fit and the opening of the next, and then taking up the story again. Thus, for example, in the early fourteenth-century *Áns rímur bogsveigis* (III, 49–68; IV, 1–9) the confrontation between Án and Ketill at the farmer's house (equivalent to chap. 4 of the saga) is related partly in one fit, partly in another, with a number of verses in the conclusion of the third *ríma* and in the *mansǫngvar* of the fourth delaying the conclusion of the scene in which Án avenges himself on the evil Ketill.[83]

82. Finnur Jónsson 1904, xviii–xix.
83. See Ólafur Halldórsson 1973, 73–74, concerning the date of the saga.

Perhaps no other fact so clearly underscores the sense that something quite new and unique has taken place in the long history of the Nordic legendary materials than the writing of *Skíðaríma*, the only mock-heroic text of its kind to come from the Icelandic Middle Ages. Although the oldest surviving manuscript of the *ríma* dates only to 1737, references to it from the sixteenth century make it clear that the text is considerably older.[84] Björn K. Þórólfsson concludes on the basis of linguistic and stylistic evidence that *Skíðaríma* was written in the first half of the 1400s, whereas previous researchers had sometimes been inclined to assign it to the fourteenth century.[85] The *ríma*—consisting of over two hundred verses without divisions into *rímnaflokkar*—tells of how a vagrant, Skíði, wanders from one chieftain's house to another, making his living by begging and regaling the households with stories. On one such occasion, he forgets to cross himself and is subsequently visited by Þórr, who takes him to Óðinn's hall. There Skíði is asked to arbitrate between Heðinn and Hǫgni, the two feuding champions of *Sǫrla þáttr*. For a time, things go well, but Skíði's frequent references to the Christian God so enrage the old pagan deities and legendary warriors that a colossal battle breaks out. It is described at length, and after Skíði has killed or maimed a number of the old gods, including Njǫrðr, Loki, and Baldr, he wakes up, only to find himself black and blue, nearly toothless, and in possession of some of the items he had acquired in his dream. Thus everyone is convinced that Skíði's story must be something more than "just" a dream. The *ríma* is humorously narrated and demonstrates that its author knew a great many of the *fornaldarsǫgur* and *riddarasǫgur*, as Konrad Maurer points out in his study of *Skíðaríma*.[86] Among the figures included in the poem are those made familiar in such sagas as *Hrólfs saga Gautrekssonar*, *Gǫngu-Hrólfs saga*, *Sǫrla þáttr*, *Norna-Gests þáttr*, **Hrómundar saga Gripssonar*, *Heiðreks saga*, and *Hálfs saga ok Hálfsrekka*.

Since at least the time of the *Batrachomyomachia* the opportunity to lampoon heroic texts by using the elevated language of epic to treat a trivial subject has been a popular, and distinct, form of versified parody. Roughly contemporary works, such as Chaucer's *Nun's Priest's*

---

84. For a discussion of the oldest text and works on it, see Homan 1975, 16–21; on the earliest references to it, beginning with an entry for 1195 in *Gottskálksannáll*, but written in the sixteenth century, see pp. 91–114.

85. Björn K. Þórólfsson 1934, 385–86. His conclusion is based on features of the poem's language and structure, e.g., rhymes such as *sér: er* and the presence of *mansǫngvar*.

86. Maurer 1869, 3–70; on the structure of, and influences on, the *ríma*, see pp. 3–55.

Tale in England and Wittenwiler's *Der Ring* on the Continent, suggest that the mock-heroic text experienced an increase in popularity throughout Europe at this time, and certainly there is much about *Skíðaríma* which justifies our assigning it to this literary category. Despite the fact that the protagonist is described as an ugly and quarrelsome *gǫngumaðr* 'vagrant,' the poet frequently employs the formal metaphoric language of skaldic verse to refer to him; among the *kenningar* for 'man' and 'hero' used for Skíði are *auðar Baldr* 'Baldr of riches' (st. 12), *laufa viðinn* 'tree of swords' (st. 52), *laufa lundr* 'grove (tree) of swords' (st. 67), and *fleina lundrinn* 'the grove (tree) of arrows' (st. 128). The large number of heroes known in *fornaldarsǫgur* named in the poem should probably be understood as a parody of the affection the *rímur* show for such lists of personages. And when the kings of the sagas give gifts to heroes, they tend to be heirloom weapons or ships laden with men and supplies; but when Óðinn offers Skíði his selection of a *kjǫrgripr* 'costly gift' (st. 100) from the kingdom, the "hero" here asks for a new tip for his staff and some butter! The poet perfects this parodic style in his narration of the battle, in which realistic descriptions that might have been culled from the eddas or the sagas trade off with such burlesque scenes as the following:

Sló til Gunnars Sigurður hringr,
sá var arfi Gjúka,
augnabrúinin á honum springr,
ei mun góðu lúka.

Gunnar was struck by Sigurðr 'ring,'
the heir of Gjúki,
his eyebrow is cut,
it will not end well.

Svó hjó hann til Sigurðar hrings,
að sverð stóð fast í tǫnnum;
hér hefir næsta komið til kings
með kǫrskum frægðarmǫnnum.

Such he hewed at Sigurðr 'ring.'
that the sword stood fast in his teeth;
here it has nearly come to ruin
with the powerful men of renown.

(sts. 155–56)[87]

One conclusion to be drawn from the testimony of *Skíðaríma* is that already by the period 1400 to 1450 the excesses of the *rímur* tradition were sufficiently well known in Iceland that a mock-heroic poem could be written at all and, further, could be appreciated to the degree that its

87. The appellation *hringr* 'ring' should probably be interpreted as 'mailed,' as the name Sigurðr Hringr (the father of Ragnarr loðbrók) would seem out of place here. The translation 'come to ruin' for *komið til kings* follows Finnur Jónsson's comment (1926–28, 210) that the phrase "may mean 'leads to destruction' (*blive til undergang*); the word [*kingr*] is obscure and otherwise unattested; may be related to *kingja* 'to swallow, consume' (*at sluge*)."

popularity, as indicated by the later manuscript activity, suggests.[88] It is periodically maintained—in a derogatory sense—that the *rímur* are intended for the "common man," individuals ill prepared or unable to appreciate the greatness of a *Njáls saga* or the complex beauty of skaldic verse.[89] To whatever extent this statement may be true for the other *rímur*—and the references to wealthy patrons in them would seem to deny the possibility—the argument certainly cannot be made for *Skíðaríma*, which demands of its audience a sophisticated knowledge of the legendary tradition and its idiom. This breadth of popular knowledge, together with the foreign loanwords of the text—for example, *Ekki sómir ammors vess / ǫllum bauga skorðum* 'Amorous verses do not befit all ring-bearers (women)' (st. 4)—suggests that the author was a highly sophisticated and learned individual, in touch with the mainstream of European literary trends.

Creation and refinement of the *rímur* were surely caused by a great many factors. Some of the aspects of Icelandic literary culture which fostered the genesis of the *rímur* have been summarized by Sir William Craigie, who suggests that the *rímur* satisfied two needs exhibited in the poetry of the thirteenth and fourteenth centuries: the need for a new form of verse to replace skaldic verse, which was in decline, and the need for "a kind of poetry which would be more in line with the sagas in telling a continuous tale instead of presenting a succession of separate incidents in a concise form."[90] Both of these needs, he maintains, were addressed by the development of the *rímur*. Indicative of the need for such an artistic reform in the thirteenth century are the numerous *prose* translations of the versified French *chansons*, for Norse literature lacked the possibility of retelling the tales in lengthy narrative poetry at that point. Whereas England had its metrical romances, Germany its *Endreim* poems, and France its *chansons*, no such poetry existed in Scandinavia. A need existed and it is unsurprising that a literary form developed which was capable of filling the gap. Just as the appearance of *knittelvers* apparently transformed the state of Old Swedish letters, so the development of *rímur* was a momentous event in Icelandic culture. It held out the possibilities not only of a new literary mode with which to entertain, but also of the subsequent renewal of an important narrative, as well as metrical, tradition. And the evident ability of the *rímur* to fulfill both functions led to its dominance of Icelandic literature for hundreds of years.

88. Cf. Homan 1975, 9 et passim.
89. Cf. Hallberg 1962, 145.
90. Craigie 1952, I, 281–82.

Sǫgumaðr, kvæðari, and rímari

I have examined here the genres that took up the traditions central to the *fornaldarsǫgur;* it remains to be seen if some general principles about their historical relationships and intertwining can be suggested. Although any single rule of transmission runs the risk of overgeneralizing, the examples above of the matrix composed of the extant *fornaldarsǫgur, rímur,* and ballads (leaving aside questions of preexisting eddic poetry, hypothetical ballads, and so on) result in a diachronic model for the composition of heroic multiforms in medieval Scandinavia in which the traditional legendary material is converted into either an essentially prose Icelandic saga or a versified form. If the poetic text is Icelandic, then the manifestation will be as *rímur;* if it is non-Icelandic, the tradition will be realized as a ballad. This simple rule is based on the opposition of Iceland and the other Scandinavian countries as a distinctive feature where these versified genres are concerned. That is, heroic ballads and heroic *rímur* are in complementary distribution in the Nordic region; geographically and linguistically, they are mutually exclusive.[91] The relationship may be even more vexed in that, of all the *fornaldarsǫgur,* the materials of only two (*Vǫlsunga saga* and *Hrólfs saga Gautrekssonar*) were rendered into both ballads and traditional *rímur* (those from before 1600).

Rímur frequently come about as a secondary development from written *fornaldarsǫgur,* while at the same time written sagas were sometimes fashioned from the *rímur.* Thus, in the later periods, *fornaldarsǫgur* and *rímur* exercised considerable influence on one another. The ballads, on the other hand, were essentially a receptive category, drawing primarily on the saga materials and the tradition itself, but rarely contributing back into the system. Clearly the coexistence of the *fornaldarsǫgur* and *rímur* in Iceland allowed for greater synergism than was possible for the ballad, which, with regard to the *fornaldarsǫgur* traditions, was essentially nonexistent in Iceland. Moreover, written sagas become more common during the later medieval period, whereas no such practice was true of the ballads until the recordings by the aristocracy in the sixteenth century. Minor exceptions to this principle of saga-ballad relations occur, as when a postulated *Týrfingr ballad was said to have influenced the nature of a hypothetical *Ormars saga, but there are no substantiated examples of ballads having been the

---

91. This is not to suggest that heroic ballads have never existed in Iceland, only that we have no such texts.

fundamental sources for subsequent sagas or *rímur*, a finding very much in keeping with Vésteinn Ólason's conclusion regarding the genesis of the Nordic ballad and the Icelandic *rímur*.[92] Although it naturally figures into the model, the distinction between oral and written texts need not preoccupy us here. Whether the contributing materials were heard from a traditional raconteur, heard while being read aloud from a manuscript, or simply read is an important issue with regard to contextualization and to other aspects of our understanding of the tales and their environment, but it does not significantly alter the path of generic transformation.

As a sort of palimpsest on Lönnroth's model of saga communications with regard to the *íslendingasǫgur*, the model of '*fornaldarsǫgur-rímur*-ballad communications' given here emerges from the preceding observations on the disposition of the legendary materials in the later medieval and early post-Reformation periods. I have elsewhere avoided the well-documented, contemporary, native term *sǫgumaðr* 'sagaman' (which might mean anything from 'oral tradition bearer' to 'saga writer'); its use here is meant to imply the creative impulse of an *individual* who fashions (or refashions) the tale. *Rímari* 'rhymer' and *kvæðari* 'balladeer' (use of the Faroese term is not intended to preclude other traditions) likewise imply the intervention of an individual who recasts the material, perhaps only in very small ways (as with the slight variations in the ballad texts) or possibly by shifting the received material into an entirely different genre (as when sagas were rewritten as *rímur*).

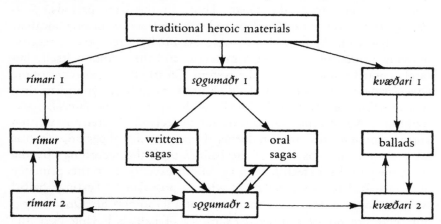

92. Cf. Vésteinn Ólason 1978a, 33. The disposition of the materials relating to the very late *Illuga saga Gríðarfóstra* remains an open question. Davið Erlingsson (1975) maintains that either (1) the saga and the ballad have both been derived from common preexisting material, or (2) the saga developed from the ballad.

Designations such as '*sǫgumaðr* 2' refer to any subsequent reworking of the material; in theory texts could be, and were, "recycled" through the system in many different forms.

To take an earlier example, at one point a written, but now lost, *Hrómundar saga Gripssonar* was created; that text was further developed into a *rímur*; and it is this work that was subsequently recast as the extant prose *fornaldarsaga*. Although there is some uncertainty on the point, some of the extant Sigurðr ballads (for example, *DgF* 2, *DgF* 3, *Landstad* 9, *CCF* 1) may have derived partially from the lost *Sigurðar saga*, partially from oral tradition.[93] Similarly, a set of traditional materials (mythological, legendary, genealogical) were at some point brought together to form the extant *Hálfs saga ok Hálfsrekka*, one of the many later manuscripts of which probably formed the basis for a Faroese ballad (*Álvur kongur, CCF* 14), which was in turn the ultimate source for the much altered Swedish ballad *Stolt Herr Alf.*

An important by-product of the saga-*rímur*-ballad network was the reinvigoration of the legendary materials: certainly one of the most fascinating aspects of the northern heroic tradition is its astonishing stability and durability. Although monsters may multiply or decrease from one telling to the next and familial relations go slightly awry in one version or another, such alterations are relatively minor when compared to the remarkable resiliance some of the traditions have enjoyed. Modulation within certain limits is not only to be expected, but is even a necessary component if the tradition is to avoid stagnation. Even when these changes are fairly great (as, for example, when the father takes over the role of the suitor in the fight against the berserker in the *Kung Speleman* multiform of *Heiðreks saga,* or when Angantýr and Hjálmar are identified as brothers in the corresponding Danish ballads), the basic story is hardly obscured. Despite all manner of geographical, linguistic, and literary obstacles, the *fornaldarsǫgur* and their traditions reveal an almost uncompromising fidelity to their place among the inherited store of Nordic narrative materials.

93. Cf. Liestøl 1970, 24–36.

Epilogue

In discussing the mechanisms by which oral traditional literature is composed and presented, Albert Lord maintains that details of compositional technique are always subordinate to the story: "The tale's the thing."[1] It is a maxim that may be justifiably applied to the materials under consideration here: to whatever extent details connected with our heroic tales may change due to the passage of time or to changes in taste or to the unique demands a genre may make on the tale, the fundamental story comes through. The tale is, indeed, the thing.

Even as this heroic legacy was being collected and published (and thereby dying out as a living oral tradition) in its last traditional outpost, the Faroe Islands, the literary transformation of the *fornaldarsǫgur* was entering a new phase elsewhere in Europe. Throughout the 1840s, in Germany and in Switzerland, Richard Wagner was busily researching and sketching out the plan for his *Ring* operas. With this stupendous drama the *fornaldarsǫgur*, as exemplified by *Vǫlsunga saga*, would achieve their greatest notoriety in the modern world.[2] But Wagner was not the first modern writer to be influenced by the *fornaldarsǫgur*. Already in the early eighteenth century one of the first attempts at a Swedish novel, Olof Broman's *Stilpo Thorgilssons Historia* (ca. 1705), the story of a Viking who sets off in search of adventure at foreign courts, had been patterned, both in style and in content, after the

1. Lord 1960, 68.
2. Richard Wagner, *Der Ring des Nibelungen: Ein Bühnenfestspiel für drei Tage und einen Vorabend* (Leipzig: n.p., 1853).

fornaldarsǫgur.[3] This early modern attempt at a recreation of the past in the mold of the *fornaldarsǫgur* was soon followed by others, written by such diverse figures as Friedrich Klopstock, Sir Walter Scott, William Morris, Viktor Rydberg, H. Rider Haggard, and, of course, Wagner. Nor has the generative power of these heroic texts waned in modern times: there is little doubt but that the adventures of Röde Orm of Höganäs in Frans G. Bengtsson's novels owe much to the *fornaldarsǫgur,*[4] and in even more recent years, a popular series of rewritten *fornaldarsǫgur* has taken shape under the pen of Poul Anderson.[5]

What sets all of these texts apart, of course, is that they are no longer traditional, no longer part of a common stock of knowledge. Still, it is a long and largely unbroken literary chain that connects the earliest *fornaldarsaga* references to our modern world. Recited, retold, read, recast, and enjoyed, the *fornaldarsǫgur* corpus has displayed both surprising longevity and surprising popularity through ten or more centuries. The sagas' ability to fire the imagination of so many artists in such different cultural settings is naturally great testimony to their intrinsic power. The success of the tales can be measured thus not only in the pleasure they have brought their audiences, but also in their resilience over time and in their transmutability across genres.

The conditions for the formation of the extant *fornaldarsǫgur,* their function in the world of the late Middle Ages, and the subsequent fate of the tales have been my topics here. In the course of such a discussion, it has been possible to review much of the previous thinking about these texts, but the current volume is meant to be anything but a survey. It has a particular point of view that is theoretically and methodologically informed by both sides of the free-prose and book-prose debate. It has been possible to see how the texts in their current forms draw on traditional themes, inherited poetry, and learned works, but it is equally important to bear in mind that they were also shaped by individual writers who created poetry and interpolated episodes. We have further seen how the power of the stories secured their place in later purely poetic innovations in the literary repertoire of the north. The results of both stages in the evolution of the tales sometimes fare poorly in the minds of modern readers when compared to the literary

---

3. Olof Broman, *Stilpo Thorgilssons Historia*. Partially reprinted in Knut Barr, "Olof Broman: Vår förste romanförfattare," *Samlaren* 18 (1897): 1–90.

4. Frans G. Bengtsson, *Röde Orm*. Vol. I: *Hemma och i österled*. Vol. II: *Sjöfarare i västerled, en berättelse från okristen tid* (Stockholm: P. A. Norstedt och söner, 1941–45).

5. E.g., Poul Anderson, *Hrolf Kraki's Saga* (New York: Ballantine, 1973).

monuments of the classical age of the sagas, but it should be remembered that the *fornaldarsǫgur* played an important aesthetic and cultural role in fourteenth- and fifteenth-century Iceland. Treating these thirty or so narrative traditions as a unit has, I trust, made this group of sagas more understandable from literary, folkloric, and historical points of view. In the headlong rush away from the historicist interests of previous periods, much of the scholarship in this century on this fascinating genre of Old Norse literature has tended to emphasize atomistic approaches. Although there can be little doubt that such positivistic contributions will continue to enrich our understanding of the *fornaldarsǫgur,* source- and motif-centered research cannot remain the sole area of scholarly investigation. It has been my intention here to validate other avenues of extraliterary exploration—specifically those tied to the issues of function, of genre analysis and genre mutability, and of the attitudes of the Icelanders toward their past—in the hope that such an analysis will raise yet further questions about, and approaches to, the *fornaldarsǫgur.*

As we have seen, the foundations of the *fornaldarsǫgur* are the traditional characters and plots whose histories in Scandinavia may stretch back many centuries in some cases, although of these earlier periods we know very little. It is not until the postclassical saga period that the *fornaldarsǫgur* as a literary genre appear. Many of the same heroes and heroic deeds also appear later in Scandinavia in ballads, *rímur,* and folklore. Can we account in general terms for the relationship between these three stages, the preliterate, the late medieval, and the modern? To some extent specific historical connections between the various manifestations of the same tradition (for example, the dissemination of a particular text via manuscripts) account for the relationship, although not all later multiforms result directly from the earlier *fornaldarsǫgur.* A parallel to this situation may be drawn from the botanical world in the substance called mycelium, the vegetative part of fungus which exists virtually everywhere in temperate climates. For unknown reasons it will suddenly form a fruiting body which presses up through the earth as a cluster of mushrooms. Like this mycelium, the material of the *fornaldarsǫgur,* the "tradition," runs unrecorded through a vast expanse of Scandinavian history and oral tradition, and suddenly emerges in a somewhat altered written form in the late Middle Ages as the *fornaldarsǫgur,* and then surfaces again in the seventeenth, eighteenth, and nineteenth centuries as texts collected from oral tradition. The discourse, the story, the tradition, is one thing, an orally transmitted sense of the tale; the various manifestations of the tradition are something else again, literary monuments that can be expressed in different forms—sagas, ballads, and *rímur*. The multifarious relations between these phenomena represent a remarkable challenge to, and opportunity for, our understanding of the heroic legacy in the later Middle Ages.

Despite the obvious appeal these stories had in the later Middle Ages, it would be misleading to suggest that they won uniform praise even in those centuries, for the *fornaldarsǫgur* have not been without their detractors, either in medieval or in modern times. The medieval authors of the *fornaldarsǫgur* were ever prepared to defend their works, and the modern student of them, echoing the author of *Hrólfs saga Gautrekssonar* (chap. 46), cannot avoid the temptation to advise those who do not care for them to look elsewhere for their amusement.

Appendix

The *fornaldarsǫgur* and Examples of Related Ballads and *rímur*[1]

Saga	Ballad(s)[2]	Pre-1600 *rímur*[3]
Áns saga bogsveigis		*Áns rímur bogsveigis*
Ásmundar saga kappabana	*Sniolvs kvæði* CCF 91	
Bósa saga		*Bósarímur*
Egils saga ok Ásmundar		*Egils rímur einhenda*
Gautreks saga		
Gǫngu-Hrólfs saga		*Gǫnguhrólfsrímur*
Gríms saga loðinkinna		
Hálfdanar saga Brǫnufóstra		*Brǫnurímur*
Hálfdanar saga Eysteinssonar		*Hálfdanarrímur Eysteinssonar*
Hálfs saga ok Hálfsrekka	*Álvur kongur* CCF 14; *Stolt Herr Alf* VB VII:352–55, 380–83	
Heiðreks saga	*Angelfyr og Helmer kamp* DgF 19; *Hjálmar og Angantýr* CCF 15; *Arngrims synir* CCF 16; *Gátu rima* CCF 17; *Kung Speleman* VB XII:394–96	
Helga þáttr Þórissonar		
Hrólfs saga Gautrekssonar	*Finnur hin fríði* CCF 26; *Ívint Herintsson* CCF 108; *Kvikisprakk Hermoðson* Ldsd 12	*Hrólfs rímur Gautrekssonar*
Hrólfs saga kraka		*Bjarkarímur*

183

Saga	Ballad(s)[2]	Pre-1600 rímur[3]
Illuga saga Gríðarfóstra	Herr Hylleland henter sin Jomfru DgF 44; Kappin Illhugi CCF 18; Kappen Illhugin Ldsd 2	
Ketils saga hængs	Rosmer DgF 41; Gǫngurólvs kvæði CCF 29; Rolf Gangar Ldsd 5	
Norna-Gests þáttr	Nornagests ríma CCF 4	
Ǫrvar-Odds saga	Angelfyr og Helmer kamp DgF 19; Hjálmar og Angantýr CCF 15; Arngríms synir CCF 16	
Ragnars saga loðbrókar	Regnfred og Kragelil DgF 22; Karl og Kragelil DgF 23; Ormekampen DgF 24; Gests ríma ella Áslu ríma CCF 3; Ragnars kvæði CCF 2; Lindarormen Ldsd 11	
Ragnarssona þáttr		
Sǫrla saga sterka	Sella ríma CCF 86	
Sǫrla þáttr		Sǫrlarímur
Sturlaugs saga starfsama		Sturlaugsrímur
Tóka þáttr Tókasonar		
Vǫlsunga saga	Sivard Snarensvend DgF 2; Sivard og Brynhild DgF 3; Frændehævn DgF 4; (Grimhilds Hævn DgF 5);[4] Sjúrðar kvæði CCF 1; Sigurð svein Ldsd 9; Sivert Snarensvend VB III: 64–67	Vǫlsungsrímur
Yngvars saga viðfǫrla		
Þorsteins þáttr bæjarmagns		
Þorsteins saga Víkingssonar		Þorsteins rímur Víkingssonar

(Probable) Lost *fornaldarsǫgur*[5]

*Andra saga jarls
*Ásmundar saga flagðagæfu
*Gríms saga ok Hjálmars
*Haralds saga Hringsbana
*Hróks saga svarta
*Hrómundar saga Gripssonar
*Huldar saga
*Illuga saga eldhússgóða[6]
*Ormars saga
*Sigurðar saga Fáfnisbana
*Skjǫldunga saga
*Úlfhamssaga[6]
*Þóris saga háleggs

---

1. For the most part only those works with substantial ties to the *fornaldarsaga* in question have been included; I have generally been guided in these and other questions by Knut Liestøl's observations, although not in all cases. Thus, I have regarded *Illuga saga eldhússgóða* as a lost *fornaldarsaga*, but do not list *Blakken som spente ihel kong Eirik* or *Steinfinn Fefinnsson* as ballads related to *Ǫrvar-Odds saga*, the connections being based on too slight a similarity of motifs in my view. Note that the following list is representative, not exhaustive; no attempt has been made to list all variants within a national tradition, especially in the case of unpublished materials, which are only cited when no printed texts exist.

2. All references to ballads are in alphabetical order by national tradition to the following collections: DgF—*Danmarks gamle Folkeviser,* ed. Svend Grundtvig; CCF—*Føroya kvæði. Corpus Carminum Faeroensium,* ed. Svend Grundtvig and J. Bloch, rev. ed. N. Djurhuus; Ldsd—*Norske Folkeviser,* ed. M. B. Landstad; VB—*1500- och 1600-talens visböcker,* ed. Adolf Noreen, Henrik Schück, J. A. Lundell, and Anders Grape. Unless the ballads are cited elsewhere in the text, they do not appear separately in the bibliography. Only the main titles are listed.

3. For those *rímur* not separately listed in the bibliography, see Björn K. Þórólfsson 1934 for detailed discussions and information on manuscripts and locations.

4. *Grimhilds Hævn* displays considerable consistency with the German Nibelung tradition and is generally regarded as being based on southern Germanic, rather than Nordic, materials.

5. There is a great deal of variation as to status among these titles: in some cases, the title may simply be another name for an extant saga (e.g., *Hróks saga svarta* and *Hálfs saga*); in other cases the existence of the saga is certain, parts of it even being known (e.g., *Skjǫldunga saga*); whereas in others (for example, *Hrómundar saga Gripssonar*), a prose saga exists, but it is a modern version based on the *rímur,* although the metrical romance was in turn fashioned after the lost saga.

6. Björn K. Þórólfsson (1934, 236), however, regards the *rímur,* on which this judgment is made as *æfintýrarímur* 'adventure *rímur,*' as distinct from those derived from the mythical-heroic sagas.

Abbreviations

AA	*American Anthropologist*
ÅNOH	*Aarbøger for nordisk Oldkyndighet og Historie*
ANF	*Arkiv för nordisk filologi*
APhS	*Acta Philologica Scandinavica*
Arv	*Arv: Tidskrift för nordisk folkminnesforskning*
AT	*The Types of the Folktale: A Classification and Bibliography.* Ed. Antti Aarne. 2d. rev. ed. Stith Thompson. FFC, 184. Helsinki: Suomalainen Tiedeakatemia. Academia Scientarium Fennica, 1961.
BA	Bibliotheca Arnamagnæana
CCF	*Føroya kvæði. Corpus Carminum Faeroensium.* Ed. Svend Grundtvig and J. Bloch. Rev. ed. N. Djurhuus. 6 vols. Copenhagen: Munksgaard, 1945–72.
DgF	*Danmarks gamle Folkeviser.* Ed. Svend Grundtvig. 12 vols. 1853–63; rpt. Copenhagen: Universitets-Jubilæets Danske Samfund, 1966–76.
EA	Editiones Arnamagnæanæ
FFC	Folklore Fellows Communications
GHÅ	Göteborgs högskolas årsbok
ÍF	Íslenzk fornrit
JAF	*Journal of American Folklore*
JEGP	*Journal of English and Germanic Philology*
Ldsd	*Norske Folkeviser.* Ed. M. B. Landstad. Christiania: Chr. Tönsberg Forlag, 1853.
ML	*The Migratory Legends: A Proposed List of the Types with a Systematic Catalogue of the Norwegian Variants.* Ed. Reidar Th. Christiansen. FFC, 175. Helsinki: Suomalainen Tiedeakatemia. Academia Scientarium Fennica, 1958.
MM	*Maal og Minne*

186

MS	*Medieval Scandinavia*
Saga-Book	*Saga-Book of the Viking Society*
SÁMR	Stofnun Árna Magnússonar á Íslandi Rit
SS	*Scandinavian Studies*
SUGNL	Samfund til Udgivelse af gammel nordisk Litteratur
TSB	*The Types of the Scandinavian Medieval Ballad: A Descriptive Catalogue.* Ed. Bengt R. Jonsson et al. Skrifter utgivna av Svenskt Visarkiv, 5. Stockholm: Svenskt Visarkiv, 1978.
ZDA	*Zeitschrift für deutsches Altertum und deutsche Literatur*
ZDP	*Zeitschrift für deutsche Philologie*

Bibliography

Alphabetization of non-English characters: å = aa; ä, æ = ae; ö, ø, ǫ = oe; ü = ue; ð, Ð = d; þ, Þ follows z. Icelandic names are filed under the patronymic.

English Translations of the *fornaldarsǫgur*

Partial translations are listed only in instances where no complete translation exists.

Ásmundar saga kappabana:
  "Hildibrand's Death Song." Trans. Lee M. Hollander. *Old Norse Poems*. New York: Columbia University Press, 1936. Pp. 52–55.
Bósa saga:
  Pálsson, Hermann, and Paul Edwards, trans. *Gautrek's Saga and Other Medieval Tales*. New York: New York University Press; London: University of London Press, 1968. Pp. 57–88.
  Pálsson, Hermann, and Paul Edwards, trans. *Seven Viking Romances*. Harmondsworth: Penguin, 1985. Pp. 199–227.
Egils saga einhenda ok Ásmundar berserkjabana:
  Pálsson, Hermann, and Paul Edwards, trans. *Gautrek's Saga* (cited above). Pp. 89–120.
  Pálsson, Hermann, and Paul Edwards, trans. *Seven Viking Romances* (cited above). Pp. 228–57.
Gautreks saga:
  Pálsson, Hermann, and Paul Edwards, trans. *Gautrek's Saga* (cited above). Pp. 23–55.
  Pálsson, Hermann, and Paul Edwards, trans. *Seven Viking Romances* (cited above). Pp. 138–70.

188

Gǫngu-Hrólfs saga:
Pálsson, Hermann, and Paul Edwards, trans. *Göngu-Hrólfs Saga.* Toronto: University of Toronto Press, 1980.
Hálfdanar saga Eysteinssonar:
Pálsson, Hermann, and Paul Edwards, trans. *Seven Viking Romances* (cited above). Pp. 171–98.
Helga þáttr Þórissonar:
Pálsson, Hermann, and Paul Edwards, trans. *Gautrek's Saga* (cited above). Pp. 141–47.
Pálsson, Hermann, and Paul Edwards, trans. *Seven Viking Romances* (cited above). Pp. 276–81.
Simpson, Jacqueline, trans. *The Northmen Talk: A Choice of Tales from Iceland.* London: Phoenix House, 1965. Pp. 175–80.
Hervarar saga ok Heiðreks konungs:
Kershaw, Nora, trans. *Stories and Ballads of the Far Past.* Cambridge: The University Press, 1921. Pp. 87–150.
Tolkien, Christopher, ed. and trans. *Saga Heiðreks konungs ins vitra; the Saga of King Heidrek the Wise.* London: Thomas Nelson and Sons, 1960.
Hrólfs saga Gautrekssonar:
Pálsson, Hermann, and Paul Edwards, trans. *Hrolf Gautreksson: A Viking Romance.* Toronto: University of Toronto Press, 1972.
Hrólfs saga kraka:
Jones, Gwyn, trans. *Eirik the Red and Other Icelandic Sagas.* New York: Oxford University Press, 1980. Pp. 221–318.
Mills, Stella M. *The Saga of Hrolf Kraki.* Oxford: Blackwell, 1933.
Hrómundar saga Gripssonar:
Kershaw, Nora, trans. *Stories and Ballads of the Far Past.* Cambridge: The University Press, 1921. Pp. 62–78.
Norna-Gests þáttr:
Kershaw, Nora, trans. *Stories and Ballads of the Far Past.* Cambridge: The University Press, 1921. Pp. 14–37.
Qrvar-Odds saga:
Edwards, Paul, and Hermann Pálsson, trans. *Arrow-Odd: A Medieval Novel.* New York: New York University Press; London: London University Press, 1970.
Pálsson, Hermann, and Paul Edwards, trans. *Seven Viking Romances* (cited above). Pp. 25–137.
Ragnars saga loðbrókar:
Schlauch, Margaret, trans. *The Saga of the Volsungs. The Saga of Ragnar Lodbrok Together with the Lay of Kraka.* 1930; rpt. New York: AMS Press, 1978. Pp. 185–256.
Sǫrla þáttr:
Kershaw, Nora, trans. *Stories and Ballads of the Far Past.* Cambridge: The University Press, 1921. Pp. 43–57.
Magnússon, Eiríkr, and William Morris, trans. *Three Northern Love Stories and Other Tales.* London: Ellis and White, 1875. Pp. 189–210, 245–46.

Sturlaugs saga starfsama:
   Zitzelberger, Otto J., ed. and trans. *The Two Versions of Sturlaugs saga starfsama.* Düsseldorf: Triltsch, 1969.
Vǫlsunga saga:
   Anderson, George K., trans. *The Saga of the Völsungs, Together with Excerpts from the "Nornageststháttr" and Three Chapters from the "Prose Edda."* Newark: University of Delaware Press, 1982.
   Byock, Jesse L., trans. *The Saga of the Volsungs: The Norse Epic of Sigurd the Dragon Slayer.* Berkeley: University of California Press, 1990.
   Finch, R. G. *The Saga of the Volsungs.* London: Thomas Nelson and Sons, 1965.
   Magnússon, Eiríkr, and William Morris, trans. *Volsunga saga: The Story of the Volsungs and the Nibelungs, with Certain Songs from the Elder Edda.* London: Ellis, 1870.
   Schlauch, Margaret, trans. *The Saga of the Volsungs. The Saga of Ragnar Lodbrok Together with the Lay of Kraka.* 1930; rpt. New York: AMS Press, 1978. Pp. 43–181.
Yngvars saga:
   Edwards, Paul, and Hermann Pálsson, trans. *Vikings in Russia: Yngvar's Saga and Eymund's Saga.* Edinburgh: Edinburgh University Press, 1989. Pp. 44–68.
Porsteins saga Víkingssonar:
   Anderson, Rasmus B., trans. *Viking Tales of the North: The Sagas of Thorstein, Viking's Son, and Fridthjof the Bold.* Chicago: Scott, Foresman, 1901. Pp. 1–73.
Porsteins þáttr bæjarmagns:
   Pálsson, Hermann, and Paul Edwards, trans. *Gautrek's Saga* (cited above). Pp. 121–40.
   Pálsson, Hermann, and Paul Edwards, trans. *Seven Viking Romances* (cited above). Pp. 258–75.
   Simpson, Jacqueline, trans. *The Northmen Talk: A Choice of Tales from Iceland.* London: Phoenix House, 1965. Pp. 180–97.

Editions

ADAM OF BREMEN. *Adam von Bremen: Hamburgische Kirchengeschichte [Gesta hammaburgensis ecclesiae pontificum].* Ed. Bernhard Schmeidler. Scriptores rerum germanicarum. 3d ed. Hanover: Hahn, 1917.
ÆTTARTǪLUR. *Flateyjarbok: En Samling af norske Konge-sagaer med inskudte mindre Fortællinger om Begivenheder i og udenfor Norge samt Annaler.* Ed. Guðbrandur Vigfússon and C. R. Unger. 3 vols. Norske historiske kildeskriftfonds skrifter, 4. Christiania: P. T. Malling, 1860–68. I, 24–29.
AF UPPLENDINGA KONUNGUM. *Hauksbók, udg. efter de arnamagnæanske Håndskrifter No. 371, 544 og 675, 4to, samt forskellige Papirshåndskrifter.* Ed. Eiríkur Jónsson and Finnur Jónsson. Copenhagen: Det kongelige nordiske Oldskrift-Selskab, 1892–96. Pp. 456–57.

ÁLA FLEKKS SAGA. *Drei Lygisǫgur: Egils saga einhenda ok Ásmundar berserkjabana, Ála flekks saga, Flóres saga konungs ok sona hans.* Ed. Åke Lagerholm. Altnordische Saga-Bibliothek, 17. Halle: M. Niemeyer, 1927. Pp. 84–120.

ALFRÆÐI ÍSLENZK. *Alfrœði íslenzk: islandsk encyklopædisk Litteratur. I: Cod. Mbr. AM. 194, 8vo.* Ed. Kr. Kålund; *II: Rímtǫl.* Ed. Nataniel Beckman and Kr. Kålund; *III: Landalýsingar m. fl.* Ed. Kr. Kålund. SUGNL, 37, 41, 45. Copenhagen: S. L. Møller, 1908–18.

ÁLVUR KONGUR. *CCF.* I, 376–98.

ANGANTÝR OG HJÁLMAR REFRAIN. *Íslenzk fornkvæði: Islandske folkeviser.* Ed. Jón Helgason. 8 vols. EA, B:17. Copenhagen: Munksgaard, 1962–81. VIII, 127.

ANGELFYR OG HELMER KAMP. *DgF.* I, 250–58; X, 15–16.

ÁNS RÍMUR BOGSVEIGIS. *Íslenzkar miðaldarímur. II: Áns rímur bogsveigis.* Ed. Ólafur Halldórsson. SÁMR, 4. Reykjavík: Stofnun Árna Magnússonar á Íslandi, 1973.

———. Younger Version. "*Áns rímur bogsveigis:* Two Nineteenth Century Icelandic Metrical Romances, Edited from Manuscripts ÍB. 38, 8vo and LBS. 2466, 8vo of the Landsbókasafn Íslands." Ed. Shaun F. D. Hughes. 2 vols. Diss. University of Washington, 1972.

ÁNS SAGA BOGSVEIGIS. *Fornaldar Sǫgur Nordrlanda, eptir gömlum handritum.* Ed. C. C. Rafn. 3 vols. Copenhagen: n.p., 1829–30. II, 323–62.

ÁRNASON, JÓN. *See* Trunt, trunt.

ARNGRÍMS SÝNIR. *CCF.* I, 402–25.

ÁSMUNDAR SAGA KAPPABANA. *Zwei Fornaldarsögur.* "*Hrólfssaga Gautrekssonar*" und "*Ásmundarsaga kappabana*" nach Cod. Holm. 7, 4to. Ed. Ferdinand Detter. Halle: M. Niemeyer, 1891. Pp. 77–100.

ATLAQVIÐA. *Edda: Die Lieder des Codex Regius nebst verwandten Denkmälern. I: Text.* Ed. Gustav Neckel, 5th rev. ed. Hans Kuhn. Heidelberg: Carl Winter. Universitätsverlag, 1983. Pp. 240–47.

BARNIÐ OG ÁLFKONAN. *Íslenzkar þjóðsögur og æventýri.* Ed. Jón Árnason. 2d rev. ed. Árni Böðvarsson and Bjarni Vilhjálmsson. 6 vols. Reykjavík: Bókaútgáfan þjóðsaga, 1961. I, 46–47.

BATTLE OF BRUNNANBURH. *The Anglo-Saxon Minor Poems.* Ed. Elliott van Kirk Dobbie. Anglo-Saxon Poetic Records, 6. New York: Columbia University Press, 1942. Pp. 16–20.

BATTLE OF MALDON. *The Anglo-Saxon Minor Poems.* Ed. Elliott van Kirk Dobbie. Anglo-Saxon Poetic Records, 6. New York: Columbia University Press, 1942. Pp. 7–16.

BEOWULF. *Beowulf and the Fight at Finnsburg.* Ed. Fr. Klaeber. 3d ed. Boston: D. C. Heath, 1950.

BJARKARÍMUR. *Hrólfs saga kraka og Bjarkarímur.* Ed. Finnur Jónsson. SUGNL, 32. Copenhagen: S. L. Møller, 1904. Pp. 109–63.

BLÓMSTRVALLA SAGA. *Blómstrvalla saga.* Ed. Theodor Möbius. Leipzig: G. Engelmann, 1855.

BÓSA RÍMUR. *Íslenzkar miðaldarímur. III: Bósa rímur.* Ed. Ólafur Halldórsson. SÁMR, 5. Reykjavík: Stofnun Árna Magnússonar á Íslandi, 1974.

BÓSA SAGA. Older Version. *Die Bósa-Saga in zwei Fassungen nebst Proben aus den*

Bósa-rímur. Ed. Otto Luitpold Jiriczek. Strassburg: Verlag von Karl J. Trübner, 1893. Pp. 3–63. (AM 586, 4to. Unless specified, all references are to this version.)

——. Younger Version. *Die Bósa-Saga.* Ed. Jiriczek. Pp. 65–138. (AM 360B, 4to.)

DIPLOMAS. *Diplomatarium islandicum. Íslenzkt fornbréfasafn.* Ed. Jón Þorkelsson. 12 vols. Copenhagen: Hið íslenzka bókmentafélag, 1857–1932.

——. *Islandske originaldiplomer indtil 1450: Tekst.* Ed. Stefán Karlsson. EA, A:7. Copenhagen: Munksgaard, 1963.

DÍSA LEGGUR INN SKREIÐ. *Íslenzkar þjóðsögur og æventýri.* Ed. Jón Árnason. 2d rev. ed. Árni Böðvarsson and Bjarni Vilhjálmsson. 6 vols. Reykjavík: Bókaútgáfan þjóðsaga, 1961. I, 566.

DOLOPATHOS. See Johannis de Alta Silva.

DUNSTANUS SAGA. *Dunstanus saga.* Ed. Christine E. Fell. EA, B:5. Copenhagen: Munksgaard, 1963.

EBBE SKAMMELSON. *DgF.* VI, 197–252.

EDDA SNORRA STURLUSONAR. *Edda Snorra Sturlusonar: Udgivet efter håndskrifterne.* Ed. Finnur Jónsson. Copenhagen: Gyldendalske boghandel. Nordisk forlag, 1931.

EGILS SAGA OK ÁSMUNDAR. *Drei Lygisǫgur: Egils saga einhenda ok Ásmundar berserkjabana, Ála flekks saga, Flóres saga konungs ok sona hans.* Ed. Åke Lagerholm. Altnordische Saga-Bibliothek, 17. Halle: M. Niemeyer, 1927. Pp. 1–83.

EGILS SAGA SKALLAGRÍMSSONAR. *Egils saga.* Ed. Sigurður Nordal. ÍF, 2. 1933; rpt. Reykjavík: Hið íslenzka fornritafélag, 1979.

EIRÍKS SAGA RAUÐA. *Hauksbók, udg. efter de arnamagnæanske Håndskrifter No. 371, 544 og 675, 4to, samt forskellige Papirshåndskrifter.* Ed. Eiríkur Jónsson and Finnur Jónsson. Copenhagen: Det kongelige nordiske Oldskrift-Selskab, 1892–96. Pp. 423–44.

EIRÍKS SAGA VÍÐFǪRLA. *Eiríks saga viðfǫrla.* Ed. Helle Jensen. EA, B:29. Copenhagen: C. A. Reitzels forlag, 1983.

EIRÍKUR KRAFINN KAUPSTAÐAR SKULDAR. *Íslenzkar þjóðsögur og æventýri.* Ed. Jón Árnason. 2d rev. ed. Árni Böðvarsson and Bjarni Vilhjálmsson. 6 vols. Reykjavík: Bókaútgáfan þjóðsaga, 1961. I, 562.

EILÍFR GOÐRÚNARSON, ÞÓRSDRÁPA. *Den norsk-islandske Skjaldedigtning. A: Tekst efter Håndskrifterne.* Ed. Finnur Jónsson. 2 vols. Copenhagen and Christiania: Gyldendalske Boghandel. Nordisk Forlag, 1912. I, 148–52.

ELIS SAGA OK RÓSAMUNDU. *Elis saga ok Rosamundu.* Ed. Eugen Kölbing. Heilbronn: Henninger, 1881.

THE FIRST GRAMMATICAL TREATISE. *The First Grammatical Treatise.* Ed. Hreinn Benediktsson. University of Iceland Publications in Linguistics, 1. Reykjavík: Institute of Nordic Linguistics, 1972.

FLATEYJARBÓK. *Flateyjarbok: En Samling af norske Konge-sagaer med inskudte mindre Fortællinger om Begivenheder i og udenfor Norge samt Annaler.* Ed. Guðbrandur Vigfússon and C. R. Unger. 3 vols. Norske historiske kildeskriftfonds skrifter, 4. Christiania: P. T. Malling, 1860–68.

FLÓRES SAGA KONUNGS OK SONA HANS. *Drei Lygisǫgur: Egils saga einhenda ok Ásmundar berserkjabana, Ála flekks saga, Flóres saga konungs ok sona hans.* Ed. Åke

Lagerholm. Altnordische Saga-Bibliothek, 17. Halle: M. Niemeyer, 1927. Pp. 121–77.

FORNSVENSKA LEGENDARIET. *Ett Forn-Svenskt Legendarium, innehållande Medeltids Kloster-Sagor om Helgon, Påfvar och Kejsare ifrån det I:sta till det XIII:de Århundradet.* Ed. George Stephens and F. A. Dahlgren. Samlingar utgivna av Svenska Fornskrift-Sällskapet. 3 vols. Stockholm: P. A. Norstedt och Söner, 1847–74.

FRIÐPJÓFS SAGA INS FRÆKNA. *Die Friðþjófssaga in ihrer Uberlieferung untersucht und in der ältesten Fassung.* Ed. Gustaf Wenz. Halle: M. Niemeyer, 1914.

FUNDINN NOREGR. *Flateyjarbok: En Samling af norske Konge-sagaer med inskudte mindre Fortællinger om Begivenheder i og udenfor Norge samt Annaler.* Ed. Guðbrandur Vigfússon and C. R. Unger. 3 vols. Norske historiske kildeskriftfonds skrifter, 4. Christiania: P. T. Malling, 1860–68. I, 219–21.

GATU RÍMA. *CCF.* I, 426–27.

GAUTREKS SAGA. Older Version. *Die Gautrekssaga in zwei Fassungen.* Ed. Wilhelm Ranisch. Palaestra, 40. Berlin: Mayer und Müller, 1900. Pp. 50–73. (AM 194C, fol., etc.)

——. Younger Version. *Die Gautreksaga.* Ed. Ranisch. Pp. 1–49. (AM 590b–c, 4to. Unless specified, all references are to this version.)

GEIRMUNDAR PÁTTR HELJARSKINNS. *Sturlunga saga efter membranen Króksfjarðarbók udfyldt efter Reykjarfjarðarbók.* Ed. Kr. Kålund. 2 vols. Copenhagen: Det kongelige nordiske Oldskrift-Selskab, 1906–11. I, 1–6.

GIBBONS SAGA. *Gibbons saga.* Ed. R. I. Page. EA, B:2. Copenhagen: Munksgaard, 1960.

GÍSLA SAGA SÚRSSONAR. *Vestfirðinga sǫgur.* Ed. Björn K. Þórólfsson and Guðni Jónsson. ÍF, 6. 1943; rpt. Reykjavík: Hið íslenzka fornritafélag, 1972. Pp. 1–118.

GǪNGU-HRÓLFS SAGA. *Fornaldar Sǫgur Nordrlanda, eptir gömlum handritum.* Ed. C. C. Rafn. 3 vols. Copenhagen: n.p., 1829–30. III, 235–364.

GOTTSKÁLKS ANNÁLL. *Islandske Annaler indtil 1578.* Ed. Gustav Storm. Christiania: Det norske historiske Kildeskriftfond, 1888. Pp. 297–378.

GRETTIS SAGA ÁSMUNDARSONAR. *Grettis saga Ásmundarsonar.* Ed. Guðni Jónsson. ÍF, 7. 1936; rpt. Reykjavík: Hið íslenzka fornritafélag, 1964.

GRÍMS RÍMUR OG HJÁLMARS. *Rímnasafn: Samling af de ældste islandske Rimer.* Ed. Finnur Jónsson. 2 vols. SUGNL, 35. Copenhagen: S. L. Møller, 1905–22. II, 114–31.

GRÍMS SAGA LOÐINKINNA. *Fornaldar Sǫgur Nordrlanda, eptir gömlum handritum.* Ed. C. C. Rafn. 3 vols. Copenhagen: n.p., 1829–30. II, 141–57.

GRIPLUR. *Rímnasafn: Samling af de ældste islandske Rimer.* Ed. Finnur Jónsson. 2 vols. SUGNL, 35. Copenhagen: S. L. Møller, 1905–22. I, 351–408.

GRŒNLENDINGA SAGA. *Eyrbyggja saga: Grœnlendinga sǫgur.* Ed. Einar Ól. Sveinsson and Matthías Þórðarson. ÍF, 4. 1935; rpt. Reykjavík: Hið íslenzka fornritafélag, 1957.

GUNNLAUGR MÚNK. See *Jóns saga helga eptir Gunnlaugr múnk.*

GYLFAGINNING. See *Edda Snorra Sturlusonar.*

HÁKONAR SAGA HÁKONARSONAR. *Icelandic Sagas and Other Historical Documents Re-*

lating to the Settlements and Descents of the Northmen on the British Isles. II: Hákons saga and a Fragment of Magnús saga. Ed. Gudbrandur Vigfússon. Rerum Britannicarum Medii AEvi Scriptores or Chronicles and Memorials of Great Britain and Ireland during the Middle Ages. London: Her Majesty's Stationery Office, 1887–94. Pp. 1–360.

HÁLFDANAR SAGA BRǪNUFÓSTRA. *Fornaldar Sǫgur Nordrlanda, eptir gömlum handritum*. Ed. C. C. Rafn. 3 vols. Copenhagen: n.p., 1829–30. III, 559–91.

HÁLFDANAR SAGA EYSTEINSSONAR. *Hálfdanar saga Eysteinssonar*. Ed. Franz Rolf Schröder. Altnordische Saga-Bibliothek, 15. Halle: M. Niemeyer, 1917.

HÁLFS SAGA OK HÁLFSREKKA. *Hálfs saga ok Hálfsrekka*. Ed. Hubert Seelow. SÁMR, 20. Reykjavík: Stofnun Árna Magnússonar á Íslandi, 1981.

HALLA FER Í KAUPSTAÐ. *Íslenzkar þjóðsögur og æventýri*. Ed. Jón Árnason. 2d rev. ed. Árni Böðvarsson and Bjarni Vilhjálmsson. 6 vols. Reykjavík: Bókaútgáfan þjóðsaga, 1961. I, 496–97.

HARALDS RÍMUR HRINGSBANA. *Íslenzkar miðaldarímur. I: Haralds rímur Hringsbana*. Ed. Ólafur Halldórsson. SÁMR, 3. Reykjavík: Stofnun Árna Magnússonar á Íslandi, 1973.

HAUKSBÓK. *Hauksbók, udg. efter de arnamagnæanske Håndskrifter No. 371, 544 og 675, 4to, samt forskellige Papirshåndskrifter*. Ed. Eiríkur Jónsson and Finnur Jónsson. Copenhagen: Det kongelige nordiske Oldskrift-Selskab, 1892–96.

HÁVAMÁL. *Edda: Die Lieder des Codex Regius nebst verwandten Denkmälern. I: Text*. Ed. Gustav Neckel. 5th rev. ed. Hans Kuhn. Heidelberg: Carl Winter. Universitätsverlag, 1983. Pp. 17–44.

HEIÐREKS SAGA. *Heiðreks saga (Hervarar saga ok Heiðreks konungs)*. Ed. Jón Helgason. SUGNL, 48. Copenhagen: J. Jørgensen, 1924.

HEIMSKRINGLA. *Snorri Sturluson. Heimskringla*. Ed. Bjarni Aðalbjarnarson. 3 vols. ÍF, 26–28. Reykjavík: Hið íslenzka fornritafélag, 1941–51.

HELGAQVIÐA HUNDINGSBANA I, II. *Edda: Die Lieder des Codex Regius nebst verwandten Denkmälern. I: Text*. Ed. Gustav Neckel. 5th rev. ed. Hans Kuhn. Heidelberg: Carl Winter. Universitätsverlag, 1983. Pp. 130–39, 150–61.

HELGA PÁTTR PÓRISSONAR. *Flateyjarbok: En Samling af norske Konge-sagaer med inskudte mindre Fortællinger om Begivenheder i og udenfor Norge samt Annaler*. Ed. Guðbrandur Vigfússon and C. R. Unger. 3 vols. Norske historiske kildeskriftfonds skrifter, 4. Christiania: P. T. Malling, 1860–68. I, 359–62.

HELREIÐ BRYNHILDAR. *Edda: Die Lieder des Codex Regius nebst verwandten Denkmälern. I: Text*. Ed. Gustav Neckel. 5th rev. ed. Hans Kuhn. Heidelberg: Carl Winter. Universitätsverlag, 1983. Pp. 219–22.

HERR HYLLELAND HENTER SIN JOMFRU. *DgF*. II, 94–102.

HERVARAR SAGA. See *Heiðreks saga*.

HILDEBRANDSLIED. *Altdeutsche Texte*. Ed. Heinz Mettke. Leipzig: VEB Bibliographisches Institut, 1970. Pp. 51–52.

HJÁLMAR OG ANGANTÝR. *CCF*. I, 399–401.

HJÁLMPÉRSSAGA OK QLVIS. "*Hjálmpérs saga*: A Scientific Edition." Ed. Richard L. Harris. Diss. University of Iowa, 1970.

HRÓA PÁTTR HEIMSKA. *Fornmanna sögur, eptir gömlum handritum útgefnar að tilhlutun hins Norrœna fornfrœða félags.* Ed. Þ. Guðmundsson et al. 12 vols. Copenhagen: Popp, 1825–37. V, 252–66.

HRÓLFS SAGA GAUTREKSSONAR. Older Version. *Zwei Fornaldarsögur.* "*Hrólfssaga Gautrekssonar*" *und* "*Ásmundarsaga 'kappabana*" *nach Cod. Holm. 7, 4to.* Ed. Ferdinand Detter. Halle: M. Niemeyer, 1891. Pp. 1–78. (Stock. Perg. 7, 4to. Unless specified, all references are to this version.)

———. Younger Version. *Fornaldar Sǫgur Nordrlanda, eptir gömlum handritum.* Ed. C. C. Rafn. 3 vols. Copenhagen: n.p., 1829–30. III, 55–190. (AM 590b–c, 4to.)

HRÓLFS SAGA KRAKA. *Hrólfs saga kraka.* Ed. Desmond Slay. EA, B:1. Copenhagen: Munksgaard, 1960.

HRÓMUNDAR SAGA GRIPSSONAR. *Fornaldar Sǫgur Nordrlanda, eptir gömlum handritum.* Ed. C. C. Rafn. 3 vols. Copenhagen: n.p., 1829–30. II, 363–80.

HULDAR SAGA. *Sagan af Huld, hinni miklu og fjölkunnugu trölldrotningu.* [Akureyri: Oddur Björnsson, 1911].

HÚNGRVAKA. *Biskupa sögur.* Ed. Jón Sigurðsson and Guðbrandur Vigfússon. 2 vols. Copenhagen: Hið íslenzka bókmentafélag, 1858–78. I, 57–86.

HVERSU NOREGR BYGGÐIST. *Flateyjarbok: En Samling af norske Konge-sagaer med inskudte mindre Fortællinger om Begivenheder i og udenfor Norge samt Annaler.* Ed. Guðbrandur Vigfússon and C. R. Unger. 3 vols. Norske historiske kildeskriftfonds skrifter, 4. Christiania: P. T. Malling, 1860–68. I, 21–29.

ILLUGA RÍMUR ELDHÚSSGOÐA. Described in Björn K. Þórólfsson, *Rímur fyrir 1600,* pp. 443–44. (AM 612d and 612e, 4to.)

ILLUGA SAGA GRÍÐARFÓSTRA. *Fornaldar Sǫgur Nordrlanda, eptir gömlum handritum.* Ed. C. C. Rafn. 3 vols. Copenhagen: n.p., 1829–30. III, 648–60.

ISLANDSKE ORIGINALDIPLOMER. *See* Diplomas.

ÍSLENDINGABÓK. *Íslendingabók: Landnámabók.* Ed. Jakob Benediktsson. ÍF, 1. Reykjavík: Hið íslenzka fornritafélag, 1968. Pp. 1–28.

JOHANNIS DE ALTA SILVA. *Historia Septem Sapientum. II: Johannis de Alta Silva Dolopathos sive de Rege et Septem Sapientibus.* Ed. Alfons Hilka. Heidelberg: C. Winter, 1913.

JOHN TALES. "Juneteenth." Ed. J. Mason Brewer. In *Tone the Bell Easy.* Special issue, *Publications of the Texas Folk-lore Society* 10 (1932), 9–54.

JÓNSBÓK. *Jónsbók. Kong Magnus Hakonssons Lovbog for Island, vedtaget paa Altinget 1281, og Réttarbœtr; de for Island givne Retterbøder af 1294, 1305 og 1314. Udgivet efter Haandskrifterne.* Ed. Ólafur Halldórsson. Copenhagen: S. L. Møller, 1904.

JÓNS SAGA HELGA EPTIR GUNNLAUGR MÚNK. *Biskupa sögur.* Ed. Jón Sigurðsson and Guðbrandur Vigfússon. 2 vols. Copenhagen: Hið íslenzka bókmentafélag, 1858–78. I, 213–60.

JÓNS SAGA HELGA HIN ELZTA. *Biskupa sögur.* Ed. Jón Sigurðsson and Guðbrandur Vigfússon. 2 vols. Copenhagen: Hið íslenzka bókmentafélag, 1858–78. I, 149–202.

KAPPEN ILLHUGIN. Ldsd. Pp. 22–28.

KAPPIN ILLHUGI. *CCF.* I, 428–34.

KARLAMAGNÚS SAGA. *Karlamagnús saga ok kappa hans. Fortællinger om Keiser Karl*

Magnús ok hans Jævninger i norsk Bearbeidelse fra det trettende Aarhundrede. Ed. C. R. Unger. Christiania: H. J. Jensen, 1860.

KETILS SAGA HÆNGS. *Fornaldar Sǫgur Nordrlanda, eptir gömlum handritum*. Ed. C. C. Rafn. 3 vols. Copenhagen: n.p., 1829–30. II, 107–39.

KIRIALAX SAGA. *Kirialax saga*. Ed. Kr. Kålund. SUGNL, 43. Copenhagen: S. L. Møller, 1917.

KJALNESINGA SAGA. *Kjalnesinga Saga; Jökuls þáttr Búasonar, Víglundar saga, Kroka-Refs saga, Þorðar saga hreðu, Finnboga saga, Gunnars saga Keldugnupsfífls*. Ed. Jóhannes Halldórsson. ÍF, 4. Reykjavík: Hið íslenzka fornritafélag, 1959.

KONUNGSSKUGGSJÁ. *Speculum Regale. Konungs-skuggsjá. Konge-speilet. Et philosophisk-didaktisk skrift, forfattet i Norge mod slutningen af det tolfte aarhundrede*. Ed. R. Keyser et al. Christiania: Carl C. Werner, 1848.

KUNG SPELEMAN. *1500- och 1600-talens visböcker*. Ed. Adolf Noreen et al. 12 vols. Skrifter utgifna af Svenska Litteratursällskapet, 7. Stockholm-Uppsala: [Edv. Berlings boktryckeri A.B.], 1884–1925. XII, 394–96.

LANDNÁMABÓK. *Íslendingabók: Landnámabók*. Ed. Jakob Benediktsson. ÍF, 1. Reykjavík: Hið íslenzka fornritafélag, 1968. Pp. 29–397. (Unless specified, all references are to this text.)

———. *Landnámabók: Melabók AM 106.112 fol*. Ed. Johannes C. H. R. Steenstrup et al. Copenhagen and Kristiania: Kommissionen for Det arna-magnæanke Legat, 1921.

LAXDŒLA SAGA. *Laxdœla saga*. Ed. Einar Ólafur Sveinsson. ÍF, 5. Reykjavík: Hið íslenzka fornritafélag, 1934.

LǪGMANNSANNÁLL. *Islandske Annaler indtil 1578*. Ed. Gustav Storm. Christiania: Det norske historiske Kildeskriftfond, 1888. Pp. 231–84.

MAGNÚSS SAGA ERLINGSSONAR. See *Heimskringla*.

MÁGUS SAGA JARLS. Older Version. *Fornsögur Suðrlanda. Isländska bearbetningar af främmande romaner från medeltiden*. Ed. Gustaf Cederschiöld. Lund: Fr. Berling, 1884. Pp. 1–42.

———. Younger Version. *Riddarasögur*. Ed. Bjarni Vilhjálmsson. 6 vols. Reykjavík: Íslendingasagnaútgáfan. Hauksdalsútgáfan, 1949–54. II, 135–429.

MARÍU SAGA. *Maríu saga. Legender om jomfru Maria og hendes jertegn*. Ed. C. R. Unger. Norske Oldskriftselskabssamlinger, 11–12, 14, 15. Kristiania: Brögger og Christie, 1871.

MORKINSKINNA. *Morkinskinna*. Ed. Finnur Jónsson. SUGNL, 53. Copenhagen: Jørgensen, 1928–32.

NIBELUNGENLIED. *Das Nibelungenlied*. Ed. Karl Bartsch and Helmut de Boor. Deutsche Klassiker der Mittelalters. 20th ed. Wiesbaden: Brockhaus, 1972.

NJÁLS SAGA. *Brennu-Njáls saga*. Ed. Einar Ólafur Sveinsson. ÍF, 12. 1954; rpt. Reykjavík: Hið íslenzka fornritafélag, 1971.

NORNAGESTSRÍMA. *CCF*. I, 248–53.

NORNA-GESTS ÞÁTTR. *Flateyjarbok: En Samling af norske Konge-sagaer med inskudte mindre Fortællinger om Begivenheder i og udenfor Norge samt Annaler*. Ed. Guðbrandur Vigfússon and C. R. Unger. 3 vols. Norske historiske kildeskriftfonds skrifter 4. Christiania: P. T. Malling, 1860–68. I, 346–59. (Gks 1005, fol. Unless specified, all references are to this version.)

———. *Fornaldar Sǫgur Nordrlanda, eptir gömlum handritum.* Ed. C. C. Rafn. 3 vols. Copenhagen: n.p., 1829–30. I, 313–42. (Gks 2845, 4to.)

———. *Norrøne Skrifter af sagnhistorisk Indhold.* Ed. Sophus Bugge. Det nordiske Oldskriftselskabs Samlingar, 6. Christiania: Det nordiske Oldskriftselskab, 1864. Pp. 45–79. (AM 62, fol.)

NÝI ANNÁLL. *Islandske Annaler indtil 1578.* Ed. Gustav Storm. Christiania: Det norske historiske Kildeskriftfond, 1888. Pp. 285–96.

QRVAR-ODDS SAGA. Older Version. *Qrvar-Odds saga.* Ed. R. C. Boer. Leiden: E. J. Brill, 1888. (Stock. Perg. 7, 4to. Unless specified, all references are to this version.)

———. Younger Version. *Qrvar-Odds saga.* Ed. Boer. (Parallel texts.)

ÓLAFS RÍMA HARALDSSONAR. *Rímnasafn: Samling af de ældste islandske Rimer.* Ed. Finnur Jónsson. 2 vols. SUGNL, 35. Copenhagen: S. L. Møller, 1905–22. I, 1–18.

ÓLÁFS SAGA TRYGGVASONAR. See *Heimskringla.*

ÓLAFS SAGA TRYGGVASONAR, AF ODDR SNORRASON. *Saga Ólafs Tryggvasonar, af Oddr Snorrason, munk.* Ed. Finnur Jónsson. Copenhagen: G. E. C. Gads forlag, 1932.

ÓLAFS SAGA TRYGGVASONAR EN MESTA. *Óláfs saga Tryggvasonar en mesta.* Ed. Ólafur Halldórsson. 2 vols. EA, A:1,2. Copenhagen: Munksgaard, 1958–.

ORKNEYINGA SAGA. *Orkneyinga saga.* Ed. Finnbogi Guðmundsson. ÍF, 34. Reykjavík: Hið íslenzka fornritafélag, 1965.

ORMAALEN UNGE. Ldsd. Pp. 99–110.

ORMARS RÍMUR. *Early Icelandic Rímur, MS No. 604, 4to of the Arna-Magnæan Collection in the University Library of Copenhagen.* Ed. and with an intro. Sir William A. Craigie. Corpus Codicum Islandicorum Medii AEvi, 11. Copenhagen: Levin og Munksgaard, 1938. Pp. 55–61.

ÓRMS ÞÁTTR STÓRÓLFSSONAR. *Flateyjarbok: En Samling af norske Konge-sagaer med inskudte mindre Fortællinger om Begivenheder i og udenfor Norge samt Annaler.* Ed. Guðbrandur Vigfússon and C. R. Unger. 3 vols. Norske historiske kildeskriftfonds skrifter, 4. Christiania: P. T. Malling, 1860–68. I, 521–32.

PHYSIOLOGUS. *The Icelandic "Physiologus."* Ed. Halldór Hermannsson. Islandica, 26. Ithaca: Cornell University Press, 1938.

PRESTER JOHN. *Der Priester Johannes.* Ed. Friedrich Zarncke. Leipzig: Königlich Sächsische Gesellschaft der Wissenschaften, 1879.

PROVERBS. Kålund, Kristian. "En islandsk ordsprogsamling fra det 15de århundrede med tillæg af andre tilhørende, samtidige optegnelser [Småstykke 7, 1886]." In *Småstykker 1–16.* Copenhagen: SUGNL, 1884–91. Pp. 39–52.

RAGNARS KVÆÐI. CCF. 215–43.

RAGNARS SAGA LOÐBRÓKAR. *Vǫlsunga saga ok Ragnars saga loðbrókar.* Ed. Magnus Olsen. SUGNL, 36. Copenhagen: S. L. Møller, 1906–8. Pp. 111–222.

RAGNARSSONA ÞÁTTR. *Danakonunga sǫgur.* Ed. Bjarni Guðnason. ÍF, 35. Reykjavík: Hið íslenzka fornritafélag, 1982. Pp. 78–83.

REGINSMÁL. *Edda: Die Lieder des Codex Regius nebst verwandten Denkmälern. I: Text.* Ed. Gustav Neckel. 5th rev. ed. Hans Kuhn. Heidelberg: Carl Winter. Universitätsverlag, 1983. Pp. 173–79.

RÉMUNDAR SAGA KEISARASONAR. *Rémundar saga keisarasonar.* Ed. Sven G. Broberg. SUGNL, 38. Copenhagen: S. L. Møller, 1909–12.

RÍMBEYGLA (AM 625, 4to). See *Alfræði íslenzk.*

ROMAN DE SEPT SAGES DE ROME. *Le Roman des Sept Sages.* Ed. Jean Misrahi. 1933; rpt. Geneva: Slatkine, 1975.

RÓMVERJA SAGA. *Rómveriasaga (AM 595, 4to).* Ed. Rudolf Meissner. Palaestra, 88. Berlin: Mayer und Müller, 1910.

SAGA MAGNÚS GÓÐA OK HARALDS HARÐRÁÐA. *Morkinskinna.* Ed. Finnur Jónsson. SUGNL, 53. Copenhagen: Jørgensen, 1928–32. Pp. 1–286.

SAXO GRAMMATICUS. *Saxo Grammaticus: The History of the Danes. I: Text.* Trans. Peter Fisher. Ed. Hilda Ellis Davidson. Totowa, N.J.: Rowman and Littlefield, 1979.

——. *Saxonis Gesta Danorum.* Ed. J. Olrik and H. Ræder. Copenhagen: Levin and Munksgaard, 1931.

SEN'DEH CHEATS THE WHITE MAN. *Kiowa Tales.* Coll. and ed. Elsie Clews Parsons. Memoirs of the American Folk-lore Society, 22. New York: American Folk-lore Society, 1929.

SJÚRÐAR KVÆÐI. *CCF.* I, 1–214.

SKÁLDSKAPARMÁL. See *Edda Snorra Sturlusonar.*

SKÍÐARÍMA. *Rimnasafn: Samling af de ældste islandske Rimer.* Ed. Finnur Jónsson. 2 vols. SUGNL, 35. Copenhagen: S. L. Møller, 1905–22. I, 10–40.

SǪGUBROT AF FORNKONUNGUM. *Danakonunga sǫgur.* Ed. Bjarni Guðnason. ÍF, 35. Reykjavík: Hið íslenzka fornritafélag, 1982. Pp. 46–71.

SǪRLA RÍMUR. *Rimnasafn: Samling af de ældste islandske Rimer.* Ed. Finnur Jónsson. 2 vols. SUGNL, 35. Copenhagen: S. L. Møller, 1905–22. II, 85–111.

SǪRLA SAGA STERKA. *Fornaldar Sǫgur Nordrlanda, eptir gömlum handritum.* Ed. C. C. Rafn. 3 vols. Copenhagen: n.p., 1829–30. III, 408–52.

SǪRLA PÁTTR. *Flateyjarbok: En Samling af norske Konge-sagaer med inskudte mindre Fortællinger om Begivenheder i og udenfor Norge samt Annaler.* Ed. Guðbrandur Vigfússon and C. R. Unger. 3 vols. Norske historiske kildeskriftfonds skrifter, 4. Christiania: P. T. Malling, 1860–68. I, 275–83.

STEINFINN FEFINNSON. Ldsd. Pp. 33–42.

STOLT HERR ALF. *1500- och 1600-talens visböcker.* Ed. Adolf Noreen et al. 12 vols. Skrifter utgifna af Svenska Litteratursällskapet, 7. Stockholm-Uppsala: [Edv. Berlings boktryckeri A.B.], 1884–1925. VII, 352–54, 381–83.

STURLAUGS SAGA STARFSAMA. *Fornaldar Sǫgur Nordrlanda, eptir gömlum handritum.* Ed. C. C. Rafn. 3 vols. Copenhagen: n.p., 1829–30. III, 592–647.

STURLUNGA SAGA. *Sturlunga saga efter membranen Króksfjarðarbók udfyldt efter Reykjarfjarðarbók.* Ed. Kr. Kålund. 2 vols. Copenhagen: Det kongelige nordiske Oldskrift-Selskab, 1906–11.

STURLU PÁTTR. *Sturlunga saga efter membranen Króksfjarðarbók udfyldt efter Reykjarfjarðarbók.* Ed. Kr. Kålund. 2 vols. Copenhagen: Det kongelige nordiske Oldskrift-Selskab, 1906–11. II, 320–28.

SVÍNFELLINGA SAGA. *Sturlunga saga efter membranen Króksfjarðarbók udfyldt efter Reykjarfjarðarbók.* Ed. Kr. Kålund. 2 vols. Copenhagen: Det kongelige nordiske Oldskrift-Selskab, 1906–11. II, 106–31.

THEODORICUS. *Historia de antiquitate regum Norwagiensum.* In *Monumenta Historica Norvegiae. Latinske Kildeskrifter til Norges Historie i Middelalderen.* Ed. Gustav Storm. Norske historiske kildeskriftfonds skrifter, 14. Kristiania: A. W. Brøgger, 1880. Pp. 1–68.

TÓKA ÞÁTTR TÓKASONAR. *Flateyjarbok: En Samling af norske Konge-sagaer med inskudte mindre Fortællinger om Begivenheder i og udenfor Norge samt Annaler.* Ed. Guðbrandur Vigfússon and C. R. Unger. 3 vols. Norske historiske kildeskriftfonds skrifter, 4. Christiania: P. T. Malling, 1860–68. II, 135–38.

TÓMAS SAGA ERKIBYSKUPS. *Thomas saga Erkibyskups. Fortælling om Thomas Becket, erkebiskop af Canterbury. To Bearbejdelser samt Fragmenter af en tredie.* Ed. C. R. Unger. Kristiania: B. M. Bentzen, 1869.

TRISTRAMS SAGA. *Saga af Tristam ok Ísönd, samt Möttuls saga.* Ed. Gísli Brynjúlfsson. Copenhagen: Det kongelige nordiske Oldskrift-Selskab, 1878.

TRÓJUMANNA SAGA. *Trójumanna saga.* Ed. Jonna Louis-Jensen. EA, A:8. Copenhagen: Munksgaard, 1963.

——. *Trójumanna saga: The Dares Phrygius Version.* Ed. Jonna Louis-Jensen. EA, A:9. Copenhagen: C. A. Reitzel, 1981.

TRUNT, TRUNT OG TRÖLLIN Í FJÖLLUNUM. *Íslenzkar þjóðsögur og æventýri.* Ed. Jón Árnason. 2d rev. ed. Árni Böðvarsson and Bjarni Vilhjálmsson. 6 vols. Reykjavík: Bókaútgáfan þjóðsaga, 1961. I, 183–84.

TÝRFINGR RIDDLES. *Íslenzkar gátur, skemtanir, vikivakar og þulur. I: Gátur.* Ed. Jón Árnason and Ólafur Daviðsson. Copenhagen: Hið íslenzka bókmentafélag, 1887. I, 103, 108.

ÚTFERÐAR SAGA OF HARALDR HARÐRÁÐI. See *Saga Magnús góða ok Haralds harðráða.*

VICTORS SAGA OK BLÁVUS. *Late Medieval Icelandic Romances. I: Victors saga ok Blávus; Valdimars saga; Ektors saga.* Ed. Agnete Loth. EA, B:20. Copenhagen: Munksgaard, 1962. Pp. 3–50.

VILHJÁLMS SAGA SJÓÐS. *Late Medieval Icelandic Romances. IV: Vilhjálms saga sjóðs; Vilmundar saga viðutan.* Ed. Agnete Loth. EA, B:23. Copenhagen: Munksgaard, 1964. Pp. 1–136.

VITA ANSKARII. *Vita Anskarii auctore Rimberto.* Ed. Georg Waitz. Scriptores rerum Germanicarum, separatim edit., 55. Hanover: Hahn, 1884.

VQLSUNGA SAGA. *Vǫlsunga saga ok Ragnars saga loðbrókar.* Ed. Magnus Olsen. SUGNL, 36. Copenhagen: S. L. Møller, 1906–8. Pp. 1–110.

VQLSUNGSRÍMUR. *Rímnasafn: Samling af de ældste islandske Rimer.* Ed. Finnur Jónsson. 2 vols. SUGNL, 35. Copenhagen: S. L. Møller, 1905–22. I, 311–47.

YNGLINGASAGA. See *Heimskringla.*

YNGVARS SAGA. *Yngvars saga víðfǫrla, jämte ett bihang om Ingvarsinskrifterna.* Ed. Emil Olson. SUGNL, 39. Copenhagen: S. L. Møller, 1912.

ÞÆTTIR UR MIÐSQGU GUÐMUNDAR BYSKUPS. *Biskupa sögur.* Ed. Jón Sigurðsson and Guðbrandur Vigfússon. 2 vols. Copenhagen: Hið íslenzka bókmentafélag, 1858–78. I, 559–618.

ÞIÐREKS SAGA. *Þiðriks saga af Bern.* Ed. Henrik Bertelsen. 2 vols. SUGNL, 34. Copenhagen: S. L. Møller, 1905–11.

ÞORGILS SAGA OK HAFLIÐA. *Þorgils saga ok Hafliða.* Ed. Ursula Brown [Dronke]. Oxford English Monographs. London: Oxford University Press, 1952.

ÞORGILS SAGA SKARÐA. *Sturlunga saga efter membranen Króksfjarðarbók udfyldt efter Reykjarfjarðarbók.* Ed. Kr. Kålund. 2 vols. Copenhagen: Det kongelige nordiske Oldskrift-Selskab, 1906–11. II, 136–328.

ÞÓRIS RÍMUR HÁLEGGS. Described in Björn K. Þórólfsson, *Rímur fyrir 1600.* (Stock. 23, 4to.)

ÞORSTEINS SAGA VÍKINGSSONAR. *Fornaldar Sǫgur Nordrlanda, eptir gömlum handritum.* Ed. C. C. Rafn. 3 vols. Copenhagen: n.p., 1829–30. II, 381–459.

ÞORSTEINS ÞÁTTR BÆJARMAGNS. *Fornmanna sögur, eptir gömlum handritum útgefnar að tilhlutun hins Norræna fornfræða félags.* Ed. Þ. Guðmundsson et al. 12 vols. Copenhagen: Popp, 1825–37. III, 175–98.

ÞORSTEINS ÞÁTTR UXAFÓTS. *Flateyjarbok: En Samling af norske Konge-sagaer med inskudte mindre Fortællinger om Begivenheder i og udenfor Norge samt Annaler.* Ed. Guðbrandur Vigfússon and C. R. Unger. 3 vols. Norske historiske kildeskriftfonds skrifter, 4. Christiania: P. T. Malling, 1860–68. I, 249–63.

Secondary Literature Cited

Acterberg, Herbert. 1930. *Interpretatio Christiana. Verkleidete Glaubensgestalten der Germanen auf deutschem Boden.* Form und Geist, 19. Leipzig: Hermann Eichblatt Verlag.

Aðalsteinsson, Jón Hnefill. 1982. "Þjóðfræði og bókmenntir." *Skírnir* 156:120–39.

Addison, James T. 1936. *The Medieval Missionary: A Study of the Conversion of Northern Europe A.D. 500–1300.* Studies in the World Mission of Christianity, 2. New York: International Missionary Council.

Allen, Richard. 1971. *Fire and Iron: Critical Approaches to "Njáls saga."* Pittsburgh: University of Pittsburgh Press.

Almqvist, Bo. 1965. "The Viking Ale and the Rhine Gold: Some Notes on an Irish-Scottish Folk-Legend and a Germanic Hero-Tale Motif." *Arv* 21:115–35.

Amory, Frederic. 1984. "Things Greek and the *Riddarasögur.*" *Speculum* 59:509–23.

Andersson, Theodore M. 1964. *The Problem of Icelandic Saga Origins: A Historical Survey.* Yale Germanic Studies, 1. New Haven: Yale University Press.

——. 1966. "The Textual Evidence for an Oral Family Saga." *ANF* 81:1–23.

——. 1967. *The Icelandic Family Saga: An Analytic Reading.* Harvard Studies in Comparative Literature, 28. Cambridge: Harvard University Press.

——. 1970. "The Displacement of the Heroic Ideal in the Family Sagas." *Speculum* 45:575–93.

——. 1975. "Splitting the Saga." *SS* 47:437–41.

——. 1980. *The Legend of Brynhild.* Islandica, 43. Ithaca: Cornell University Press.

——. 1985a. "'Helgakviða Hjǫrvarðssonar' and European Bridal-Quest Narrative." *JEGP* 84:51–75.

——. 1985b. "Kings' Sagas (*Konungasögur*)." In *Old Norse–Icelandic Literature: A Critical Guide.* Ed. Carol J. Clover and John Lindow. Islandica, 45. Ithaca: Cornell University Press, 1985. Pp. 197–238.

——. 1987. *A Preface to the "Nibelungenlied."* Stanford: Stanford University Press.

Andrews, A. Le Roy. 1914–16. "The Lygisǫgur." *Publications of the Society for the Advancement of Scandinavian Study* 2:255–63.

Arent, Margaret A. 1969. "The Heroic Pattern: Old Germanic Helmets, *Beowulf* and *Grettis saga.*" In *Old Norse Literature and Mythology: A Symposium.* Ed. Edgar C. Polomé. Austin: University of Texas Press. Pp. 130–99.

Baetke, Walter. 1951. "Christliches Lehngut in der Saga Religion." *Berichte über die Verhandlungen der Sächsischen Akademie der Wissenschaft zu Leipzig.* Phil.-Hist. Klasse, Bd. 98, Hft. 6. Pp. 7–55.

——. 1956. *Über die Enstehung der Isländersagas. Berichte über die Verhandlungen der Sächsischen Akademie der Wissenschaft zu Leipzig.* Phil.-Hist. Klasse, Bd. 102, Hft. 5. Pp. 5–108.

Bäuml, Franz H. 1980. "Varieties and Consequences of Medieval Literacy and Illiteracy." *Speculum* 55:237–65.

Bandle, Oscar. 1969. "Isländersaga und Heldendichtung." In *Afmælisrit Jóns Helgasonar. 30. júní 1969.* Ed. Jakob Benediktsson et al. Reykjavík: Heimskringla. Pp. 1–26.

——. 1988. "Die Fornaldarsaga zwischen Mündlichkeit und Schriftlichkeit: Zur Entstehung und Entwicklung der Örvar-Odds saga." In *Zwischen Festtag und Alltag. Zehn Beiträge zum Thema 'Mündlichkeit und Schriftlichkeit.'* Ed. Wolfgang Raible. ScriptOralia, 6. Tübingen: Gunter Narr Verlag. Pp. 191–213.

Barnes, Daniel R. 1970. "Folktale Morphology and the Structure of *Beowulf.*" *Speculum* 45:416–34.

Batts, Michael S. 1981. "Author and Public in the Late Middle Ages." In *Interpretation und Edition deutscher Texte des Mittelalters. Festschrift für John Asher zur 60. Geburtstag.* Ed. Kathryn Smits et al. Berlin: E. Schmidt. Pp. 178–86.

Bausinger, Hermann. 1968. *Formen der "Volkspoesie."* Grundlagen der Germanistik, 6. Berlin: Erick Schmidt.

Beck, Heinrich. 1970. "Germanische Menschenopfer in der literarischen Überlieferung." In *Vorgeschichtliche Heiligtümer und Opferplätze in Mittel- und Nordeuropa. Bericht über ein Symposium in Rheinhausen bei Göttingen in der Zeit vom 14.-16. Oktober 1968.* Ed. Herbert Jankuhn. Göttingen: Vandenhoeck & Ruprecht. Pp. 240–58.

Bekker-Nielsen, Hans. 1986. "Church and Schoolroom—and Early Icelandic Literature." In *Sagnaskemmtun. Studies in Honour of Hermann Pálsson on His 65th Birthday, 26th May 1986.* Ed. Rudolf Simek et al. Vienna: Hermann Böhlaus. Pp. 13–18.

Bell, Michael. 1983. "The Names of the Sagas: Prolegomenon and Proposal." *Skandinavistik* 13:44–50.

Ben-Amos, Dan. 1969. "Analytical Categories and Ethnic Genres." *Genre* 2:275–301 [rpt. in Ben-Amos 1976, 215–42].

——. 1976. "Introduction." In *Folklore Genres.* Ed. Dan Ben-Amos. AFS Bibliographical and Special Series, 26. Austin: University of Texas Press. Pp. ix–xlv.

Benediktsson, Jakob. 1956–78a. "Hauksbók." In *Kulturhistorisk leksikon for nordisk middelalder fra vikingetid til reformationstid.* 21 vols. Rpt. Copenhagen: Rosenkilde og Bagger, 1981–82. VI, 250–51.

——. 1956–78b. "Studieresor: Island." In *Kulturhistorisk leksikon for nordisk middelalder fra vikingetid til reformationstid.* 21 vols. Rpt. Copenhagen: Rosenkilde og Bagger, 1981–82. XVII, 341–42.

——. 1981. "Den vågnende interesse for sagalitteraturen på Island i 1600-tallet." *MM* 157–70.

Benediktz, B. S. 1964–65. "The Master Magician in Icelandic Folk-Legend." *Durham University Journal* 57(n.s. 26):22–34.

——. 1973. "Basic Themes in Icelandic Folklore." *Folklore* (London) 84:1–26.

Benson, Larry D. 1970. "The Originality of *Beowulf*." In *The Interpretation of Narrative: Theory and Practice*. Ed. Morton W. Bloomfield. Harvard English Studies, 1. Cambridge: Harvard University Press. Pp. 1–44.

Berger, John Allen. 1980. "Did Haukr Erlendsson Write *Víga-Glúms saga?*" *ANF* 95:113–115.

Berlin, Brent. 1978. "Ethnobiological Classification." In *Cognition and Categorization*. Ed. Eleanor Rosch and Barbara B. Lloyd. Hillsdale, N.J.: Lawrence Erlbaum Associates. Pp. 9–26.

Berlin, Brent, Dennis E. Breedlove, and Peter H. Raven. 1973. "General Principles of Classification and Nomenclature in Folkbiology." *AA* 75:214–42.

Berulfsen, Bjarne. 1948. *Kulturtradisjon fra en storhetstid. En kulturhistorisk studie på grunnlag av den private brevlitteratur i første halvdel av det 14. hundreår.* Oslo: Gyldendal Norsk Forlag.

Bessason, Haraldur. 1977. "Mythological Overlays." In *Sjötíu ritgerðir helgaðar Jakobi Benediktssyni 20. júlí 1977*. Ed. Einar G. Pétursson and Jónas Kristjánsson. 2 vols. SÁMR, 12. Reykjavík: Stofnun Árna Magnússonar á Íslandi. I, 273–92.

Beyer, Harald. 1956. *A History of Norwegian Literature*. Trans. Einar Haugen. Rpt. New York: New York University Press, 1979.

Bjørnbo, Axel A., and Carl S. Petersen. 1909. *Der Däne Claudius Claussøn Swart (Claudius Clavus). Der älteste Kartograph des Nordens, der erste Ptolemäus-Epigon der Renaissance. Eine Monographie*. Revised and trans. Ella Lesser. Innsburck: Verlag der Wagner'schen Universitäts-Buchhandlung.

Blanck, Anton. 1911. *Den nordiska renässansen i sjuttonhundratalets litteratur: En undersökning av den "götiska" poesiens allmänna och inhemska förutsättningar.* Stockholm: Albert Bonnier.

Blom, Ådel Gjøstein. 1982. "Innleining." *Norske mellomalderballader. I: Legendeviser.* Instituttet for sammenlignende kulturforskning, B:LXVI. Oslo: Universitetsforlaget. Pp. 9–31.

Boberg, Inger M. 1966. *Motif-Index of Early Icelandic Literature*. BA, 27. Copenhagen: Munksgaard.

Boor, Helmut de. 1918. *Die färöischen Lieder des Nibelungenzyklus*. Germanische Bibliothek: Untersuchungen und Texte, 12. Heidelberg: Carl Winter.

——. 1929. "'Heldensage ist Literaturgeschichte': Aus Anlaß von Hermann Schneiders 'Germanischer Heldensage.' " *Zeitschrift für deutsche Bildung* 5:449–66.

Bowra, Cecil M. 1952. *Heroic Poetry*. London: Macmillan.

Boyer, Regis. 1975. "Paganism and Literature: The So-called 'Pagan Survivals' in the Samtíðarsögur." *Gripla* 1:135–67.

——. 1986. "Fate as a Deus Otiosus in the *Íslendingasögur*: A Romantic View?" In *Sagnaskemmtun. Studies in Honour of Hermann Pálsson on His 65th Birthday, 26th May 1986*. Ed. Rudolf Simek et al. Vienna: Hermann Böhlaus. Pp. 61–78.

Bringéus, Nils-Arvid. 1982. "Folklorismus: Einige prinzipielle Geschichtspunkte vor schwedischem Hintergrund." In *Folklorismus; Vorträge der I. Internationalen*

Arbeitstagung des Vereins "Volkskultur um den Neusiedlersee" in Neusiedl/See 1978. Ed. Edith Hörandner and Hans Lunzer. Neusiedler Konfrontationen, 1. Neusiedl/See: Verein für regionale Volkskunde und internationale Fachkontakte. Pp. 55–72.

Brink, Bernhard ten. 1889. *History of English Literature (to Wiclif)*. Trans. Horace M. Kennedy. New York: Henry Holt.

Brøndum-Nielsen, Johannes. 1910. "De danske Folkevisers Betydning i sproglig Henseende." In *Nordisk tidskrift för vetenskap, konst och industrie*. Pp. 587–602.

Brown, Ursula. *See* Dronke, Ursula Brown.

Brückner, Wolfgang. 1969. "Kontinuitätsproblem und Kulturbegriff in der Volkskunde." In *Kontinuität? Geschichtlichkeit und Dauer als volkskundliches Problem*. Ed. Hermann Bausinger and Wolfgang Brückner. Berlin: Erich Schmidt Verlag. Pp. 31–46.

Brunvand, Jan. 1959. "Norway's Askeladden, the Unpromising Hero, and Junior-Right." *JAF* 72:14–23.

Buchan, David. 1972. *The Ballad and the Folk*. London: Routledge and Kegan Paul.

———. 1977. "Oral Tradition and Written Tradition: The Scottish Ballads." In *Oral Tradition: Literary Tradition: A Symposium*. Ed. Hans Bekker-Nielsen et al. Odense: Odense University Press. Pp. 56–68.

Buchholz, Peter. 1976. "Fornaldarsaga und mündliches Erzählen zur Wikingerzeit." In *Les vikings et leur civilisation. Problèmes actuels. Rapports scientifiques publiés sous la direction de Régis Boyer*. Ecole des Haute Etudes en Sciences Socials. Bibliothèque Arctique et Antarctique, 5. Paris: Mouton. Pp. 133–78.

———. 1980. *Vorzeitkunde: Mündliches Erzählen und Überliefern im mittelalterlichen Skandinavien nach dem Zeugnis von Fornaldarsaga und eddischer Dichtung*. Skandinavistische Studien, 13. Neumünster: Karl Wachholtz Verlag.

Bugge, Sophus. 1881–89. *Studier over de nordiske Gude- og Heltesagns Oprindelse*. 3 vols. Christiania: Alb. Cammermeyer.

———. 1908. *Norsk Sagaskrivning og Sagafortælling i Irland*. Kristiania: Grøndahl og Søns Forlag.

Byock, Jesse. 1982. *Feud in the Icelandic Saga*. Berkeley: University of California Press.

———. 1984–85. "Saga Form, Oral Prehistory, and the Icelandic Social Context." *New Literary History* 16(1):153–73.

———. 1985. "Cultural Continuity, the Church, and the Concept." *Skandinavistik* 15:1–14.

———. 1988. *Medieval Iceland: Society, Sagas, and Power*. Berkeley and Los Angeles: University of California Press.

Calame, Claude. 1986. "Mythe et conte: La légende du cyclopes et ses transformations narratives." In *Le récit en Grèce ancienne: Enonciations et représentations de poètes*. Paris: Méridiens Klincksieck. Pp. 121–51.

Caldwell, James R. 1939. "The Origin of the Story of Bǫthvar-Bjarki." *ANF* 55:223–75.

Carlyle, Thomas. n.d. *On Heroes, Hero Worship, and the Heroic in History*. New York: Dodge.

Castetter, E. F. 1944. "The Domain of Ethnobiology." *American Naturalist* 78:158–70.

Cederschiöld, Gustaf. 1884. "Inledning." In *Fornsögur Suðrlanda. Isländska bearbetningar af främmande romaner från medeltiden.* Lund: Fr. Berling. Pp. i–lxxix.

Chadwick, Hector Munro. 1912. *The Heroic Age.* Cambridge: Cambridge University Press.

Chadwick, Hector Munro, and N. Kershaw Chadwick. 1933. *The Growth of Literature.* 3 vols. Rpt. Cambridge: Cambridge University Press, 1968.

Ciklamini, Marlene. 1966a. "The Combat between Two Half-Brothers: A Literary Study of the Motif in *Ásmundar saga kappabana* and *Saxonis Gesta Danorum.*" *Neophilologus* 5:269–79, 370–79.

——. 1966b. "Grettir and Ketill Hængr, the Giant-Killers." *Arv* 22:136–55.

——. 1968. "Journeys to the Giant-Kingdom." *SS* 40:95–110.

——. 1975. "Ynglingsaga: Its Function and Appeal." *MS* 8:86–99.

——. 1984. "Veiled Meaning and Narrative Modes in *Sturluþáttr.*" *ANF* 99:139–50.

Čistov, K. 1976. "Zur Frage der theoretischen Unterschiede zwischen der Folklore und Literatur." *Studia Fennica* 20:148–58.

Clover, Carol J. 1982. *The Medieval Saga.* Ithaca: Cornell University Press.

——. 1985. "Icelandic Family Sagas (*Íslendingasögur*)." In *Old Norse–Icelandic Literature: A Critical Guide.* Ed. Carol J. Clover and John Lindow. Islandica, 45. Ithaca: Cornell University Press. Pp. 239–315.

——. 1986. "Vǫlsunga saga and the Missing Lai of Marie de France." In *Sagnaskemmtun. Studies in Honour of Hermann Pálsson on His 65th Birthday, 26th May 1986.* Ed. Rudolf Simek et al. Vienna: Hermann Böhlaus. Pp. 79–84.

Clover, Carol J., et al. 1985. "Preface." In *Old Norse–Icelandic Literature: A Critical Guide.* Ed. Carol J. Clover and John Lindow. Islandica, 45. Ithaca: Cornell University Press. Pp. 7–11.

Conroy, Patricia L. 1974. "Faroese Ballads and Oral-Formulaic Composition." Diss. University of California, Berkeley.

——. 1980. "Oral Composition in Faroese Ballads." *Jahrbuch für Volksliedforschung* 25:34–50.

Craigie, Sir William A. 1913. *The Icelandic Sagas.* Cambridge: Cambridge University Press.

——. 1952. *Sýnisbók íslenzkra rímna frá upphafi rímnakvedskapar til loka nítjándu aldar.* 3 vols. London: Thomas Nelson and Sons.

CREST (Computer Research into Early Scandinavian Texts). "A Concordance to Five Legendary Sagas: A Pilot Project." Ed. Michael Bell et al. Manuscript.

Crosby, Ruth. 1933. "Oral Delivery in the Middle Ages." *Speculum* 11:88–110.

Curschmann, Michael. 1984. "The Prologue of *Þiðreks saga:* Thirteenth-Century Reflections on Oral Traditional Literature." *SS* 56:140–51.

Curtius, Ernst Robert. 1973. *European Literature and the Latin Middle Ages.* Trans. Willard R. Trask. Bollingen Series, 36. Princeton: Princeton University Press.

Dal, Erik. 1956. *Nordisk folkeviseforskning siden 1800: Omrids af text- og melodistudiets historie og problemer især i Danmark.* Universitets-jubliæets danske samfund. Publikation, 376. Copenhagen: J. H. Schultz forlag.

Danielsson, Tommy. 1986. *Om den isländska släktsagans uppbyggnad.* Skrifter utgivna av Litteraturvetenskapliga Institutionen vid Uppsala universitet, 22. Uppsala: Almqvist och Wiksell.

Danske Viser fra Adelsvisebøger og Flyveblade, 1530–1630. 1912–30. Ed. Håkon Grüner-Nielsen. 3 vols. Copenhagen: Det danske Sprog- og Litteraturselskab.

Danske viser: Gamle folkeviser: Skæmt: Efterklang. 1962. Ed. Erik Dal. Copenhagen: Rosenkilde og Bagger.

Davidson, H. R. Ellis. 1941. "Fostering by Giants in Old Norse Saga Literature." *Medium Ævum* 10:70–85.

———. 1975. "Folklore and Literature." *Folklore* (London) 86:73–93.

———. 1976. *The Viking Road to Byzantium.* London: G. Allen and Unwin.

Debo, Angie. 1970. *A History of the Indians of the United States.* Civilization of the American Indian Series. Norman: University of Oklahoma Press.

Dehmer, Heinz. 1927. *Primitives Erzählungsgut in den Íslendingasögur.* Von deutscher Poeterey. Forschung und Darstellungen aus dem Gesamtgebiet der deutschen Philologie, 2. Leipzig: J. J. Weber.

Dorson, Richard M. 1961. "Ethnohistory and Ethnic Folklore." *Ethnohistory* 8:12–30.

Dronke, Ursula Brown. 1947–48. "The Saga of Hrómund Gripsson and Þorgilssaga." *Saga-Book* 13(2):51–77.

———. 1971. "Classical Influences on Early Norse Literature." In *Classical Influences on European Culture,* A.D. *500–1500: Proceedings of an International Conference Held at King's College, Cambridge.* Ed. R. R. Bolgar. Cambridge: Cambridge University Press. Pp. 143–49.

Dumézil, Georges. 1973a. *From Myth to Fiction: The Saga of Hadingus.* Trans. Derek Coltman. Chicago: University of Chicago Press. [Originally published in French in 1970.]

———. 1973b. *Gods of the Ancient Northmen.* Ed and trans. Einar Haugen. Publications of the UCLA Center for the Study of Comparative Folklore and Mythology, 3. Berkeley and Los Angeles: University of California Press.

Dundes, Alan. 1962. "From Etic to Emic Units in the Structural Study of Folklore." *JAF* 75:95–105.

———. 1964. "Texture, Text, and Context." *Southern Folklore Quarterly* 28:251–65.

Ebel, Else. 1977. "Kaufmann und Handel auf Island zur Sagazeit." *Hansische Geschichtsblätter* 95:1–26.

Ebel, Uwe. 1982a. "Darbietungsformen und Darbietungsabsicht in Fornaldarsaga und verwandten Gattungen." In *Beiträge zur Nordischen Philologie.* Frankfurt am Main: Haag und Herschen. Pp. 56–118.

———. 1982b. "Vorbemerkung." In *Beiträge zur Nordischen Philologie.* Pp. 7–25.

Edwards, Paul, and Hermann Pálsson. 1970. "Introduction." In *Arrow-Odd: A Medieval Novel.* New York: New York University Press. Pp. ix–xxi.

Einarsson, Bjarni. 1961. *Skjáldasögur: Um uppruna og eðli ástaskáldasagnanna fornu.* Reykjavík: Bókaútgáfa Menningarsjóðs.

———. 1975. *Litterære forudsætninger for Egils saga.* SÁMR, 8. Reykjavík: Stofnun Árna Magnússonar á Íslandi.

Einarsson, Stefán. 1949. "Alþýðjukveðskapur frá miðöldum." *Skírnir* 123:114–40.

———. 1955. "Report on Rímur." *JEGP* 54:255–61.

———. 1957. *A History of Icelandic Literature*. New York: Johns Hopkins Press for the American-Scandinavian Foundation.

———. 1966. "Heimili (skólar) fornaldarsagna og riddarasagna." *Skírnir* 140:272.

Eiríksson, Hallfreður Örn. 1975. "On Icelandic Rímur: An Orientation." *Arv* 31:139–50.

———. 1980. "Folkminnenas roll i den litterära renässansen på Island under 1800-talet." In *Folklore och nationsbyggande i Norden*. Ed. Lauri Honko. Åbo: Nordiska institutet för folkdiktning. Pp. 85–96.

Ek, Sverker. 1921. *Norsk kämpavisa i östnordisk tradition. Ett försök till tudelning av det nordiska folkvisematerialet*. GHÅ, 27. Göteborg: Högskolans Gustaf-Adolfsfond.

Eldevik, Randi. 1987. "The Dares Phrygius Version of "Trojumanna Saga": A Case Study in the Cross-Cultural Mutation of Narrative." Diss. Harvard University.

Ellis, Hilda R. *See* Davidson, H. R. Ellis.

Erlingsson, Davið. 1970. "Etiken i Hrafnkels saga Freysgoða." *Scripta Islandica* 21:2–41.

———. 1974. *Blómað mál í rímum*. Studia Islandica. Íslenzk fræði, 33. Reykjavík: Bókaútgáfa Menningarsjóðs.

———. 1975. "Illuga saga og Illuga dans." *Gripla* 1:9–42.

———. 1980. "Hjörleifur kvensami og Fergus MacLéite." *Gripla* 4:198–205.

———. 1987. "Prose and Verse in Icelandic Legendary Fiction." In *The Heroic Process: Form, Function, and Fantasy in Folk Epic*. Ed. Bo Almqvist et al. Dublin: Glendale Press. Pp. 371–93.

Faulkes, Anthony. 1983. "Pagan Sympathy: Attitudes to Heathendom in the Prologue to *Snorra Edda*." In *Edda: A Collection of Essays*. Ed. Robert J. Glendinning and Haraldur Bessason. University of Manitoba Icelandic Studies, 4. n.p.: University of Manitoba Press. Pp. 283–314.

Feilberg, Henning F. 1910. *Bjærgtagen: studie over en gruppe træk fra nordisk alfetro*. Danmarks folkeminder, 5. Copenhagen: Det Schønbergske forlag.

Feleppa, Robert. 1986. "Emics, Etics, and Social Objectivity." *Current Anthropology* 27:243–55.

Finch, Ronald George. 1962–65. "The Treatment by the Compiler of Sources in the *Vǫlsunga saga*." *Saga-Book* 16:315–53.

———. 1981. "*Atlakviða, Atlamál*, and *Vǫlsunga saga*: A Study in Combination and Integration." In *Specvlvm Norroenvm: Norse Studies in Memory of Gabriel Turville-Petre*. Ed. Ursula Dronke et al. Odense: Odense University Press. Pp. 123–38.

Finnegan, Ruth. 1977. *Oral Poetry: Its Nature, Significance, and Social Context*. Rpt. Cambridge: Cambridge University Press, 1979.

Foote, Peter. 1955–56. "Sagnaskemtan: Reykjahólar 1119." *Saga-Book* 14:226–39.

Fors, Andrew P. 1904. *The Ethical World Conception of the Norse People*. Chicago: University of Chicago Press.

Fowler, Alastair. 1982. *Kinds of Literature: An Introduction to the Theory of Genres and Modes*. Cambridge: Harvard University Press.

Frandsen, Ernst. 1935. *Folkevisen: Studier i Middelalderens poetiske Litteratur*. Copenhagen: Levin og Munksgaard.

Frank, Roberta. 1981. "Snorri and the Mead of Poetry." In *Specvlvm Norroenvm: Norse Studies in Memory of Gabriel Turville-Petre*. Ed. Ursula Dronke et al. Odense: Odense University Press, 1981. Pp. 155–70.

———. 1985. "Skaldic Poetry." In *Old Norse–Icelandic Literature: A Critical Guide*. Ed. Carol J. Clover and John Lindow. Islandica, 45. Ithaca: Cornell University Press. Pp. 157–96.

Frank, Tenney. 1909. "Classical Scholarship in Medieval Iceland." *American Journal of Philology* 30:132–52.

Frazer, Sir James G. 1921. "Ulysses and Polyphemus." In *Apollodorus: The Library*. Loeb Classical Library, 122. Rpt. Cambridge: Harvard University Press, 1979. II. 404–55.

Fry, Donald. 1977. "Polyphemus in Iceland." In *The Fourteenth Century*. Ed. Paul E. Szarmach and Bernard S. Levy. Acta, 4. Binghamton, N.Y.: Center for Medieval and Renaissance Studies, SUNY at Binghamton. Pp. 65–86.

Frye, Northrop. 1957. "Historical Criticism: Theory of Modes." In *Anatomy of Criticism: Four Essays*. Rpt. Princeton: Princeton University Press, 1973.

Gehl, Walter. 1937. *Ruhm und Ehre bei den Nordgermanen: Studien zum Lebensgefühl der isländischen Saga*. Neue deutsche Forschung, 3. Berlin: Junker und Dünnhaupt.

Geirsdóttir, Kristín. 1979. "Fáein alþýðleg orð." *Skírnir* 153:5–41.

Gelsinger, Bruce E. 1981. *Icelandic Enterprise: Commerce and Economy in the Middle Ages*. Columbia: University of South Carolina Press.

Gennep, Arnold van. 1908. "La légende de Polypheme." In *Religions, moeurs, et légendes: Essais d'ethnographie et de linguistique*. Paris: Société du Mercure de France. Pp. 155–64.

Genzmer, Felix. 1948. "Vorzeitsaga und Heldenlied." In *Festschrift Paul Kluckhohn und Hermann Schneider gewidmet zu ihren 60. Geburtstag*, "herausgegeben von ihren Tübinger Schülern." Tübingen: J. C. B. Mohr. Pp. 1–31.

Georges, Robert A., and Alan Dundes. 1963. "Toward a Structural Definition of the Riddle." *JAF* 76:111–18.

Gering, Hugo. 1880. "Der Beowulf und die islaendische Grettissaga." *Anglia* 3:74–87.

Gerschel, Lucien. 1960. "Un épisode trifonctionnel dans la saga de Hrólfr Kraki." In *Hommages à Georges Dumézil*. Collection Latomus, 45. Brussels: Latomus. Pp. 104–16.

Gíslason, Jónas. 1981. "Island (till 1700)." In *Ur nordisk kulturhistoria: Universitetsbesöken i utlandet före 1660: XVIII Nordiska historikermötet, Jyväskylä 1981: Mötesrapport I*. Studia Historica Jyväskyläensia, 22:1. Jyväskyla: Jyväskylan Yliopisto. Pp. 119–41.

Gíslason, Konrað. 1897. "Forelæsninger over ældste 'rímur.'" In *Efterladte skrifter. II: Forelæsninger og videnskabelige Afhandlinger*. Ed. Björn M. Ólsen. Copenhagen: Gyldendal. Pp. 144–215.

Gíslason, Magnús. 1977. *Kvällsvaka: En isländsk kulturtradition belyst genom studier i bondebefolkningens vardagsliv och miljö under senare hälften av 1800-talet och början av 1900-talet*. Acta Universitatis Upsaliensis. Studia Ethnologia Upsaliensia, 2. Uppsala: Almqvist och Wiksell.

Glauser, Jürg. 1983. *Isländische Märchensagas. Studien zur Prosaliteratur im spätmittelalterlichen Island.* Beiträge zur nordischen Philologie, 12. Basel and Frankfurt am Main: Helbing und Lichtenhahn.

Godzich, Wlad, and Jeffrey Kittay. 1987. *The Emergence of Prose: An Essay in Prosaics.* Minneapolis: University of Minnesota Press.

Gödel, Vilhelm. 1897. *Fornnorsk-isländsk litteratur i Sverige.* Stockholm: Ivar Hæggströms boktryckeri.

Göransson, Johan. 1749. *Svea Rikes Konungars Historia ok Ättartal, ifrån 2200 Är före Christum, intill 1749.* Stockholm: L. L. Grefing.

Gould, Chester Nathan. 1923. "The Friðþjófs Saga: An Oriental Tale." *SS* 7:219–50.

Greenway, John L. 1977. *The Golden Horns: Mythic Imagination and the Nordic Past.* Athens: University of Georgia Press.

Grimm, Jakob. 1813. "Gedanken über Mythos, Epos und Geschichte." Rpt. in *Kleinere Schriften.* Ed. K. Müllenhoff. Berlin: F. Dümmler, 1869. IV, 74–85.

——. [1883.] "Preface." In *Teutonic Mythology.* Trans. James Steven Stallybrass. New York: Dover, 1966. III, v–lv. [Originally published in German in 1844.]

Grimm, Wilhelm. 1867. *Die deutsche Heldensage.* 2d rev. ed. Berlin: Ferd. Dümmlers Verlagsbuchhandlung.

Grønbech, Vilhelm. 1955. *Vor folkeæt i oldtiden.* 2 vols. rev. ed. Copenhagen: Gyldendal.

Grüner-Nielsen, Håkon. 1945. *De færøske kvadmelodiers tonalitet i middelalderen belyst gennem nutidsoverleveringen.* Færoensia, 1. Copenhagen: Munksgaard.

Grundtvig, N. F. S. 1832. *Nordens Mythologi, eller Sindbilled-Sprog historisk-poetisk udviklet og oplyst.* 2d rev. ed. Copenhagen: J. H. Schubothes Boghandling.

Grundtvig, Svend. 1847. "Plan til en ny Udgave af Danmarks gamle Folkeviser." In *Prøve paa en ny Udgave af DgF.* 2d ed. Copenhagen: Samfundet til den danske Litteraturs Fremme. P. 19. Rpt. in the facsimile edition of *DgF,* I.

——. 1863. "Udsigt over den nordiske oldtids heroiske digtning. Tre forelæsninger." *Nordisk Universitets-Tidskrift* 9:4, 41–126.

——. 1866. "Oldnordiske Litteraturhistorie." *Historisk Tidskrift* (Copenhagen), 3e Række, 5:499–618.

——. 1882. "Meddelelse angående Færøernes Literatur og Sprog." *ÅNOH* 357–72.

Guðnason, Bjarni. 1963. *Um Skjǫldungasögu.* Reykjavík: Menningarsjóður.

——. 1969. "Gerðir og ritþróun Ragnars sögu loðbrókar." In *Einarsbók. Afmæliskveðja til Einars Ól. Sveinssonar. 12. desember 1969.* Ed. Bjarni Guðnasson et al. n.p.: "útgefndur nokkrir vinir." Pp. 28–37.

——. 1977. "Theodoricus og íslenzkir sagnaritarar." In *Sjötíu ritgerðir helgaðar Jakobi Benediktssyni 20. júlí 1977.* Ed. Einar G. Pétursson and Jónas Kristjánsson. 2 vols. SÁMR, 12. Reykjavík: Stofnun Árna Magnússonar á Íslandi. I, 107–20.

——. 1982. "Formáli." In *Danakonunga sǫgur. Skjǫldunga saga. Knýtlinga saga. Ágrip af sǫgu Danakonunga.* ÍF, 35. Reykjavík: Hið íslenzka fornritafélag. Pp. v–cxciv.

Gwyndaf, Robin. 1987. "The Cauldron of Regeneration: Continuity and Function in the Welsh Epic Tradition." In *The Heroic Process: Form, Function, and Fantasy in Folk Epic.* Ed. Bo Almqvist et al. Dublin: Glendale Press. Pp. 413–51.

Hackman, Oskar. 1904. *Die Polyphemsage in der Volksüberlieferung.* Helsinki: Frenckellska tryckeri AB.

Hallberg, Peter. 1962. *The Icelandic Saga.* Trans. Paul Schach. Rpt. Lincoln: University of Nebraska Press, 1971.

———. 1972. "Nyare studier i isländsk sagalitteratur." *Samlaren* 93:211–37.

———. 1973. "Broder Robert, Tristrams saga och Duggals leizla. Anteckningar till norska översättningar." *ANF* 88:55–71.

———. 1982. "Some Aspects of the Fornaldarsögur as a Corpus." *ANF* 97:1–35.

Halldórsson, Ólafur. 1956–78. "Rímur." In *Kulturhistorisk leksikon for nordisk middelalder fra vikingetid til reformationstid.* 21 vols. Rpt. Copenhagen: Rosenkilde og Bagger, 1981–82. XIV, 319–24.

———. 1973. "Inngangur." In *Íslenzkar miðaldarímur. II: Áns rímur bogsveigis.* SÁMR, 4. Reykjavík: Stofnun Árna Magnússonar á Íslandi. Pp. 7–84.

———. 1974. "Inngangur." In *Íslenzkar miðaldarímur. III: Bósa rímur.* SÁMR, 5. Reykjavík: Stofnun Árna Magnússonar á Íslandi. Pp. 7–34.

Halldórsson, Óskar. 1982. "Tröllsaga Bárðæla og Grettluhöfundur." *Skírnir* 156:5–36.

Halvorsen, Eyvind F. 1951. "On the Sources of the Ásmundar saga Kappabana." *Studia Norvegica* 2:1–57.

———. 1959. *The Norse Version of the "Chanson de Roland."* BA, 19. Copenhagen: Munksgaard.

Harris, Joseph C. 1972. "Genre and Narrative Structure in Some *Íslendinga þættir.*" *SS* 44:1–27.

———. 1975. "Genre in Saga Literature: A Squib." *SS* 47:427–36.

———. 1976a. "The Masterbuilder Tale in Snorri's *Edda* and Two Sagas." *ANF* 91:66–101.

———. 1976b. "Theme and Genre in Some *Íslendinga þættir.*" *SS* 48:1–28.

———. 1983. "Eddic Poetry as Oral Poetry: The Evidence of Parallel Passages in the Helgi Poems for Questions of Composition and Performance." In *Edda: A Collection of Essays.* Ed. Robert J. Glendinning and Haraldur Bessason. University of Manitoba Icelandic Studies, 4. n.p.: University of Manitoba Press. Pp. 210–42.

———. 1985. "Eddic Poetry." In *Old Norse–Icelandic Literature: A Critical Guide.* Ed. Carol J. Clover and John Lindow. Islandica, 45. Ithaca: Cornell University Press. Pp. 68–156.

Harris, Richard L. 1970a. "Introduction." In *"Hjálmþérs saga:* A Scientific Edition." Diss. University of Iowa. Pp. iv–xciv.

———. 1970b. "The Lion-Knight Legend in Iceland and the Valþjófsstaðir Door." *Viator* 1:125–45.

———. 1974. "The Deaths of Grettir and Grendel: A New Parallel." *Scripta Islandica* 25:25–53.

Haslag, Josef. 1963. *"Gothic" im siebzehnsten und achtzehnten Jahrhundert: Eine wort- und ideengeschichtliche Untersuchung.* Anglistische Studien, 1. Cologne: Böhlau.

Hastrup, Kirsten. 1982. "Establishing an Ethnicity: The Emergence of the 'Icelanders' in the Early Middle Ages." In *Semantic Anthropology.* Ed. David Parkin. Association of Social Anthropologists Monograph, 22. London: Academic Press. Pp. 145–60.

————. 1985. *Culture and History in Medieval Iceland: An Anthropological Analysis of Structure and Change.* Oxford: Clarendon Press.

————. 1986. "Tracing Tradition—An Anthropological Perspective on *Grettis saga Ásmundarsonar.*" In *Structure and Meaning in Old Norse Literature: New Approaches to Textual Analysis and Literary Criticism.* Ed. John Lindow et al. Viking Collection, 3. Odense: Odense University Press. Pp. 281–313.

Hauck, Karl. 1963. "Heldendichtung und Heldensaga als Geschichtsbewusstsein." In *Alteuropa und die moderne Gesellschaft. Festschrift für Otto Brunner.* Ed. Alexander Bergengruen and Ludwig Deike. Göttingen: Vandenhoeck & Ruprecht. Pp. 118–69.

Haug, Walter. 1963. "Theodorichs Ende und ein tibetisches Märchen." In *Märchen, Mythos, Dichtung. Festschrift zum 90. Geburtstag Friedrich von der Leyens am 19. August 1963.* Ed. Hugo Kuhn and Kurt Schier. Munich: C. H. Beck. Pp. 83–115.

————. 1975. "Andreas Heuslers Heldensagamodell: Prämissen, Kritik und Gegenentwurf." *ZDA* 104:273–92.

Heinrichs, H. M. 1976. "Mündlichkeit und Schriftlichkeit: Ein Problem der Sagaforschung." *Akten des V. Internationalen Germanisten-Kongresses Cambridge 1975.* Jahrbuch für Internationale Germanistik, Ser. A: Kongreßberichte, 2. Bern: Herbert Lang. I, 114–33.

Heinzle, Joachim. 1978. *Mittelhochdeutsche Dietrichepik: Untersuchungen zur Tradierungsweise, Überlieferungskritik umd Gattungsgeschichte später Heldendichtung.* München Texte und Untersuchungen zur deutschen Literatur des Mittelalters, 62. Zürich: Artemis.

Helgason, Jón (1866–1942). 1925. *Islands Kirke fra dens Grundlæggelse til Reformationen.* Copenhagen: G. E. C. Gads.

Helgason, Jón (1899–1986). 1924a. "Færøiske studier. I. Den eldste optegnelse av færøiske kvad." *MM* 29–37.

————. 1924b. "Indledning." In *Hervarar saga ok Heiðreks konungs.* SUGNL, 48. Copenhagen: J. Jørgensen. Pp. i–lxxxix.

————. 1934. *Norrøn Litteraturhistorie.* Copenhagen: Levin og Munksgaard.

————. 1960. "Introduction." In *Hauksbók: The Arna-Magnæan Manuscripts 371, 4to, 544, 4to, and 675, 4to.* Manuscripta Islandica, 5. Copenhagen: Munksgaard. Pp. v–xxxvii.

Helle, Knut. 1968. "Anglo-Norwegian Relations in the Reign of Hákon Hákonsson (1217–63)." *MS* 1:101–14.

Hempfer, Klaus W. 1973. *Gattungstheorie. Information und Synthese.* UniTaschenbuch, 133. Munich: Wilhelm Fink Verlag.

Hermannsson, Halldór. 1912. *Bibliography of the Mythical-Heroic Sagas.* Islandica, 5. Rpt. New York: Kraus Reprint Corp., 1966.

————. 1937. *The Sagas of the Kings and the Mythical-Heroic Sagas: Two Bibliographical Supplements.* Islandica, 26. Ithaca: Cornell University Press.

————. 1958. *The Hólar Cato: An Icelandic Schoolbook of the Seventeenth Century.* Islandica, 39. Ithaca: Cornell University Press.

Hernadi, Paul. 1972. *Beyond Genre: New Directions in Literary Classification.* Ithaca: Cornell University Press.

Herrmann, Paul. 1903. *Nordische Mythologie in gemeinverständlicher Darstellung.* Leipzig: Wilhelm Engelmann.

Herskovits, Melville J. 1948. *Man and His Works: The Science of Cultural Anthropology.* Rpt. New York: Knopf, 1967.

Heusler, Andreas. [1905.] *Lied und Epos in germanischer Sagendichtung.* Rpt. Darmstadt: Wissenschaftliche Buchgesellschaft, 1956.

———. [1908.] "Die gelehrte Urgeschichte im isländischen Schrifttum." Rpt. in *Andreas Heusler. Kleine Schriften.* Ed. Helga Reuschel, rev. ed. Stefan Sonderegger. 2 vols. Berlin: de Gruyter, 1969. II, 80–161.

———. [1909a.] "Die Anfänge der isländischen Saga." Rpt. in *Kleine Schriften,* rev. ed. Sonderegger. Berlin: de Gruyter, 1969. II, 388–460.

———. [1909b.] "Geschichtliches und Mythisches in der germanischen Heldensage." Rpt. in *Kleine Schriften,* rev. ed. Sonderegger. II, 495–517.

———. [1919.] "Altnordische Dichtung und Prosa von Jung Sigurd." Rpt. in *Kleine Schriften,* rev. ed. Sonderegger. I, 26–64.

———. 1926. "Altgermanische Sittenlehre und Lebensweisheit." In *Germanische Wiedererstehung: ein Werk über die germanischen Grundlagen unserer Gesittung.* Ed. H. Nollau. Heidelberg: Carl Winter. Pp. 156–204.

———. [1934.] "Das germanische Heldenideal." Rpt. in *Kleine Schriften,* rev. ed. Sonderegger. II, 170–74.

———. 1943. *Die altgermanische Dichtung.* 2d rev. ed. Potsdam: Akademische Verlagsgesellschaft Athenaion.

———. 1955. *Nibelungensage und Nibelungenlied: Die Stoffgeschichte des deutschen Heldenepos.* 5th ed. Dortmund: Verlagsbuchhandlung Fr. Wilh. Ruhfus.

Hildeman, Karl-Ivar. 1958a. "Den äldsta svensk-språkiga lyriken och dess ursprung." In *Medeltid på vers: Litteraturhistoriska studier.* Skrifter utgivna av Svenskt visarkiv, 1. Stockholm: Almqvist och Wiksell. Pp. 153–77.

———. 1958b. "När kom kämpavisan till Sverige?" In *Medeltid på vers.* Pp. 49–115.

Hobsbawm, Eric J. 1983. "Introduction: Inventing Traditions." In *The Invention of Tradition.* Ed. Eric Hobsbawm and Terence Ranger. New York: Cambridge University Press. Pp. 1–14.

Höfler, Otto. 1941. "Deutsche Heldensage." In *Von deutscher Art in Sprache und Dichtung.* Stuttgart: Kohlhammer. II, 73–98.

———. 1952. *Germanisches Sakralkönigtum. I: Der Runenstein von Rök und die germanische Individualweihe.* Tübingen: M. Niemeyer.

———. 1959. "Siegfried, Arminius, und die Symbolik." In *Festschrift für F. R. Schröder zu seinem 65. Geburtstage, September 1958.* Ed. Wolfdietrich Rasch. Heidelberg: Carl Winter. Universitätsverlag. Pp. 11–121.

Hofmann, Dietrich. 1971. "Vers und Prosa in der mündlich gepflegten mittelalterlichen Erzählkunst der germanischen Länder." *Frühmittelalterliche Studien* 5:135–75.

———. 1976. "Hrafnkels und Hallfreðs Traum: Zur Verwendung mündlicher Tradition im der Hrafnkels saga Freysgoða." *Skandinavistik* 6:19–36.

———. 1981. "Die *Yngvars saga viðfǫrla* und Oddr munkr inn fróði." In *Specvlvm Norroenvm: Norse Studies in Memory of Gabriel Turville-Petre.* Ed. Ursula Dronke et al. Odense: Odense University Press. Pp. 182–222.

———. 1984. "Zu Oddr Snorrasons *Yngvars saga viðfǫrla.*" *Skandinavistik* 14:106–8.

Hollander, Lee M. 1912. "The 'Faithless Wife' Motif in Old Norse Literature." *Modern Language Notes* 27:71–73.

212   Bibliography

——. 1913. "The Relative Ages of *Gautreks saga* and *Hrólfs saga Gautrekssonar.*" *ANF* 29:120–34.

——. 1916. "Notes on the *Nornagests þáttr.*" *Publications of the Society for the Advancement of Scandinavian Study* 3:105–111.

Holtsmark, Anne. 1965. "Heroic Poetry and Legendary Sagas." *Bibliography of Old Norse–Icelandic Studies* 9–21.

Homan, Theo. 1975. *Skíðaríma: An Inquiry into the Written and Printed Texts, References, and Commentaries.* Amsterdamer Publikationen zur Sprache und Literatur, 20. Amsterdam: Rodopi N.V.

Honko, Lauri. 1968. "Genre Analysis in Folkloristics and Comparative Religion." *Temenos: Studies in Comparative Religion* 3:48–66.

——. [1979–80.] "Methods in Folk Narrative Research." Rpt. in *Nordic Folklore: Recent Studies.* Ed. Reimund Kvideland and Henning Sehmsdorf. Bloomington: Indiana University Press, 1989. Pp. 23–39.

Honti, Hans. 1931. *Volksmärchen und Heldensage: Beiträge zur Klärung ihrer Zusammenhänge.* FFC, 95. Helsinki: Suomalainen Tiedeakatemia. Academia Scientiarum Fennica.

Hood, C. F. 1946. *Icelandic Church Saga.* London: Society for Promoting Christian Knowledge.

Hughes, Shaun F. D. 1976. "The Literary Antecedents of *Áns saga bogsveigis.*" *MS* 9:196–235.

——. 1978. "'Völsunga rímur' and 'Sjúrðar kvæði': Romance and Ballad, Ballad and Dance." In *Ballads and Ballad Research: Selected Papers of the International Conference on Nordic and Anglo-American Ballad Research: University of Washington, Seattle, May 2–6, 1977.* Ed. Patricia Conroy. Seattle: University of Washington Press. Pp. 37–45.

——. 1980. "Report on *rímur* 1980." *JEGP* 79:477–98.

Hume, Kathryn. 1974. "The Thematic Design of *Grettis saga.*" *JEGP* 73:469–86.

Huppé, Bernhard. 1984. *The Hero in the Earthly City: A Reading of Beowulf.* Medieval and Renaissance Texts and Studies, 33. Binghamton: Center for Medieval and Renaissance Studies, State University of New York.

Hustvedt, Sigurd B. 1930. *Ballad Books and Ballad Men: Raids and Rescues in Britain, America, and the Scandinavian North since 1800.* Cambridge: Harvard University Press.

Die Isländersaga. 1974. Ed. Walter Baetke. Wege der Forschung, 151. Darmstadt: Wissenschaftliche Buchgesellschaft.

Íslenzkar þjóðsögur. 1935–39. Ed. Ólafur Davíðsson. 2 vols. Akureyri: Þorsteinn M. Jónsson.

Jackson, W. T. H. 1960. *The Literature of the Middle Ages.* New York: Columbia University Press.

Jansen, William Hugh. 1959. "The Esoteric-Exoteric Factor in Folklore." *Fabula: Journal of Folktale Studies* 2:205–11. Rpt. in *The Study of Folklore.* Ed. Alan Dundes. Englewood Cliffs, N.J.: Prentice-Hall, 1965. Pp. 44–51.

Jansson, Valter. 1945. *Eufemiavisorna: en filologisk undersökning.* Uppsala universitets årsskrift, 1945:8. Uppsala: Lundequistska bokhandeln.

Jauss, Hans Robert. [1972.] "Theorie der Gattungen und Literatur des Mittelalters." Rpt. in *Alterität und Modernität der Mittelalterlichen Literatur: Gesammelte Aufsätze 1956–76*. Munich: Wilhelm Fink Verlag, 1977. Pp. 327–58.

Jesch, Judith. 1984. "Hrómundr Gripsson Revisited." *Skandinavistik* 14:89–105.

Jørgensen, Ellen. 1960. *Historieforskning og Historieskrivning i Danmark indtil Aar 1800*. Copenhagen: Den danske historiske Forening.

Jones, Gwyn. 1972. *Kings, Beasts, and Heroes*. New York: Oxford University Press.

Jonsson, Bengt R. 1967. *Svensk balladtradition. I: Balladkällor och balladtyper*. Svenskt visarkivs handlingar, 1. Stockholm: Svenskt visarkiv.

———. 1978. "The Ballad in Scandinavia: Its Age, Prehistory, and Early History. Some Preliminary Reflections." In *The European Medieval Ballad: A Symposium*. Ed. Otto Holzapfel et al. Odense: Odense University Press. Pp. 9–15.

———. [1989.] "Bråvalla och Lena." *Sumlen*. [In press.]

———. 1991. "Oral Literature, Written Literature, and the Ballad: Relations between Old Norse Genres." In *The Ballad and Oral Literature*. Ed. Joseph Harris. Harvard English Studies, 16. Cambridge: Harvard University Press. Pp. 139–70.

Jónsson, Finnur. 1892–96. "Inledning." In *Hauksbók, udg. efter de arnamagnæanske Håndskrifter No. 371, 544 og 675, 4to, samt forskellige Papirhåndskrifter*. Copenhagen: Det kongelige nordiske Oldskrift-Selskab. Pp. i–cxxxix.

———. 1904. "Inledning." In *Hrólfs saga kraka og Bjarkarímur*. SUGNL, 32. Copenhagen: S. L. Møller. Pp. i–xxx.

———. 1914. "De islandske folkeviser." *ÅNOH* 1–62.

———. 1917. "Sigurðarsaga og de prosaiske stykker i Codex Regius." *ÅNOH* 16–36.

———. 1920–24. *Den oldnorske og oldislandske Litteraturs Historie*. 2d ed. 3 vols. Copenhagen: G. E. C. Gads forlag.

———. 1926–28. *Ordbog til de af Samfund til Udg. af gml. nord. Litteratur udgivne Rímur samt til de afr dr. O. Jiriczek udgivne Bósarímur*. Copenhagen: J. Jørgensen.

———. 1927. "Flateyjarbók." *ÅNOH* 139–90.

Jónsson, Guðni. 1940. "Sannfræði íslenzkra þjóðsagna." *Skírnir* 114:25–57.

Jorgensen, Peter A. 1975. "The Two-Troll Variant of the Bear's Son Folktale in Hálfdanar saga Brönnufóstra and Gríms saga loðinkinna." *Arv* 31:35–43.

———. 1986. "Additional Icelandic Analogues to *Beowulf*." In *Sagnaskemmtun. Studies in Honour of Hermann Pálsson on His 65th Birthday, 26th May 1986*. Ed. Rudolf Simek et al. Vienna: Hermann Böhlaus. Pp. 201–8.

Kålund, Kristian. 1900. "Den nordiske (norrøne) oldlitteraturs samling og bevaring." In *Katalog over de oldnorsk-islandske Håndskrifter i Det Store Kongelige Bibliotek og i Universitetsbibliotek (udenfor Den arnamagnæanske Samling)*. Copenhagen: Kommissionen for Det arnamagnænske Legat.

Kalinke, Marianne. 1985. "Norse Romance (*riddarasögur*)." In *Old Norse–Icelandic Literature: A Critical Guide*. Ed. Carol J. Clover and John Lindow. Islandica, 45. Ithaca: Cornell University Press. Pp. 316–63.

———. 1990. *Bridal-Quest Romance in Medieval Iceland*. Islandica, 46. Ithaca: Cornell University Press.

Kalinke, Marianne, and P. M. Mitchell. 1985. *Bibliography of Old Norse–Icelandic Romances*. Islandica, 44. Ithaca: Cornell University Press.

Kames, Henry Home, Lord. 1762. *Elements of Criticism*. 3 vols. Facs. rpt. New York: Johnson Reprint Corp., 1967.

Karlsson, Gunnar. 1974–78. "Frá þjóðveldi til konungsríkis." In *Saga Islands: samin að tilhlutan þjóðhátíðarnafndar.* Ed. Sigurður Líndal. Reykjavík: Hið íslenzka bókmenntafélag. Sögufélagið. II, 3–54.

Karlsson, Stefán. 1970. "Ritun Reykjarfjarðarbókar. Excursus: Bókagerð bænda." *Opuscula 4.* BA, 30. Copenhagen: Munksgaard. Pp. 120–40.

——. 1979. "Islandsk bogeksport til Norge i middelalderen." *MM* 1–17.

——. 1986. "*Bóklausir menn:* A Note on Two Versions of *Guðmundar saga.*" In *Sagnaskemmtun. Studies in Honour of Hermann Pálsson on His 65th Birthday, 26th May 1986.* Ed. Rudolf Simek et al. Vienna: Hermann Böhlaus. Pp. 277–86.

Katalog öfver kongliga bibliotekets fornisländska och fornnorska handskrifter. 1897–1900. Ed. Vilhelm Gödel. Stockholm: P. A. Norstedt och söner.

Katalog over Den arnamagnæanske Håndskriftsamling. 1889–94. Ed. Konráð Gíslason et al. 2 vols. Copenhagen: Kommission for Det arnamagnæanske Legat.

Katalog over De oldnorsk-islandske Håndskrifter i Det Store Kongelige Bibliotek og i Universitetsbibliotek (udenfor Den arnamagnæanske Samling). 1900. Ed. Kr. Kålund. Copenhagen: Kommissionen for Det arnamagnæanske Legat.

Kellog, Robert. 1979. "Varieties of Tradition in Medieval Literature." In *Medieval Narrative: A Symposium.* Ed. Hans Bekker-Nielsen et al. Odense: Odense University Press. Pp. 120–29.

Ker, W. P. 1908. *Epic and Romance: Essays on Medieval Literature.* 2d rev. ed. Rpt. New York: Dover, 1957.

Koch, Marie Ludovica. 1964–65. "Le ballate popolari scandinave e la litteratura norrena, I–II." *Annali. Istituto Orientale di Napoli. Sezione germanica* 7:61–102; 8:41–76.

Kochs, Matthias. 1911. *Die Ethik der Edda.* Bonn: C. Georgi. Universitäts-Buchdruckerei und Verlag.

Kölbing, Eugen. 1876. "Beiträge zur kenntniss und kritischen Verwerthung der älteren isländischen rímurpoesie." In *Beiträge zur verleichenden Geschichte der romantischen Poesie und Prosa des Mittelalters.* Breslau: Wilh. Koebner. Pp. 137–241.

Köstlin, Konrad. 1982. "Folklorismus als Therapie? Volkskultur als Therapie?" In *Folklorismus; Vorträge der I. Internationalen Arbeitstagung des Vereins "Volkskultur um den Neusiedlersee" in Neusiedl/See 1978.* Ed. Edith Hörandner and Hans Lunzer. Neusiedler Konfrontationen, 1. Neusiedl/See: Verein für regionale Volkskunde und internationale Fachkontakte. Pp. 129–48.

Korff, Gottfried. 1980. "Folklorismus und Regionalismus: Eine Skizze zum Problem der kulturellen Kompensation ökonomischer Rückständigkeit." In *Heimat und Identität: Probleme regionaler Kultur: 22. Deutscher Volkskunde-Kongreß in Kiel vom 16. bis 21. Juni 1979.* Ed. Konrad Köstlin and Hermann Bausinger. Studien zur Volkskunde und Kulturgeschichte Schleswig-Holsteins, 7. Neumünster: Karl Wachholtz Verlag. Pp. 39–52.

Krappe, Alexandre Haggerty. 1928. "The Sources of the Saga af Herraudi ok Bósa." *Neuphilologische Mitteilungen* 29:250–56.

——. 1930. *The Science of Folklore.* New York: The Dial Press.

——. 1937. "Waberlohe." *Archiv* 172:1–10.

Krenn, Ernst. 1940. *Die Entwicklung der foeroyischen Literatur.* Illinois Studies in Languages and Literature, 26:1. Urbana: University of Illinois Press.

Krijn, Sophia A. 1925. "Sturlaugssagaen og Sturlaugsrímur." *ANF* 41:101–13.

Kristjánsson, Jónas. 1975. "*Íslendingadrápa* and Oral Tradition." *Gripla* 1:76–91.

Kuhn, Hans. 1938. "Sitte und Sittlichkeit." In *Germanische Altertumskunde.* Ed. Hermann Schneider. Munich: C. H. Beck'sche Verlagsbuchhandlung. Pp. 171–221.

———. 1952. "Heldensage vor und ausserhalb der Dichtung." In *Edda, Skalden, Saga: Festschrift zum 70. Geburtstag von Felix Genzmer.* Ed. Hermann Schneider. Heidelberg: Carl Winter. Universitätsverlag. Pp. 262–78.

Lagerholm, Åke. 1927. "Allgemeine bemerkungen über die lygisǫgur." In *Drei lygisǫgur: Egils saga einhenda ok Ásmundar berserkjabana, Ála flekks saga, Flóres saga konungs ok sona hans.* Altnordische Saga-Bibliothek, 17. Halle: M. Niemeyer. Pp. ix–xviii.

Lamm, Martin. 1908. *Olof Dalin: En litteraturhistorisk undersökning af hans verk.* Uppsala: Almqvist och Wiksell.

Lang, Andrew. 1884. "The Method of Folklore." Rpt. in *Custom and Myth.* Rev. ed. London: Longmans, Green, 1893. Pp. 10–28.

Lárusson, Magnús Már. 1960. "On the So-called 'Armenian' Bishops." *Studia Islandica* 18:23–28.

Lárusson, Ólafur. 1936. "Island." In *Befolkningen i oldtiden.* Ed. Haakon Shetelig. Nordisk kultur, 1. Stockholm: Albert Bonniers förlag. Pp. 121–37.

Lawrence, William W. 1911. *Medieval Story and the Beginnings of the Social Ideas of English-Speaking People.* New York: Columbia University Press.

———. 1928. *Beowulf and Epic Tradition.* Cambridge: Harvard University Press.

Leach, Henry Goddard. 1921. *Angevin Britain and Scandinavia.* Harvard Studies in Comparative Literature, 6. Cambridge: Harvard University Press.

Levy, Gertrude R. n.d. *The Sword from the Rock: An Investigation into the Origins of Epic Literature and the Development of the Hero.* London: Faber and Faber.

Leyerle, John. 1965. "Beowulf the Hero and the King." *Medium Ævum* 34:89–102.

Liberman, Anatoly. 1984. "Introduction." In *Vladimir Propp: Theory and History of Folklore.* Trans. Ariadna Y. Martin and Richard P. Martin. Theory and History of Literature, 5. Minneapolis: University of Minnesota Press. Pp. ix–lxxxi.

Liestøl, Knut. 1910. "Kappen Illugjen." *Syn og Segn* 16:269–86.

———. 1915a. "Nokre islendske folkeviser." *Edda* 4(3):1–27.

———. 1915b. *Norske trollvisor og norrøne sogor.* Kristiania: Olaf Norlis forlag.

———. 1916. "Stulku táttur." *MM.* Pp. 47–53.

———. 1921. "Vestnordisk og austnordisk folkevisediktning." *Edda* 16:40–55.

———. 1930. *The Origin of the Icelandic Family Sagas.* Instituttet for sammenlignende kulturforskning Ser. A:10. Oslo: H. Aschehoug. [Originally published in Norwegian in 1929 as *Upphavet til den islendske ættesaga* (Oslo: Aschehoug).]

———. 1931. "Karakteristiske drag i norsk folkediktning." *Nordisk tidskrift för vetenskap, konst och industri.* Pp. 41–56.

———. 1936. "Det norrøne folkeviseumrådet." *Nordisk tidskrift* 12:271–83.

———. 1945. "Til spørsmålet om dei eldste islendske dansekvæde." *Arv* 1:70–75.

———. 1970. *Den norrøne arven.* Scandinavian University Books. Oslo: Universitetsforlaget. [Originally published in *Norveg* 14:7–96.]

Lindblad, Gustaf. 1954. *Studier i Codex Regius av äldre Eddan.* Lundastudier i nordisk språkvetenskap, 10. Lund: Gleerup, 1954.

———. 1979. "Snorre Sturluson och eddadiktningen." *Saga och sed* 17–34.

———. 1980. "Poetiska Eddans förhistoria och skrivskicket i Codex regius." *ANF* 95:142–67.

Lindow, John. 1977. "A Mythic Model in *Bandamanna saga* and Its Significance." *Michigan Germanic Studies* 3:1–12.

———. 1985. "Mythology and Mythography." In *Old Norse–Icelandic Literature: A Critical Guide*. Ed. Carol J. Clover and John Lindow. Islandica, 45. Ithaca: Cornell University Press. Pp. 21–67.

Lindroth, Hjalmar. 1937. *Iceland: A Land of Contrasts*. Princeton: Princeton University Press.

Lindroth, Sten. 1975–81. *Svensk lärdomshistoria*. 4 vols. Stockholm: P. A. Norstedt och söners förlag.

Littleton, C. Scott. 1965. "A Two-Dimensional Scheme for the Classification of Narratives." *JAF* 78:21–27.

Löfqvist, Karl-Erik. 1935. *Om riddarväsen och frälse i nordisk medeltid. Studier rörande adelsståndets uppkomst och tidigare utformning*. Lund: H. Ohlsson.

Lönnroth, Lars. 1963–64. "Kroppen som själens spegel—ett motiv i de isländska sagorna." *Lychnos* 24–61.

———. 1964. "Tesen om de två kulturerna: Kritiska studier i den isländska sagaskrivningens sociala förutsättningar." *Islandica* 15:3–97.

———. 1965. *European Sources of Icelandic Saga-Writing: An Essay Based on Previous Studies*. Stockholm: Thule-Seelig.

———. 1965–69. "Det litterära porträttet i latinsk historiografi och isländsk sagaskrivning. En komparativ studie." *APhS* 27:68–117.

———. 1969. "The Noble Heathen: A Theme in the Sagas." *SS* 41:1–29.

———. 1971. "Hjálmar's Death-Song and the Delivery of Eddic Poetry." *Speculum* 46:1–20.

———. 1975a. "Charlemagne, Hrolf Kraki, Olaf Tryggvason: Parallels in the Heroic Tradition." In *Les relations littéraires Franco-Scandinaves au moyen âge. Actes du College de Liège (avril 1972)*. Bibliothèque de la Faculté de Philosophie et Lettres de l'Université de Liège, 208. Paris: Société d'Edition "Les Belles Lettres." Pp. 29–52.

———. 1975b. "The Concept of Genre in Saga Literature." *SS* 47:419–26.

———. 1976. *Njáls saga: A Critical Introduction*. Berkeley and Los Angeles: University of California Press.

———. 1978. *Den dubbla scenen: Muntlig diktning från Eddan till ABBA*. Stockholm: Bokförlaget Prisma.

———. 1980. "New Dimensions and Old Directions in Saga Research." *Scandinavica* 19:57–61.

Löw, Gustav. 1908–10. *Sveriges forntid i svensk historieskrivning*. 2 vols. Stockholm: C. E. Fritzel.

Lord, Albert B. 1960. *The Singer of Tales*. Harvard Studies in Comparative Literature, 24. Rpt. Cambridge: Harvard University Press, 1981.

———. 1967. "The Influence of a Fixed Text." In *To Honor Roman Jakobson: Essays on the Occasion of His Seventieth Birthday (11 October 1966)*. Janua Linguarum, Series Maior, 33. The Hague and Paris: Mouton. II, 1199–1206.

———. 1974. "Introduction." In *The Wedding of Smailagić Meho: Avdo Međeović*.

Serbo-Croatian Heroic Songs Collected by Milman Parry, 3. Cambridge: Harvard University Press. Pp. 3–34.

———. 1976. "Folklore, 'Folklorism,' and National Identity." *Balkanistica: Occasional Papers in Southeast European Studies* 3:63–73.

———. 1986. "The Merging of Two Worlds: Oral and Written Poetry as Carriers of Ancient Values." In *Oral Tradition in Literature: Interpretation in Context*. Ed. John Miles Foley. Columbia: University of Missouri Press. Pp. 19–64.

Lüthi, Max. 1976. *Once upon a Time: On the Nature of Fairy Tales*. Trans. Lee Chadeayne and Paul Gottwald. Bloomington: Indiana University Press. [Originally published in German in 1973.]

Lukman, Niels. 1976. "Ragnarr loðbrók, Sigifrid, and the Saints of Flanders." *MS* 9:7–50.

———. 1977. "An Irish Source and Some Icelandic *fornaldarsǫgur*." *MS* 10:41–57.

Magerøy, Hallvard. 1978. "Kvar står sagaforskningen i dag?" *Nordisk tidskrift* 54:164–75.

Magoun, Francis P. 1943. "Nikulás Bergson of Munkaþverá and Germanic Heroic Legend." *JEGP* 42:210–18.

———. 1944. "The Pilgrim-Diaries of Nikulás of Munkathverá: The Road to Rome." *Medieval Studies* 6:314–44.

Margeson, Sue. 1980. "The Vǫlsung Legend in Medieval Art." In *Medieval Iconography and Narrative: A Symposium*. Ed. Flemming G. Andersen et al. Odense: Odense University Press. Pp. 183–211.

Martin, John Stanley. 1973. "Some Comments on the Perception of Heathen Religious Customs in the Sagas." *Parergon* 6:37–45.

Martin, Richard P. 1989. *The Language of Heroes: Speech and Performance in the "Iliad."* Ithaca: Cornell University Press.

Matras, Christian. 1969. "Nøkur orð um rím og aldur." In *Afmælisrit Jóns Helgasonar. 30. júní 1969*. Ed. Jakob Benediktsson et al. Reykjavík: Heimskringla. Pp. 418–20.

Maurer, Konrad. 1869. "Die Skída-ríma." *Abhandlungen der K. Bayerischen Akademie der Wissenschaften*, I Kl., XII. Bd., I. Abt. Munich: Verlag der k. Akademie. Pp. 3–70.

Mayr, Ernst. 1982. *The Growth of Biological Thought: Diversity, Evolution, and Inheritance*. Cambridge, Mass.: Belknap Press.

McCreesh, Bernadine. 1979–80. "Structural Patterns in the *Eyrbyggja saga* and Other Sagas of the Conversion." *MS* 11:271–80.

———. 1980. "How Pagan Are the Icelandic Family Sagas?" *JEGP* 79:58–66.

McTurk, Rory W. 1975. "The Extant Icelandic Manifestations of *Ragnars saga loðbrókar*." *Gripla* 1:43–75.

———. 1977. "The Relationship of *Ragnar saga Loðbrókar* to *Þiðriks saga af Bern*." In *Sjötíu ritgerðir helgaðar Jakobi Benediktssyni 20. júlí 1977*. Ed. Einar G. Pétursson and Jónas Kristjánsson. 2 vols. SÁMR, 12. Reykjavík: Stofnun Árna Magnússonar á Íslandi. Pp. 568–85.

The Medieval Legacy: A Symposium. 1982. Ed. Andreas Haarder et al. Odense: Odense University Press.

Meletinsky, Eleazar, et al. 1974. "Problems of the Structural Analysis of Fairy-tales." In *Soviet Structural Folkloristics*. Ed. Pierre Maranda. Approaches to Semiotics, 42. The Hague: Mouton. Pp. 73–139. [Originally published in Russian in 1969.]

Metzner, Ernst Erich. 1972. *Zur frühesten Geschichte der europäischen Balladendichtung: Der Tanz in Kölbigk: legendarische Nachrichten, gesellschaftlicher Hintergrund, historische Voraussetzungen*. Frankfurter Beiträge zur Germanistik, 14. Frankfurt: Athenäum Verlag.

Milroy, James. 1967–68. "Story of Ætternisstapi in *Gautreks saga*." *Saga-Book* 17:206–23.

Mitchell, Stephen A. 1983. "*Fǫr Scírnis* as Mythological Model: *frið at kaupa*." *ANF* 98:108–22.

———. 1984. "On the Composition and Function of *Guta Saga*." *ANF* 99:151–74.

———. 1985a. "Scandinavian Balladry and the Old Norse Legacy: 'Álvur kongur' (CCF 14), 'Stolt Herr Alf' (ST 5), and *Hálfs saga*." *Arv* 41:123–31.

———. 1985b. "'Nú gef ek þik Óðni': Attitudes toward Odin in the Mythical-Heroic Sagas." In *The Sixth International Saga Conference 28/7–2/8 1985. Workshop Papers*. II, 777–91.

———. 1985c. "The Whetstone as Symbol of Authority in Old English and Old Norse." *SS* 57:1–31.

———. 1987. "The Sagaman and Oral Literature: The Icelandic Traditions of Hjörleifr inn kvensami and Geirmundr heljarskinn." In *Current Issues in Oral Literature Research: A Memorial for Milman Parry*. Ed. John Miles Foley. Columbus, Ohio: Slavica Publishers. Pp. 395–423.

———. 1991. "*Gråkappan* (AT 425) as Chapbook and Folktale in Sweden." In *The Ballad and Oral Literature*. Ed. Joseph Harris. Harvard English Studies, 16. Cambridge: Harvard University Press. Pp. 269–91.

Mjöberg, Jöran. 1967–68. *Drömmen om sagatiden*. 2 vols. Stockholm: Natur och Kultur.

Modéer, Ivar. 1957. "Östsmåländska bondenamn från 1500-talet." In *Personnamn från medeltid och 1500-tal*. Ed. Ivar Modéer. Anthroponymica Suecana, 2. Stockholm: Almqvist och Wiksell. Pp. 56–69.

Mogk, Eugen. 1901–9. "Nordische Literaturen. A. Norwegisch-isländische Literatur." In *Grundriss der germanischen Philologie. II:1. Literaturgeschichte*. Ed. Hermann Paul. Strassburg: Karl J. Trübner. Pp. 555–923.

Moser, Hans. 1962. "Vom Folklorismus in unserer Zeit." *Zeitschrift für Volkskunde* 58:177–209.

Motz, Lotte. 1973. "Withdrawal and Return: A Ritual Pattern in the *Grettis saga*." *ANF* 88:91–110.

Mudrak, E. 1943. *Die nordische Heldensage*. Jahrbuch für historische Volkskunde, 10. Berlin: H. Stubenrauch.

Müller, Peter E. 1813. *Ueber den Ursprung und Verfall der isländischen Historiographie*. Trans. L. C. Sander. Copenhagen: I. F. Schultz.

———. 1817–20. *Sagabibliothek med Anmærkninger og indledende Afhandlingar*. 3 vols. Copenhagen: I. F. Schultz.

Munch, P. A. 1847. *Nordmændenes Gudelære i Hedenold, tilligemed de vigtigste Heltesagn*. Christiania: Johan Dahl.

Mundt, Marina. 1971. "Omkring dragekampen i *Ragnars saga loðbrókar.*" *Arv* 27:121–40.

Nahl, Astrid van. 1981. *Originale Riddarasögur als Teil altnordischer Sagaliteratur.* Europäische Hochschulschriften. Reihe 1, Deutsche Sprache und Literatur, 447. Frankfurt: Peter Lang.

Naumann, Hans-Peter. 1978. "Die Abenteuersaga. Zu einer Spätform altisländischer Erzählkunst." *Skandinavistik* 8:41–55.

——. 1979. "Das Polyphem-Abenteuer in der altnordischen Sagaliteratur." *Schweizerisches Archiv für Volkskunde* 75:173–89.

Neckel, Gustav. 1920. "Sigmunds Drachenkampf." *Edda* 13:122–40; 204–29.

Nerman, Birger. 1913. *Studier över Svärges hedna litteratur.* Uppsala: [K. W. Appelbergs boktryckeri].

Newcomb, W. W., Jr. 1961. *The Indians of Texas, from Prehistoric to Modern Times.* Austin: University of Texas Press.

Niles, John D. 1983. *Beowulf: The Poem and Its Tradition.* Cambridge: Harvard University Press.

Nilsson, Gun. 1954. "Den isländska litteraturen i stormaktstidens Sverige." *Scripta Islandica* 5:19–41.

Nolsøe, Mortan. 1976. "Noen betrakninger om forholdet mellom ballade og sagaforelegg." *Sumlen: Årsbok för vis- och folkmusikforskning* 11–19.

——. 1978. "The Faroese Heroic Ballad and Its Relation to Other Genres." In *The European Medieval Ballad: A Symposium.* Ed. Otto Holzapfel et al. Odense: Odense University Press. Pp. 61–66.

——. 1987. "The Heroic Ballad in Faroese Tradition." In *The Heroic Process: Form, Function, and Fantasy in Folk Epic.* Ed. Bo Almqvist et al. Dublin: Glendale Press. Pp. 395–412.

Nordal, Sigurður J. 1933. "Formáli." In *Egils saga Skalla-Grímssonar.* ÍF, 2. Reykjavík: Hið íslenzka fornritafélag. Pp. v–cv.

——. 1940. *Hrafnkatla.* Studia Islandica. Íslenzk fræði, 7. Reykjavík: Ísafoldarprentsmiðja h.f.

——. 1952. "Time and Vellum. Some Remarks on the Economic Conditions of Early Icelandic Literature." Presidential Address. *Modern Humanities Research Association Annual Bulletin* 24:15–26.

——. 1953. "Sagalitteraturen." In *Litteraturhistoria. B: Norge og Island.* Nordisk kultur, 8:B. Stockholm: Albert Bonniers förlag. Pp. 191–93.

——. 1957. *The Historical Element in the Icelandic Family Sagas.* W. P. Ker Memorial Lecture, 15. Glasgow: Jackson and Son.

Nordiska Kämpa Dater, i en Sagoflock samlade om forna Kongar och Hjältar. 1737. Ed. Erik J. Biörner. Stockholm: Joh. L. Horrn.

Nordiske Fortids Sagaer, efter den udgivne islandske eller gamle nordiske Grundskrift. 1829–30. Trans. C. C. Rafn. 3 vols. Copenhagen: Poppske Bogtrykkeri.

Nordiske Kæmpe-Historier efter islandske Haandskrifter fordanskede. 1821–26. Trans. C. C. Rafn. 3 vols. Copenhagen: H. F. Popp.

Nordström, Johan. 1934. *De Yverbornes Ö: Sextonhundratalsstudier.* Stockholm: Albert Bonniers.

Norrøn Fortællekunst. Kapitaler af den norsk-islandske middelalderlitteraturshistorie. 1965. Ed. Hans Bekker-Nielsen et al. n.p.: Akademie Forlag.

Norsk folkediktning. 1958. Ed. Knut Liestøl and Moltke Moe. 2d rev. ed. Olav Bø and Svale Solheim. 3 vols. Oslo: Det norske samlaget.

Okpewho, Isidore. 1987. "'Once upon a Kingdom . . . ': Benin in the Heroic Tradition of Subject Peoples." In *The Heroic Process: Form, Function, and Fantasy in Folk Epic.* Ed. Bo Almqvist et al. Dublin: Glendale Press. Pp. 613–50.

Ólason, Vésteinn. 1976. "Nýmæli í íslenzkum bókmenntum á miðöld." *Skírnir* 150:68–87.

———. 1978a. "Ballad and Romance in Medieval Iceland." In *Ballads and Ballad Research: Selected Papers of the International Conference on Nordic and Anglo-American Ballad Research: University of Washington, Seattle, May 2–6, 1977.* Ed. Patricia Conroy. Seattle: University of Washington Press. Pp. 26–36.

———. 1978b. "Frásagnarlist í fornum sögum." *Skírnir* 152:166–202.

———. 1978c. "The Icelandic Ballad as a Medieval Genre." In *The European Medieval Ballad: A Symposium.* Ed. Otto Holzapfel et al. Odense: Odense University Press. Pp. 67–74.

———. 1982. *The Traditional Ballads of Iceland: Historical Studies.* SÁMR, 22. Reykjavík: Stofnun Árna Magnússonar á Íslandi.

———. 1983. "Kveðið um Ólaf helga." *Skírnir* 157:48–63.

———. 1984. "Íslenzk sagnalist—erlendur lærdómur: þróun sérkenni íslenzkra fornsagna í ljósi nýrra rannsókna." *Tímarit Máls og menningar* 2:174–89.

———. 1985. "Saint Olaf in Late Medieval Icelandic Poetry." In *Narrative Folksong: New Directions: Essays in Appreciation of W. Edson Richmond.* Ed. Carol L. Edwards and Kathleen E. B. Manley. Boulder, Colo.: Westview Press. Pp. 2–17.

Olesen, Tryggvi J. 1957. "Book Collections of Mediaeval Icelandic Churches." *Speculum* 32:502–10.

———. 1959. "Book Collections of Icelandic Churches in the Fourteenth Century." *Nordisk tidskrift för bok- och biblioteksväsen* 46:111–23.

———. 1960. "Book Collections of Icelandic Churches in the Fifteenth Century." *Nordisk tidskrift för bok- och biblioteksväsen* 47:90–103.

Olmer, Emil. 1902. *Boksamlingar på Island 1179–1490 enligt diplom.* GHÅ, 8. Pp. 1–84.

Olrik, Axel. 1890. "Om Svend Grundtvigs og Jörgen Blochs Føroyjakvæði og færøske ordbog." *ANF* n.s. 2:146–61.

———. 1892. *Kilderne til Sakses Oldhistorie: En literaturhistorisk Undersøgelse. I: Forsøg på en Tvedelning af Kilderne til Sakses Oldhistorie.* Copenhagen: Otto B. Wroblewski's Boghandel [*Særtrykk af ÅNOH,* 1892].

———. 1894. *Kilderne til Sakses Oldhistorie: En literaturhistorisk Undersøgelse. II: Norrøne Sagaer og danske Sagn: En literaturhistorisk Undersøgelse.* Copenhagen: G. E. C. Gad.

———. 1898. "Tvedelning af Sakses kilder, et genmæle." *ANF* n.s. 10:47–93.

———. 1903–10. *Danmarks Heltedigtning: en Oldtidsstudie.* 2 vols. Copenhagen: G. E. C. Gad.

———. 1904. "Et dansk vers fra Erik af Pommerns tid." *Danske Studier* 210–16.

———. 1909. "Epische Gesetze der Volksdichtung." *ZDA* 51:1–12. [Trans. "Epic Laws of Folk Narrative." In *The Study of Folklore.* Ed. Alan Dundes. Englewood Cliffs, N.J.: Prentice-Hall, 1965. Pp. 129–41.]

———. 1921. *Nogle Grundsætninger for Sagnforskning*. Ed. Hans Ellekilde. Danmarks Folkeminder, 23. Copenhagen: Det Schønbergske Forlag.

Olson, Oscar Ludvig. 1916. *The Relation of the "Hrólfs Saga Kraka" and the "Bjarka-rímur" to "Beowulf": A Contribution to the History of Saga Development in England and the Scandinavian Countries*. Chicago: University of Chicago Libraries.

O'Neil, Wayne. 1970. "The Oral-Formulaic Structure of the Faroese *kvæði*." *Fróðskaparrit* 18:39–68.

Paasche, Fredrik. 1924. *Norges og Islands litteratur indtill utgangen av middelalderen*. Norsk litteraturhistorie, 1. Kristiania: H. Aschehoug.

———. 1948. *Hedenskap og kristendom: Studier i norrøn middelalder*. Oslo: H. Aschehoug.

Pálsson, Hermann. 1962. *Sagnaskemmtun Íslendinga*. Reykjavík: Mál og Menning.

———. 1969. "Um eðli Íslendingasagna." *Skírnir* 143:42–63.

———. 1971. *Art and Ethics in Hrafnkel's Saga*. Scandinavian University Books. Copenhagen: Munksgaard.

———. 1974. "Icelandic Sagas and Medieval Ethics." *MS* 7:61–75.

———. 1975. "Um gæfumenn og ógæfu í íslenzkum fornsögum." In *Afmælisrit Björns Sigfússonar*. Ed. Björn Teitsson et al. Reykjavík: Sögufélag. Pp. 135–53.

———. 1979a. "Early Icelandic Imaginative Literature." In *Medieval Narrative: A Symposium*. Ed. Hans Bekker-Nielsen et al. Odense: Odense University Press. Pp. 20–30.

———. 1979b. "Towards a Definition of the Fornaldarsögur." Paper presented at Fourth International Saga Conference, Munich.

———. 1982a. "Fornaldarsögur." In *Dictionary of the Middle Ages*. New York: Charles Scribner's Sons. V, 137–43.

———. 1982b. *Sagnagerð. Hugvekjur um fornar bókmenntir*. Reykjavík: Almenna bókafélagið.

Pálsson, Hermann, and Paul Edwards. [1968.] *Gautrek's Saga and Other Medieval Tales*. Rpt. New York: New York University Press, 1970.

———. 1971. *Legendary Fiction in Medieval Iceland*. Studia Islandica, 30. Reykjavík: Heimspekideild Háskóla Íslands og Bókútgáfa Menningarsjóðs.

Panzer, Friedrich. 1910–12. *Studien zur germanischen Sagengeschichte. I: Beowulf. II: Sigfrid*. Munich: C. H. Beck'sche Verlagsbuchhandlung.

———. 1925. "Zur Erzählung von Nornagest." In *Vom Werden des deutschen Geistes: Festgabe Gustav Ehrismann zum 8. Oktober 1925 dargebracht von Freunden und Schülern*. Ed. Paul Merker und Wolfgang Stammler. Berlin und Leipzig: Walter de Gruyter. Pp. 27–34.

Parsons, Elsie Clews. 1929. "Introduction." In *Kiowa Tales*. Memoirs of the American Folk-lore Society. New York: American Folk-lore Society. Pp. i–xxii.

Pentikäinen, Juha. 1978. *Oral Repertoire and World View: An Anthropological Study of Marina Takalo's Life History*. FFC, 219. Helsinki: Academia Scientarium Fennica. Suomalainen Tiedeakatemia.

Phillpotts, Bertha S. 1931. *Edda and Saga*. Home University Library, 150. London: Thornton Butterworth.

Pipping, Rolf. 1938. "Ordspråkstudier. I. Ordspråk i funktion. A. Grettis saga." *Studier i nordisk filologi* 37:5–40.

Pizarro, Joaquín Martínez. 1976–77. "Transformations of the Bear's Son Tale in the Sagas of the Hrafnistumenn." *Arv* 32–33:263–81.

Ploss, Emil E. 1966. *Siegfried—Sigurd, der Drachenkämpfer: Untersuchungen zur germanisch-deutschen Heldensage: Zugleich ein Beitrag zur Entwicklungsgeschichte des alteuopäischen Erzählgutes.* Beihefte der Bonner Jahrbücher, 17. Cologne: Böhlau.

Pörtner, Rudolf. 1971. *Die Wikinger-Saga.* Dusseldorf and Vienna: Econ Verlag GmbH.

Power, Rosemary. 1984. "Journeys to the North in the Icelandic Fornaldarsögar." *Arv* 40:7–26.

———. 1985a. "An Óige, an Saol agus an Bás, *Feis Tighe Chónain* and 'Þórr's Visit to Útgarða-Loki.'" *Béaloideas* 53:217–94.

———. 1985b. "Le Lai de Lanval and Helga þáttr Þórissonar." *Opscula* 8:158–61.

Pritsak, Omeljan. 1981. *The Origin of Rus'. I: Old Scandinavian Sources Other than the Sagas.* Harvard Ukrainian Research Institute Monograph Series. Cambridge: Harvard University Press.

Propp, Vladimir. 1968. *Morphology of the Folktale.* Trans. Laurence Scott. 2d rev. ed. Publications of the American Folklore Society: Bibliographic and Special Series, 9; Indiana University Research Center in Anthropology, Folklore, and Linguistics. 10. Austin: University of Texas Press. [Originally published in Russian in 1928.]

———. 1984. "The Principles of Classifying Folklore Genres." In *Vladimir Propp: Theory and History of Folklore.* Trans. Ariadna Y. Martin and Richard P. Martin. Theory and History of Literature, 5. Minneapolis: University of Minnesota Press. Pp. 39–47.

Raglan, Lord. 1933. "Tradition in Anthropology." *Polynesian Society Journal* 42:321–23.

Ranisch, Wilhelm. 1935. "Die Dichtung von Starkaðr." *ZDA* 72:113–28.

Ranke, Kurt. 1934. *Die zwei Brüder. Eine Studie zur vergleichenden Märchenforschung.* FFC, 114. Helsinki: Suomalainen Tiedeakatemia. Academia Scientarium Fennica.

———. 1969. "Orale und literale Kontinuität." In *Kontinuität? Geschichtlichkeit und Dauer als volkskundliches Problem.* Ed. Hermann Bausinger and Wolfgang Brückner. Berlin: Erich Schmidt Verlag. Pp. 102–17.

Recke, Ernst von der. 1907. "Folkevisestudier, Vestnordisk Indflydelse i Dansk." *Danske Studier* 79–120.

Reuschel, Helga. 1933. *Untersuchungen über Stoff und Stil der Fornaldarsaga.* Bausteine zur Volkskunde und Religionswissenschaft, 17. Bühl-Baden: Konkordia.

Richmond, W. Edson. 1983. "Introduction." In *Handbook of American Folklore.* Ed. Richard M. Dorson. Bloomington: Indiana University Press. Pp. xi–xii.

Righter-Gould, Ruth. 1975. "A Structural Analysis of the Fornaldar Sögur Nordrlanda." Diss. Cornell University.

———. 1978–79. "*Áns saga bogsveigis:* A Legendary Analog to *Egils saga.*" *MS* 11:265–70.

———. 1980. "The *Fornaldar Sögur Norðurlanda:* A Structural Analysis." *SS* 52:423–41.

Röhrich, Lutz. 1962. "Die mittelalterlichen Redaktionen des Polyphem-Märchens und ihr Verhältnis zur außerhomerischen Tradition." *Fabula* 5:48–71.

Rokkjær, Carl C. 1964. "Rímur og folkeviser." *APhS* 26:100–108.

Rosenberg, Bruce A. 1977. "Oral Literature in the Middle Ages." In *Oral Tradition: Literary Tradition: A Symposium.* Ed. Hans Bekker-Nielsen et al. Odense: Odense University Press. Pp. 440–50.

Ross, Margaret Clunies. 1981. "An Interpretation of the Myth of Þórr's Encounter with Geirrøðr and His Daughters." In *Specvlvm Norroenvm: Norse Studies in Memory of Gabriel Turville-Petre.* Ed. Ursula Dronke et al. Odense: Odense University Press. Pp. 370–91.

Rubow, Paul V. 1936. "De islandske Sagaer." In *Smaa kritiske Breve.* Copenhagen: Levin and Munksgaard. Pp. 7–25.

Sagadebatt. 1977. Ed. Else Mundal. Oslo: Universitetsforlaget.

Salmonsson, Anders. 1984. "Some Thoughts on the Concept of Revitalization." *Ethnologia Scandinavica.* Pp. 34–47.

Sauer, Marianne. 1971– . "Nornagests þáttr." In *Kindlers Literatur Lexikon.* 2d ed. Zürich: Kindler Verlag. VIII, 6789.

Sauvé, James. 1970. "The Divine Victim: Aspects of Human Sacrifice in Viking Scandinavia and Vedic India." In *Myth and Law among the Indo-Europeans: Studies in Indo-European Comparative Mythology.* Ed. Jaan Puhvel. Publications of the UCLA Center for the Study of Comparative Folklore and Mythology, 1. Berkeley and Los Angeles: University of California Press. Pp. 173–91.

Sawicki, Stanislaw. 1939. *Die Eufemiavisor: Stilstudien zur nordischen Reimliteratur des Mittelalters.* Skrifter utgivna av Kungl. humanistiska vetenskapssamfundet i Lund, 28. Lund: C. W. K. Gleerup.

Schach, Paul. 1957–59. "Some Observations on *Tristrams saga.*" *Saga-Book* 15:102–29.

——. 1964. "Tristan and Isolde in Scandinavian Ballad and Folktale." *SS* 36:281–97.

——. 1969. "Some Observations on the Influence of *Tristrams saga ok Ísöndar* on Old Icelandic Literature." In *Old Norse Literature and Mythology: A Symposium.* Ed. Edgar C. Polomé. Austin: University of Texas Press. Pp. 81–129.

——. 1975. "Antipagan Sentiment in the Sagas of Icelanders." *Gripla* 1:105–34.

——. 1982. Rev. of Peter Buchholz, *Vorzeitkunde. Speculum* 57:868–70.

Schier, Kurt. 1970. *Sagaliteratur.* Sammlung Metzler, 78. Stuttgart: J. B. Metzlersche Verlagbuchhandlung.

——. 1971– . "Fornaldarsögur." In *Kindlers Literatur Lexikon.* 2d ed. Zürich: Kindler Verlag. IV, 3610–3613.

——. 1977. "Einige methodische Überlegungen zum Problem von mündlicher und literarischer Tradition im Norden." In *Oral Tradition: Literary Tradition: A Symposium.* Ed. Hans Bekker-Nielsen et al. Odense: Odense University Press. Pp. 98–115.

——. 1983. *Märchen aus Island.* Die Märchen der Weltliteratur. Cologne: Eugen Diedrichs Verlag.

Schlauch, Margaret. 1930. "Another Analogue of *Beowulf.*" *Modern Language Notes* 45:20–21.

——. 1934. *Romance in Iceland.* Princeton: Princeton University Press.

Schneider, Hermann. 1928–34. *Germanische Heldensage.* 3 vols. Grundriss der germanischen Philologie, 10, 1/3. Berlin: de Gruyter.

——. 1955. "Einleitung zu einer Darstellung der Heldensage." *Beiträge zur Geschichte der deutschen Sprache und Literatur* (Tübingen) 77:71–82.

Schøning, Gerhard. 1771. *Norges Riiges Historie, Første Deel, indeholdende Riiges ældste Historie fra dets Begyndelse til Harald Haarfagers Tiider.* Sorsøe: Heineck [sic] Mumme og Faber.

Scholz, Manfred Günter. 1975. "Zur Hörerfiktion in der Literatur des Spätmittelalters und der frühen Neuzeit." In *Literatur und Leser. Theorien und Modelle zur Rezeption literarischer Werke.* Ed. Günter Grimm. Stuttgart: Reclam.

——. 1980. *Hören und Lesen. Studien zur primären Rezeption der Literatur in 12. und 13. Jahrhundert.* Wiesbaden: Franz Steiner.

——. 1984. "On Presentation and Reception Guidelines in the Germanic Strophic Epic in the Late Middle Ages." *New Literary History* 16:137–52.

Schomerus, Rudolf. 1936. *Die Religion der Nordgermanen im Spiegel christlicher Darstellung.* Leipzig: Robert Noske.

Schröder, Franz Rolf. 1928. "Motivwanderungen im Mittelalter." *Germanisch-romanische Monatsschrift* 16:7–13.

——. 1955. "Mythos und Heldendichtung." *Germanisch-romanische Monatsschrift* 36:1–22.

[Schrøter.] *J. H. Schrøters optegnelser af Sjúrðar kvæði (Ny. Kgl. Saml. 345, 8°).* 1951–53. Ed. Christian Matras. Færoensia, 3. Copenhagen: Munksgaard.

Schück, Henrik. 1891. "Våra äldsta historiska folkvisor." *Historisk tidskrift* (Stockholm) 11:281–318.

——. 1935. *Sveriges litteratur intill 1900.* Rev. ed.; rpt. Stockholm: Hugo Gebers förlag, 1952.

See, Klaus von. [1966.] "Germanische Heldensage. Ein Forschungsbericht." In *Edda, Saga, Skaldendichtung: Aufsätze zur skandinavischen Literatur des Mittelalters.* Heidelberg: C. Winter, 1981. Pp. 107–53.

——. 1981a. *Germanische Heldensage: Stoffe: Probleme: Methoden: eine Einführung.* 2d unrev. ed. Wiesbaden: Athenaion, 1981.

——. 1981b. "Das Problem der mündlichen Erzählprosa im Altnordischen. Der Prolog der Þiðreks saga und der Bericht von der Hochzeit in Reykjahólar." *Skandinavistik* 11:90–95.

Seznec, Jean. 1953. *The Survival of the Pagan Gods: The Mythological Tradition and Its Place in Renaissance Humanism and Art.* Trans. Barbara F. Sessions. Bollingen Series, 38. Rpt. New York: Harper Torchbooks, 1961.

Shils, Edward A. 1971. "Tradition." *Comparative Studies in Sociology and History* 13:122–59.

——. 1978. *Tradition.* Chicago: University of Chicago Press.

Sigmundsson, Finnur. 1966. *Rímnatal.* 2 vols. Reykjavík: Rímnafélagið.

Sigurds saga i middelalderens billedkunst. 1972. Ed. Martin Blindheim. Oslo: Universitets Oldsaksamling.

Sigurðsson, [Síra] Helgi. 1891. *Safn til bragfræði íslenzkra rímna að fornu og nýju.* Reykjavík: [Ísafoldarprentsmiðja].

Simek, Rudolf. 1986. "Elusive Elysia, or: Which Way to Glæsisvellir? On the Geography of the North in Icelandic Legendary Fiction." In *Sagnaskemmtun. Studies in Honour of Hermann Pálsson on His 65th Birthday, 26th May 1986.* Ed. Rudolf Simek et al. Vienna: Hermann Böhlaus. Pp. 247–76.

Simpson, Jacqueline. 1963. "Grímr the Good, a Magical Drinking Horn." *Études Celtiques* 10:489–515.

——. 1965. *The Northmen Talk: A Choice of Tales from Iceland.* London: Phoenix House.

——. 1966. "Otherworld Adventures in an Icelandic Saga." *Folklore* (London) 77:1–20.

——. 1967. "Some Scandinavian Sacrifices." *Folklore* (London) 78:190–202.

Skard, Sigmund. 1980. *The Classical Tradition in Norway.* Oslo: Universitetsforlag.

Skautrup, Peter. 1944–70. *Det danske sprogs historie.* 5 vols. Copenhagen: Gyldendal.

Skovgaard-Petersen, Inge. 1956–78. "Saxo." In *Kulturhistorisk leksikon for nordisk middelalder fra vikingetid til reformationstid.* 21 vols. Rpt. Copenhagen: Rosenkilde og Bagger, 1981–82. XV, 49–57.

——. 1985. "Starkad in Saxo's Gesta Danorum." In *History and Heroic Tale: A Symposium.* Ed. Tore Nyberg et al. Odense: Odense University Press. Pp. 207–21.

Sønderholm, Eric. 1978. "The Importance of the Oldest Danish Ballad Manuscripts for the Dating of the Ballad Genre." In *Ballads and Ballad Research: Selected Papers of the International Conference on Nordic and Anglo-American Ballad Research: University of Washington, Seattle, May 2–6, 1977.* Ed. Patricia Conroy. Seattle: University of Washington Press. Pp. 231–37.

Sørensen, Preben Meulengracht. 1977. *Saga og samfund: En indføring i oldislandsk litteratur.* Copenhagen: Berlingske forlag.

Solheim, Svale. 1970. "Færøysk-norsk i folkevisediktninga." *Fróðskaparrit* 18:297–306.

Speirs, John. 1959. *Medieval English Poetry: The Non-Chaucerian Tradition.* London: Faber and Faber.

Sprogelige og historiske Afhandlinger viede Sophus Bugges Minde. 1908. Kristiania: H. Aschehoug. Pp. 285–94.

Steblin-Kaminskij, M. I. 1966. "An Attempt at a Semantic Approach to the Problem of Authorship in Old Icelandic Literature." *ANF* 81:24–34.

Steenstrup, Johannes C. H. R. 1891. *Vore Folkeviser fra Middelalderen. Studier over Visernes Æsthetik, rette Form og Alder.* Copenhagen: R. Klein.

——. 1918. "De danske Folkevisers ældste Tid og Visernes Herkomst." *Historisk Tidskrift* (Copenhagen) 9:232–54, 355–97.

Stefánsson, Magnús. 1974. "Frá goðakirkju til biskupskirkju." In *Saga Íslands.* Ed. Sigurður Líndal. Reykjavík: Hið íslenzka bókmenntafélag; Sögufélagið. III, 111–260.

Steffen, Richard. 1898. *Enstrofig nordisk folklyrik i jämförande framställning.* Bidrag till kännedom om de svenska landsmålen ock [sic] svenskt folklif, 16:1. Stockholm: P. A. Norstedt och söners förlag.

Steffensen, Jón. 1975. *Menning og meinsemdir: Ritgerðasafn um mótunarsögu íslenzkrar þjóðar og baráttu hennar við hungur og sóttir.* n.p.: Sögufélagið.

Stein, Gertrude. 1935. "What Is English Literature." In *Lectures in America.* Rpt. New York: Random House, 1975. Pp. 11–58.

Stephens, George. 1883. *Prof. S. Bugge's Studies on Northern Mythology Shortly Examined.* London and Edinburgh: Williams and Norgate ["overprint from

'Mémoires de la Société royal des Antiquaires du Nord,' Copenhagen 1882–84"].

Storm, Gustav. 1888. "Forord." In *Islandske Annaler indtil 1578*. Christiania: Det norske historiske Kildeskriftfond. Pp. i–lxxxiv.

Ström, Åke. 1966. "Die Hauptriten des wikingerzeitlichen nordischen Opfers." In *Festschrift Walter Baetke. Dargebracht zu seinem 80. Geburtstag am 28. März 1964*. Ed. Kurt Rudolph et al. Weimar: Böhlau. Pp. 330–42.

Ström, Folke. 1948. *Den egna kraftens män: en studie i forntida irreligiositet*. GHÅ, 54:2. Göteborg: Elanders boktryckeri AB.

———. 1981. "Poetry as Instrument of Propaganda. Jarl Hákon and His Poets." In *Specvlvm Norroenvm: Norse Studies in Memory of Gabriel Turville-Petre*. Ed. Ursula Dronke et al. Odense: Odense University Press. Pp. 440–58.

Strömbäck, Dag. 1963a. "The Dawn of West Norse Literature." *Bibliography of Old Norse–Icelandic Studies* 7–24.

———. 1963b. "Uppsala, Iceland, and the Orient." In *Early English and Norse Studies Presented to Hugh Smith in Honour of His Sixtieth Birthday*. Ed. Arthur Brown and Peter Foote. London: Methuen. Pp. 178–90.

———. 1970. "En orientalisk saga i fornnordisk dräkt." In *Folklore och filologi: Valda Uppsatser utgivna av Kungliga Gustav Adolfs Akademien 13.8 1970*. Acta Academiae Regiae Gustavi Adolphi, 48. Uppsala: Lundquistska bokhandeln. Pp. 70–105.

Suhm, Peter Friderich. 1782. *Historie af Danmark I: Fra de ældste Tider til Aar 803*. Copenhagen: Brødrene Berlings Skrifter.

Sveinsson, Einar Ólafur. 1929. *Verzeichnis isländischer Märchenvarianten, mit einer einleitenden Untersuchung*. FFC, 83. Helsinki: Academia Scientiarum Fennica. Suomalainen Tiedeakatemia.

———. 1932. "Keltnisk áhrif á íslenzkar ýkjusögur." *Skírnir* 106:100–123.

———. 1935. "Um rímur fyrir 1600 og fleira." Rpt. in *Við uppspretturnar. Greinasafn*. Reykjavík: Helgafell, 1956. Pp. 200–217.

———. 1936. "Nafngiftir Oddaverjar." In *Bidrag till nordisk filologi tillägnade Emil Olson juni 1936*. Lund: Gleerup. Pp. 190–212.

———. 1937. *Sagnaritun Oddaverja: Nokkrar athuganir*. Studia Islandica. Islenzk fræði, 1. Reykjavík: [Ísafoldarprentsmiðja h.f.].

———. 1940. *Um íslenzkar þjóðsögur*. Reykjavík: [Ísafoldarprentsmiðja h.f.].

———. 1944. "Lestrarkunnátta Íslendinga í fornöld." *Skírnir* 118:173–97.

———. 1953. *The Age of the Sturlungs: Icelandic Civilization in the Thirteenth Century*. Trans. Jóhann S. Hannesson. Islandica, 36. Ithaca: Cornell University Press.

———. 1956a. "Läs- och skrivkunnighet på Island under fristatstiden." *Scripta Islandica* 7:5–20.

———. 1956b. "Um Ormar hinn unga, kappann Illhuga, bækur og dansa." In *Nordæla: Afmæliskveðja til prófessors, dr. phil. og litt. og jur. Sigurðar Nordals ambassadors Íslands í Kaupmannahöfn sjötugs 14. september 1956*. Ed. Halldór Halldórsson et al. [Reykjavík]: Helgafell. Pp. 55–74.

———. 1957. "Celtic Elements in Icelandic Tradition." *Béaloideas* 25:3–24.

———. 1958. *Dating the Icelandic Sagas: An Essay in Method*. Trans. Gabriel Turville-Petre. Viking Society Text Series, 3. London: Viking Society for Northern Research.

———. 1960. "Nugae metricae." *Saga och sed* 118–29.

———. 1971. "Jón Árnason (1819–1888). In *Leading Folklorists of the North*. Ed. Dag Strömbäck. Scandinavian University Books. Oslo: Universitetsforlaget. Pp. 419–35.

Svennung, J. 1967. *Zur Geschichte des Goticismus*. Skrifter utgivna av Kungliga Humanistiska Vetenskapssamfundet i Uppsala, 44:2B. Stockholm: Almqvist och Wiksell.

Sweringen, Grace Flemming van. 1909. "Women in the Germanic Hero-Sagas." *JEGP* 8:501–12.

———. 1915. "The Main Literary Types of Men in the Germanic Hero-Sagas." *JEGP* 14:212–25.

Sydow, Carl W. von. 1911. Rev. of Friedrich Panzer, *Studien zur germanischen Sagengeschichte*, in *Anzeiger für deutsches Altertum* 35:123–31.

———. 1918. "Sigurds strid med Fåvne. En studie rörande hjältesagans förhållande till folkdiktningen." *Lunds Universitets Årsskrift*, NS, Avd. 1, Bd. 14, Nr. 16.

———. 1927. "Hjältesagans framväxt med särskild hänsyn til Sigurdsdiktningen." *ANF* 43:221–44.

Taylor, Paul Beekman. 1970. "Icelandic Analogues to the Northern English Gawain Cycle." *Journal of Popular Culture* 4:93–106.

Thompson, Claiborne W. 1977. "Moral Values in the Icelandic Sagas: Recent Reevaluations." In *The Epic in Medieval Society: Aesthetic and Moral Values*. Ed. Harald Scholler. Tübingen: Max Niemeyer Verlag. Pp. 347–60.

Thompson, Stith. 1932–36. *Motif-Index of Folk Literature*. 6 vols. Indiana University Studies 96–97, 100–101, 105–6, 108–12. Bloomington: Indiana University Press.

———. 1946. *The Folktale*. New York: Holt, Rinehart and Winston.

———. 1970. "Unfinished Business: The Folktale." In *Medieval Literature and Folklore Studies: Essays in Honor of Francis Lee Utley*. Ed. Jerome Mandel and Bruce A. Rosenberg. New Brunswick, N.J.: Rutgers University Press, 1970. Pp. 213–22.

Thorp, Mary. 1940. *The Study of the Nibelungenlied: Being the History of the Study of the Epic and Legend from 1755 to 1937*. Oxford: Clarendon Press.

Thuren, Hjalmar. 1908. *Folkesangen paa Færøerne*. Folklore Fellows Publications. Northern Series, 2. Copenhagen: And. Fred Høst og Søns Forlag.

Togeby, Knud. 1961–70. "Nordiske folkeviser." In *Vor kulturarv*. Ed. Per Krarup et al. 6 vols. Copenhagen: Forlaget for faglitteratur, 1961–70. II, 300–303.

———. 1971–74. "Den europæiske litteratur." In *Verdens litteraturhistorie*. Ed. F. J. Billeskov Jansen et al. 12 vols. Copenhagen: Politiken. II, 197–578.

Toldberg, Helge. 1961. "Traditionen om Presbyter Johannes i Norden." *ANF* 86:231–57.

Tolkien, Christopher. 1955–56. "The Battle of the Goths and the Huns." *Saga-Book* 14:141–63.

Tómasson, Sverrir. 1977. "Hvenær var Tristrams sögu snúið?" *Gripla* 2:47–78.

Toorn, M. C. van den. 1955. *Ethics and Morals in Icelandic Saga Literature*. Van Gorcum's Litteraire Bibliotheek, 9. Assen: Van Gorcum.

———. 1964. "Über die Ethik in den Fornaldarsagas." *APhS* 26:19–66.

Tuck, Anthony. 1972. "Some Evidence for Anglo-Scandinavian Relations at the End of the Fourteenth Century." *MS* 5:75–86.

Turville-Petre, E. O. Gabriel. 1953. *Origins of Icelandic Literature*. Oxford: Clarendon Press.

——. 1964. *Myth and Religion of the North: The Religion of Ancient Scandinavia*. New York: Holt, Rinehart and Winston.

Tveitane, Mattias. 1969. "Europeisk påvirkning på den norrøne sagalitteraturen: Noen synspunkter." *Edda* 56:73–95.

Tylor, Edward B. 1871. *Primitive Culture: Researches into the Development of Mythology, Philosophy, Religion, Art, and Custom*. 2 vols. London: John Murray.

Tynjanov, Jurij. 1971. "On Literary Evolution." In *Readings in Russian Poetics: Formalist and Structuralist Views*. Ed. Ladislav Matejka and Krystyna Pomorska, trans. C. A. Luplow. Cambridge: MIT Press, 1971. Pp. 66–78. [Originally published in Russian in 1927.]

Uecker, Heiko. 1972. *Germanische Heldensage*. Sammlung Metzler, 106. Stuttgart: J. B. Metzlersche Verlagsbuchhandlung.

——. 1980. "Isländersaga contra Heldensage." *Skandinavistik* 10:81–88.

Utley, Francis Lee. 1965. "Some Implications of Chaucer's Folktales." *Laographia* 22:588–94.

Vajda, Laszló. 1975. "Zum Polyphem-Abenteuer." *Ethnologische Zeitschrift* (Zürich), H. 1, 245–57.

Vedel, Valdemar. 1903. *Helteliv: En Studie over Heltedigtningens Grundtræk*. Copenhagen: Det nordiske Forlag.

Velure, Magne. 1977. "Folklorisme: oppattliving av forntida." *RIG* 60:76–87.

Vigfússon, Guðbrandur. 1878. "Prolegomena." In *Sturlunga saga Including the Islendinga Saga of Lawman Sturla Thordsson and Other Works*. 2 vols. Oxford: Clarendon Press. Pp. xvii–ccxiv.

Vries, Jan de. 1915. *Studiën over Færösche balladen*. Haarlem: H. D. Tjeenk Willink & Zoon.

——. 1928. "Die westnordische Tradition der Sage von Ragnar Lodbrok." Rpt. in *Kleine Schriften zur Literatur- und Geistesgeschichte*. Ed. Klaas Heeroma and Andries Kylstra. Berlin: de Gruyter, 1965. Pp. 285–330.

——. 1941–42. *Altnordische Literaturgeschichte*. 2 vols. Grundriss der germanischen Philologie, 15–16. Rpt. Berlin: de Gruyter, 1964–67.

——. 1954. *Betrachungen zum Märchen, besonders in seinem Verhältnis zu Heldensage und Mythos*. FFC, 150. Helsinki: Suomalainen Tiedeakatemia. Academia Scientiarum Fennica.

——. 1956. *Altgermanische Religionsgeschichte*. 2d rev. ed. Grundriss der germanischen Philologie, 12. 2 vols. Berlin: de Gruyter.

——. 1963. *Heroic Song and Heroic Legend*. Trans. B. J. Timmer. Oxford Paperbacks, 69. London: Oxford University Press. [Originally published as *Heldenlied en Heldensage* (Utrecht and Antwerp: Uitgeverij Het Spectrum N.V., 1959).]

Walker, Roger M. 1971. "Oral Delivery or Private Reading? A Contribution to the Debate on the Dissemination of Medieval Literature." *Forum for Modern Language Studies* 7:36–42.

Wallace, Anthony F. C. 1956. "Revitalization Movements." *AA* 58:264–81.

——. 1968. "Nativism and Revivalism." In *International Encyclopedia of the Social Sciences*. n.p.: Macmillan and Free Press. Pp. 75–80.

Wallen, C. C. 1970. "Klimatförändringar under sommaren över Norske havet och Danmarksstredet." *Ymer* 90:225–26.

Walter, Ernst. 1971. "Die lateinische Sprache und Literatur auf Island und Norwegen bis zum Beginn des 13. Jahrhunderts. Ein Orientierungsversuch." *Nordeuropa. Jahrbuch für nordische Studien* 4:195–230.

Watkins, Calvert. 1987. "How to Kill a Dragon in Indo-European." In *Studies in Memory of Warren Cowgill (1929–1985). Papers from the Fourth East Coast Indo-European Conference, Cornell University, June 6–9, 1985*. Ed. Calvert Watkins. Studies in Indo-European Language and Culture, 3. Berlin: de Gruyter. Pp. 270–99.

Wax, Rosalie H. 1969. *Magic, Fate, and History: The Changing Ethos of the Vikings*. Lawrence, Kans.: Coronado Press.

Weber, Gerd W. 1969. *Wyrd. Studien zum Schicksalsbegriff der altenglischen und altnordischen Literatur*. Frankfurter Beiträge zur Germanistik, 8. Bad Homburg von der Höhe: Gehlen.

——. 1972. "'Fact' und 'Fiction' als Maßstäbe literarischer Wertung in der Saga." *ZDA* 101:188–200.

——. 1978. "Die Literatur des Nordens." In *Neues Handbuch der Literaturwissenschaft*. Ed. Willi Erzgräber. Wiesbaden: Akademische Verlagsgesellschaft Athenaion. Pp. 487–518.

——. 1981. "Irreligiosität und Heldenzeitalter. Zum Mythencharakter der altisländischen Literatur." In *Specvlvm Norroenvm: Norse Studies in Memory of Gabriel Turville-Petre*. Ed. Ursula Dronke et al. Odense: Odense University Press. Pp. 474–505.

——. 1986. "The Decadence of Feudal Myth—towards a Theory of *riddarasaga* and Romance." In *Structure and Meaning in Old Norse Literature: New Approaches to Textual Analysis and Literary Criticism*. Ed. John Lindow et al. Viking Collection, 3. Odense: Odense University Press. Pp. 415–54.

Wessén, Elias. 1928. "Om de nordiska folkvisornas språkform." *Nysvenska studier* 8:43–69.

Westhuizen, J. E. van der. 1973. "The Saga of Icelanders—Possibilities of Ethical Criticism." *Proceedings of the First International Saga Conference. University of Edinburgh. 1971*. Ed. Peter Foote et al. London: Viking Society for Northern Research. Pp. 435–61.

Whitman, Cedric. 1958. *Homer and the Homeric Tradition*. Cambridge: Harvard University Press.

Widding, Ole. 1964. "Carl C. Rafn 1795–1864." *Bibliography of Old Norse–Icelandic Studies* 7–22.

——. 1965. "Islændingesagaer." In *Norrøn Fortællekunst. Kapitler af den norsk-islandsk middelalderlitteraturs historie*. Ed. Hans Bekker-Nielsen et al. n.p.: Akademisk Forlag, 1965. Pp. 72–91.

Wieselgren, Per. 1935. *Quellenstudien zur Vǫlsungasaga*. Acta et Commentationes Universitatis Tartuensis, B 34.3. Tartu: K. Mattiesens Buchdruckerei.

Wikander, Stig. 1964. "Från indisk djurfabel till isländsk saga." *Vetenskaps-societeten i Lund. Årsbok* (1964). Lund: Gleerup. Pp. 89–114.

Wiley, E. O. 1981. *Phylogenetics: The Theory and Practice of Phylogenetic Systematics.* New York: John Wiley and Sons.

Wundt, Wilhelm. 1908. "Märchen, Sage, und Legende als Entwicklungsformen des Mythos." *Archiv für Religionswissenschaft* 11:200–222.

Zumthor, Paul. 1972. *Essai de poétique médiévale.* Paris: Editions du Seuil.

——. 1987. *La lettre et la voix de la "littérature" médiéval.* Paris: Editions du Seuil.

Þorkelsson, Jón. 1888. *Om Digtningen på Island i det 15. og 16. Århundrede.* Copenhagen: Andr. Fred. Høst og Søns Forlag.

Þórólfsson, Björn K. 1934. *Rímur fyrir 1600.* Safn Fræðafélagsins um Ísland og Íslendinga, 9. Copenhagen: Hið íslenzka fræðafélag.

——. 1950. "Dróttkvæði og rímur." *Skírnir* 124:175–209.

Þorsteinsson, Björn. 1956–78a. "Englandshandel: Island." In *Kulturhistorisk leksikon for nordisk middelalder fra vikingetid til reformationstid.* 21 vols. Rpt. Copenhagen: Rosenkilde og Bagger, 1981–82. III, 665–68.

——. 1956–78b. "Hansan: Island." In *Kulturhistorisk leksikon for nordisk middelalder fra vikingetid til reformationstid.* 21 vols. Rpt. Copenhagen: Rosenkilde og Bagger, 1981–82. VI, 213–15.

——. [1957.] "Island." *Det nordiske syn på forbindelsen mellem Hansastæderne og Norden: Det nordiske historikermøde i Århus, 1957.* N.p.: n.p., n.d. Pp. 165–95.

——. 1970. *Enska öldin í sögu Íslendinga.* Reykjavík: Mál og Menning.

——. 1978. *Íslenzk miðaldasaga.* Reykjavík: Sögufélag, 1978.

Þorsteinsson, Steingrímur J. 1973. "Icelandic Folktales." *Scandinavica* 12:85–99.

Index

Alphabetization of non-English characters: å = aa; ä, æ = ae; ö, ø, ǫ = oe; ü = ue; ð, Đ = d; þ, Þ follows z. Icelandic names are filed under the patronymic.

Library of Congress Cataloging-in-Publication Data

Mitchell, Stephen Arthur.
  Heroic sagas and ballads / Stephen A. Mitchell.
    p. cm. — (Myth and poetics)
  Includes bibliographical references and index.
  ISBN 0-8014-2587-5 (cloth : alkaline paper)
  1. Sagas—History and criticism. 2. Oral tradition—History and criticism. 3. Old
Norse literature—History and criticism. I. Title. II. Series.
PT7181.M5 1991
839'.609—dc20   91-9899

Ingram Content Group UK Ltd.
Milton Keynes UK
UKHW040612230323
419035UK00001B/87